Contents

List of tables and figures

viii

Contributors

Jonathan Bradbury is Reader in Politics and Head of the Department of Political and Cultural Studies at Swansea University. He is co-convenor of the PSA Territorial Politics Specialist Group and has published widely on multi-level politics in the UK, electoral politics and political parties, public policy and constitutional change (j.p.bradbury@swansea.ac.uk).

Rosie Campbell is Senior Lecturer in the Department of Politics, Birkbeck, University of London. She has written widely on gender and voting behaviour, political participation and representation. Her book *Gender and the Vote in Britain* was published by the ECPR press in 2006. Recent publications include 'Do Women Need Women MPs?' co-authored with Sarah Childs and Joni Lovenduski, *British Journal of Political Science* 2010 (r.campbell@bbk.ac.uk).

Sean Carey is a Lecturer in Politics at the University of Sheffield. He is the author of a number of articles and chapters on voting behaviour in Britain and public attitudes to European integration (s.carey@shef.ac.uk).

Sarah Childs is Professor of Politics and Gender at the University of Bristol. She has written extensively on women's political representation, both conceptually and empirically. Her book, *Women and British Party Politics* was published in 2008 and her current research includes a major project on the Conservative Party, *Women and the Conservative Party: From Iron Lady to Kitten Heels*, with Paul Webb, will be published in 2011. (s.childs@bristol.ac.uk).

John Curtice is Professor of Politics at Strathclyde University. He was co-director of the *British Election Study* from 1983 to 1997, has been a co-editor of NatCen's *British Social Attitudes* survey annual reports since 1994, and a co-director of the *Scottish Social Attitudes* survey since 1999. Recent publications include *Has Devolution Worked* (co-ed; Manchester University Press) and *Revolution or Evolution?: The 2007 Scottish Elections* (co-author; Edinburgh University Press). (j.curtice@strath.ac.uk).

David Cutts is a Research Fellow at the Institute for Social Change, University of Manchester. He has published on a wide range of topics, including geographical and contextual effects in voting and attitudes, voter turnout, party campaigning, political engagement and participation. He has also published a number of journal articles on the Liberal Democrats. (david.cutts@man.ac.uk).

David Denver is Professor of Politics, Lancaster University. Among many other works, he is the author of *Elections and Voters in Britain* (2nd ed., Palgrave, 2007) (d.denver@lancaster.ac.uk).

Jocelyn Evans is Professor of Politics at the University of Salford. He is the author of *Voters and Voting* (Sage, 2004) and has recently edited, with Kai Arzheimer, *Electoral Behaviour* (2008) in the Sage Library of Political Science, as well as authoring numerous articles on various aspects of voting and party competition in Northern Ireland, France and Europe. He is co-editor of *Parliamentary Affairs*, and series editor for Palgrave Macmillan's *French Politics, Society and Culture* series. He is currently working on a series of forecast models for French and European elections, as well as a project on candidate profile effects on voter choice. (j.a.evans@salford.ac.uk).

Ed Fieldhouse is Professor of Social and Political Science and Director of the Institute for Social Change at the University of Manchester. His research spans civic and political engagement, voting and elections and immigration and diversity, with a particular focus on the role of place in political behaviour. Previous work on the Liberal Democrats includes *Neither Left Nor Right? The Liberal Democrats and the Electorate*, with Andrew Russell. His most recent book is *The Age of Obama: the changing places of minorities in British and American Society*, with Tom Clark and Robert Putnam. (e.fieldhouse@man.ac. uk).

Steven Fielding is Professor of Political History in the School of Politics and International Relations at the University of Nottingham where he is also Director of the Centre for British Politics (steven.fielding@ nottingham.ac.uk).

Justin Fisher is Professor of Political Science and Director of the Magna Carta Institute at Brunel University. He has published extensively on party finance, elections and parties, and is co-editor (with Christopher Wlezien) of the *Journal of Elections, Public Opinion and Parties*. (justin.fisher@brunel.ac.uk).

Ruth Fox is Director of the Parliament and Government Programme at the Hansard Society. Her research interests include third party politics and the history of the Liberal Party: her PhD concerned the strategy and philosophy of the Liberal Party 1970–83. (r.fox@hansard.lse.ac.uk).

Andrew Gamble is Professor of Politics, a Fellow of Queens' College and Head of the Department of Politics and International Studies at the University of Cambridge. He is joint editor of *The Political*

Quarterly and a Fellow of the British Academy. He has published widely on British politics, public policy, and political economy. (amg59@cam.ac.uk).

Andrew Geddes is Professor of Politics and Head of the Department of Politics at the University of Sheffield. He has researched and written extensively on British, European and EU immigration politics and on British relations with the EU, including *Migration and Mobility in the European Union* (with Christina Boswell, Palgrave Macmillan, forthcoming 2011). (a.geddes@shef.ac.uk).

Jane Green is a Lecturer in Politics at the University of Manchester. She was the author, with Phil Cowley, of the Conservative chapter for the 2005 Geddes and Tonge election volume, *Britain Decides*. She has written several papers on the Conservative party in opposition, and works widely on British politics and comparative political behaviour, researching parties and candidate competence ratings, party strategies, public opinion dynamics, voter turnout and electoral choice. She gained her D.Phil. at Nuffield College, Oxford, in 2007, and was the BBC World Service election expert for the election night coverage in the 2005 and 2010 elections. (jane.green@manchester.ac.uk).

James Mitchell is Professor of Politics, University of Strathclyde in Glasgow. He is author of, Devolution in the UK (2009) and co-author of Voting for a Scottish Government: The Scottish Parliament election of 2007 (2010), both published by Manchester University Press. (j.mitchell@strath.ac.uk)

Andrew Russell is Senior Lecturer in Politics at the University of Manchester and co-author, with Ed Fieldhouse, of *Neither Left Nor Right? The Liberal Democrats and the Electorate* (Manchester University Press, 2005). He is Co-Director of the Democracy, Citizens and Elections Research Network, has undertaken various research for the Electoral Commission and has published widely on British politics (andrew.russell@manchester.ac.uk).

Martin Smith is Professor of Politics and Director of Research and Innovation in the Faculty of Social Sciences at the University of Sheffield. He has published widely on British politics and public policy and his most recent book is *Power and the State*, Palgrave Macmillan, 2009. He is also editor of the journal *Political Studies*. (m.j.smith@ shef.ac.uk).

Jonathan Tonge is Professor of Politics at the University of Liverpool and President of the Political Studies Association of the United Kingdom. He was Principal Investigator of the ESRC's 2010 Northern Ireland election survey. Recent books include *Abandoning the Past? Former Political Prisoners and Reconciliation in Northern Ireland* (2010); *Politics in Ireland: Convergence and Divergence in a two-polity* *island* (2009); *Northern Ireland* (2006) and *Sinn Fein and the SDLP; From Alienation to Participation* (2005); Recent journal articles include items in the *British Journal of Politics and International Relations; Political Psychology; Electoral Studies, Party Politics and Political Studies.* (j.tonge@liv.ac.uk).

Arno Van Der Zwet is completing a PhD at Strathclyde University comparing the Scottish National Party and the Frisian National Party. (arno.van-der-zwet@strath.ac.uk).

Stephen Ward is Reader in Politics at the University of Salford. His research interests are in the area of the Internet and politics, where he has analysed the role of the Internet in elections in a range of countries since 1997. His publications include: *Making a Difference? A comparative view of the role of the Internet in election politics*, (Lexington Books 2008), co-edited with Richard Davis, Diana Owen and David Taras. (s.j.ward@salford.ac.uk).

Richard Whitman is Professor of Politics at the University of Bath and Associate Fellow, Europe at Chatham House. His current research interests include the external relations and foreign and security and defence policies of the EU, and the governance and future priorities of the EU. He has published in a variety of academic journals including *International Affairs, European Foreign Affairs Review, Contemporary Security Policy, Journal of European Public Policy*, and *Journal of Common Market Studies.* He is the author of *From Civilian Power to Superpower? The International Identity of the European Union* (Macmillan, 1998), and co-editor with Ian Manners of *The Foreign Policies of European Union Member States* (Manchester University Press, 2000). His most recent book is *The European Neighbourhood Policy in perspective: context, implementation and impact* (Palgrave, 2010), co-edited with Stefan Wolff. (r.g.whitman@bath.ac.uk).

Dominic Wring is Reader in Political Communication at Loughborough University, author of The Politics of Marketing the Labour Party, editor of Political Communications: the British General Election 2005, chair of the International Political Science Association's Research Committee for Political Communication and co-founder of the UK Political Studies Association's Media and Politics Group. (d.j.wring@lboro.ac.uk).

Preface

The extraordinary aftermath of the 2010 general election—the exciting and unpredictable five days in May that produced the Conservative/ Liberal Democrat coalition—has overshadowed both the campaign itself and even the result. Neither should be forgotten.

First, the campaign was unlike all previous ones because of the novelty of the three televised leaders' debates which dominated the energies and time of the party leaders, the media coverage and the polls. There has not been enough soul searching in either the political or the media worlds about the rise and fall of 'Cleggmania' and the impact, or lack of them, of the debates.

Second, the results are in themselves significant. Andrew Geddes and Jon Tonge argue in their conclusion to this book that 'The UK can no longer be understood as a two-party system and biases within the electoral system make single-party government less likely, particularly for the Conservative Party'. John Curtice reinforces this conclusion with a typically acute analysis which points out that the Conservative promise to reduce disparities in the size of constituency electorates will only eliminate some of the disadvantage suffered by the Conservatives. 'Single-member plurality will still be likely to produce a hung parliament', he argues. That possibility, or perhaps fear, has far-reaching implications for the behaviour of not just the coalition partners but also Labour, and its new leader, as they seek to minimise their time in opposition.

As politicians and journalists speculate about the duration of the coalition, this book suggests that the electoral conditions which led to its formation may not be an aberration but may result in further hung parliaments where no single party gains an overall Commons majority.

This collection of essays is invaluable in its depth and breadth, covering these and other often neglected parts of the campaign. The 'Britain Votes' volume, published by the Hansard Society in collaboration with Oxford University Press after each general election, is derived from a special edition of the Society's *Parliamentary Affairs* journal. The journal and this publication are central to the Society's goal of explaining the British parliamentary system in an easily understood and accessible way.

Peter Riddell
Chair
Hansard Society

© The Author [2010]. Published by Oxford University Press on behalf of the Hansard Society
doi:10.1093/pa/gsq040

Acknowledgements

A large number of debts have been incurred in producing this volume. We thank all the contributors for their pieces, which they delivered without complaining about our very tight deadlines. We are particularly grateful to Professor Steven Fielding (Nottingham University) and Professor Jocelyn Evans (Salford University) who, as editors of *Parliamentary Affairs*, have provided unstinting support. Steven and Sue Simpson, in the Centre for British Politics at Nottingham, were instrumental in organising an excellent post-election conference at which many of the ideas of the contributors here were 'road-tested'. Vanessa Lacey, Rachel Mill and Hilary Lamb at Oxford University Press have been consistently helpful and enthusiastic, adjectives equally applicable to Ruth Fox, the Director of the Parliament and Government programme at the Hansard Society. Andrew thanks Federica for feigning a modicum of interest in British electoral politics and Jacopo and Beatrice for their general enthusiasm about everything. Jon wishes to thank BBC Radio 5 Live's Tony Livesey, Jonathan Aspinwall and Helen Thompson for involving him in dealing with difficult questions throughout their election coverage; the same thanks are extended to Arif Ansari, political editor of BBC North West. Jon also thanks Maria, Joseph and Connell for their considerable forbearance in coping with an election obsessive.

Introduction

How Britain Got Hung

Long in advance of its arrival, the 2010 election looked likely to be the most closely fought contest since 1992. 'New Labour' appeared ideologically and politically exhausted. The party staggered on under a leader who had eschewed the chance of electoral glory in 2007. Gordon Brown had been wary of testing the depth of his popularity amid a brief honeymoon period following his 'coronation' as Prime Minister. Since then, leader and party had been burdened by acute global economic problems and an apparent lack of a clear domestic vision. The Conservatives had revived under David Cameron, but the extent and depth of this revival remained uncertain. The Liberal Democrats had stabilised under Nick Clegg after changing leader twice within two years, but, pre-election, the orthodoxy was they might be squeezed in a close Labour–Conservative fight.

Clearly there were uncertain elements to the contest. All three main parties had leaders who had not been at the helm at the previous general election. The agreement between those leaders to take part in the first-ever televised debates during the campaign added another new dimension, with unpredictable consequences. Further elements which potentially made the contest more difficult to predict included geographical variability, with Scotland, in contrast to the South of England, seemingly impervious to David Cameron's charms; the possible impact of huge disparities in campaign finance available to the (rich) Conservatives and (poor) Labour and the switches in allegiance of several newspapers.

Beyond the global recession and banking crisis, the period prior to the election had been marked by an extraordinary humiliation of many MPs amid prolonged coverage, led by the *Daily Telegraph*, of what quickly became known simply as the 'expenses scandal'. Amid rows over the claims by MPs for reimbursement for duck houses and moat cleaning and with police charges pressed in some cases, the reputation

© The Author [2010]. Published by Oxford University Press on behalf of the Hansard Society
doi:10.1093/pa/gsq032

of elected representatives at Westminster sunk to an all-time low. As the furore failed to subside, it tended to be overlooked that the majority of MPs were blameless. Many of those alleged to have committed the worst excesses did not contest the 2010 election and it was uncertain whether incumbency would influence local constituency outcomes, or lead to higher support for political parties without representation at Westminster.

Yet all these unpredictable aspects did not mask the message apparent from the opinion polls that a hung parliament was a strong probability, the first time Britain had 'been hung' since February 1974. Whilst seemingly secure in their lead in the polls, the Conservatives were not polling sufficiently strongly to obtain an overall majority, given constituency and efficacy biases. Smaller Labour constituencies and larger 'wasted' Conservative majorities added to the size of Cameron's task, already formidable in requiring a swing to the Conservatives not achieved by any previous leader of the party. Nonetheless there had been periods prior to the campaign when the Conservatives had threatened fulfilment of their aspiration for a decisive majority. From 2006 to 2009, the Conservatives gained over 1700 council seats and 69 councils at the annual round of council elections. In May 2008, the Crewe and Nantwich by-election was won on a 17.6% swing from Labour. However, the Conservatives peaked in their poll ratings at this point, whilst Labour's poll ratings began to recover from Spring 2009 onwards. Under Nick Clegg, Liberal Democrat support rose gently from Spring 2008, whilst the polls continued to indicate a significant (if declining, as the election drew near) level of support for 'others'.

A realistic assessment of these respective rankings pointed to one outcome; the Conservatives winning the most seats, but not enjoying an overall majority. Surprisingly, bookmakers continued to offer short odds on a Conservative overall majority, despite the evidence to the contrary provided even by forecasts based upon *actual* votes cast over the inter-election period in local elections.[1] To the end, layers displayed reluctance to believe in Labour's powers of seat retention, offering generous odds on the party obtaining more than 240 seats even after the (magnificently accurate) election night exit poll for BBC, ITV and Sky predicted that party would retain a credible 255 seats. The apparent suspension of belief was more widely spread. Given the likelihood of a hung parliament and the probable need for a Conservative–Liberal Democrat deal, what was striking about the coverage of the campaign was the absence of serious consideration of how such a coalition—formal or informal—might look or operate. This dearth of discussion reflected political and electoral cultures still rooted in majoritarian politics based upon a two-party system, even if such a system has existed in representational but not electoral form since the 1970s.

The purpose and plan of the volume

This volume is divided into four sections, designed to cover the nature, outcomes, geography and issues of the election campaign. Whilst numerous aspects of the election are covered, the volume seeks to address core questions in terms of the result; why was Labour ousted from power, after winning three consecutive elections? To what extent can the Conservatives' partial victory be attributed to Cameron's rebranding of his party or to Labour's failings? To what degree does the rise and fall of 'Cleggmania' highlight the soft basis of Liberal Democrat support? What factors explain the considerable national and regional variations in party support? Beyond the result, the volume assesses the key issues that influenced the result—and asks why. There is a detailed analysis of the coverage and finance of the campaign and an assessment of how the Conservative–Liberal Democrat coalition government was formed. We also step back a little from the intensity of the campaign battle to examine the longer term effects of New Labour's 13 years in power and its effects on British politics. We also look ahead and ask whether the British electoral system is now so fragmented that it may be incapable in the future of delivering single-party majority government.

Section 1 analyses the results and their impact. David Denver notes how the Labour government's partial recovery during the year prior to the election, a traditional feature in an election novel in many other respects, was crucial in denying the Conservatives the ultimate prize of an overall majority. Denver also highlights the considerable fluctuations in geographic performance of the parties (with Scotland a huge outlier to the overall result) whilst emphasising that these differences represent continuity not change. In his overview of what took place, Denver emphasises that, for all the excitement of the campaign and closeness of the contest, democratic revival, as measured by increased turnout, was modest (the queues outside certain polling stations owed everything to incompetence). Following this overview of the election outcome, the impact of the results in highlighting the diminishing capacity of the First-Past-the-Post (FPTP) system to produce majoritarian government is demonstrated by John Curtice. In indicating how FPTP can no longer be relied upon to produce such an outcome, Curtice demonstrates how the electorate's preference for the supposed 'big two' parties has diminished, as support for nationalists, others and, of course the Liberal Democrats, has grown since the 1970s. Unless the electorate punishes the Liberal Democrats for participation in the coalition government, or there is an unforeseen erosion of nationalist sentiment, FPTP is likely to remain not fit for one of its purposes: the yielding of a decisive result. The consequences of the inability of a single plurality system to yield its supposedly desired majority government result are explored in the piece by Ruth Fox.

She examines how the Conservatives and Liberal Democrats quickly overcame the lack of knowledge and blueprint in terms of coalition-building to form a power-sharing administration. Fox accounts for the momentous five days following the election during which the political landscape was re-shaped and much conventional wisdom about British politics was stood on its head.

Section 2 assesses the campaigns of the main parties, viewed beyond the inadequate prism of four weeks of hectic campaigning and instead analysed over the full inter-election period. Andrew Gamble begins this section by reflecting on how Labour was positioned at the end of ten years of Blair as Prime Minister and assesses the unpromising inheritance bequeathed to Gordon Brown. Steven Fielding then assesses Brown's performance in office and the impact of Labour's defeat. While no party can claim to have decisively won the 2010 general election, it is clear that Labour was by far the biggest loser. Fielding highlights the inadequacies which prevented the party being in a post-election position to seriously engage with the Liberal Democrats in a way which some senior Labour figures had envisaged. Jane Green offers a quizzical assessment of the fillip to the Conservative Party provided by David Cameron. Whilst the party appeared pre-election to be cruising serenely to victory and its 2009 annual conference in Manchester had the unmistakeable feeling of a government in waiting, Green indicates how, notwithstanding the election semi-victory (which does indeed matter!) the revival of support for the Conservative Party has not been spectacular. In their analysis of Liberal Democrat fortunes, Cutts, Fieldhouse and Russell suggest that the 2010 election was a case of *plus ca change* despite the near hysteria generated by Nick Clegg's opening leadership debate performance. The biases of the electoral system and a lack of a strong social base for the Liberal Democrats remain the biggest culprits.

In Section 3, the election beyond England is assessed to tease out national variations and highlight how the Conservatives' (and Liberal Democrats') mandate is more contested in the other nations of the UK. This is particularly striking in Scotland, where, as James Mitchell and Arno van der Zwet declare, the Conservative brand remains toxic. Gordon Brown remained popular, whilst the Liberal Democrats, who ditched two Scottish leaders in quick succession, lost ground. Labour's continued dominance in Wales is highlighted by Jonathan Bradbury. In Northern Ireland, the new alliance between the Conservative and the Ulster Unionist Party proved utterly ineffective, costing the latter its only parliamentary seat.

Section 4 begins with an assessment of potentially important aspects of the campaign and how they affected the parties. Sarah Childs and Rosie Campbell assess why the 2010 general election saw only modest representational gains for women while the campaign saw less focus on leading women politicians than on the wives of the three main party leaders. Justin Fisher's exploration of party finance highlights the imbalance in resources. Labour could only spend half of what the party threw at the 2005 election, when victory seemed assured, whilst the Conservatives returned to their traditional position as the best-funded party. Fisher shows why this sizeable advantage did not translate straightforwardly into a Conservative victory. Labour hoped that the equality of opportunity afforded in the televised leadership debates might neutralise the inequalities of campaign spending. However, as the contribution by Steve Ward and Dominic Wring demonstrates, hostile press coverage, allied to Brown's 'failures' in those debates, exacerbated Labour's plight.

Finally Section 5 of the volume explores some of the issues within the campaign. The election was overshadowed by two stark issues, the economy and Afghanistan. Whilst tri-partisanship was evident on the latter, largely neutralising it, as Richard Whitman discusses, as a major foreign policy election issue, the economy elicited sharp debate over the timing and nature of spending reductions. These arguments contained an air of unreality, for, as Martin Smith relates, none of the parties wished to be entirely frank over the sheer scale of pruning required, nor its likely impact. Smith also pinpoints important underlying differences between the Conservatives and Labour about the respective roles of the state and market that are certain to be key dividing lines in the years to come as the Conservative–Liberal Democrat coalition takes an axe to public spending. Recent elections have seen Europe (2001) or immigration (2005) featuring as part of Conservative dog whistle campaigns. Sean Carey and Andrew Geddes show why immigration was high on the list of concerns of the electorate, a major issue in the contest and argued over in every leadership debate. They assess how immigration forced its way onto the agenda in a spectacularly visible manner in Rochdale as the campaign entered its final week, even if, like Cleggmania, its impact was unpredictable. After all, the Liberal Democrats lost seats and Labour won Rochdale.

1   C. Rallings, M. Thrasher and G. Borisyuk, 'Forecasting the 2010 General Election Using Local Election Data', presented at the International Symposium on Methods and Models for UK Election Forecasting, Democracy, Citizens and Elections Research Network, University of Manchester, 19–20 March 2010.

DAVID DENVER

The Results: How Britain Voted

The results of the 2010 general election were dramatic in two main ways. Firstly, the Conservatives made significant gains but fell just short of an overall majority of seats in the House of Commons. The second dramatic feature, however, was something that did not happen. Unexpectedly, given campaign polls, the Liberal Democrats failed to make any significant advance in popular support and actually fell back in terms of the number of seats won. These outcomes had immediate effects on the subsequent formation of a government and in the longer term could have a major impact on the shape and conduct of British politics. Another—perhaps less dramatic but nonetheless notable—feature of the election was that there was an increase in voter turnout. This article examines patterns of party support and turnout in some detail, but focuses first on the lead-up to the election by considering trends in party support over the inter-election period as a whole and in the 'hot' campaign during the last few weeks before polling.

The inter-election cycle of party support

The years between the 2005 and 2010 general elections saw something of a reversion to what was once thought to be an inevitable cycle of support for the major parties. From the 1950s on, governing parties generally became unpopular between elections and the main opposition benefitted—having large leads in the opinion polls, making numerous gains in local elections and winning seats in parliamentary by-elections. As the next general election approached, however, support usually flowed back to the governing party. 'Mid-term blues' were forgotten and the big opposition leads previously recorded were whittled away. Although there were occasional 'random shocks' (such as the election of a new party leader) producing sudden changes in the parties' fortunes, the effect of these was usually short-lived and the basic pattern was quickly re-established. Recent electoral cycles have not clearly conformed to this familiar pattern, however. Between 2001 and 2005, for

© The Author [2010]. Published by Oxford University Press on behalf of the
Hansard Society
doi:10.1093/pa/gsq017

example, support for the government certainly declined but there was no recovery at all in the last few months before the election was called. If anything, indeed, there was a further decline.

Trends in party support between 2005 and 2010 are shown in Figure 1. Looking first at Labour, the party experienced a very brief 'honeymoon' with the electorate after the 2005 election but then, with Tony Blair as Prime Minister, its support fell fairly steadily for two years. In June 2007, the first 'random shock' occurred when Gordon Brown replaced Blair and made a favourable impression in his first few months in office. In autumn 2007, however, Brown's apparent dithering over whether or not to call a general election coincided with a sharp reduction in support. Another boost was occasioned by the onset of the economic crisis in late 2008 but this upturn proved to be very short-lived. From summer 2009, however, Labour's standing with the electorate improved steadily, if slowly, and the upward trend was maintained through to March 2010. This was, then, a fairly clear example of the classic cycle of support for the governing party.

David Cameron took over as Conservative leader in December 2005 and immediately had a favourable impact on the party's poll ratings. Within a year the Conservatives had overtaken Labour and this lead was maintained—apart from the few months of the 'Brown bounce'—for the rest of the cycle. The peak of Conservative fortunes was in the summer of 2008, but thereafter the trend was downwards and the gap

Figure 1. Trends in party support 2005–March 2010.

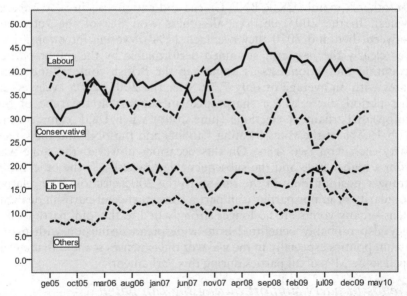

Note: For each month the graph shows the mean percentage intending to vote for each party on the basis of results from five firms which polled consistently throughout the period: Communicate Research, ICM, IpsosMORI, Populus and YouGov.

between the two main parties became significantly smaller. Over the period as a whole, however, the strength of the Conservatives was reflected to some extent in parliamentary by-elections and, more convincingly, in the annual rounds of local elections. In the 13 by-elections that took place the Conservatives won two seats from Labour (Crewe and Nantwich and Norwich North), held three and lost none. In each round of local elections the Conservatives easily outpolled the other parties, gaining numerous seats and councils in the process. After the 2009 elections the Conservatives were by far the largest party in local government in England and Wales, holding 48% of all council seats (compared with 23% for Labour and 21% for the Liberal Democrats) and controlling 209 of the 373 councils.[1] These cumulative local election successes have an importance beyond the merely local, since they can encourage a party's supporters and councillors can be valuable and effective campaigners in a general election.

The Liberal Democrats, meanwhile, changed leaders twice after 2005. In March 2006 Menzies Campbell took over from Charles Kennedy and he, in turn, was replaced by Nick Clegg in December 2007. These changes both produced a small fillip for the Liberal Democrats (probably due to the attendant publicity for the party), but the effects were not dramatic or long lasting. Nonetheless, from early 2009 the position of the Liberal Democrats slowly improved and as the election drew near they were not far off the level of support that they had achieved in 2005.

Perhaps the most remarkable aspect of Figure 1 is the level of support for 'others' (mainly UKIP, BNP, Greens and nationalists in Scotland and Wales). In the 2005 election, all others won 8% of the votes but between then and 2010 they averaged 11% of voting intentions. This was clearly the best ever sustained performance by the minor parties (counting the nationalists as 'minor' in the British context) and compares with an average of only 7.7% over the 2001–2005 cycle. As in that period, there was a sharp spike in support at the time of the European Parliament elections (June 2009) when UKIP came second with 16.5% of the votes (beating Labour) and the BNP and the Green party each won two seats. On this occasion, however, the spike was from a higher base and the subsequent decline still left the others in a stronger position than in the run-up to the 2005 election. The relative popularity of minor parties is in part a consequence of partisan dealignment—many voters are no longer strongly tied to the 'old' parties—but they also probably benefitted from widespread disillusion with mainstream politics especially in the wake of the expenses scandal that enveloped some MPs of all parties during this Parliament.

Trends in party support during the campaign

Gordon Brown announced on Tuesday April 6th that the election would take place one month later on May 6th and the dissolution of

Parliament on Monday April 12th signalled the formal start of the 'short' campaign. In fact, of course, the parties had been in campaigning mode long before that. 'Permanent campaigning' is thought by many to be a defining aspect of modern electoral politics and it is certainly the case that at both national and local levels (especially in key marginal seats) campaign preparations and activity are under way many months before an election is due. Nonetheless, the 'official' campaign sees a substantial increase in activity and saturation media coverage. Moreover, there remains much to play for. The proportion of voters saying that they decided which party to support during the campaign has steadily increased over the years and reached almost 40% in 2010. Even those who have made up their minds need to be reinforced and mobilised during the campaign.

The importance of the short campaign period in 2010 was heightened by the fact that it was punctuated by the first-ever televised campaign debates between the major party leaders, reflecting and almost certainly reinforcing the growing personalisation of politics. These were held on three consecutive Thursdays—April 15th, 22nd and 29th. The first was watched by 9.4 million viewers and was accompanied by enormous media ballyhoo. The second debate had an average audience of 4 million and the third was watched by about 7.5 million people. The media frenzy surrounding the debates did not vary in line with the audiences, however.

Figure 2 charts the trend in voting intentions according to the daily polls undertaken by YouGov, from the day that the election date was announced through to the actual result on polling day (and the pattern is very similar if a 'poll of polls' is used). The first week was generally thought somewhat lacklustre by commentators and saw little change in support for the major parties, although there appears to have been a slight improvement in the position of the Liberal Democrats and a slight decrease in support for others. In the second week, however, the first televised leaders' debate shattered the somnolent atmosphere. By general consent the Liberal Democrat leader, Nick Clegg, made the best impression and, as the graph shows, the impact on public opinion was electric. Two YouGov polls over the weekend following the debate put the Liberal Democrats in the lead. Although they declined from this peak during the next week, they largely held on to their new-found eminence and were consistently running second to the Conservatives. The latter's ship steadied somewhat but Labour slipped into third place. There was no clear 'winner', in the second leaders' debate but it was widely thought that David Cameron came off best in the third. Whether as a result of this or not, the Conservatives inched forward in the penultimate and also the last week of campaigning while the other parties remained close together stuck in the high twenties. The final polls produced on the evening of polling day are summarised in Table 1. With one exception Conservative support was estimated reasonably accurately but all

Figure 2. Trends in voting intentions during the 'short' campaign.

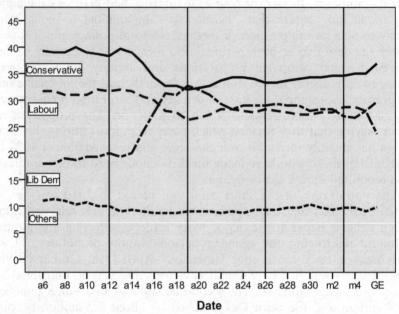

Date

Note: The data are three-day moving averages of figures reported in YouGov's tracking polls for the *Sun* and *Sunday Times*. The vertical lines mark each Monday of the campaign.

underestimated Labour's vote share, although not by much in most cases. Liberal Democrat support was consistently overestimated—indeed two companies had them in second place while another two had them running neck and neck with Labour. The sudden, last-minute evaporation of this support is one of the mysteries of the election.

The national result

The shares of votes and the number of seats won by the major parties in 2010 (in Great Britain) and changes from 2005 are shown in Table 2. The Conservatives made a modest advance in terms of vote share but there was a larger drop in Labour support to produce a net swing of 5.1% from Labour to the Conservatives. This was enough to enable the Conservatives to take 87 seats from Labour (on the basis of 2005 notional results) while none moved in the opposite direction. The Conservatives' vote share also improved relative to the Liberal Democrats and 12 seats duly switched from the latter to the former. In this case, however, two seats went against the general tide (Eastbourne and Wells). As well as losses to the Conservatives, the decline in Labour support resulted in the party losing five seats to the Liberal Democrats and one each to Plaid Cymru and the Green party. In terms of votes, the most successful of the 'other' parties was UKIP with 3.2% of votes (+0.9 from 2005) whereas the BNP won 1.9% of votes

1. Final opinion poll results

Firm	Con (%)	Lab (%)	Lib Dem (%)	Other %
Populus	37	28	27	8
ComRes	37	28	28	7
ICM	36	28	26	10
IpsosMori	36	29	27	8
Angus Reid	36	24	29	11
Opinium	35	27	26	12
YouGov	35	28	28	9
Harris	35	29	27	9
TNS BMRB	33	27	29	11
Election result	37	30	24	10

Source: UK polling report.

2. Share of votes and number of seats won (Great Britain) and changes from 2005

	Share of votes (%)	Change 2005–2010	Number of seats	Change 2005–2010
Conservative	36.9	+3.7	305	+95
Labour	29.7	−6.4	258	−90
Liberal Democrat	23.6	+1.0	57	−5
UKIP	3.2	+0.9	0	0
SNP/Plaid Cymru	2.3	0.0	9	+1
BNP	1.9	+1.2	0	0
Green	1.0	−0.1	1	+1
Other	1.5	−0.2	1	−3

Notes: The Speaker, who was not opposed by the Conservatives, Labour or Liberal Democrats, is treated as an 'other'. The change in seats is calculated on the basis of 'notional' 2005 results in England and Wales due to boundary changes. The data here and throughout the article exclude the delayed election in one constituency.

(+1.2) and the Green Party 1.0% (−0.1) although both of these parties had many more candidates than in 2005. Despite losing support, the Green Party was the only 'other', apart from the Speaker, to win a seat (Brighton Pavilion).

The distribution of votes in 2010 was produced, of course, by a relatively complex 'flow of the votes' when compared with the 2005 election, with voters switching in all directions and moving into and out of non-voting. Survey data are required to reveal these ebbs and flows and we can use the British Election Study post-election internet poll to construct such a table based on voters' recall of what they did in 2005. The results are shown in Table 3 and suggest that the Conservatives did best and Labour worst in retaining previous supporters. Direct switching between the two biggest parties heavily favoured the Conservatives who also did best from the circulation of non-voters. The Liberal Democrats picked up more from Labour than the Conservatives while losing more to the latter. They also beat Labour among previous non-voters and were the most favoured party among

3. Flow of the vote between 2005 and 2010

Vote in 2005

Vote 2010	Conservative (%)	Labour (%)	Lib Dem (%)	Other (%)	Did not vote (%)	Too young %
Conservative	76	9	12	17	7	16
Labour	1	50	7	10	6	16
Lib Dem	6	13	58	11	7	19
Other	5	4	7	32	3	2
Did not vote	13	23	16	30	77	48
n	2736	3973	1406	971	2511	633

Source: BES pre-campaign and post-election polls. The data have been weighted to the 2010 outcome as well as for demographics.

those who were too young to vote in 2005. Overall, the picture of electoral change provided by these data is obviously more complex than a simple reading of the election results might suggest.

Variations in changes in party support

Table 4 shows changes in party shares of votes across English regions and in Scotland and Wales. The national trend is replicated, to a greater or lesser extent, across England and Wales, but the result in Scotland stands out as a clear exception. Here, in contrast to the rest of the country, Labour improved upon its 2005 performance and there was a sharp reduction in support for the Liberal Democrats. The Conservatives did advance—but by very little. Scotland has moved in the opposite direction to the rest of the country in previous elections, most notably perhaps in 1959, which was the start of a process which saw a steady weakening of Conservatism in Scotland relative to England. It seems unlikely, however, that the 2010 election will herald further long-term electoral changes. Rather, the deviation of Scottish voters can be largely explained in terms of two short-term factors. First, Labour's success stemmed in part from the fact that the SNP is the incumbent Scottish government and—since incumbents usually attract criticism—this blunted the SNP attack as the main challenger to Labour. More important, however, is the significance of Scottish identity in relation to changes in the leaderships of Labour and the Liberal Democrats. Under a popular Scottish leader, Charles Kennedy (who was more liked in Scotland than elsewhere, according to BES data) the Liberal Democrat share of Scottish votes improved by much more in 2005 than in other parts of Britain. Having dumped Kennedy and then another Scottish leader (Menzies Campbell) in favour of a manifestly 'posh' southerner in the interim, it was always likely that the appeal of the Liberal Democrats in Scotland would wane in 2010, and so it proved. Labour, meanwhile, had replaced the less-than-loved Tony Blair with Gordon Brown, a Fifer with deep roots in Scottish society and an unmistakeable Scottish accent. As one of their own, Scottish

4. Changes in party shares of votes in regions

	Con	Lab	Lib Dem	SNP/PC	Other
North East	+4.2	−9.3	+0.3	—	+4.8
North West	+3.0	−5.7	+0.2	—	+2.3
Yorkshire/Humber	+3.4	−8.9	+2.2	—	+3.3
East Midlands	+4.1	−9.2	+2.3	—	+2.7
West Midlands	+4.5	−8.1	+1.9	—	+1.7
Eastern	+3.8	−10.5	+2.3	—	+4.2
London	+2.6	−2.3	+0.2	—	−1.0
South East	+4.3	−8.2	+0.8	—	+2.9
South West	+4.2	−7.4	+2.1	—	+1.0
Wales	+4.7	−6.5	+1.7	−1.3	+1.3
Scotland	+0.9	+3.1	−3.7	+2.2	−2.5

voters consistently rated the Prime Minister much more positively than voters in the rest of the UK. In the final YouGov campaign poll in Scotland, for example, 43% of respondents thought that Brown was doing a good job and 39% a bad job as Prime Minister whereas similar questions in UK-wide polls consistently produced large negative majorities. Brown's Scottishness may have been a disadvantage in some parts of the country but it was a definite advantage in Scotland.

In England and Wales, London had clearly the smallest Labour decline and the most niggardly Conservative increase. In addition, uniquely, there was a fall in support for others. In the latter case, rises for the BNP and UKIP were offset by sharp falls in votes for the Green party and 'other others' such as Respect. The large concentrations of ethnic minority and Muslim voters in London may explain the limited damage that Labour suffered especially given that the Iraq war was a highly salient issue in 2005. Although survey data would be required to test this suggestion in detail, some support for it is given by the fact that across England there is a significant positive correlation (0.502, $n = 531$) between change in Labour's vote share and the percentage of ethnic minority residents in a constituency. The more there were of the latter, the less badly Labour did.

Much greater variations in both the direction and extent of changes in party support would be expected at constituency level, since general elections are more than simply national contests between party leaders (notwithstanding the impression given by the leaders' debates). Local personalities, issues, events and traditions as well as constituency campaigning at the grass roots all have a part to play. In 2010, indeed, we would expect even more variation than normal because of the constituency boundary changes that were implemented in England and Wales. Of the 573 constituencies outside Scotland (where there was no change) only 81 were unaltered when compared with 2005. For the remainder, we have estimates of what the distribution of votes would have been in 2005 had people voted in the new constituencies as they actually did in the old.[2] These 'notional results'—which are used to measure changes in party support—are enormously valuable but they are estimates, not exact figures, and it would be miraculous if there were not some error in all cases and significant under- or over-estimates of votes in a few. Nonetheless, the general accuracy of the estimates (and the impressive continuity in the geographical distribution of votes) is illustrated by the correlations coefficients measuring the association between the parties' estimated shares of votes in 2005 and actual shares in 2010 which are 0.972 for the Conservatives, 0.936 for Labour and 0.905 for the Liberal Democrats ($n = 629$ in all cases). Restricting analysis to unchanged constituencies does not produce significantly different statistics.

Even so, there remains considerable variation in the extent of change and, in some constituencies, its direction. Outside Scotland, Conservative support declined in 36 constituencies while Labour's rose in 37. Over the country as a whole, the share won by the Liberal Democrats fell in 252 seats, stayed the same in three and increased in the remainder. Even when changes were in the expected direction their magnitude varied hugely. Conservative increases, for example, ranged from less than one percentage point to more than 16 (in Hartlepool) while Labour decreases peaked at almost 24 points in Barnsley East (which might be explained by an overestimate of original Labour strength). The range of outcomes for the Liberal Democrats is truly spectacular—from a drop of 16 points in Orpington to a gain of 25 points in Redcar. The latter exemplifies the role of local issues since the government's apparent inability to prevent the run-down of the steel industry in the area resulted in Labour being severely punished by the voters.

Although specifically local factors explain many constituency variations and thus make it difficult to generalise, it is worth looking for systematic patterns. A first step is to consider how changes in support for the various parties were inter-related and Table 5 reports the relevant correlation coefficients. Not unexpectedly the Conservatives did worse where the other main parties did better, and vice versa. It is worth noting, however, that there is no significant relationship between changes in Conservative support and the performance of UKIP. This seriously undermines simplistic assertions that UKIP costs the Conservatives seats and perhaps even cost them a clear majority in the 2010 election (since there were 21 seats where the Conservatives lost by a smaller number of votes than UKIP obtained). Indeed, on the basis of these data it is more plausible to claim that UKIP cost Labour votes—the more the former improved their position, the worse the performance of the latter. The BNP also seems to have weakened Labour (the coefficient is statistically significant and negative), presumably drawing support from elements of the white working class alienated from their former party. Nonetheless, Labour's fortunes were most strongly linked to the ups and downs of the Liberal Democrats.

It might reasonably be expected that the nature of party competition in different constituencies would affect changes in party support (for

5. Correlations between changes in vote shares

	Change % Con	Change % Lab	Change % Lib Dem	Change % Nat	Change % UKIP
Change % Con	—	—	—	—	—
Change % Lab	−0.288	—	—	—	—
Change % Lib Dem	−0.270	−0.519	—	—	—
Change % Nat	−0.375	0.193	−0.557	—	—
Change % UKIP	0.053	−0.131	0.065	0.031	—
Change % BNP	−0.008	−0.274	0.043	−0.401	−0.131

Note: Significant coefficients are printed in bold. The n for coefficients involving Conservatives, Labour and Liberal Democrats only is 629; for these parties and the nationalists it is 98, and the BNP 245 and UKIP 588. The Speaker's seats in 2005 and 2010 are excluded.

6. Changes in overall vote shares in different electoral contexts (England only)

Top two parties in 2005

	Con Lab	Con Lib Dem	Lab Con	Lab Lib Dem	Lib Dem Con	Lib Dem Lab
Con	+3.6	+4.2	+4.6	+3.4	+3.6	+5.0
Lab	−10.0	−6.8	−7.5	−6.0	−5.4	−5.8
Lib Dem	+3.4	+0.4	+0.8	+0.7	+0.7	+1.3
(n)	(127)	(80)	(192)	(84)	(39)	(9)

example, due to tactical voting) and Table 6, which is restricted to England, due to the complexities of the party systems in Scotland and Wales, presents data enabling us to check this suggestion. In fact, variations in the parties competing for first and second places appear to have had remarkably little effect on changes in party support. In constituencies where the Conservatives led Labour the latter party did particularly badly and the Liberal Democrats appear to have benefitted. Apart from these cases, however, there are no marked differences across the various categories.

There is ample evidence that the quality and intensity of local campaigning affects election outcomes[3] and in the inter-election period before 2010 there was much comment on the effort being put into target seats by the Conservatives, largely funded, apparently, by Lord Ashcroft. There was also some poll evidence during the campaign that the party was doing better in these seats than in the country as a whole. An elementary analysis of the election results suggests that the strategy did indeed have some impact where the party was in competition with Labour. In seats that were either safely held (80) or hopeless (247) for the Conservatives, they had their smallest advances (+3.0 and +3.5 points on average). Better results came in seats held but potentially at risk (+4.2; $n = 20$), those marginally held (+5.2; $n = 27$), probable gains (+4.2; $n = 33$) and possible gains (+4.6; $n = 77$).[4]

In the cases of Conservative-Liberal Democrat competition, safe and hopeless seats again had relatively small increases (+3.6 in both cases, $ns = 52$ and 25). However, the Conservatives made least headway in the ten constituencies where they were very closely behind the Liberal Democrats. Overall, the rewards for all the effort and money put in may appear modest. It should be remembered, however, that the Conservatives' opponents would have been targeting the same seats and that any edge in seats that are not safe or hopeless is worth having. On the other hand, the modest benefits to the Conservatives should act as a reminder that no amount of direct mail, leaflets or advertising hoardings is a substitute for the essential mobilising activities on the ground—canvassing and the get out the vote operation on polling day—that are the hallmarks of an effective local campaign.

During the 2005–2010 Parliament, the scandal relating to MPs' expenses made headlines for weeks on end and there were numerous prophecies that an enraged electorate would wreak terrible vengeance on sitting MPs when the chance came. All incumbents, it was suggested, could be tarred with the expenses brush and suffer at the polls. In line with this kind of thinking, a record number of incumbents stood down in 2010. We can make an initial assessment of the extent to which incumbents were punished by the voters by comparing the performance of incumbent MPs of each party with that of new candidates selected to replace an outgoing MP. This is done in Table 7 and it is clear that the most apocalyptic fears or hopes raised by the expenses scandal simply failed to materialise. In all parties, incumbents overall achieved a better performance than new candidates selected to defend seats where the incumbent had resigned. It may be, of course, that these new candidates were being punished for the sins of their departed colleagues.

The patterns of changes in party support across constituencies between the 2005 and the 2010 general elections were complicated and were affected not just by being mostly based on estimates of the 2005 results, but also by a number of purely local factors. This can be illustrated by looking at the worst and best Conservative performance. If we compare the actual Conservative vote share with that predicted on the basis of 2005 performance then their worst results include a constituency where a former party leader retired (Folkestone and Hythe), one

7. Mean changes in party vote shares (incumbents versus non-incumbents)

Con-held seats		Lab-held seats		Lib Dem-held seats	
Mean change % Con		Mean change % Lab		Mean change % LDem	
Incum	Non-incum	Incum	Non-incum	Incum	Non-incum
+4.2	+2.9	−5.1	−7.4	+0.6	−4.7
(152)	(55)	(242)	(106)	(53)	(10)

where the former MP was heavily embroiled in the expenses scandal (Bromsgrove), one where they faced a popular local MP (Westmorland and Lonsdale) and one where they faced the Liberal Democrat leader (Sheffield Hallam). On the other hand, their best results included Crewe and Nantwich where they had won an intervening by-election, Montgomery where the Liberal Democrat MP was colourful but controversial, and Cardiff Central and Hartlepool for no very obvious reasons. There were, of course, nationwide movements in votes in response to national issues and personalities (although the response was different in Scotland), but the extent of local variation in 2010 was probably greater than has been seen for some time.

Patterns of party support in 2010

When we turn from change between elections to variations in absolute levels of support for the parties, we are on territory that is much more familiar in that the patterns are very similar to those evident in previous elections. To begin with, regional variations in party support (Table 8) show that, with the exception of London, there remains a broad north–south division. Labour's strongest areas outside London remain Scotland, Wales and the three northernmost English regions. In each of these, it was the largest party. On the other hand, Labour trailed the Conservatives in the Midlands and came a poor third in the south and east of England. Conservative support across regions is a mirror image of that for Labour but the Liberal Democrats have a relatively even spread of support across the country although, as usual, they did rather better than average in the south of England and, on this occasion, rather poorly in Scotland. A north–south division is even more apparent in terms of seats won. In Scotland, Wales and northern England, despite making gains, the Conservatives won only 51 seats compared with 168 for Labour and 33 for the Liberal Democrats. In the Eastern, South East and South West regions, in contrast, the tally was 162 for the Conservatives, 10 for Labour and 23 for the Liberal Democrats.

Correlation coefficients measuring the associations between the shares of the vote obtained by the parties in the constituencies and a standard set of socio-demographic variables are shown in Table 9 and the data contain few surprises in respect of the major parties, even though the census data are now somewhat dated.

The Conservatives, as might be expected, had a larger share of the vote in constituencies where there were more professional and managerial workers, owner occupiers, older voters, people with degrees and in more rural areas. They performed less well where there were more manual workers, social renters, younger people, and students, those having no educational qualifications and no car, people belonging to ethnic minorities and in more urban areas. The pattern of Labour support was almost a mirror image of that for the Conservatives while that for the Liberal Democrats was, broadly, a paler reflection of it.

8. Party shares of votes and seats won in regions (row %)

	Con	Lab	Lib Dem	SNP/PC	Other
North East	23.7	43.6	23.6	—	9.1
Seats	2	22	2		
North West	31.7	39.4	21.6	—	7.3
Seats	22	47	6		
Yorkshire/Humber	32.5	34.7	22.9	—	9.9
Seats	18	32	3		
East Midlands	41.2	29.8	20.8	—	8.2
Seats	31	15	0		
West Midlands	39.5	30.6	20.5	—	9.4
Seats	33	24	2		
Eastern	47.1	19.6	24.0	—	9.3
Seats	52	2	4		
London	34.5	36.6	22.1	—	6.8
Seats	28	38	7		
South East	49.3	16.2	26.2	—	8.3
Seats	74	4	4		2
South West	42.8	15.4	34.7	—	7.1
Seats	36	4	15		
Wales	26.1	36.2	20.1	11.3	6.3
Seats	8	26	3	3	
Scotland	16.7	42.0	18.9	19.9	2.5
Seats	1	41	11	6	

Unlike the Conservatives, however, the Liberal Democrat vote was slightly stronger where there were more young people and students. This may reflect impressionistic accounts during the campaign that younger people were the most impressed by Nick Clegg's performance in the leaders' debates. The large numbers of UKIP and BNP candidates in 2010 enables us to present a similar analysis of variations in these parties' votes. The coefficients for UKIP are an unusual mixture. The party did best where there was a high proportion of older people, owner occupiers and in rural areas but also prospered where there were more manual workers and people lacking educational qualifications. On the other hand, UKIP did worse in areas where there were more professionals, students and people with degrees (which are characteristic of more middle-class areas) but also where there were more social renters, people with no car and ethnic minorities (characteristic of more working-class areas). The BNP clearly did better in urban working-class areas—there are strong positive correlations with proportion of manual workers, social renters, people with no educational qualifications and having no car—and significantly less well the more professionals and managers, people employed in agriculture, owner occupiers, students and people with a degree there were in a constituency.

In sum, despite the change in the fortunes of the major parties, the geographical and hence social bases of their support remained much as they have been in the past. The emerging profiles of support for UKIP and the

9. Bivariate correlations between party shares of vote in 2010 and constituency characteristics

	Conservative	Labour	Liberal Democrat	UKIP	BNP
% Prof./ Managerial	0.553	−0.532	0.317	−0.152	−0.558
% Manual Workers	−0.602	0.591	−0.349	0.116	0.573
% Owner occupiers	0.603	−0.552	0.088	0.295	−0.123
% Social renters	−0.676	0.680	−0.247	−0.227	0.306
% Aged 18–24	−0.406	0.313	0.094	−0.304	−0.076*
% Aged 65+	0.293	−0.409	0.162	0.343	−0.073*
% In agriculture	0.296	−0.481	0.232	0.186	−0.235
Persons per hectare	−0.315	0.387	−0.031*	−0.291	−0.021*
% With degrees	0.164	−0.238	0.351	−0.378	−0.582
% No qualifications	−0.538	0.582	−0.424	0.139	0.642
% Students	−0.344	0.216	0.180	−0.334	−0.175
% With no car	−0.738	0.737	−0.218	−0.319	0.225
% Ethnic minority	−0.229	0.343	−0.078	−0.301	0.005*
(*n*)	(630)	(630)	(630)	(556)	(337)

Note: All coefficients are significant at the 0.01 level except those asterisked.

BNP suggest that the two find support in different sorts of areas. In interpreting the data in Table 9, however, it should be borne in mind not only that the social data are rather out of date but that on their own the figures tell us nothing about the party choices of the people belonging to the various groups involved—for that, surveys and polls are required. Rather, correlations provide information about the relationship between the characteristics of constituencies and levels of party support.

Turnout

The level of turnout in general elections has been the subject of considerable debate since the post-war low figure of 59.1% in 2001 which was followed by only a slight increase to 61.3% in 2005.[5] During the campaign there were predictions of a 'bumper' turnout in some quarters. These were fuelled partly by the increased proportions of poll respondents saying that they were 'certain' to vote but also by a report from the Electoral Commission, that large numbers of people were downloading electoral registration forms from its website (although one wonders how all of these people were missed off the electoral register in the first place, since registration is compulsory). On polling day itself, there were reports of long queues forming at some polling stations (not to mention polling stations running out of ballot papers). In fact these were due to the incompetence of election officials rather than to a huge turnout. Turnout did increase to 65.3%, although this is still a good deal lower than at any general election between 1950 and 1997.

Table 10 shows that turnout increased in every region but by most in London and the North West which had been among the lowest turnout regions in 2005. As with support for the main parties, there remains something of a north–south divide in turnout with the three northern English regions having the poorest record. The new constituency boundaries restrict our ability to analyse turnout change at constituency level—since the notional vote figures are not intended to be reliable in respect of turnout—but it seems clear that turnout increased almost everywhere. Among the 140 unchanged constituencies only nine experienced a fall in turnout and in five of these cases the decline was by less than one percent.[6]

The across-the-board nature of the rise in turnout suggests that we should look for nationwide explanations. The televised debates between party leaders (and the ensuing 'Cleggmania') probably increased the interest of the electorate, but perhaps more important is that the election result was universally expected to be close and on that basis more electors than of late took the trouble to cast a ballot. Elections in which a close outcome is predicted usually have higher turnouts than those which look to be easy victories for one side or the other. As Anthony King wrote in the *Daily Telegraph* after the 2001 turnout debacle: 'Just provide the voters with a closely fought election…and, make no mistake, they will again turn out in their droves'. If we substitute 'semi-respectable numbers' for 'droves', then that is what happened in 2010.

As usual, the level of 2010 turnout varied considerably across constituencies. Having been held by Liverpool Riverside for the previous three elections, the turnout wooden spoon passed to Manchester Central (44.3%). At the other end of the scale, the highest turnout (77.3%) was recorded in East Renfrewshire. To put this into

10. Regional and national turnout in 2010

	Turnout 2005	Turnout 2010	Change 05–10
North East	57.4	60.9	+3.5
North West	57.3	62.3	+5.0
Yorkshire/Humber	59.1	63.2	+4.1
East Midlands	62.7	66.6	+3.9
West Midlands	60.7	64.5	+3.8
Eastern	64.0	67.6	+3.6
London	57.8	64.6	+6.8
South East	64.7	68.0	+3.3
South West	66.5	69.1	+2.6
Wales	62.6	64.8	+2.2
Scotland	60.8	63.8	+3.0
Great Britain	61.3	65.3	+4.0

11. Bivariate correlations between turnout in 2010 and constituency characteristics

% Professional and Managerial	0.645	% in agriculture	0.370
% Manual Workers	-0.669	Persons per hectare	-0.390
% Owner occupiers	0.650	% Ethnic minority	-0.244
% Social renters	-0.691	% With degrees	0.362
% Private renters	-0.125	% With no car	-0.788
% Aged 18–24	-0.396		
% Aged 65+	0.287	Constit. marginality 05	0.459

Notes: All coefficients are significant at the 0.01 level. $n = 630$ (Speaker's seat excluded) except for 2005 marginality from which Wyre Forest (Independent victory in 2005) and Glasgow North East (Speaker's seat 2005) are also excluded ($n = 628$).

perspective, it is worth remembering that it is a lower figure than the overall turnout in the 1992 election (77.9%). More generally in 2010, only five constituencies had turnouts in the 40s, 109 in the 50s, 370 in the 60s and 146 in the 70s.

As with the distribution of support for the major parties, in examining turnout variations across constituencies, we encounter a highly predictable and familiar pattern. Table 11 shows correlations between the level of turnout and census variables indicating the socio-economic characteristics of constituencies as well as their marginality (or 'notional marginality' in many cases) in 2005. In general—and it is nothing new—the coefficients for the social variables indicate that, despite the overall increase in turnout, Britain continues to be divided into relatively low turnout and relatively high turnout constituencies and the two are very different in social terms. The former are mainly urban, working-class and poor; the latter rural and suburban, middle-class and relatively affluent. It is perhaps worth noting, however, that although most coefficients are of the same order as they were in 2005, the proportion of ethnic minority residents is not such a strongly negative influence on turnout (-0.254) as it was in 2005 (-0.402).

The closeness of the contest in a constituency in the previous election (marginality) is also regularly associated with turnout levels. Parties put greater campaign efforts into more marginal seats (paying little attention to those that are either very safe or hopeless for them) and, unsurprisingly, these efforts usually bear fruit in higher turnouts. In 2010, however, many voters would have been quite unaware of the marginality status of their new constituency. The correlation coefficient (0.459) remains substantial but it is noticeably smaller than the equivalent coefficient in 2005 (0.712). This suggests that in addition to differential campaigning the electorate's awareness of how safe or marginal their seat is plays some part in determining whether or not they vote.

The electoral system

It must be doubtful whether the electoral system used to elect the House of Commons has ever been subject to as much attention in an election as it was in 2010. In part, this was because Labour, in what was widely interpreted as an act of desperation, held out the offer of a referendum on changing the system. In part also, it derived from commentators recognising that the bias of the electoral system against them made it difficult for the Conservatives to win an overall majority of seats. In 2005, the operation of the electoral system had been massively to the advantage of Labour which won 56.6% of the seats with only 36.2% of the votes. The ratio of votes for the two leading parties was approximately 52:48 in Labour's favour, but the ratio of seats was 64:36. In 2010, the Conservatives won a greater share of the votes but only 48.3% of the (non-Northern Ireland) seats. The two party ratio of votes was 55:45 but there was no 'winner's bonus' and the ratio of seats was only 54:46. This bias against the Conservatives arises in part because, despite the implementation of new constituency boundaries, seats won by the Conservatives have more electors (average 72,477) than those won by Labour (average 68,407). In addition turnout was higher in Conservative seats (68.3%) than in Labour seats (61.2%). The effect is that elected Conservative MPs averaged 23,866 votes and elected Labour MPs 19,383. It need hardly be said that the system is very disproportional for the Liberal Democrats who took just 9% of seats with almost 24% of votes. The problem for the Liberal Democrats—shared to some extent by the Conservatives—is that results under the first-past-the post system are affected by the geographical distribution, as well as the sheer amount, of votes and their support is not very effectively distributed for this purpose. The new government (or at least the dominant Conservative element in it) has accorded a high priority to a further boundary review with greater emphasis on equalising electorates. The expectation is that this will reduce electoral system bias against the party, but whether it will do so to a significant extent remains to be seen.

Explaining the outcome

Although the primary focus of this article has been on the election results themselves it seems appropriate to conclude with a few brief thoughts on how the outcome of the 2010 election might be explained. The deviation of Scotland from the national trends has already been considered but the reason why the Conservatives beat Labour fairly comfortably elsewhere is related, in that it probably boils down to the fact that the electorate preferred David Cameron to Gordon Brown. Recent electoral research in Britain has stressed that evaluations of party leaders have come to play a larger part in voters' decisions than previously.[7] Partly, this is because the personalities and characteristics, the strengths, weaknesses and likeability of the party leaders (and even the clothes worn by their wives) have come to play a much larger part in media coverage of politics. This increased emphasis was highlighted in 2010, of course, by the leaders' debates. Although Nick Clegg made a serious impact on the public in these, the more important fact is that throughout the campaign—and for a long time before—Cameron comfortably led Brown as the electorate's preferred Prime Minister. By the end of the campaign, according to the BES rolling surveys, 33% were for Cameron, 25% for Brown and 22% for Clegg. At the same time, although neither of the leading contenders were particularly liked, Cameron was consistently liked more than Brown scoring 4.4 to Brown's 3.7 (on a 0–10 dislike-like scale) as the campaign drew to a close. In the results article in the 2005 volume in this series I concluded that 'to a considerable extent... the future electoral fate of the Conservatives is tied up with the leadership succession'.[8] In the event, Cameron's succession provided the long-awaited electoral fillip although it was also critical that Brown succeeded Blair as Prime Minister and leader of the Labour party.

On the other hand, policies and performance do continue to play a part in voters' calculations and in this respect the Conservatives were far from clearly preferred to Labour. When BES respondents were asked during the campaign which party was likely to deal best with the issue that they had nominated as the most important to them, the two parties were virtually neck and neck. As the election loomed, 26% chose the Conservatives and 25% Labour (with 12% suggesting the Liberal Democrats and 26% saying that no party would do so). Clearly, voters still harboured doubts about the ability of the Conservatives to perform in office. It is possible that this explains why the Conservative victory over Labour—although substantial—was not big enough to deliver them an overall majority of seats.

Finally, I referred at the outset to the last-minute evaporation of support for the Liberal Democrats. Although some pollsters claim that the later interviews conducted for their final polls did indicate some draining away of Liberal Democrat support, this does seem to have been very much a last-minute development. We have seen that there is some evidence that those most attracted to the Liberal Democrats by Clegg's performance in the debates tended to be first-time voters. Young people tend to have a relatively low level of interest in politics and a greater propensity not to turn out at the moment of truth and this may explain the gap between support for the Liberal Democrats in opinion polls and the real poll. However, the surge and decline of the Liberal Democrats in the 2010 election campaign remains something of a mystery.

---

1   Local election data are taken from the series of *Local Elections Handbooks* produced by C. Rallings and M. Thrasher of the Local Government Chronicle Elections Centre, University of Plymouth.

2   'Notional' 2005 results in constituencies with changed boundaries are taken from C. Rallings and M. Thrasher, *Media Guide to the New Parliamentary Constituencies*, Local Government Chronicle Elections Centre, University of Plymouth, 2007.

3 See, for example, D. Denver, G. Hands and I MacAllister, 'The Electoral Impact of Constituency Campaigning in Britain, 1992–2001', *Political Studies*, 52, 2004, 289–306.

4 Seats were classified as 'safe' or 'hopeless' where the relevant majority was more than 15%, 'potentially at risk' or 'possible gain' where it was between 5 and 15% and 'marginally held' or 'probable gain' where it was less than 5%.

5 All turnout figures are provisional and based on valid votes cast (excluding, therefore, voters who did vote in the election but whose ballots—for whatever reason—were rejected as invalid). For the most part, numbers of rejected votes are small but it is worth noting that in the Buckingham constituency of the Speaker, no fewer than 1067 ballots were rejected.

6 The four with more significant turnout declines form two odd small clusters—Blaenau Gwent (−4.3) and Rhondda (−1.5) on the one hand and Dorset West (−1.8) and Dorset South (−1.3) on the other.

7 See H. Clarke, D. Sanders, M. Stewart and P. Whiteley, *Performance Politics and the British Voter*, Cambridge University Press, 2009.

8 D. Denver, 'The Results: How Britain Voted' in A. Geddes and J. Tonge (eds), *Britain Decides*, Palgrave, 2005.

Five Days in May: A New Political Order Emerges[1]

The post-election arithmetic could not have been more finely balanced. Sixty-five per cent of voters had spoken at the ballot box but it was not at all clear what they had said. No party could secure an overall majority of 326 seats on its own and only a combination of the Conservatives and Liberal Democrats together could command a significant majority of seats in the House of Commons. A progressive 'rainbow alliance' embracing Labour, the Lib Dems, the SNP, Plaid Cymru, the SDLP and the sole Green MP, was widely discussed, and although such an alliance, even if it could be formed, could claim the support of 53% of those who voted on 6 May, it could muster just 328 seats in the Commons, thus providing only a perilously thin majority.[2]

The electoral arithmetic thus pointed in the direction of some form of alliance or arrangement between the Conservatives and the Liberal Democrats but conflicts between ideological traditions and instincts, personal relationships and party interests, plunged Westminster politics into uncharted territory in the week following polling day as the potential political outcomes were worked through. What eventually emerged after five days of negotiations was an outcome barely mentioned before polling day: a formal Conservative–Liberal Democrat coalition that substantially reshaped the political landscape. David Cameron and Nick Clegg proclaimed the emergence of a 'new politics' through a coalition they believed had the potential for 'era changing, convention-challenging, radical reform'.[3] How the coalition came into being, the lessons that can be drawn from it, and the political projections that can be made from the organisational and policy commitments on which the coalition is based all provide a foundation for making an interim assessment about how politics may be shaped in the immediate years to come.

doi:10.1093/pa/gsq030

Party positioning

The Conservative dilemma in the aftermath of the election was whether they should try to form a minority administration, the preference of many Tory MPs, or a coalition. Whereas before the election most commentators assumed that a coalition would not be on the agenda for any of the parties, Cameron appears to have dismissed the idea of minority government almost immediately. He believed that the economic problems facing the country were so serious that they required strong, stable government which a minority administration, sustained at best by a confidence and supply agreement (support in votes of confidence and on the Budget), could not provide. The result would be a rapid second general election with no reason to believe that the outcome would be significantly different. There was a risk that the public might blame the Conservatives for an unwanted second election by failing to respond positively to the public's dissatisfaction with politics as usual. In spite of repeated warnings about the dangers of a hung parliament from Conservative politicians, City analysts and some journalists, the public had nonetheless voted for this outcome, implying they had no confidence in any single party to govern the country and therefore desired that the politicians talk to and co-operate with each other. A second election might indeed be won but probably not with a sufficiently large majority to justify the political upheaval and the economic risk, as Labour found in 1974 when the party barely improved its position between the February and October general elections. Faced with political disappointment in Conservative ranks, and with his reputation and career on the line, Cameron wanted instead an outcome that would shake up the political kaleidoscope. A formal coalition with the Liberal Democrats might provide strong, stable government for years rather than months to come, combining together the support of 59% of the voters. Such boldness could also enable him to seize the political initiative. As he indicated in the foreword to the final coalition agreement, he was 'uninspired' by the prospect of minority government.[4] That a coalition would also enable him to tame the more strident elements on the right flank of his party was a further benefit.

Given the scale of the party's failure, Labour emerged from the election in relatively buoyant mood. Having feared an electoral meltdown and coming third in the share of the total vote, an outcome that denied the Conservatives outright victory was better than anticipated. Nonetheless, recognising the scale of the defeat and looking at the balance of MPs, some concluded that the party should go into opposition, suffering the short-term consequences in the hope of preserving its reputation and credibility for the longer term. The Conservatives might not have won an overall majority but Labour had certainly lost it and had no claim to continue to govern even if, constitutionally, the Prime Minister had the right to try to form an administration. But then there were some, particularly on the Blairite wing of the party, who saw a remote opportunity to fulfil the New Labour mission: there was perhaps a chance to repair the historic fracture of the centre-left through a realignment of Labour and the Liberal Democrats in a new progressive alliance.

The problem was that although ideologically a Labour–Lib Dem agreement might appear more credible and politically cohesive than a Conservative–Lib Dem arrangement, and would be a deal with which most Liberal Democrat activists would be more naturally comfortable, the arithmetic did not add up. A 'rainbow alliance' could not command sufficient support in the House of Commons: able to rely at best on just 328 seats—which assumed that every MP in the bloc would always support the coalition—such an administration would have been inherently unstable, susceptible to every self-interested claim made against it by the minor parties. Mutual antagonism between Labour and the SNP also meant that most Labour calculations about the prospects for a 'rainbow alliance' did not include the SNP's six MPs thus reducing any potential alliance to minority government status.

None of the options on the table were particularly palatable for the third party. Former leader Paddy Ashdown summed up their dilemma when he declared that the British electorate had 'invented a deliciously painful torture mechanism for the Liberal Democrats because our instincts go one way but the mathematics go the other'.[5]

For a party that had leapt 10% in the polls as a result of Clegg's performance in the first party leaders debate, and had hopes of leapfrogging over Labour into second place, 'Cleggmania' had proved a false dawn as they emerged from the election with five fewer seats than in the previous parliament, though a point higher share of the vote. In historical context, however, it was a good result: only in 2005 had the party secured more seats in the post-war period and it was their equal second best result since 1929.

Despite failing to make a significant electoral breakthrough, the campaign nonetheless established the Liberal Democrats collectively, and Nick Clegg in particular, as serious political players in the mind of the public and media in a way the party had not been perceived for many decades. As a consequence, holding the balance of power, the party was now under considerable pressure: having asserted the credentials of three party politics would it now retreat from serious decision-making because the options available to it on both left and right might have difficult consequences?

Like Cameron, Clegg and the Liberal Democrat strategists soon concluded that minority government was not an attractive proposition. Standing passively on the sidelines was not a risk-free approach. They feared that they would share the blame for the quick collapse of a minority administration and suffer the consequences at a second election. A confidence and supply agreement was regarded as the worst of all

possible worlds: every day the party would face line-by-line votes on policies they opposed and over which they exercised no influence, but which
they would be forced to either support or risk bringing down the government. The poor state of the party's finances also meant that the party
could not afford a quick second election. The party's strategic options
therefore narrowed to a coalition with the Conservatives in some form.

In essence, the leadership faced a profound choice: would they stick
to the Ashdown strategy that had clearly aligned the party on the
centre-left since the abandonment of equidistance in the mid-1990s, or
would they accept the arithmetic conclusion of the election result and
jump to the centre-right? Could a party that believed in co-operative
politics, and whose support for electoral reform necessarily implied
support for coalitions, simply walk away, particularly at a time of great
economic uncertainty, when faced with the prospect of having to reach
a deal with a party that was not its natural partner of choice? The key
question was whether the parties could negotiate a satisfactory policy
agreement in which the clarity of the mathematical equation was buttressed politically and ideologically.

Inter-party talks

The morning after the election, Nick Clegg announced that he would
talk first with the Conservative Party on the grounds that having won
the most votes and seats it had a mandate to form the government. The
onus was now, he stressed, on the Conservative Party 'to prove that it is
capable of seeking to govern in the national interest'.[6] The Liberal
Democrats had been preparing for this moment for some time. Six
months prior to the general election the party nominated a team of four
MPs to prepare the way for how, and on what basis, it would conduct
inter-party negotiations. This team operated in parallel to the party's
manifesto and general election preparation teams in order that there
were clearly established priorities. The membership of all three teams
consequently overlapped. Danny Alexander MP led the preparations for
the election manifesto and sat on the general election planning group
and the coalition negotiating group (although this latter group was
never formally named as such). Andrew Stunnell MP, regarded as
having his finger firmly on the pulse of Liberal Democrat activism, had
experience of inter-party negotiations at local government level and was
a member of both the general election planning and coalition negotiating groups. Fellow MPs Chris Huhne and David Laws, regarded as two
of the party's best negotiators, completed the team. Huhne brought
negotiating experience from his time in Europe and in business and
Laws, in his capacity as the party's Policy Director, had advised the
Scottish Liberal Democrats during the inter-party negotiations that followed the 1999 Scottish Parliament elections.

The first meeting with the Conservative negotiating team—MPs
William Hague, George Osborne and Oliver Letwin and Edward

Llewellyn, the Conservative Leader's Chief of Staff—took place at the Cabinet Office on the morning of Saturday 8 May following direct discussions on the telephone between Cameron and Clegg the night before. The talks were almost entirely political in nature: the civil servants had little role beyond providing the room and facilitating the arrangements for the gathering that morning. The discussions proved to be friendly and constructive and it rapidly became clear that the Conservatives wanted a deal.

David Cameron had indicated the day before that he wanted to make a 'big, open and comprehensive offer'.[7] He had laid out where the broad policy negotiating lines would be: more powers to the EU and anything that looked like a weakening of immigration or defence policy were ruled out; but there was common ground around the need for education reform, new measures to establish a low-carbon economy, urgent reform of the political system, reform of the tax system and protection of civil liberties and the scrapping of ID cards. He made clear his belief that the election result meant 'it is reasonable to expect that the bulk of the policies in our manifesto should be implemented'.[8] In a statement to Conservative Party supporters on the Saturday evening, he noted nonetheless that the party could 'give ground, both in the national interest and in the interest of forging an open and trusting partnership', on areas such as reducing taxes on the lowest paid, in return for which he hoped the Lib Dems would give ground on their stance regarding the tackling of the national deficit.[9]

Beyond policy, the scale of the deal being offered by the Conservatives became even clearer when discussions turned to how a formal coalition would work. Here, the Conservatives tabled an offer that astounded their Lib Dem counterparts: 20 ministerial positions of which five would be in Cabinet. But for the Liberal Democrats two key sticking points remained. First, the instinct of many of their supporters was still to prefer Labour: for many, a coalition with the Conservatives would be an act of unforgivable apostasy. And second, the offer of an all-party committee of inquiry on political and electoral reform was simply not strong enough. Electoral reform was at the heart of the party's raison d'etre. An all-party committee would risk the issue simply being kicked into the long grass.

Over the weekend talks were also underway, albeit informally, between leading Liberal Democrats and Labour MPs: a 'rainbow alliance' had not yet been fully ruled out. But an obstacle to the talks was the prospect of the deeply unpopular Gordon Brown remaining as Prime Minister. Thus the Labour leader's announcement on Monday 10 May that he would stand down at the next party conference in September cleared the way for formal discussions to take place.

The Liberal Democrat negotiating team faced Lord Mandelson, Lord Adonis, Ed Miliband MP, and one of Brown's closest confidantes, Ed Balls MP. These negotiations faced two major obstacles: one was the weakness of the electoral arithmetic on which a progressive 'rainbow alliance' would be based; the second was that the Liberal Democrats were being asked to negotiate with a Labour Party whose long-term leader was unknown.

In contrast to the positive atmosphere of the negotiations with the Conservatives, it rapidly emerged that the first set of talks with Labour were chilly and generally unproductive. The second meeting of the two teams the following day was somewhat warmer and at a policy level more productive, but it soon became clear that the Labour negotiating team did not have a mandate for their discussions. Whilst the talks were going on, senior Labour MPs, including former cabinet ministers such as John Reid and David Blunkett, were being interviewed on television rejecting the prospect of a deal they deemed unworkable because of the arithmetic. It was also becoming increasingly clear internally that some Cabinet Ministers would refuse to serve.

Negotiations are naturally perceived differently by each side depending on the particular stance of each participant. The Liberal Democrats emerged disappointed from the first set of talks, unclear about whether Labour really wanted a deal: only Mandelson and Adonis—both advocates of electoral reform and progressive realignment—were thought to want a positive outcome to the talks and Labour was perceived to have offered little by way of concessions in the policy discussions. When senior Labour members were then seen on TV rejecting the very notion of a deal, the approach foundered. From the Labour perspective, however, things looked very different. Policy concessions were reportedly identified and offered during the talks, including tax changes to benefit those earning under £10,000, an end to the proposed third runway at Heathrow, and the scrapping of ID cards. Tempered by a realism about the difficulties of governance borne of 13 years in power, Labour perceived that the Lib Dems were naïve about what could realistically be achieved by a government with a barely workable majority, and were hankering after policies which Labour had already considered in office and had dismissed as unworkable. The Labour hierarchy was concerned that they were effectively being invited to take part in a 'Dutch auction' of policy commitments regardless of cost or the prospects for implementation. And above all, they feared that they were being used by the Liberal Democrats to force the Conservatives into greater concessions, specifically on electoral reform—a fear confirmed when the Conservative's lead negotiator, William Hague, announced on the Monday evening, 10 May, that they would 'go the extra mile' and make a final offer of a referendum on the Alternative Vote electoral system.[10]

Liberal Democrat attitudes to the Labour talks split in large part along a generational axis. A significant number of Liberal Democrat parliamentarians and activists—former leaders Ashdown, Kennedy and Campbell among them—would have preferred a progressive coalition despite the obvious difficulties posed by the parliamentary arithmetic. Those Liberal Democrats whose commitment to the historic task of realignment of the left was reinforced by disdain for 1980s Thatcherism were instinctively anti-Conservative. The prospect of a government that encompassed Simon Hughes on the Liberal left and Bill Cash on the Conservative right was anathema. But within Liberal Democrat ranks there was a younger generation—the 'Orange Book' Liberals, including the party leader Nick Clegg himself—who did not instinctively loathe the Conservative Party in the same way, and who were just as likely to be suspicious of a Labour Party that they perceived to be the purveyor of big state solutions and instinctively illiberal on issues such as civil liberties. But the latter group within the party could never have convinced the former to support a coalition with the Conservatives unless they believed that serious discussions with Labour had been entered into in good faith and that it was clear that a deal was simply not possible.

By Monday evening, when it became clear that a deal had not been struck, there was some disquiet, particularly in the media, about the length of time it might take to reach an agreement. The four days Ted Heath had taken to negotiate with the Liberal leader Jeremy Thorpe after the inconclusive February 1974 general election was seen as a benchmark, if only because it was the only point of reference available. By the morning of Tuesday 11 May, there was thus increasing pressure on the parties to resolve the impasse. Fear of how the financial markets above all would respond to a hung parliament had defined much of the pre-general election commentary on the issue and yet, when the event came to pass, the markets were not overly affected. On the afternoon after the election the FTSE 100 fell by 4% or nearly 200 points; but when the markets reopened the following Monday, the index recovered ground, seemingly affected more by the efforts of EU member states to address the sovereign debt crisis rather than the ebb and flow of domestic UK politics. All the talk about the prospect of a hung parliament and its implications prior to polling day had served to prepare the City and international opinion on the issue: the market had 'priced in' the possibility of an uncertain result. More influential than the financial pressures were the twin concerns of the media and party management. If the negotiations were protracted there was real concern that at some point an impatient media would turn against the negotiators. Conservative and Liberal Democrat party members—parliamentarians and activists alike—had also been remarkably disciplined and control of each party's 'message' throughout the talks had been very tight. However, both sides recognised that this would not continue indefinitely.

A programme for government

With no prospect of a Labour–Liberal Democrat deal being struck, Gordon Brown resigned on the evening of Tuesday 11 May, five days after the election. The decision appeared to catch the other parties unprepared as a formal deal had not yet been finalised.

Unlike his Conservative counterpart, the Liberal Democrat leader needed the formal agreement of his party to enter the coalition: his party's rules imposed a 'triple-lock' on the negotiations. First, he needed the majority support of the parliamentary party and the Federal Executive; second, unless there was a three-quarters majority of each group in favour of the proposals, then a majority would have to be secured at a Special Conference and finally, if a majority of two-thirds was not secured at the Special Conference, then the consent of a majority of all members of the Party would have to be sought. Thus, that night the Liberal Democrat parliamentarians and Federal Executive hastily convened to discuss the deal, endorsing it with the required majority. But not before it became clear that many of the party's senior parliamentarians, including former leaders Charles Kennedy, Paddy Ashdown and David Steel, had serious reservations about the proposed course of action, with Kennedy subsequently confessing afterwards that he had abstained.

The following day the Conservatives and Liberal Democrats jointly published their coalition negotiation agreement which set out in-principle commitments on deficit reduction, the spending review, taxation, banking reform, immigration, political reform, pensions and welfare policy, education, relations with the EU, civil liberties and the environment.[11] That the document had been concluded in haste, and had not involved civil servants in the drafting, was evidenced by the patchy presentation and the absence of any costings.

Nick Clegg was appointed Deputy Prime Minister and was joined by four other Liberal Democrat MPs in the Cabinet: David Laws as Shadow Chief Secretary to the Treasury, Danny Alexander as Secretary of State for Scotland, Chris Huhne as Secretary of State for Energy and Climate Change and Vince Cable as Secretary of State for Business, Innovation and Skills. In the days that followed, 15 other Liberal Democrat MPs joined the government ensuring the party's voice was heard across a broad range of departments.

Just over a week later, the coalition formally launched its 'Programme for Government' setting out in detail, across 31 identified policy areas and over 400 individual commitments, what it planned to do over the course of the following five years. Whilst there were clearly areas of common ground, the fact that there were to be 29 policy reviews and five commissions was indicative of the significant differences that existed between the two parties. The parties simply agreed to differ when it came to votes on electoral reform, transferable tax allowances to recognise marriage in the tax system, nuclear power and fox hunting.

Whilst not papering over the differences, the two party leaders were at pains to stress that the document encompassed a strong emphasis both on responsibility and individual liberty, that it was a synthesis of the Conservatives' Big Society vision and the Liberal Democrats' focus on the citizen.[12] And, above all, the document stressed that the deficit reduction programme would take precedence over all other measures.[13]

The Coalition Agreement for Stability and Reform was also published, setting out how the working practices of government would be adapted to take account of the operational requirements of a coalition. It made clear that application of 'the principle of balance' would underpin the approach taken by both parties to 'all aspects of the conduct of the Government's business, including the allocation of responsibilities, the Government's policy and legislative programme, the conduct of its business and the resolution of disputes'.[14] The agreement is particularly notable for detailing the role and influence that Deputy Prime Minister Nick Clegg would exert over the machinery of government: the right to nominate Liberal Democrat ministers and to be fully consulted should their removal or a wider ministerial reshuffle be required; joint agreement with the Prime Minister regarding the allocation of portfolios between the parties; full participation in cabinet committees and sub-committees and the power to commission papers from the Cabinet Secretariat in order, like the Prime Minister, 'to have a full and contemporaneous overview of the business of Government'.[15]

Two new committees were established to help manage the coalition process within government, co-ordinated through the Cabinet Secretariat. The Coalition Committee is a full cabinet committee co-chaired by the Prime Minister and the Deputy Prime Minister with an equal number of representatives drawn from each party. In the event that an issue cannot be resolved by a Cabinet Committee, then either the Chair or Deputy Chair has the right to remit the issue to the Coalition Committee for consideration, though the Cabinet Office guidance made clear that 'the use of this right will be kept to a minimum'.[16] An informal working group—the Coalition Operation and Strategic Planning Group—was also established to consider the longer-term strategic planning of government business and report as necessary to the Coalition Committee.[17] With just four members— Oliver Letwin, Danny Alexander, Francis Maude and Lord Wallace of Tankerness—the purpose of this group is to deal with day-to-day problem solving and to look ahead at the political and legislative landscape and try to ensure that there will be no surprises, and that where known difficulties are anticipated these are dealt with at an early enough stage that a resolution of sorts can be reached between the parties before a crisis hits and plunges the coalition into chaos.

Arithmetic versus ideology

Cameron and Clegg both argued that the coalition deal was based on more than just arithmetic: they had, during their negotiations, found many areas of common ground. But taking the agreement as a whole is there sufficient philosophical congruence between the parties and, particularly from the Liberal Democrat perspective, where does the coalition deal leave them strategically? Did Clegg and his negotiating team drive a hard bargain that will be to the long-term advantage and renaissance of their party or, under pressure, did they accept a deal that threatens their future identity and electoral prospects? And is the coalition arrangement strong enough ideologically, strategically and organisationally to last a full five-year term?

The Liberal Democrat manifesto set out four core thematic policy areas: fair taxes, a fair start for children, a green and sustainable economy and a comprehensive clean up of politics. Having deliberately co-ordinated the work of the manifesto planning group with that of the coalition negotiating group prior to the election, it is against these themes that the coalition agreement should, from a Liberal Democrat perspective, be judged. On this score, the commitments to press ahead with further House of Lords reform, including moving to election by proportional representation, fixed term parliaments, and a bill to abolish ID Cards and repeal other laws deemed to restrict freedoms and civil liberties are all policies where the party may deliver on its agenda. Similarly, increasing the personal allowance income tax threshold for low earners, restoring the earnings link to pensions, the introduction of a pupil premium to support pupils from disadvantaged backgrounds, and moves to a green economy through support for low-carbon energy production all fit with the Liberal Democrats' core agenda.

On the other side of the political balance sheet, the Conservative Party retained much of its economic policy framework with the exception of cuts to inheritance tax which, though not abandoned, was side-lined in favour of the Liberal Democrat desire to increase the personal income tax allowance to £10,000. The Liberal Democrats made major concessions on two Conservative flagship policies, accepting transferable tax allowances for married couples whilst retaining the right to abstain in any parliamentary votes and agreeing to £6 billion of public expenditure cuts in the current financial year. The Conservatives retained their free schools programme and the ring-fencing of the NHS budget. Agreeing to the renewal of Trident was also a significant concession by the Liberal Democrats and one for which they did not secure an abstention opt-out, agreeing simply that the renewal programme would be 'scrutinised to ensure value for money' and that the party would continue 'to make the case for alternatives'.[18] And several Liberal Democrat policy priorities that featured prominently in their election campaign such as the citizen's pension and earned citizenship for illegal immigrants did not make it into the agreement.

Overall the Conservatives got the better of the deal in the economic arena, and the Liberal Democrats the political and constitutional reform agenda. Across other policy areas the division of influence between the parties is more mixed. Ultimately the test of who got the better part of the deal will come down to whether the opportunity to secure a referendum on the Alternative Vote proves, in the long term, more strategically valuable to the Liberal Democrats than the cost of being associated with the economic and associated social policies of the next few years.

In a government in which the Conservatives outnumber the Liberal Democrats by a ratio of 5:1 the party may struggle to earn sufficient independent credit for the policies it is most committed to and ensured were part of the coalition agreement. Given the broader political and economic landscape, the challenges the party will face are more likely to come from the policies it failed to prevent rather than those it was responsible for introducing. Generally, the public lacks detailed knowledge of the policies of each party. Those that matter most are therefore the flagship commitments that define the party in the public mind. For example, the Liberal Democrats have attracted many young voters in recent years (Ipsos MORI estimates that 30% of 18–24 year olds voted for them at the election[19]) in part because of their opposition to the lifting of the tuition fees cap. If the review of higher education funding recommends this, then the Liberal Democrats have the option to abstain. However, senior Liberal Democrats, including former leader Sir Menzies Campbell, have indicated that this will not be enough and they may vote against any such legislation. Similarly, the agreement sets out proposals to facilitate the building of new nuclear power stations. Again, the Liberal Democrats are opposed to this and have the option to abstain. But abstention may not be enough to insulate the party from the political consequences of these policies in terms of a loss of support among Liberal Democrat supporters. The party may not support the policies but it will be hard for it to escape the accusation that it has facilitated their introduction. And if a significant number of senior Liberal Democrats choose to vote against policies where they have been provided with an abstention opt-out, or against measures like the budget where there is no opt-out, then the relationship between the coalition partners could rapidly become severely strained.

It would require three-quarters of the Liberal Democrat parliamentary party to vote against the government on an issue in order to bring down the administration. As just over a third of the party are now members of the payroll vote, it is unlikely that the coalition would pursue a policy knowing that it risked its very existence. But the possibility of a small number of disaffected backbenchers voting on principle against key pieces of legislation is likely to be a continuing worry. Unrest in the party ranks could prove useful over time as it may give the party leader additional leverage to argue for further concessions. On the other hand, it will present two specific challenges to the health of the coalition. First, it will make the internal management of the

Conservative Party more difficult and thereby exacerbate tensions. If rebellion, even on a small scale, breaks out in Liberal Democrat ranks it may prove difficult to stop it spreading to the Conservative back-benches where a significant number of Conservative MPs are uneasy about key coalition policies such as the proposed changes to Capital Gains Tax, the introduction of fixed term Parliaments and the mechanism to be used for an early dissolution of Parliament. Second, how such divisions are perceived by the electorate will then be crucial: a coalition riven with regular disagreement may make the 'new politics' distinctly unattractive and make it more difficult to win a campaign for electoral reform that would make such coalitions a regular feature of British politics. On the other hand, if the two coalition party leaders can finesse rebellion within their ranks, providing an outlet for dissent without ultimately risking the coalition, then the tone and culture of politics may fundamentally change.

The broader economic landscape is also crucial to how the Liberal Democrats are perceived by the electorate and how internally it manages potential dissension in the ranks. The party campaigned against the Conservatives' proposed £6 billion of tax cuts in the 2010–2011 financial year arguing that it would damage the prospects for economic growth and risk a double-dip recession. And yet in the face of this Conservative negotiating red line, the party agreed and signed up to the scale of the cuts programme. Similarly, it campaigned during the general election against a 'Tory VAT bombshell' and yet the coalition's first budget raised VAT to 20%. Although there may have been good reasons for changing direction in light of rapidly changing economic circumstances—namely advice from the Governor of the Bank of England and the deteriorating economic situation in mainland Europe, particularly Greece and Spain—these u-turns will be difficult to explain to the electorate generally and to Liberal Democrat voters in particular. Labour had proposed, prior to the election, to halve the national deficit within four years: the coalition proposes to go much further than this, reducing the debt by a further £40 billion to balance the books by 2015. Tensions within the Liberal Democrats are likely to emerge at their most acute from autumn 2010 when the results of the Spending Review, and the details about how departments are to reduce spending by 25% over four years, are known. It is at this point that Liberal Democrat MPs will have to directly confront the consequences of cuts to services and jobs in their constituencies in areas such as education. All the parties are agreed about the need for a programme of deficit reduction. The political dividing line will focus on the scale and speed of that programme: the Liberal Democrats may bear the brunt of public anger if people feel that they failed to use their influence to sufficiently ameliorate policies, such as, for example, the coalition's emergency budget proposals to increase VAT, freeze child benefit for three years and impose a two-year freeze on public sector pay.

The one issue above all others that may give the Liberal Democrat leadership pause to consider their strategy is the referendum on the Alternative Vote. If the referendum is lost then the rationale for Liberal Democrat involvement in the coalition becomes unclear. Electoral reform is the single issue that most clearly defines the Liberal Democrats' raison d'etre: if a move to the Alternative Vote cannot be delivered because the Conservatives will not support what is after all the Liberal Democrats second choice policy (they would prefer the Single Transferable Vote system), then many Liberal Democrat MPs and activists will question why they should support a predominantly Conservative government that is implementing economic and social policies with which they do not agree and whose approach threatens their electoral prospects in the long term. There is already potential for significant differences between local Liberal Democrat activists and the national leadership on, for example, the scale and impact of the cuts agenda, reduced powers for local education authorities as a result of the Academies Bill and the proposed election of local police commissioners. These differences could develop into a more damaging schism if local activists pay a heavy electoral price for the stance taken by the party at Westminster without securing the holy grail of electoral reform in return.

The Liberal Democrats have also signed up to the Conservative proposal to reduce the number of parliamentary seats by 10% and equalise the size of constituencies. If the rules governing the boundary redistricting process are radically revised by the next election then the party could also suffer. They have signed up to the proposal without a clear sense of what impact it will have on their electoral fortunes: the Conservatives on the other hand have been working on this policy for months and have a clear idea of how it will benefit them.

Having entered a coalition with the Conservatives the Liberal Democrat's electoral prospects may be irrevocably altered. In a poll conducted on 5 May, Ipsos MORI found that if no party achieved an overall majority then 22% of Liberal Democrat voters would prefer the party to work with the Conservatives, but 40% of them preferred that they work with Labour.[20] Research by YouGov similarly found that 43% of Lib Dem voters described themselves as centre-left or left compared with just 29% who described themselves as centrist and 9% as centre-right or right wing.[21] Overall, 18 Liberal Democrat seats are vulnerable to a swing to Labour of just one in four voters or less.[22] It will not take much for the party's future electoral prospects to be ravaged.

However, the Conservatives will also be vulnerable should Liberal Democrat voters desert: they could lose up to 38 seats if just one in three Lib Dem voters switch to Labour.[23] Ultimately then it is in both party's mutual interest to keep the coalition going as long as possible.

In light of the scale of public spending cuts and tax rises, it will serve neither party to face an early second general election.

Changing the culture of politics?

If the coalition lasts, it will have an impact on the way government and parliament operates; on how the Conservative and Liberal Democrat parties are managed; and on how election campaigns are conducted in the future.

Governing will necessarily be a slower process as decisions will have to command the support of both coalition parties. The instantaneous demands of online journalism, 24-hr news, and the blogosphere may therefore pose significant challenges for the coalition as and when difficulties arise: rapid rebuttal may not always be possible. Unlike the Conservative Party, the Liberal Democrats have strong but often cumbersome internal democratic machinery for policy development and authorisation and it is not yet clear how their internal party procedures will mesh with the speed of decision-making required inside government.

In Parliament the Liberal Democrats are more disadvantaged by the coalition arrangements than are the Conservatives: they have lost the publicity value of the leader's slot at Prime Minister's Questions, and Labour is now able to project itself as the only voice of opposition. They have also lost their entitlement to Short Money and, with no obvious alternative source of income to plug the financial gap, over 20 members of the party's staff have consequently been made redundant. It will be difficult for the party to sustain an independent policy development process with reduced resources at headquarters and only a handful of special advisers on which it can rely. Indeed, the party may have made a fundamental error in agreeing to a prior Conservative commitment to limit the number of special advisers across government. With only five cabinet ministers the special advisers working for the Liberal Democrats are limited both in number and in terms of policy coverage. In time this problem may be resolved by newly established backbench parliamentary party committees spanning several government departments, with responsibility for both orchestrating independent policy development and the management of the party's backbench contributions and therefore its profile in the Commons Chamber. This in turn may have repercussions for party management within the Conservative Party: the elections to the 1922 Committee shortly after Parliament reconvened demonstrated the determination of backbenchers to preserve some independence from frontbench influence. Given that there are four government departments not fronted by a Conservative Secretary of State and the Deputy Prime Minister leads on political and constitutional reform, Conservative backbenchers may in time be pushing to create their own mechanisms to develop policy and a clear party identity in the House of Commons in these areas.

In time we may also see a change in the nature of party campaigning. If the Liberal Democrats are to have any hope of maintaining a distinct identity then they need to shift to a more European style of campaigning, focusing on parallel messages of achievement and restraint. They will need to sharply identify and promote those policy areas they can claim responsibility for—their achievements—as well as those policies that they have stopped the Conservatives implementing—where they have exercised a restraining influence. Nick Clegg took a decision not to take on responsibility for a government department. In large part this was to avoid the danger of being overloaded as management of the coalition will necessarily absorb much of his time. But his stance also enables him to roam more freely across the full breadth of government policy, beyond his political and constitutional reform brief, maintaining a strong Liberal Democrat presence on a range of issues. The increasingly presidential style of election campaigns means that he will bear the heaviest burden of responsibility for maintaining his party's distinct identity.

Having entered the coalition the party must also at some point answer the vital question of what its exit strategy will be, particularly if the Alternative Vote referendum is lost. At present that remains unclear: the party knows the question is a critical one but it does not yet have the answer to it.

1   I am grateful to Peter Riddell, Chair of the Hansard Society, for his advice and comments on an earlier draft. This article draws on a number of off the record interviews and ad hoc conversations with senior politicians and party staff during and after the general election campaign. For reasons of political sensitivity they asked that their identity not be revealed. I am grateful for their time and consideration.

2   For information on the arithmetic nuances associated with forming either a majority or minority government see R. Blackburn, R. Fox, O. Gay, L. Maer, *Who Governs: Forming a Coalition or a Minority Government in the Event of a Hung Parliament*, Hansard Society, 2010, pp. 6–7.

3   HM Government, *The Coalition: Our Programme for Government*, 20.5.10, p. 7. (www. programmeforgovernment.hmg.gov.uk/)

4   Ibid.

5   Paddy Ashdown Interviewed on the *BBC*'s Andrew Marr Programme on 9.5.10. (www.news.bbc.co.uk/1/hi/programmes/andrew_marr_show/8670862.stm)

6   Nick Clegg Statement on the Results of the Election, 7.5.10. (www.libdems.org.uk/news_detail. aspx?title=Nick_Clegg's_statement_on_the_results_of_the_election&pPK=910a0064-f1e8-430c-afb6-49ccc4fd32e0)

7   David Cameron Press Release, 'National interest first', 7.5.10. (www.conservatives.com/News/Speeches/2010/05/David_Cameron_National_interest_first.aspx)

8   Ibid.

9   David Cameron e-mail to Conservative Party Supporters Quoted in Andrew Sparrow's Election 2010 Blog for the *Guardian*, 9.5.10. (www.guardian.co.uk/global/2010/may/09/general-election-2010-hung-parliament)

10 Statement by William Hague, 10.5.10. (www.news.bbc.co.uk/1/hi/uk_politics/election_2010/8673807.stm)

11 Conservative Liberal Democrat Coalition Negotiations Agreements—Reached on 11.5.10, Published 12.5.10. (www.libdems.org.uk/press_releases_detail.aspx?title=Conservative_Liberal_Democrat_coalition_agreements&pPK=2697bcdc-7483-47a7-a517-7778979458ff)

12 HM Government, *The Coalition: Our Programme for Government*, 20.5.10, p. 8.

13 Ibid., p. 35.

14 Cabinet Office, Coalition Agreement for Stability and Reform, May 2010, p. 1. (www.cabinetoffice.gov.uk/media/409174/stabilityreformmay2010.pdf)

15 Ibid., p. 2.

16 Cabinet Office, Cabinet Committee System, May 2010, p. 1. (www.cabinetoffice.gov.uk/media/409188/cabinetcommitteesystemmay2010.pdf)

17 Ibid., p. 2.

18 HM Government, The Coalition: Our Programme for Government, 20.5.10, p. 15. (www.programmeforgovernment.hmg.gov.uk/)

19 Ipsos MORI, General Election 2010—An Overview. (www.ipsos-mori.com/Assets/Docs/News/General_Election_2010-An_Overview.PDF)

20 Ibid.

21 YouGov/The Sun Survey Results, 5.5.10, p. 6. (www.today.yougov.co.uk/sites/today.yougov.co.uk/files/YG-Archives-Pol-Suntrackers-100505.pdf)

22 T. Horton, *Electoral Opportunities for Labour from a Lib Dem-Tory Pact*, Fabian Society, 2010, p. 3.

23 Ibid., p. 4.

JOHN CURTICE

So What Went Wrong with the Electoral System? The 2010 Election Result and the Debate About Electoral Reform

One feature of the outcome of the 2005 UK general election stands out above all others—no one party secured an overall majority of seats. As a result the election was followed by the formation of a coalition government for the first time in peacetime since the 1930s; indeed it was the first time ever in modern British politics that a coalition between two whole parties was formed afresh immediately after a general election. The mould of single-party alternating majority government, a mould to which British politicians have become accustomed in the post-war era, was finally broken.

This article examines why the first past the post (or single-member plurality) electoral system failed to deliver an overall majority for any one party in 2010. In particular it asks whether this failure was a one-off event, or was an outcome that is likely to be repeated should the system continue to be used in future. It then considers the implications of this analysis for the debate about electoral reform in Britain, a debate that has now acquired new force following the commitment made by the new Conservative/Liberal Democrat coalition government to holding a referendum on replacing the current system with the Alternative Vote.

The argument for first past the post

At the heart of the debate about the merits or otherwise of the single-member plurality electoral system is an argument about the function of elections in a parliamentary system of government.[1] Some argue that the principal purpose of an election in such a system is to produce a

© The Author [2010]. Published by Oxford University Press on behalf of the Hansard Society
doi:10.1093/pa/gsq018

body of legislators whose views broadly mirror those of society as a whole. If that body is representative of public opinion then the decisions it makes should reflect majority opinion, a seemingly desirable state of affairs in a democracy. Those who uphold this view typically argue that parliamentary elections are best held using some form of proportional representation.

However, one likely price of such an arrangement is that who forms the government does not simply depend on who has won most votes, but also on post-election negotiations between the parties so that a coalition or minority government can be formed. For those on the other side of the argument, this is too high a price to pay. They argue that it is more important that the electorate should determine directly who forms the next government than that the legislature should reflect precisely the distribution of opinions and political preferences across the electorate. Otherwise, it is suggested, voters lose the power to hold a government accountable by removing it from office. Those who uphold this view thus favour an electoral system that more or less guarantees an overall majority to whichever party comes first in votes, even if that party fails to secure anything like half the votes, thereby ensuring that elections become a choice between an incumbent single-party government and an opposition alternative.[2]

The apparent tendency for single-member plurality to promote and sustain a system of single-party government that alternates between two parties was most famously identified in the early 1950s by Maurice Duverger. In what became known as 'Duverger's Law', he stated that, 'The simple majority electoral system favours the two-party system'.[3] Two principal reasons have been identified as why this is the case.[4] The first is a 'mechanical' one; if there is only one winner in a constituency, then that winner will rarely, if ever, be a third party that has secured relatively few votes across the country as a whole. The second is a 'psychological' one. If indeed it is the case that a third party is unlikely to secure representation, then voters are discouraged from voting for it in the first place.

However, the claim that single-member plurality facilitates alternating single-party government rests not only on the way it makes life difficult for third parties, but also on the way in which it treats the two largest parties. In particular, it has been argued that the system rewards the party that comes first in votes more generously than the party that runs second. This property was summarised—again in the early 1950s—as a 'cube law', which states that if the two largest parties divide the votes they win between them in the proportion A:B, the seats that they win will be divided in the proportion $A^3:B^3$.[5] In practical terms what this formula means is that when the outcome of an election is close to being a dead heat between the top two parties, a 1% switch of votes from one of those parties to the other will result in as many as 3% of the seats changing hands. So a party that wins, say,

51% of the votes cast for the two largest parties is likely to secure as many as 53% of the seats won by those two parties. As a result even if third parties do win a few seats, it is likely that, even in the event of a narrow outcome, whoever has come first will have an overall majority of seats.

Although such a system is not proportional it can be regarded as 'fair', at least so far as its treatment of the top two parties is concerned. Single-member plurality provides a bonus to whoever comes first, irrespective of which is the party that occupies that position. But clearly it is important that the system should be even handed in awarding that bonus. If one party would secure 53% of the seats on the back of 51% of the vote won by the two largest parties, then the other principal party should also secure 53% of the seats in the same circumstances. Otherwise, it would apparently be easier for one party to win an overall majority than the other. Indeed it might even be possible for a party to win a majority even though it did not secure most votes, an outcome that would seem to deny rather than facilitate voters' ability to determine who should form the next government directly through the ballot box.

We have then identified four crucial foundations to the argument that single-member plurality facilitates a system of alternating single-party majority government, such as the UK has hitherto enjoyed in the post-war period. These are that the system:

(i) should discourage people from voting for third parties,
(ii) reward such votes as are cast for third parties with few seats,
(iii) give a 'bonus' of seats to whoever comes first in votes, and
(iv) to award that 'bonus' in an even-handed fashion.

In the remainder of this article, we will assess whether single-member plurality largely continues to exhibit these features in Britain, or whether the outcome of the 2010 election is symptomatic of changes in voting patterns that have undermined the ability of the system to perform in the manner anticipated by Duverger's Law and the cube law.

Discouraging third parties

So, our first consideration is whether single-member plurality is continuing to prove effective at discouraging people from voting for third parties. To address this, in Table 1 we summarise the votes cast across the UK as a whole in all elections held since 1922, which was the first election to be held following the partition of Ireland and the first at which the Labour Party replaced the Liberals as the principal opposition to the Conservatives. We show three statistics: the proportion of votes cast for Conservative and Labour combined (hereafter the 'two-

1. Trends in party support, UK 1922–2010

	Conservative and Labour (%)	Liberal/Alliance/Liberal Democrat (%)	Others (%)
1922	68.2	28.8	3.0
1923	68.7	29.1	1.6
1924	80.1	17.8	2.1
1929	75.2	23.5	1.3
1931	91.6	7.0	1.4
1935	91.3	6.7	2.0
1945	87.6	9.0	3.4
1950	89.5	9.1	1.4
1951	96.8	2.6	0.6
1955	96.1	2.7	1.2
1959	93.2	5.9	0.9
1964	87.5	11.2	1.3
1966	89.9	8.5	1.5
1970	89.5	7.5	3.0
1974 (February)	75.1	19.3	5.6
1974 (October)	75.1	18.3	6.7
1979	80.8	13.8	5.4
1983	70.0	25.4	4.6
1987	73.1	22.6	4.4
1992	76.3	17.8	5.8
1997	73.9	16.8	9.3
2001	72.4	18.3	9.4
2005	67.6	22.0	10.4
2010	65.1	23.0	11.9

Between 1922 and 1945 the figures include a small number of votes cast in 'university seats' elected by single transferable vote. In 1922 Liberal includes both Liberal and National Liberal.

Sources: C. Rallings and M. Thrasher, *British Electoral Facts 1832–2006*, Ashgate, 2007; 2010 Nuffield Election Study data set compiled by Robert Ford.

party vote'), votes cast for the Liberal Party and its successors, and votes secured by all other parties.]

The top half of the table shows how, once Labour had replaced the Liberals as the Conservatives' principal opposition, voter sympathies soon concentrated themselves on Labour and the Conservatives. Within ten years nine of every ten votes were cast for one or other of those two parties. The proportion remained at or around that figure for the next 30 years. Indeed in the early 1950s the figure was as high as 96%, and the Liberal Party appeared to be on the verge of extinction. It is little wonder that it was at this time that Duverger's Law should have emerged in the academic literature.

But in February 1974 there was a dramatic change. Nearly one in four votes were cast for parties other than the Conservatives and Labour. With nearly one in five votes, the Liberal Party secured what was by far its biggest share of the vote at any election since 1929. At the same time, support for other, smaller parties also reached its highest level since the partition of Ireland. In particular, the Scottish National Party won one-fifth of the vote in Scotland, while in Northern Ireland the fracturing of the unionist vote and the termination of the link between the Ulster Unionist party and the Conservative party meant that electoral politics in the province became wholly divorced from the party system in the rest of the UK.

This heralded a new pattern that was to persist for the next three decades or so, with the proportion of the vote won by Conservative and Labour combined oscillating around the three-quarters mark. The one further development of note during this period was that support for 'Others' increased markedly in 1997 to a new high, thanks primarily to votes secured by a wholly new 'Referendum Party' that campaigned for a referendum on Britain's membership of the European Union.

However, the last two elections, including 2010, have seen yet a further erosion of the two-party vote, and it is now at a lower level than at any time since 1922. Although the Liberal Democrats may not have fulfilled the high expectations generated by the opinion polls during the 2010 election campaign, at 23% their share of the UK vote was still the second highest share Britain's main third party has secured at any time since 1929. Meanwhile, the share of the vote won by 'Others' reached yet another all-time high. Indeed, even if we leave Northern Ireland to one side, no less than 9.8% of votes in Great Britain were cast for an 'other' candidate, the highest proportion recorded at any election since the First Reform Act.

So, the single-member plurality electoral system has never looked less effective at discouraging voters from supporting smaller parties than it does now. Never before in the history of British politics has the share of the vote won by the two largest parties been consistently as low as it has been at recent elections. Indeed, so far as votes cast are concerned, it is difficult to argue any longer that the UK is a two-party system at all.[6]

But what of the translation of votes cast by third parties into seats? Table 2 shows the number of seats won by third parties at each election since 1922, distinguishing between those won by the Liberal Party and its successors, those won by other smaller parties and candidates standing in Great Britain and those won by others standing in Northern Ireland. In so doing we also indicate for elections held between 1992 and 1945 the number of such seats that were won by candidates standing in one of the university seats, where the election was conducted using the single transferable vote rather than single-member plurality. These seats should clearly be discounted in assessing the degree to which third parties were able to win seats under single-member plurality.[7]

Gradually during the inter-war period, Liberal Party representation in the Commons, together with that of other parties, was squeezed. By 1950 only a dozen MPs represented parties other than Conservative and

2. Seats won by third parties in UK general elections 1922–2010

	Liberal/Alliance/Liberal Democrat	Others (GB)	Others (NI)
1922	115 (3)	12 (1)	2
1923	158 (2)	6 (1)	2
1924	40 (3)	12 (1)	0
1929	59 (2)	7 (2)	2
1931	36 (2)	3 (2)	2
1935	21 (1)	9 (3)	2
1945	12 (1)	21 (7)	4
1950	9	1	2
1951	6	0	3
1955	6	0	2
1959	6	1	0
1964	9	0	0
1966	12	0	1
1970	6	2	4
1974 (February)	14	11	12
1974 (October)	13	14	12
1979	11	4	12
1983	23	4	17
1987	22	6	17
1992	20	7	17
1997	46	11	18
2001	52	10	18
2005	62	12	18
2010	57	10	18

Figures in brackets between 1922 and 1945 are seats won in 'university seats' elected by single transferable vote. In 1922 Liberal includes both Liberal and National Liberal.
Sources: C. Rallings and M. Thrasher, *British Electoral Facts*. http://news.bbc.co.uk/1/shared/election2010/results/.

Labour, and in the subsequent 20 years that figure was never greater than a baker's dozen. However, the growth in third-party support in February 1974, together with the fracturing of Northern Ireland's politics, had a clear impact on third-party representation—all of a sudden there were now some three dozen or so MPs representing parties other than Conservative or Labour. Still, given the extent of third-party support (a quarter of the vote) this was still a miserly reward (just 6% of the seats). The degree to which the system discriminated against Britain's main third-party formation was further emphasised in 1983, when a quarter of the vote brought the Liberal/SDP Alliance just 4% of the seats.

However, in recent years the Liberal Democrats have been far more successful at winning seats, even though the party has never quite managed to emulate the share of the vote won by the Alliance in 1983. In 2005 the party won more seats than it had done at any time since 1923. And while the party's tally fell back slightly (despite an increase in its share of the vote) in 2010, at 57 it was still the equal second highest number of single-member plurality seats to be won by Britain's main third force since that date.

The explanation for this change is reasonably straightforward. The Liberal Democrat vote has become geographically somewhat less evenly spread. When the Liberal/SDP Alliance made its advance in 1983, its vote was very evenly spread—the standard deviation of its share of the vote across every constituency was just 7.3. At recent elections, in contrast, the equivalent figure has been between 10.4 and 11.[8] And as the party's vote has become more unevenly spread, so it has become more likely to come first in some places rather than perpetually either second or third everywhere.

Discrimination against third parties is not an invariant feature of single-member plurality. Rather, the degree to which it does so depends on the geography of those parties' support. The more geographically concentrated a third party's vote, the less effective the system is at denying it representation. Thus, while first past the post does still discriminate against the Liberal Democrats (even in 2010 the party still only won 9% of the seats), an increase in the geographical concentration in that support means that it now does so less effectively. Coupled with the seats won by the (relatively concentrated) support won by nationalist and Northern Ireland parties, this development has at the last three elections produced a House of Commons in which there have been as many as 80–90 third-party MPs—and thus inevitably a House that is more likely to be hung.

Marginal seats → foundation 3.

But what about the second key property ascribed to single-member plurality—a tendency to reward whichever party comes first in votes with a 'bonus' of seats, so that the lead of the first party over the second party in the House of Commons is an exaggerated reflection of its lead in the country as a whole. In particular, can it still be argued that this tendency is in line with the expectations of the 'cube law'?

A moment's reflection indicates that the degree to which single-member plurality will exaggerate the lead of the largest party over the second party must depend on how many constituencies are closely fought—or marginal—between those two parties. If 3% of the seats are to change hands as a result of a 1% swing in votes from party A to party B, then it must be the case that in 3% of the seats the lead of party B over party A is less than 2% of the vote. This requirement was formulated more formally by two statisticians, Maurice Kendall and Alan Stuart, who demonstrated that if the cube law was to operate, the frequency distribution of the Conservative (or Labour) share of the two-party vote across all constituencies needs to approximate a normal distribution with a standard deviation of 13.7.[9] It can also be shown that, if this condition is satisfied, then in the event that the Conservative and Labour parties were to have the same shares of the two-party vote across the country as a whole, 30% of constituencies would be ones where the Conservative share of the two-party vote would be between 45 and 55%.[10] We can term these seats 'marginal seats'.

Table 3 shows how far these conditions have been satisfied at each election since 1955. First it shows the number of seats that were marginal, as we have defined that term, and the proportion of all seats won by Conservative and Labour that fell into that category. Thereafter it indicates, the standard deviation of the two-party vote across all constituencies, together with the kurtosis, a measure of the degree to which the distribution conforms to a normal distribution. A normal distribution is often described as a 'bell'-shaped curve, and the kurtosis indicates whether the height of that bell is as high as it would be if the distribution were normal.

A striking story emerges. In the 1950s the frequency distribution of the two-party vote did come close to meeting the stipulations identified by Kendall and Stuart. The standard deviation was close to the 13.7 mark, while there was only a slightly negative kurtosis—an indication that at the centre of the distribution there were somewhat fewer seats than would occur if it were normal. Still, at around the 160 mark, the proportion of seats that were marginal was only a little less than the 30% required for the cube law to operate. It is thus little surprise that during this period the electoral system did exaggerate small leads in votes into quite large leads in seats—thus, for example, in 1955 a

3. Changing distribution of two-party vote 1955–2010

	Marginals		Two-party vote	
	Number	%	Standard deviation	Kurtosis
1955	166	27.2	13.5	−0.25
1959	157	25.7	13.8	−0.29
1964	166	27.3	14.1	−0.45
1966	155	25.6	13.8	−0.46
1970	149	24.5	14.3	−0.27
1974 (February)	119	19.9	16.1	−0.68
1974 (October)	98	16.4	16.8	−0.82
1979	108	17.8	16.9	−0.87
1983	80	13.2	20.0	−1.05
1987	87	14.4	21.4	−1.03
1992	98	16.1	20.2	−1.03
1997	114	19.6	18.1	−0.85
2001	114	19.7	18.3	−0.82
2005	104	18.8	19.7	−0.96
2010	85	15.0	22.2	−1.08

Marginal seat: Seat where Conservative share of two-party vote (overall Conservative share of two-party vote—50%) lies within the range of 45–55%.
Two-party vote: Votes cast for Conservative and Labour combined.
Table based only on seats won by Conservative or Labour at that election and contested by both parties.
Source: Curtice, 'Neither Representative nor Accountable' and author's calculations.

Conservative lead over Labour of just over three points in terms of votes was translated into an 11-point lead—and an overall majority of 59—in terms of seats.

But here too something changed in February 1974. The number of marginal seats suddenly fell to 119, or no more than one in five of the total. Meanwhile, the standard deviation of the two-party vote increased to 16.1. There were even fewer marginal seats in the second election of that year, held in October. It was in truth no accident that the February 1974 election produced the first hung parliament of the post-war era or that the October 1974 election only gave Labour an overall majority of four, a majority that soon disappeared, thereby leaving the minority Labour government dependent on, first, the Liberals and then other parties for support. Not only had there been a notable increase in the number of third-party MPs at those elections, but also the ability of the electoral system systematically to exaggerate the lead of the largest party over the second largest had also been seriously eroded.

The principal reason for this erosion was long-term change in the geography of Conservative and Labour support.[11] Beginning with the pattern of movement between the 1955 and 1959 elections, Conservative support became increasingly concentrated in the South and Midlands of England together with more rural areas. Labour, meanwhile, performed better in Scotland, the North of England and more urban constituencies. Initially, this development had little impact on the number of marginal seats. But waves of the same pattern at successive elections meant that, by the early 1970s, constituencies that were already relatively strong for the Conservatives were becoming more so, while the opposite happened in seats where Labour was relatively strong. As Britain diverged politically, so fewer seats were left where both parties had a chance of winning.

Meanwhile, as in the case of third-party support and representation, the pre-1974 status quo was never restored. Indeed by 1983 just one in eight seats were marginal while the standard deviation of the two-party vote had reached 20. True, there was some reversal of the decline in marginal seats in the 1990s—not least because in the 1997 and 2001 elections Labour were relatively successful in the South of England and the Midlands—but even so the character of the frequency distribution of the two-party vote still fell far short of what was required for the cube law to operate. With some 80–90 MPs now representing third parties, a hung parliament had in truth become a rather likely prospect.

In fact, the chances of such a parliament occurring increased further in 2010, thanks to a further fall in the number of marginal seats, which have now fallen to a level only a little above that which pertained in the 1980s. For once again, previously Conservative and previously Labour Britain diverged. On average, the Conservative share of the two-party vote increased by 10.2 points in seats that the party had already won in 2005, while it increased by only 6.3 points in seats Labour were defending.[12] The sharpest manifestation of this divergence was in heavily Labour Scotland, where, in contrast to the rest of the country, there was a small net (total vote) swing from the Conservatives to Labour. However, divergence on much the same scale was also evident within England and Wales, not least because Labour's vote held up relatively well in seats with high ethnic minority populations.

Bias → foundation 3,4.

Still, at this point the reader might be asking themselves an important question. If the exaggerative quality of the electoral system has indeed been eroded for some time, why did a hung parliament not occur before 2010? Part of the answer is that at most recent elections, the winning party has enjoyed a handsome lead in votes, let alone seats, as typified by the Conservatives' 15-point lead over Labour in 1983, and Labour's 12.5-point lead over the Conservatives in 1997. Such large leads might well be expected to produce overall majorities, despite the growth in third-party representation and the fall in the number of marginal seats. However, in 2005 Labour enjoyed no more than a three-point lead over the Conservatives, yet still emerged with a very comfortable overall majority of 66. How was this possible? And, indeed, why, given what happened in 2005, was the seven-point lead that the Conservatives obtained in 2010 still insufficient to secure an overall majority?

The answer lies in a marked failure of single-member plurality these days to treat Labour and the Conservatives in an equal-handed manner. Instead it has come to reward Labour more favourably than the Conservatives. There are in fact a number of possible different reasons why such a 'bias' can emerge under first past the post, and it is the Conservatives' misfortune that most of these have come together to work against them at recent elections.

Table 4 provides a simple introduction to the trends over time in the two most obvious potential sources of bias.[13] The first such potential source is that the seats won by party A have more voters in them than do those won by party B. If that is the case then the average vote won by party A across every constituency will be less than that party's overall share when the votes cast for each party are totalled across the country as a whole. So the first statistic displayed in Table 4 is the difference between the mean Conservative share of the two-party vote across every constituency and the party's overall share of that vote totalled across the whole country.

The second main potential source of bias arises if one party's vote is more efficiently distributed than another's. A party's vote is distributed efficiently if the seats it does win are secured with relatively small majorities, while those it loses are lost badly. Such a pattern would mean

4. Measures of bias 1955–2010

Conservative percentage two-party vote

	Mean – overall	Median – mean	Median – overall
1955	+0.3	+0.6	+0.9
1959	+0.4	+0.8	+1.2
1964	+0.1	+0.4	+0.5
1966	−0.3	+0.2	−0.1
1970	−0.9	+0.8	−0.1
1970[a]	−0.1	+0.5	+0.4
1974 (February)	−0.1	−0.5	−0.5
1974 (October)	−0.3	+1.4	+1.1
1979	−0.7	−0.5	−1.2
1979[a]	−0.1	+0.9	+0.9
1983	−0.5	+1.7	+1.2
1987	−0.8	+1.4	+0.6
1992	−1.2	−0.0	−1.2
1992[a]	−0.2	−0.7	−0.9
1997	−0.4	−1.6	−2.0
2001	−1.4	−1.5	−2.9
2001[a]	−1.1	−1.4	−2.5
2005	−2.1	−1.1	−3.2
2005[a]	−1.5	−1.0	−2.5
2010	−1.3	−0.8	−2.1

[a]Notional results based on estimates of what the outcome would have been if that election had been fought on the new constituency boundaries that were introduced at the subsequent election. The 2001 redistribution (together with a reduction in the number of seats) was confined to Scotland.
Two-party vote: Votes cast for Conservative and Labour combined.
Figures based on all seats in Great Britain. Northern Ireland excluded.
Source: Author's calculations.

that most of the votes won by that party helped it to win seats rather than wasted either stoking up large majorities or losing out narrowly.

One way of identifying whether one party's vote is more or less efficiently distributed is to compare the mean share of the two-party vote it wins across every constituency with the median value of that statistic across all constituencies. This is done in the second column of the table. If a party's vote is more efficiently distributed then its median share of the two-party vote should be higher than the mean, for that indicates it has managed to win more than its mean share in over half of all constituencies—and, of course, who wins most seats depends not on who wins most votes overall, but on who wins most votes in the median constituency.

Table 4 suggests that until 1997 no one party was particularly disadvantaged. True, the Conservatives' mean share of the two-party vote tended to be smaller than their overall share, and especially so as a set of constituency boundaries grew older.[14] For most of the post-war period the population of Great Britain has shifted away from the more Labour inclined urban areas and northern half the country, and thus the longer a set of constituency boundaries have been in place, so the greater the degree to which Labour seats have become relatively smaller. However, the process has been at least partially corrected by the periodic redrawing of constituency boundaries. This can be discerned by looking at the figures in the table that show what would have happened if an election had been fought on the new boundaries that were introduced at the next election and comparing them with the figures for the actual result for that election as fought on the old boundaries.

In any event, this tendency for Conservative held seats to be bigger was for most of the post-war period counteracted by a tendency for the Conservative vote to be more efficiently distributed (though one notable occasion when this was not the case was February 1974 when, as a result, Labour won four more seats than the Conservatives despite winning 0.7% less of the UK vote). This was because Labour had a tendency to win more seats than the Conservatives by large majorities.[15] Thanks to this counterbalance the overall level of bias (as measured by the difference between the median and the overall Conservative share of the two-party vote in the final column of the table) was usually relatively small.

However, this pattern changed in the 1990s. From 1997 onwards it has been Labour's vote that has been the more efficiently distributed.[16] At that election the Conservatives lost ground particularly heavily in seats they were defending, while Labour's ability to capture seats from the Conservatives was further enhanced by tactical votes from Liberal Democrat supporters who wished to ensure the local Conservative was defeated. Consequently, the Conservatives came a relatively good second in too many seats, and it is a pattern that has not subsequently been fully reversed.[17]

At the same time, the advantage that Labour has derived from winning seats that are smaller has also been relatively big at the last three elections, including in 2010, despite the implementation of two boundary reviews that between them reduced the number of seats in Scotland and updated those in England and Wales. There are two main reasons for this. First, the boundary review implemented in 2010 was based (in England) on electorates that were by then already ten years old. Second, no attempt has been made to reduce the over-representation of (Labour inclined) Wales, while the reduction in the number of constituencies in Scotland failed in practice to wholly remove the disparity between the size of the average English and that of the average Scottish constituency. Thus in 2010 the average seat in Wales contained just 56,626 voters, that in Scotland, 65,234, while the average constituency in England had 71,909. On average across Great Britain as a whole, seats won by the Conservatives in 2010 had 3733 more names on the electoral register than did those won by Labour.

However, the effective 'size' of a constituency does not only depend on the number of people on the electoral register, but also on what proportion of those registered to vote actually cast their ballot. While turnout has commonly been lower on average in Labour-held than in Conservative held seats, the gap widened markedly in 1992, and has not since subsequently significantly narrowed once again. Thus in 2010 the turnout in the average seat won by the Conservatives was, at 68.4%, some seven points higher than that in the average seat won by Labour (61.1%). This ensured that the 3733 difference between the two types of seat in the number of persons on the electoral register proved to be one of 7894 in the number of people who actually turned out to vote.

So thanks to a myriad of developments, it has become more difficult nowadays for the Conservatives to secure an overall majority than it is Labour. Labour might have been able to win a safe majority with just a three-point lead in 2005, but before the 2010 election it was antici- pated that in the absence of a radical change in the electoral geography of Britain, the Conservatives would require a lead of nearly 11 points over Labour in order to secure a bare overall majority. And so it came to pass that the seven-point lead the Conservatives actually obtained proved not to be enough.

Implications

All four foundations that lie behind the claim that single-member plur- ality facilitates alternating single-party majority government have been seriously eroded in the UK. The system is no longer effective at denying third parties votes and is now significantly less effective than it once was at denying them seats. Meanwhile, the system now exaggerates the lead of the largest party over the second party in a systematic manner to a much lesser extent than in the past, while it certainly now fails to treat the two largest parties in an even-handed manner. In uncovering these changes, we have discovered that far from adhering reliably to any general law, the link between votes and seats under single-member plurality is in fact heavily contingent on the geography of party support.

The collective impact of the four developments on the prospects that future elections in the UK under single-member plurality might enable the electorate to choose directly between two alternative majority gov- ernments is illustrated in Table 5. This takes as its starting point the outcome of the 2010 election (shown in bold) and then shows what the outcome in seats would be for various other possible Conservative leads over Labour (based on votes cast in Great Britain only). We make two assumptions to produce these calculations. First, we assume that support for the Liberal Democrats and other smaller parties remains at the same level in every constituency as it was in 2010. Second, in each case we assume that changes in the level of Conservative and Labour support occur uniformly in each and every constituency. Thus, for example, our calculation for what would happen in the event of a

5. How single-member plurality works now

Conservative percentage lead over Labour (GB)	Seats (UK)			
	Conservative	Labour	Liberal Democrat	Others
−2.7	239	326	59	26
0.0	255	306	61	28
4.1	282	281	59	28
7.3	307	258	57	28
11.2	327	233	62	28

Source: Author's calculations.

11.2 point Conservative lead over Labour, that is almost four points above what the party obtained in 2010, is based on the assumption that the Conservative vote increases by just under two points everywhere while Labour's vote falls by nearly two points everywhere. In short, we assume that the electoral geography of Britain remains as it was in 2010.

Two features of the table are striking. The first is the extent of the disadvantage suffered by the Conservatives. On the current electoral geography Labour only needs a little under a three-point lead in votes in order to secure an overall majority. That is a more demanding target than Labour needed in the wake of the 2005 election (on the boundaries that pertained at that election)—then Labour could have secured a majority while still one point behind the Conservatives—but it is still a far less demanding target than the 11-point lead required for an overall majority by the Conservatives.

The second striking feature is the size of the gap between these two targets—a range of no less than 14 points. Following the fall in the number of marginal seats that range is even wider than the near 11 point one that obtained after 2005. Indeed it has never previously been wider. It simply means that, given the current electoral geography of Britain and levels of third-party support, single-member plurality is now highly likely to produce a hung parliament—and thus its continued use is now very difficult to defend on the grounds that it facilitates a two-party system of alternating single-party majority government.

The future

One of these features—the bias against the Conservatives—is due to be addressed by the new coalition government. It aims to reduce the disparities in the size of constituency electorates. It remains to be seen how successful it will be, but even if it is, it should be apparent from our analysis above that it will only eliminate some of the disadvantage suffered by the Conservatives.[18] Moreover, there is no reason to believe that this step will reduce the range of outcomes that would produce a hung parliament. The Conservatives might be able to win a majority on a nine- or ten-point lead—but Labour then be unable to do so on a four or five point one. The range might perhaps be narrowed a little by a second commitment of the new government—to cut the number of MPs by 50 to 600—but any effect is only likely to be small.[19] Single-member plurality will still be likely to produce a hung parliament.

Meanwhile the public are due to be given an opportunity to vote in a referendum on whether single-member plurality should be replaced with the Alternative Vote. Under this system voters place candidates in the order of preference, 1, 2, 3, and in the event that no candidate secures over half of the first preference vote, the votes cast for those candidates with the fewest votes are successively eliminated and redistributed in accordance with the second and subsequent preferences expressed by those voters until someone reaches the 50% target. Far from proportional, the system would still leave the Liberal Democrats at a considerable disadvantage. Nevertheless because the party is often the second preference of Conservative and Labour voters it would sometimes manage to leapfrog into first place, and thereby win some extra seats.[20] And more seats for the Liberal Democrats means hung parliaments become yet more likely. But as should now be clear, they are now quite likely to occur under single-member plurality anyway.

1   R. Plant, *The Plant Report: A Working Party on Electoral Reform*, the *Guardian*, 1991; G. Bingham Powell Jr, *Elections as Instruments of Democracy: Majoritarian and Proportional Visions*, Yale University Press, 2000.

2   See, for example, P. Norton, 'The Case for First Past the Post', *Representation*, 34, 1997, 84–8.

3   M. Duverger, *Political Parties: Their Organisation and Activity in the Modern State*, Methuen, 1954, p. 217. See also G. Cox, *Making Votes Count*, Cambridge University Press, 1997.

4   K. Benoit, 'Duverger's Law and the Study of Electoral Systems, *French Politics*, 4, 2006, 69–83.

5   D. Butler, 'An Examination of the Results' in H. Nicholas (ed.), *The British General Election of 1950*, Macmillan, 1951; G. Gudgin and P. Talyor, *Seats, Votes and the Spatial Organisation of Elections*, Pion, 1979; R. Taagerpera and M. Shugart, *Seats and Votes: The Effects and Determinants of Electoral Systems*, Yale University Press, 1989.

6   Indeed, according to the formula for the effective number of (electoral) parties developed by Laakso and Taagepera, the UK now has as many as 3.7 effective parties. M. Laakso and R. Taagerpera, 'Effective Number of Parties: A Measure with Application to Western Europe', *Comparative Political Studies*, 12, 1979, 3–27.

7   It should also be noted that until 1950 24 MPs were elected (by plurality rule) in double member rather than single member constituencies.

8   For further details see J. Curtice, 'Neither Representative nor Accountable: First Past the Post in Britain', in B. Grofman, A. Blais and S. Bowler (eds), *Duverger's Law of Plurality Voting*, Springer, 2009, and A. Russell and E. Fieldhouse, *Neither Left nor Right? Liberal Democrats and the Electorate*, Manchester University Press, 2005.

9   M. Kendall and A. Stuart, 'The Law of Cubic Proportions in Election Results', *British Journal of Sociology*, 1, 1951, 183–97.

10 J. Curtice and M. Steed, 'Electoral Choice and the Production of Government: The Changing Operation of the Electoral System in the UK Since 1955', *British Journal of Political Science*, 12, 1982, 249–98.

11 Curtice and Steed, 'Electoral Choice'; J. Curtice and M. Steed, 'Proportionality and Exaggeration in the British Electoral System', *Electoral Studies*, 5, 1986, 209–28; Curtice, 'Neither Representative nor Accountable'.

12 Seats not won by either Conservative or Labour in 2010 are not included in this calculation.

13 C. Soper and J. Rydon, 'Under-representation and Electoral Prediction', *Australian Journal of Politics and History*, 4, 1958, 94–106. For a more complex approach see D. Rossiter, R. Johnston, C. Pattie,

D. Dorling I. MacAllister and H. Tunstall, 'Changing Biases in the Operation of the UK's Electoral System, 1950–1997' *British Journal of Politics and International Relations*, 1, 1998, 133–64, and R. Johnston, D. Rossiter and C. Pattie, 'Integrating and Decomposing the Sources of Electoral Bias: Brooke's Method and the Impact of Redistricting in Great Britain', *Electoral Studies*, 18, 1999, 367–78.

14 The set of boundaries first implemented in 1955 exhibited a small bias to the Conservatives because on that occasion, unlike those created thereafter, the English boundary commission deliberately created smaller seats in rural areas. See D. Rossiter, R. Johnston and C. Pattie, *The Boundary Commissions: Redrawing the UK's Map of Parliamentary Constituencies*, Manchester University Press, 1999.

15 D. Butler, *The Electoral System in Britain*, 2nd edn. Clarendon Press, 1963; R. Johnston, C. Pattie, D. Dorling and D. Rossiter, *From Votes to Seats: The Operation of the UK Electoral System Since 1945*, Manchester University Press, 2001.

16 J. Curtice and M. Steed, 'Appendix 2: The Results Analysed' in D. Butler and D. Kavanagh (eds), *The British General Election of 1997*, Macmillan, 1997; J. Curtice, 'The Electoral System: Biased to Blair?', *Parliamentary Affairs*, 54, 2001, 803–14.

17 The Conservatives have also 'wasted' a higher proportion of their vote than Labour in losing in (the now larger number of) seats won by third parties. For example, in 2010 the average Conservative share of the vote in seats won by third parties was 28.4%, while that for Labour was just 16.6%.

18 G. Borisuyk, C. Rallings, M. Thrasher and R. Johnston, 'Parliamentary Constituency Boundary Reviews and Electoral Bias: How Important are Variations in Constituency Size?', *Parliamentary Affairs*, 63, 2010, 4–21.

19 Curtice and Steed, 'Exaggeration and Proportionality'.

20 An opinion poll conducted by ComRes for *The Independent* newspaper (27.4.10), found that 68% of Labour supporters and 41% of Conservatives would have given a second preference vote to the Liberal Democrats. If these and the other figures obtained by the poll were to have been in evidence in the ballot box in an Alternative Vote election in 2010, the Liberal Democrats would probably have won around 80 seats.

ANDREW GAMBLE

New Labour and Political Change

Labour lost office in May 2010 after 13 years in government. It was the longest period of continuous government in Labour's 100 year history as a party, surpassing even the 11.5 years the party served in government from 1940 to 1951, during the first 5 of which the party was a part of the Wartime Coalition Government. Under Tony Blair Labour won three general elections, the first two with large parliamentary majorities. For the first time Labour was able to develop policy through three Parliaments and had the opportunity to reshape institutions and the agendas of debate.

How far did Labour succeed in changing British politics between 1997 and 2010? What if anything has it left behind? It would be surprising if there was no legacy. Governments undo less of the policies and the institutions that they inherit than is sometimes imagined or than their rhetoric suggests. A few quangos are abolished and new departures boldly announced, but genuine changes of direction are rather rare, and tend to occur not at general elections but during Parliaments.[1] Many of the new initiatives that a new government announces with such panache in the first few weeks and months after the general election fizzle and die and attention moves away to other matters. In many general elections victory often goes to the party that can most plausibly promise change. Many voters it is suggested grow tired of incumbents and can be tempted to vote for the challenger. The task therefore for the challenger is to find a way to become associated with change and a brighter future. Labour's campaign song in 1997 'Things can only get better' is the message of every opposition seeking to supplant an incumbent government. Governments have authority and experience on their side, and these will often prevail. What oppositions have is hope and change.

Did Labour deliver change? The party was keen to associate itself with change in 1997, even styling itself as 'New Labour' in order to emphasise to voters that the party was different, and that this was not the old Labour party presenting itself for election. But some observers

doi:10.1093/pa/gsq031

thought that the Labour party was all that had changed, that new Labour, as Martin Jacques and Stuart Hall argued, may have had a project of change for the party but lacked one for the country.[2]

Approaches to new Labour

In evaluating the impact of Labour's longest period in government different contexts need to be considered. The first is the pattern of general elections themselves, and the way in which some of them come to be seen as ushering in major political change. Some elections are regarded as watersheds, particularly 1906, 1945 and 1979. All three are seen as marking a major shift in the direction of policy, reflecting changes in the electorate, changes in ideology and changes in external circumstances. There has been a dispute over whether 1997 is a watershed election like 1945 and 1979, or whether it led mainly to a change in government personnel rather than a change in policy direction.

Three broad positions have been developed on this question. The first approach emphasises continuity and sees the policies adopted by Labour after 1997 as staying within the paradigm established by the Thatcher Government in the 1980s and maintained and consolidated by the Major Government in the 1990s,[3] just as the Conservative Government of 1951–64 stayed within the paradigm established by the Attlee Government. A key question whenever a new government is elected, is how much it reverses of the major legislation of its predecessor, or whether it is content to govern within the limits it inherits. The second interpretation of the new Labour era is that it was a period of radical ideological and policy renewal, codified in the ideas of the Third Way.[4] On this reading Labour found a way to combine social justice and economic efficiency, which had eluded all previous governments, as well as developing a new electoral strategy which its opponents were eventually forced to copy.

The third interpretation regards new Labour as not particularly new, but a continuation of old Labour. This discounts the rhetoric employed by the supporters and the critics of the new Labour project both of whom for different reasons suggest that new Labour represented a major break in Labour party traditions. It became common on the Left for example to argue that new Labour was no longer a social democratic party but a neo-liberal centrist party, or even according to Tony Benn a second Conservative party, and for a time a more successful one. Supporters of the new Labour project had an equal interest in emphasising the newness and in claiming that Labour had been reborn, and was quite different from the Labour party of the 1960s and 1970s, even though obeisance could still be paid to figures in the more distant Labour past, because this lay at the heart of the electoral strategy. The counter-argument is that new Labour is not as new as is claimed, and that to understand new Labour the appropriate context is the Labour party itself, the traditions, institutions and historical development of the Labour movement.[5]

Governments can be in office for a very long while and do very little. Other governments can be in office for a short time and achieve a lot. Since 1945 there have been three governments that have been sustained in office for at least three elections, the Conservative Government of 1951–1964, the Conservative Government of 1979–1997 and the Labour Government of 1997–2010. Then there have been governments that held office for much shorter periods but which are regarded as taking decisions of major importance, such as the Attlee Government between 1945 and 1951, and the Heath Government of 1970–1973, when it secured Britain's entry into the European Community.

Another important way of understanding British politics is to think in terms of long cycles. For the Labour party there have so far been three major cycles since the party became a mass party and a contender for government after 1918. The first of these cycles ran from 1918 to 1948 and the second from 1948 to 1978 and the third between 1978 and 2008. The first cycle was dominated by 'The Forward March of Labour', the period when the Labour movement despite setbacks steadily enlarged its support and its organisational strength until its great electoral triumph in 1945 which saw the enactment of a Labour programme which shaped British politics and government for the next 30 years.[6] The second cycle starts from the zenith of Labour's achievement in 1948–1949, but when the forward momentum was already weakening, and the party was shortly to lose office and be in opposition for 13 years. Labour struggled to cope with defeat and the unexpected resilience of the Conservatives, and was convulsed by ideological and policy conflicts. Office was regained in 1964 and held with one interruption for the next 15 years, but the expectations raised by the Wilson Government were quickly disappointed, and the second government between 1974 and 1979 was weak and struggled to manage the consequences of stagflation and British economic decline. The most recent period began in 1979 with the defeat of the Labour party in the 1979 election and the triumph of Thatcherism. The Labour party split in opposition and suffered its worst electoral result since 1945 in 1983. It regrouped and reformed under Neil Kinnock, but progress was slow and the party was to suffer two further election defeats in 1987 and 1992. But the groundwork for recovery had been laid and under Tony Blair's leadership the party succeeded in ousting the Conservatives in 1997 and winning the next two general elections as well. The financial crash in 2008 removed however one of the major elements in Labour's success, its reputation for economic competence, where it had enjoyed a lead over the Conservatives since Black Wednesday in 1992 (the exit of the pound from the exchange rate mechanism, ERM), and in 2010 the party lost office, and faced a new period of uncertainty and rebuilding.

A second set of cycles relevant to evaluating the new Labour era are two 16 year political cycles. The first began in 1976 with the IMF crisis which marked the beginning of the political ascendancy of the Conservatives under Margaret Thatcher and led to four consecutive Conservative elections victories. It was terminated by the 1992 ERM crisis. This marked the beginning of the political ascendancy of Labour, first under John Smith, then under Tony Blair, leading again to the dominance of one party for an extended period. This period was terminated by the 2007–2008 financial crash, which marked the beginning of a new political ascendancy for the Conservatives, and was duly confirmed by electoral advance, if not an outright victory in 2010, and the formation of the Coalition between the Liberal Democrats and the Conservatives. Whether this new period will be an extended period of Conservative ascendancy is as yet uncertain. It could just as easily signal a return to a period of frequent alternations of the parties in Government as was the case between 1964 and 1979. At that time it gave rise to critical analyses of the harmful effects of adversary politics in the UK, in particular the frequent and damaging reversals of policy by British Governments, every time there was a change in the party in control.[7] Although there was considerable evidence that the adversary politics thesis was exaggerated, and ignored the much continuity in government policy between different party administrations, it did capture the more polarised nature of politics in the 1960s and the 1970s, and the way in which it was reflected in the very frequent reversals of party fortunes. The years between 1979 and 2010 have been very different, dominated by two long periods of single party rule, and in each case the weakness of the opposition.

Electoral strategy

All these contexts need to be considered in addressing the question of the degree to which the parameters of British politics changed during the new Labour era. Three main areas will be explored: electoral strategy, new politics and policy agendas.

One of the most obvious ways in which the new Labour has reshaped British politics has been in the new styles of politics it introduced. Not all of this began with new Labour, and much of it was borrowed from across the Atlantic, particularly from the strategy pioneered by Clinton in his successful pursuit of the Democratic nomination in 1992. What the strategists for new Labour took from Clinton was how to rebuild the electoral appeal and credibility of a left of centre political party after a long period of the ascendancy of the right. Repositioning the party and triangulating issues became key ideas for this new kind of electoral politics. It meant that no policy stance should be declared off-limits on principle, if electoral calculation determined that it was necessary to win votes.[8]

These ideas were deeply opposed by many in the Labour party, but they did prove extraordinarily effective. The lesson from Clinton's campaign was clear. First determine the issues on which your opponent appeared particularly strong among voters; then devise a plan to wrest control of the issue from them. Blair was determined to seize the initiative in this way on several key issues from the Conservatives, including economic competence, crime and patriotism. Labour had traditionally been weak on all three. The purpose in rebranding Labour as new Labour was to demonstrate that there were in principle no areas of policy on which Labour could not appeal to voters, and could not be trusted more than the Conservatives. Blair also pioneered the technique of appealing to voters, particularly centrist voters and swing voters, by disagreeing with his party, and even picking fights with sections of it. Debate inside the Labour party had become quite narrow, confined by a series of taboos and assumptions which were easy targets for opponents, and helped remind many voters why they disliked the Labour party so much. Blair's decision to replace Clause IV of the party constitution with a new wording had little direct importance for policy, since it had long ceased to guide the party in office. But Clause IV still had considerable symbolic significance, because for many it was the guarantee that the party was still a socialist party, with a mission to transform the economy and the society into a quite different kind of society than the present capitalist society. Hugh Gaitskell had tried to change Clause IV after Labour's third election defeat in 1959, but he failed. Tony Blair's success in 1995 marked the ascendancy he had established within the party, and more than any other action it helped identify the party as one that was changing, and was genuinely offering something new.

The success of Labour's strategy after 1994 was shown not only by the three election victories, but also by the disarray into which the Conservatives were plunged. The Conservatives changed their leader four times between 1997 and 2005, a sure sign that they could not find an adequate response to new Labour. In 2001 and even 2005 the Conservatives were unable significantly to raise their share of the vote, in sharp contrast to every previous period when they had been in opposition for a whole parliament. For many Conservatives Tony Blair appeared to be a magician who had cast a spell on the British people, and had stolen Conservative policies and votes. In some ways this new Labour strategy was not new at all, or perhaps only really new for the Labour party. It echoed in many ways the successful Conservative statecraft of the past which in the 1990s seemed to have deserted them. Under Blair Labour was determined to occupy the centre ground of British politics by making sure that on those issues that most mattered to voters it was either ahead of the Conservatives or only a little way behind them. The Conservatives found they no longer had a monopoly of certain issues. Labour was now determined to compete across the board. New Labour combined flexibility with ruthlessness, a winning combination when it came to attracting votes. At the heart of this conception of politics was the idea of the Big Tent, which was big enough to include almost everyone. This pluralist conception was a long way from the tribal politics which had so often defined Labour. The Conservatives in the past had often conceived politics in this way, using ideas such as One Nation and the Middle Way, which had played a similar role to the Third Way. This form of statecraft was always ideology-lite. Much greater attention was paid to responding to what voters found important rather than to sticking to party dogmas and principles. Such a statecraft appears to its critics as unprincipled, but to its supporters it simply means that it is not bound by fixed principles.

The electoral strategy developed by new Labour helped transform the electoral prospects of the Labour party and in so doing changed British politics. The surest sign of its success was in the way it changed the Conservative party. The strategy developed by David Cameron after he won the leadership in 2005 imitated in important respects the strategy of new Labour. Cameron incautiously described himself as the heir to Blair shortly after he became Leader, and while there are many differences, the key Blairite message that to win elections in Britain it is necessary to occupy the centre ground and deny it to your opponents, has been truly learnt.[9] The most spectacular example in fact has been the formation of the coalition government between the Conservatives and the Liberal Democrats after the indecisive election result in 2010. As Ruth Fox and Peter Riddell also discuss in their contribution to this volume, David Cameron after recovering from his initial disappointment at not having secured an absolute majority realised the great opportunity which the election result had presented to him. It allowed him to achieve what Tony Blair had failed to achieve, a realignment of British politics, a big tent involving the full participation of two of the three major national parties. The realignment of the centre left which had been the aspiration of so many progressives had been transformed by Cameron into a realignment on the centre right. It allowed him to proclaim himself as a Liberal Conservative with more confidence that at any time since he had assumed the leadership. For the moment it silenced the right of his party, because it was the means by which he put the Conservatives back into government, and ended 13 years of Labour government.

Another aspect of Labour's winning electoral strategy was the party's success in positioning itself as the party most trusted by voters to handle the issues rated as most important to them. Economic competence was the most significant. Labour was ahead of the Conservatives on the economy from 1992 and only definitively lost its lead after the beginnings of the credit crunch in 2007. For much of the period of the Labour's ascendancy Labour was also ahead on most other issues as well, including even crime for a while. The Labour leadership under Kinnock, Smith and Blair gradually disengaged from many former policy positions, until finally Labour could be presented to the electorate in an entirely new light. This flexibility and adroitness and nimble positioning were something the Conservatives had lost, but they rediscovered it under Cameron. The set of techniques and skills which Labour developed were much derided as spin, and famously lampooned by the BBC series 'In the Thick of It', but they were something which no party was able to do without, because they were essential tools for operating in the new political environment created by modern media and a disengaged electorate. Blair and Cameron have both been accused by critics in their parties of abandoning core principles and beliefs, but both achieved electoral success, although in the case of Cameron it has so far been only partial. Both showed that in competitive electoral politics it is essential to seize the initiative. Opportunities to shape political attitudes, to lead from the front and to create entirely new political alignments in politics are rare. Most politicians work within the constraints of the existing patterns of values, beliefs and interests of their electorates. Blair and Cameron have showed themselves master of the new politics, with Cameron's audacious embrace of coalition making him even bolder than Blair.

New politics

One of the promises of new Labour was that it offered not just an electoral strategy but a new politics, to counter the disillusion with the shortcomings of both statist social democracy and statist neo-liberalism. Many of the original ideas that animated new Labour were finding ways to make government more decentralised and more participative. It would be closer to the people. The heart of this new politics was to be a strong self-governing and pluralist civil society. The role of the state in such a society would be enabling, seeking to help families, businesses and voluntary associations to be independent and self-governing, rather than trying to impose outcomes from above. Disengagement and disaffection with politics did not begin in 1997. They were strong features of the 1990s, and the aim of Labour's new politics was to reverse creeping disaffection with politics and politicians, and to renew civic purpose and confidence. New Labour wanted to reject top-down solutions, the 'Whitehall knows best' culture of statist social democracy. But it also wanted to reject the neo-liberal position which was to be suspicious of the state in theory, but more than willing to use the state in practice, often in very illiberal ways. The result had been to undermine the sense of a public interest and public domain.

Labour promised in 1997 to reverse this through a major series of constitutional reforms, including devolution of powers to Wales and Scotland, freedom of information legislation, incorporation of the

European Convention on human rights into British law, the return of self-government for London, new regional assemblies, reform of the House of Lords, and elected mayors. Taken together this was the most radical set of constitutional changes since the advent of universal suffrage. Critics were quick to point out that it fell short of the new constitutional settlement and written constitution which many constitutional reformers sought. Many of the reforms were introduced piecemeal and lacked coherence, leaving behind numerous loose ends. The devolved institutions at first struggled to gain legitimacy, and turnout at their elections has generally been low, while the extension of devolution to England in the shape of the North East Assembly was roundly rejected by voters there.

What is undeniable however is that although timid and inconsistent the constitutional reform programme has permanently transformed British politics. It may yet come to be seen as the biggest legacy of the Blair Government.[10] The most permanent and irreversible change has been the devolution of powers to Scotland and Wales. The establishment of the Welsh Assembly and the Scottish Parliament, approved in subsequent referendums, created a dynamic towards a federal union. It would now be impossible for a Westminster Government to withdraw the powers that have been granted, and all the pressure has been for more powers to be devolved, and for the Westminster Parliament to address the anomalies created for England by the character of the devolution settlement. This is the most significant development in British territorial politics since the exit of Ireland from the United Kingdom.

The constitutional reforms did not however succeed in ending disaffection from politics. The rise of new Labour initially boosted membership of the Labour party and the turnout at the 1997 general election was over 70 per cent, in line with what it had been in elections of the previous 20 years. But turnout slumped at the 2001 General Election, and only marginally recovered in 2005. It rose slightly again in 2010, but was still below the 1997 figure, and a long way below the high figures of the elections in the immediate post-war period. Party membership soon continued its decline, and the cynicism and lack of trust in politicians and the political process which were so much in evidence before 1997 and were temporarily displaced by the enthusiasm for Tony Blair and new Labour, came back with renewed force. Tory sleaze became Labour sleaze, and then with the MPs expenses scandal in 2009 became the sleaze of the whole political class, from which very few politicians escaped unscathed. The public rage against politicians of all parties acquired a new intensity at the end of the new Labour period. The exposure of MPs expenses was an accident waiting to happen, and several MPs had warned their colleagues about it. What made it possible was another constitutional reform, the Freedom of Information Act. Much criticised for being too weak, it was too strong for MPs to protect their privacy. MPs had voted for the Act, but many evidently thought it would never be applied to them.

Another promise of the new politics was that new Labour promised to bring government much closer to the people, and to reshape the public sector so that services were delivered which were much more in line with what citizens wanted. The ambition was to reverse the contraction of the public ethos and the public domain, by finding ways to make the public sector legitimate again, and not just for those who were dependent on public services in some way, but for the whole community. The government energetically pushed through reforms in the way in which the public sector is managed and monitored, but it was too often divided over its aims. The tension between Tony Blair and Gordon Brown which emerged at the heart of government was in part a dispute over how best to reform the state, and to deliver the big improvement in public services which the public wanted.[11] Many Blairite ministers and Blair himself wanted to experiment with more radical methods of service delivery, involving greater choice, more providers, and greater pluralism. Brown and the Treasury favoured close detailed central control over spending. One of the consequences of the latter was that the enabling state increasingly came to resemble the old command state, and this bred growing resentment at increasing government interference—in particular the big extension of the techniques associated with the new public management, the target and audit culture, and performance indicators. Under new Labour true decentralisation of services was limited, and instead there was a considerable increase in government interference and government monitoring. The ease with which Labour came to be identified with the promotion of a nanny state showed how seriously it was failing to achieve its original objectives.

The decentralist agenda in British politics has been championed by all parties when in opposition, but in government none has yet succeeded in actually implementing it, because none have been ready to devolve real powers to subordinate bodies. Localism has always clashed with the centralist traditions of British government, and governments concerned with improving delivery of core public services never in the end trust local governments or the voluntary sector sufficiently to hand over control to them. The reason is partly self-preservation. Voters still blame central government when things go wrong, and disclaiming responsibility by saying that central government no longer has responsibility does not work. The one area where there was real devolution was to Scotland, and to a smaller extent in Wales.

One of the difficulties that the new politics faced was that the conditions for renewing civic engagement in public life had drastically changed, most obviously through the new role played by the media. New Labour politicians recognised that the media had become the crucial gatekeepers of the relationship between politicians and the public, but they attempted to deal with it by developing a media strategy of their own which they hoped would enable them to control the news agenda, and prevent the government becoming the victims of the media in the manner of the Major Government. Although this worked for a time, in the long run it proved ruinous for the government's reputation and for any attempt to introduce a new politics. The culture of spin and news management was turned back against the government by the media, which made the government's attempt to manipulate the media an all-consuming news story.

Policy agendas

The Blair Government set out to combine economic efficiency with social justice, free markets with universal welfare. In his Fabian pamphlet on the Third Way Blair set out four broad policy objectives for his government: a dynamic knowledge-based economy; a strong civil society; a modern government based on partnership and decentralisation and a foreign policy based on international cooperation.[12] For the first ten years the economic policy of the Blair Government appeared to be successful. There was no financial crisis of the kind which attended Labour Governments in the past; inflation stayed low, unemployment stayed low, and there was steady uninterrupted growth in each of the ten years. The government consolidated and extended the financial growth model which it inherited from the Conservatives, and which depended on flexible labour markets, relatively low business taxes, the development of a strong financial services industry and the development of strategies to make all citizens financial agents. Labour went further by giving the Bank of England operational independence over the setting of interest rates, and redressing the underfunding of major parts of the public sector. It invested heavily in the science base and introduced a number of supply side policies aimed at raising productivity. Productivity in British industry remained stubbornly low, and the prize of raising the long-term growth potential of the British economy was not achieved. But Labour did show itself to be pro-business, pro-enterprise and pro-market. This was perhaps the first Labour Government towards which the business community was not actively hostile. The old battlelines between capital and labour which had dominated economic policy-making throughout the twentieth century were finally erased. The consensus between the parties on markets and private ownership as the best way to secure prosperity was confirmed.

At the beginning of its tenure Labour went further. So anxious was the government to win the confidence of the markets and show that Labour could be trusted with the economy that the Chancellor, Gordon Brown, stuck rigidly to the plans for public spending inherited from the Conservatives. Brown argued that public finances had to be put on a sound footing and he was determined to bear down on public debt. The squeeze proved so severe that by the end of the Parliament in 2001 the Blair Government was spending less on core public services as a percentage of GDP than John Major's Government had been.[13] The government however by this means established a reputation for prudence and for putting financial stability first. In the next nine years the position changed dramatically. Starting from the plans announced in 1999 the government presided over a very rapid increase in public spending, including the fastest ever increase of funds for the NHS and education. By 2008 the resources available to the NHS had more than doubled and as a percentage of GDP rose from 6% to over 9%. Britain began to approach European levels of spending on welfare.

The record on the economy is therefore very mixed. At one level the government did continue neo-liberal policies and worked to promote prosperity within that framework. But at the same time it can also be viewed as a rather orthodox social democratic government in its devotion to increasing public spending, using the conventional instruments of the command state to do so. It was the most successful period of economic management in the history of Labour Governments because for ten years growth was not interrupted, and this delivered a rising trend of public spending. The sure sign of its success was that by 2007 the Conservatives under Cameron were promising to match Labour's spending totals, and in particular to protect the NHS. The Conservatives declared that they would use the 'growth dividend' differently, allocating more to reducing taxes, but they also accepted that public spending would continue to rise. The Conservatives were content to compete on the new political centre ground which Labour had carved out.

Much of this was swept away by the credit crunch and the financial crash which followed in 2008, and the recession in 2009. Labour lost its reputation for economic competence, as the banking crisis changed into a fiscal crisis and then a sovereign debt crisis, which the Conservatives, and the Coalition Government, attempted to blame on Labour's economic stewardship. But crucial parts of the new consensus remained, including the ringfencing of the NHS and overseas aid, as well as a commitment to make the tax system fairer. It suited the Coalition to distance themselves as much as possible from Labour's record, and in particular Gordon Brown's, but in many respects they continued Labour's policies and approach to the economy. The Conservatives were very keen not to be labelled in the way they had been in the 1980s, when they presided over a substantial increase in inequality in Britain, and their policies were widely perceived as harsh and uncaring. The actual scale of the cuts in the 1980s was less than the scale planned by the Coalition in 2010, but the political context was very different. The Conservatives did not need to lower taxes on the rich in 2010, because Labour had largely maintained the low tax regime on income and wealth which the Conservatives had established in the 1980s. In 2010 the Conservatives accepted that certain core public services should be protected, at the same time as they proposed a radical reshaping of the state, which would involve much greater decentralisation and the handing over of many functions to providers in the voluntary and private sectors. The Big Society was the big idea of the Conservatives in the 2010 election but how far they were prepared to act on it, or how far the traditional centralist impulses of the British state would reassert themselves remained uncertain. The direction of change had been anticipated by new Labour and was foreshadowed in many of the plans and instincts of the early period of the Labour Government, even if not ultimately delivered. But this was why David Cameron was keen to declare himself the heir to Blair, because he regarded some of the paths which Blair had mapped out as the way the state should be reshaped. If the Coalition survives the stresses of the cuts the way that policy is likely to develop in the future may well continue to draw on some new Labour ideas.

In a longer perspective the Blair Government is likely to be seen as quite contradictory, with both a decentralising and a centralising impulse working together. It may therefore appear as a transitional period, but one none the less very important for signposting what was to come. Labour's exploration of new ways of delivering state services, and a new emphasis on pluralism are likely to prove influential for the future. During Labour's period in office its ambition to improve the delivery and quality of public services produced mixed results. Many aspects of the target regime proved counter productive because they demotivated professionals. Efforts to revive morale in the public sector and restore the public service ethos did not meet much success. The government found it very difficult to persuade citizens that services had improved, even though many objective measures showed that they had. The aim of a more decentralised welfare state, based on the continuance of state funding for public services but delivery through a wide range of alternative providers[14] has made some progress but much less than the early new Labour thinkers hoped. As a result the strategic aim which Labour set itself, of improving state-funded public services to the point that the middle classes would be happy to go on using them and paying for them, was only partially achieved. It seemed to have been won when Cameron and Osborne pledged to maintain Labour's spending totals. But once the banks crashed and the recession hit the Conservatives reverted to a much older tradition of sound fiscal management, and saw the opportunity for a major reduction in the size and the scope of the state. The social democracy that was such a powerful political force for a hundred years in British politics, may have had a last fling with the Labour Government elected in 1997. Although at the time many denied it was a social democratic government at all, in retrospects its social democratic character is likely to become more and more obvious.

As noted above the Coalition Government formed in 2010 did not have to concern itself about redistributing income and wealth to the rich, because Labour had generally left the rich alone. This was not accidental, but a central feature of the economic and political strategy which new Labour pursued. The government stressed opportunity, investment in human capital, and the establishment of minimum levels of provision. Pursuing this agenda it instituted a series of measures to combat poverty, reduce disadvantage and discrimination. These included the minimum wage, Sure Start, family and pensioner tax credits, welfare to work, as well as the improvements in the quality of education and health services, and the creations of a third arm of the welfare state, asset-based welfare, with the introduction of the child trust fund. Many of these innovations appeared permanent, but in the new climate of austerity after the 2010 election the Coalition Government announced major cuts in the welfare budget, the scrapping of major innovative schemes such as the child trust fund, as well as average cuts of 25% in departmental budgets. Overall the share of government spending in GDP which had risen to 42% before the crash, and had risen further to 47.5% to stave off economic collapse, now was scheduled to shrink back to 38% by 2015. If a reduction in the size of the public sector of this magnitude is achieved, all the increases of the Labour years will be wiped out, and the UK will be heading back towards a residual welfare state. The measures in the budget to soften the impact on the poor and low income families will be overtaken by the impact of the tax increases and the reduction in services on which the poor rely. The result of this reshaping of the state is likely to lead to a further rise in inequality and to very high regional unemployment. The scale of the private sector and export recovery required to avoid the latter has never been achieved before, and there is little likelihood of it occurring in the next few years, especially given the problems of Britain's largest market, the Eurozone.

Conclusion

The fate of the Coalition and its ambitious deficit reduction plans will play a big role in shaping the way in which the new Labour era comes to be viewed. The changes which Labour introduced after 1999 were incremental and gradual but were sustained until 2008, and pushed British welfare standards a long way towards European levels of provision. The issue was always whether such improvements could be sustained, if there was a serious economic downturn. There were many warning signs that the British economy was becoming increasingly unsustainable and that public and private borrowing were both too high. But few predicted the global storm that was about to break. The policies that are now emerging to deal with the deficit is handled may well be crucial in determining the direction of British politics and the future of the public sector.

In other areas the Labour legacy may be more lasting. Many of the constitutional changes will not be reversed. Continuities in fields like defence, foreign policy, European policy, are likely to be far more apparent than the breaks. How radical the new regime emerging in economic policy will be is as yet unclear, but it will not be a fresh start or a reversion to an earlier model. It will be powerfully shaped by the new Labour era.

1   R. Rose, *Do Parties Matter*, Macmillan, 1984.
2   M. Jacques and S. Hall, 'Wrong', *Marxism Today*, Special Issue, November–December 1998.
3   R. Heffernan, *New Labour and Thatcherism: Political Change in Britain*, Palgrave, 2001.
4   A. Giddens, *The Third Way*, Polity, 1998.
5   S. Fielding, *The Labour Party: Continuity and Change in the Making of New Labour*, Palgrave, 2003.
6   E. Hobsbawm, *The Forward March of Labour Halted?*, Verso, 1981.
7   S. Finer, *Adversary Politics and Electoral Reform*, Wigram, 1975.
8   P. Gould, *The unfinished Revolution: How the modernisers saved the Labour party*, Little, Brown, 1998.
9   T. Bale, *The Conservative Party: From Thatcher to Cameron*, Polity, 2010.
10 V. Bogdanor, *The New British Constitution*, Hart, 2009.
11 A. Seldon, *Blair Unbound*, Pocket Books, 2008.
12 Blair, *The Third Way*, Fabian Society, p. 7.
13 Maurice Mullard, 'New Labour, New Public Expenditure', *The Political Quarterly*, 72, 2001, 310–21.
14 IPPR, *Building Better Partnerships*, IPPR, 2001.

STEVEN FIELDING

Labour's Campaign: Things Can Only Get ... Worse?[1]

None of the three main parties won the 2010 general election, but Labour was undoubtedly the biggest loser. Although it did not suffer the wipe-out many members feared, the election was another staging point in the graduated dissolution of the party's 1997 coalition. Labour received 29 per cent of the vote, down 6.2 per cent from 2005 and its lowest share since 1983; the size of the Parliamentary Labour Party consequently fell to 258 MPs, its smallest number since 1987. Having claimed the Conservatives wanted to return Britain to the 1980s, it was Labour that, electorally speaking, now found itself back in Thatcher's decade.

Table 1 shows that the party's decline is especially striking in relation to its total vote. Between 1997 and 2010, Labour lost 4.9 million voters or two-fifths of those who supported Tony Blair in 1997. In net terms, just under half had gone to the Conservatives and Liberal Democrats, while the rest went to either minor (mainly far-right) parties or non-voting. Much of this decline occurred between 1997 and 2001, but the 167 seat majority that underpinned Labour's second term meant it did not provoke much agonising within the party. By 2005, Labour's problems were more apparent. However, plotting to replace Blair then Gordon Brown became a convenient displacement activity for a party that would not—or could not—confront a more basic problem: how to regain its lost 'core' and 'swing' supporters.

During the government's third term, circumstances became uniquely difficult for the party. The Conservatives found in David Cameron a leader who made the main opposition party look credible while the economy was cast into a deep recession. Thus, if it was to win a fourth term, what some still called 'New Labour' would have to renew itself in circumstances far more challenging than those faced by Blair and Brown while in opposition during the 1990s.

Given this context, Labour's 2010 campaign had merit. This was an election no one thought it could win. Instead strategists believed they

The Author [2010]. Published by Oxford University Press on behalf of the
Hansard Society
doi:10.1093/pa/gsq026

1. Labour's decline, 1997–2005

General election	Votes cast (per cent)	Total vote (in millions)	Difference from previous election (in millions)
1997	43.2	13.5	
2001	40.3	10.7	−2.8 (−20.7%)
2005	35.2	9.5	−1.2 (−12.6%)
2010	29.0	8.6	−0.9 (−12.8%)
Difference	−14.2	−4.9 (36.3%)	

might prevent the Conservatives from gaining a Commons majority and ensure Labour remained the biggest party, thereby creating the basis for a coalition with the Liberal Democrats. Labour plausibly appealed to 'swing' and 'core' voters, defended its record but looked to the future. Unfortunately, most people had stopped listening—the damage had already been done—under Brown but also Blair. The campaign made the best of a bad job—but a bad job it undoubtedly was.

A *missed opportunity?*

When, after a 13-year wait, Brown became its leader in June 2007, Labour was in a weakened state. Despite its 69-seat majority, in 2005 more people had abstained from voting than had supported Labour.[2] Moreover, after the election, Blair spent much of his time as Prime Minister avoiding speculation about when he was going to leave office.

When Blair reluctantly announced his resignation date, some of his supporters wanted to stand a candidate against Brown. Others believed a leadership election in which the contenders debated the party's direction would restore its position in the country. As it was generally assumed Brown would easily defeat any rival, no credible candidate came forward, so his election became a 'coronation'—which critics claimed undermined his legitimacy as Prime Minister.

Brown appreciated that he could only reverse Labour's unpopularity by establishing how different he was to Blair. This was never going to be easy—since 1994 he had been the second most significant party figure. As Prime Minister, Brown consequently talked of his being 'a new government with new priorities'. He encouraged attempts to reposition its policies. Brown claimed that he sought a 'new consensus' based around a 'new constitutional settlement' and, in contrast to Blair, promised to take Cabinet seriously and give more powers to Parliament. Much of this activity marked just a change of tone and most of his initiatives came to nothing.

In July, a Populus poll revealed that nearly 60 per cent did not think Brown represented a 'significant change' from Blair. There was, even so, a modest rise in Labour support during the summer: according to ICM, the party regained a lead over the Conservatives for the first time since December 2005. The basis for this 'Brown bounce' is unclear but events—thwarted terror attacks, floods and an outbreak of foot and mouth—saw the Prime Minister manage these threats to Britain's security with aplomb. Some close to Brown talked of holding an election, if only to destabilise the Conservatives; this objective gave way to the feeling that an autumn contest would really be a good idea.[3]

During August, the party made serious preparations: journalists were primed and media speculation went into overdrive. However, in September, the party commissioned private polls that suggested Labour's support was weak and so an election would not increase its majority. For Brown, winning more seats than did Blair in 2005 was the whole purpose of the exercise: it would allow him to claim a personal mandate; anything less would undermine his authority. He now backed off, allowing the Conservatives to claim the Prime Minister had 'dithered' and was 'weak'. To make matters worse, Brown denied he had considered holding an election, a disbelieved claim that undermined his crumbling reputation as a serious man of substance.

Brown the leader

Academics have long debated the importance of a party's leader to its electoral support. They now agree that while the leader is rarely enough to determine the outcome of an election outright, they can exert a significant impact, especially in close contests in which partisanship is weak.[4] The 'leadership effect' is nonetheless hard to measure: disaggregating it from other influences on voting patterns is almost impossible.

What can be measured is the media's tendency to personalise politics.[5] Under Blair, Labour exploited this process, projecting itself through its leader so his persona highlighted the party's message.[6] Initially, Brown's persona was also deemed useful. At a time when some thought the public had tired of Blair's actorly style, Brown's uncertain grasp of media presentation but presumed firm understanding of policy was presented in positive terms. This was exemplified in the poster produced during preparations for the abortive 2007 election: 'Not Flash—Just Gordon'.

Once his honeymoon was over, Brown's approach to presentation looked more troubling. The Prime Minister was mocked for his awkward attempts to smile on camera during an April 2009 statement on MPs' expenses published on the Number 10 Youtube site. Amateur psychiatrists shared their views about the origins of Brown's lack of ease in public. To the astonishment of some, such issues became a fit subject for public debate—most notably when the BBC's Andrew Marr forced Brown to deny during an interview in September 2009 that he relied on anti-depressants. The source for Marr's story was a blogger who admitted he had no proof for his speculations.

Whatever the cause, as even his closest supporter Ed Balls put it, Brown 'couldn't be the leader that people wanted'.[7] YouGov polls show that from January 2008 to April 2010 Brown consistently trailed

Cameron when people were asked who would make the best Prime Minister. In May 2008, Brown fell as low as 17 per cent, at which point Cameron enjoyed a 22 per cent advantage: during 2009 Brown lagged by an average of 14 per cent behind his Conservative counterpart.

The financial crisis

Matters of substance also effected how people viewed Brown's premiership. According to Peter Watt, Labour's General Secretary during his first months as leader, Downing Street 'was a total shambles: there was no vision, no strategy, no co-ordination. It was completely dysfunctional'.[8] The misjudgements underlying the election-that-never-was typified Brown's leadership; it would not be the last time he was found wanting.

In his last Budget as Chancellor, Brown cut the basic rate of income tax from 22p to 20p to show he could be as nice to swing voters as Blair and win positive headlines in the right-wing press. An unintended consequence was, however, that five million low earners would be worse off. As Brown had also abolished the 10p rate at which they would start paying tax, they would now do so at 20p. Despite numerous warnings, Brown only acknowledged this when Labour MPs rose up in dismay in May 2008 and forced a humbling climb-down. This last minute change of heart damaged his authority and still did not prevent Labour losing the London mayoralty. A year later, the pattern was repeated over the government's refusal to allow 36,000 Gurkha veterans to live in the country in whose interests they had fought. By the time he finally offered concessions, they came too late to prevent a humiliating Commons defeat, further demonstrating the Prime Minister's uncanny ability to alienate his own MPs and the public.[9]

The lost Gurkha vote occurred just a week before the *Daily Telegraph* published unedited MPs' expenses claims, setting off a massive wave of public outrage. The *Telegraph* took particular aim at Labour, starting its revelations by reproducing the claims of Cabinet members. If Brown came out unscathed, the same could not be said of all his colleagues. Brown might have mitigated the damage to the government had he responded early and decisively: instead Cameron did that and so further outflanked the Prime Minister.

The most significant issue to confront Brown was the international financial crisis. The bankruptcy of Northern Rock, which preoccupied the government during the autumn of 2007, was but the first instalment of the threatened collapse of the whole financial sector. After some hesitation, Brown and Chancellor Alistair Darling acted to prevent the demise of some of Britain's leading banks by taking huge stakes in institutions such as HBOS. This prevented them failing and so dragging down the rest of the economy with them.

In tackling the emergency in this way, Brown encouraged other governments to adopt an interventionist approach; he also took the lead in coordinating efforts to stave off an even deeper international recession. For this, he won the praise of prominent economists and other world leaders. These rediscovered leadership skills even gave the Prime Minister some relief at home as Labour started to rise in the polls. However, Brown's achievements on the world stage were never enough to allow him to completely escape his domestic troubles. The plaudits he received at the G20 summit in April 2009 were undercut by the resignation of Damian McBride, one of his closest aides, who was exposed promoting rumours about leading Conservatives' private lives.

Despite his efforts, the economy still fell into the worst recession since the 1930s, which made Brown's earlier claims that Labour had ended 'boom and boost' look hollow. As Chancellor he promised prudence but, in saving the banks, the government intervened massively in the economy, thereby throwing its finances deeply into the red. To help retrieve matters, ministers therefore had to countenance raising income tax. In November 2008, Darling announced that in 2011 he would increase the top rate of income tax from 40p to 45p, a measure that would be felt by only the top 1 per cent of earners. In April 2009, such was the depth of the crisis in the public finances, Darling said he would raise the top rate to 50p.

Commentators—notably in the Murdoch press—presented these measures as marking the end of New Labour. In November 2008, the *Sun* pictured a tombstone on its front page on which was carved 'RIP New Labour'. The accompanying story surveyed 'The life and death of Blair's baby' which had, it claimed, finally succumbed to 'socialism'.[10] When the paper announced its support for Cameron during Labour's 2009 conference, only its timing could have surprised anyone. Brown reinstated Peter Mandelson to the Cabinet in October 2008 to reinforce the government's New Labour credentials. In response to this onslaught, Mandelson stated that it was the 'times that have changed, not New Labour' and it remained in favour of 'people becoming very rich, as long as they pay their taxes'.[11] His old magic, however, no longer worked.

Winning back the lost voters

Prior to 1997, New Labour had persuaded voters it could best serve all their interests by reconciling the apparently irreconcilable. It promised to improve public services but not increase income tax and satisfy aspirations to rise up the social ladder while building a fairer society. Until he became fixated with Iraq, Blair had bound these different elements together. However, as government spending rose, from 40.6 to 44.1 per cent of the Gross Domestic Product during 1997–2007, the public began to favour reducing taxes over increasing spending.[12] Yet, during this period, Labour had not made Britain a much fairer society, although it had reduced child poverty by one-third.[13] So, already losing the support of swing voters and having made but a modest difference to the lives of most core supporters, the financial crisis threatened to completely unravel the New Labour coalition.

Some in the party hoped the crisis would push Labour leftwards. Even if this sentiment had not been based on hope more than reality, it did not sit well with Brown's cautious approach. The Prime Minster wanted to make Britain fairer but he was unconvinced enough voters shared his vision. That was why as Chancellor he had redistributed modestly and by 'stealth' and appealed to what he presumed were most voters' conservative instincts.[14] New Labour had followed this strategy from its inception—but with Blair at its head it usually presented a coherent case to the nation. Under Brown, Labour only gave voters confused signals, notably in the case of the reduction of the starting rate of tax.

Not everyone called for more radicalism. In July 2009, John Denham, Secretary of State for Communities, argued that by defining 'fairness solely in terms of society's response to those in greatest need', Labour, 'is badly out of step with popular sentiment'. Highlighting strategic differences within the Cabinet Denham implicitly criticised Harriet Harman's Equality Bill, which aimed to reduce the gap between rich and poor through legislative means. Instead of passing this measure, Denham asserted, Labour should better understand the concerns of those on middle incomes - one of New Labour's original precepts.

Some younger Blairites sought less familiar territory. James Purnell, who left the Cabinet in June 2009 after calling for Brown's resignation wanted 'to open up New Labour, reinvent it and then eventually move beyond it' and from the backbenches argued the party should stop slav- ishly following the demands of swing voters.[15]

The impending election meant ministers had to focus on tangible ways of winning back Labour's lost voters. Mandelson and Darling felt that could be done through demonstrating the government's economic competence, by being open about the need for massive cuts, given that public spending was set to account for 53 per cent of GDP by 2010. Brown and Ed Balls, however, wanted to be able to promise some future spending in health and education at least, thereby creating a clear dividing line between Labour and the Conservatives. Cameron's party could then be cast as interested only in an ideologically driven attack on the public services. When Darling made his 2009 Pre-Budget Report in December 2009, Brown seemed to have prevailed. Mandelson was reportedly furious it proposed tax rises for the middle class but failed to spell out detailed cuts. This he allegedly described as a 'core vote' strategy.[16]

By the March 2010 Budget, Brown had been weakened by yet another attempted coup, and in return for his support, Darling shifted the Pre-Budget Report's original emphasis. He announced that a re-elected Labour government would cut spending on a scale 'deeper and tougher' than under Margaret Thatcher and halve the deficit by the end of the next Parliament. If this sounded like the Conservatives that was deliberate.[17] Yet differences between the two parties remained. Darling would not start cutting until 2011 to allow the economy to recover. He would also raise more revenue through taxing the better off, and to that end, Darling proposed raising £6 billion by increasing National Insurance on higher earners.

The Budget, then, set the parameters for the campaign. Labour presented itself to swing voters as economically competent while casting the Conservatives as threatening the futures of many voters—core as well as swing.

The positive/negative strategy

The party that fought the 2010 campaign was a shadow of its former self. By 2010, membership had fallen to as low as 150,000, one-third of what it had been in 1997. If there were fewer—and older—troops in the constituencies, there was less money available to the national party. As a result, Labour employed just one-third of the staff it had used in 2005. On the verge of bankruptcy in 2007, the party's finances had, however, improved somewhat by 2010, largely thanks to those trade unions that contributed 80 per cent of its income. As Justin Fisher's contribution to this volume demonstrates, Labour's resources were stretched and it could not afford to spend money like Cameron.

Strategists knew that if the election became a *referendum* on the government's record the party was sunk, so wanted to turn the campaign into a *choice* between the Conservatives and Labour—the Liberal Democrats barely featured in anyone's thinking. If they could do that, strategists believed they had some hope of winning back some swing voters; otherwise, Labour would be forced to go negative and maximise its chances with core voters.

The voters' desire for 'change' was, however, so overwhelming, Labour's definition of the future was irrelevant. A MORI poll taken in March 2010, for example, showed that 55 per cent 'strongly agreed' and a further 21 per cent 'tended to agree' with the proposition that 'Britain needs a fresh team of leaders'.[18] This meant that Labour increasingly focused on scaring core voters about the threat posed by Conservative 'change'. The party's televised election broadcasts illustrated this shift in tone. The second and third were upbeat about 'brilliant Britain' and outlined how Labour would make it even better. The final broadcast, however, outlined 'a nightmare on your streets', showing officious men with clip boards visiting hitherto happy families on 'middle and modest incomes' to take away their child tax credits and baby bond payments.

If the Conservative campaign focused on Brown—his smiling face was often found on their posters—Labour repaid the compliment by concentrating much of their fire on Cameron. The Conservative leader was designated a lightweight, who lacked Brown's experience. Very much as John Major had said of Blair in 1997, Brown predicted Cameron would be 'found out'. 'At the end of the day', he said, 'people are going to choose how they vote on the basis of substance and they are going to look below the superficialities, the public relations and the tactics'.[19] Labour's main line of attack was that Cameron led an unreformed Thatcherite party, the basis for a poster depicting him as Gene Hunt, the politically incorrect detective from the television series *Ashes to Ashes*, set at the height of Thatcherism. Unfortunately, Hunt was a cult hero and Labour inadvertently made Cameron look something approaching 'cool'.

The sunshine manifesto

Labour's manifesto launch went as well as could be expected. Its title 'A future fair for all' along with its sunshine logo promoted the party's initially optimistic approach and was launched in a new NHS hospital to demonstrate Labour's ongoing commitment to public services.

Ed Miliband who had coordinated the drafting of the manifesto since 2007 claimed it proved the party remained best qualified to lead 'the next phase of national renewal'. The elements Miliband high-lighted—raising the minimum wage and using post offices as commu-nity banks—suggested it also marked a return to the concerns of core Labour voters.[20] Yet Brown claimed people 'will be surprised by the pro-business nature of the manifesto, the pro-enterprise nature of the manifesto and pro-industry nature of the manifesto'.[21] In truth, the document tried to appeal to both core and swing voters by arguing that only government (suitably reformed) could ensure a fair society and an efficient economy. Post-launch briefings confirmed the extent to which the manifesto—like Labour's campaign at this point—looked in contrasting directions. One unnamed 'senior figure' said the party was now no longer interested in wooing the wealthy; yet Mandelson suggested Labour remained the party of 'aspiration'.[22]

Ed Miliband was correct when he claimed that the manifesto con-tained a 'big argument', about government being on the side of the people. But manifesto launches are just the start of a campaign. It is the job of the leader to embody and articulate their party's manifesto message; but Brown was not trusted with that task. He was conse-quently filmed attending small meetings of Labour supporters, saying very little. These photo opportunities left the Prime Minister, according to one journalist, 'looking less like a world leader than a hostage being moved from safe house to safe house under close guard'.[23]

The debates

The leadership debates forced Brown centre stage. Labour agreed to participate because such was its lowly poll position few felt it had much to lose. Some strategists even hoped they would show Brown to be a man of substance while exposing Cameron.

The debates certainly provided the Prime Minister with a unique platform the first one being watched by 9.4 million, one in four of whom said it had changed their minds.[24] Brown was, however, unable to exploit this opportunity. According to YouGov, viewers rated him as performing the worst of the three leaders: only 19 per cent thought he did best in the first; 29 per cent in the second and 25 per cent in the final debate. Given their low expectations about Brown's performance, the best that might be said is that, overall, the debates did not make voters think any worse of him.

The debate format was not kind to Brown. The large number of questions and the tight limit on the length of answers meant that if he did enjoy a greater grasp of the issues he could not demonstrate it. Viewers were in any case impressed more by how a leader spoke and the extent to which he seemed personable. Those watching did not like it when a leader went negative—something Brown had to do to undermine Conservative 'change'. He was in truth doomed to fail. MORI polling showed that voters considered Brown the best equipped and most capable of the three leaders; but whatever he said they just did not want him to be their Prime Minister.[25]

The first debate proved the most crucial of the three by dramatically boosting Nick Clegg. Brown's strategy had been to highlight the danger Cameron posed to the recovery and he drew him into arguments that knocked the Conservative leader off his game. He also wanted to demonstrate how far the Labour and the Liberal Democrats agreed on policy, repeatedly claiming 'I agree with Nick'—not to boost Clegg but to isolate Cameron. This approach might have inadvertently helped fuel 'Cleggmania'.

Not only did the first broadcast fail to change perceptions of Brown, it propelled the Liberal Democrats into second place according to some opinion polls. For a time, Labour looked completely irrelevant as the media focused on the battle between the two 'change' parties. Indeed, so disenchanted was the Labour camp, after the second debate the party wrote to Britain's broadcasters to complain about how far the debates dominated their news coverage. There was more than a grain of truth to the charge—but the genie having escaped the bottle, there was little Labour could do to ram it back in.

Bigotgate and the I-word

With Labour looking like it might come third in the popular vote, it was decided to let Brown loose on the public during the last full week of campaigning. Accompanied by Sarah Brown, his 'human shield', Brown was despatched to meet 'real people'. However, the danger inherent to this approach was exposed in what will be the best-remembered moment of the election: 'bigotgate'.

In a visit to the marginal constituency of Rochdale, the Prime Minister—temporarily separated from his wife—became involved in a discussion with Mrs Gillian Duffy, a grandmother and long-time Labour voter. Duffy claimed she was 'ashamed of saying I'm Labour' and shared with Brown a number of her grievances. The exchange nonetheless was seemingly good humoured and he answered her points respectfully. Immediately after this, Brown entered his car and, forgetting he was wearing a live microphone, complained to an aide about having to engage with 'a sort of bigoted woman'. Journalists played Brown's remarks back to Duffy and her look of shock was splashed across the media for days. The Prime Minister was also filmed listening, slumped in his seat, to a recording of his own words in a BBC radio studio. His despairing reaction provoked the US comedian Jon Stewart to note that 'you can actually see the moment when his political career leaves his body'.

Brown immediately made a pilgrimage to the Duffy home to offer his apologies and even issued one to Labour members. He had given up a moment for which all journalists—especially those employed by the right-wing press—had been praying. The *Sun*, desperate to obtain Duffy's story, was willing to pay her a considerable amount if she also said she would now vote Conservative. In the end, the *Mail on Sunday* signed her up for a story in which Duffy said she would not vote at all.

'Bigotgate' occurred the day before the final leaders' debate, during which Brown acknowledged his gaffe when he said: 'There's a lot to this job [of Prime Minister]. And as you saw yesterday, I do not get all of it right. But I do know how to run the economy in the good times and the bad'. Memorable it might have been—and it dominated the media for a few days—but how far 'bigotgate' hurt Labour's performance is moot. Most of those who disliked Brown had already made up their minds; and Labour—without Duffy—even managed to win Rochdale, from the Liberal Democrats.

The Liberal Democrats

It might not have appeared that way at the time but Labour was better prepared for Cleggmania than the Conservatives. Insofar as it prevented a Cameron majority, some in the party even welcomed it. Indeed, the BBC's Political Editor Nick Robinson quoted a 'senior Labour figure' saying after the first leaders' debate that a hung parliament—in which presumably Labour and the Liberal Democrats would cooperate—would be 'the ultimate fulfilment of the New Labour mission'.[26]

Appreciating how unlikely retaining its Commons majority would be, Labour had prepared for a rapprochement with the Liberal Democrats for some time. The party's object was twofold: to encourage Liberal Democrat supporters to vote tactically at the election and to lay the foundations for a post-election arrangement between the two parties. In this process, the promise of electoral reform was central.[27] A cabinet subcommittee was formed in June 2009 to look into reforming politics in light of the MPs' expenses controversy, but specifically to develop proposals regarding elections to the Lords and Commons. While caution prevailed, some ministers wanted to hold a referendum on electoral reform on the same day as the election, to bind the Liberal Democrats close to Labour.[28] Instead in February 2010, Brown announced plans to legislate for a referendum as the keystone in his attempt to build a 'progressive consensus'.

Therefore, while Cleggmania took everyone by surprise, Labour was ready to engage with the Liberal Democrats. In the aftermath of the first debate, Brown consequently stressed how far the two parties agreed on constitutional reform—and how far the Conservatives opposed such change.[29] The Transport Secretary Lord Adonis—a former Liberal Democrat—even argued that Clegg's manifesto was 'basically a social democratic document'.[30] Constitutional reform had the added advantage of making Labour look like a party of 'change' and suggesting the Conservatives really favoured the status quo.[31]

Interpreting the result

By election-day support for Labour was slightly lower than where it had been at the start of the campaign, having recovered from a slump caused by Cleggmania. Despite all its sound and fury, therefore, the campaign barely altered the party's lowly position. Nonetheless, Labour had helped prevent the Conservatives winning a Commons majority. There were, however, not enough Labour MPs to make a coalition with the Liberal Democrats viable. Given the context, then, the campaign might be described as a qualified failure.

As the party had long known, Labour had lost the support of voters on average and above-average incomes on a disproportionate scale (Table 2). During the campaign, it tried to persuade such swing voters that it could deliver a 'future fair for all' and that Conservative 'change' threatened them. It failed. Among the richest and poorest social groups, Labour did less badly; the party's negative emphasis, which came to the fore during the last week, had shored up support among core supporters.

Brown had confirmed his shortcomings. The Prime Minister had prevented the world economy from slipping over the edge, but that was clearly not enough to prevent most Britons wanting him out. He was the fourth most significant reason Conservative (35 per cent) and Liberal Democrat (33 per cent) voters gave for their party choice. In contrast, only 20 per cent of Labour voters said Brown's qualities had influenced them, making it the joint sixth most important reason for supporting the party.[32] It is likely then that another leader would have improved Labour's result but it is impossible to say exactly by how much, given the vagaries of when and how such a person (let alone who) would have

2. Labour's 2010 vote by social class

Social class	Labour share
AB (upper middle/middle)	29 (+1)
C1 (lower middle)	26 (−6)
C2 (skilled working)	22 (−18)
D (working)	44 (−4)

Figure in brackets: difference from 2005.
Source: Ipsos-MORI.

taken over. In any case, Labour carried too much baggage to allow a new face to completely transform its fate: but they would have made a coalition with the Liberal Democrats more possible.

Many members were actually relieved when 6 May dawned. Given Labour's flawed leader and the difficult circumstances they concluded Labour might have done much worse. In terms of votes, members and income the party was certainly down—well down—but not quite out. If nearly 30 per cent of voters rallied to the party in such a context surely with a new leader and a period of renewal in opposition Labour could quickly bounce back?

Labour's defeat was, however, part of a progressive downward trend evident across three elections. It is arguable that Brown's failure to transform the party—more than the financial crisis—was what condemned Labour to defeat. A survey undertaken by Stan Greenberg a few days after the poll nonetheless suggested that while renewal remained a priority Labour's position was recoverable.

As Table 3 indicates, in terms of embodying the 'right kind of change' Labour came out the worst of the main parties, the same being the case with regard to which had the right approach to immigration. However, attitudes to Labour and the Conservatives were not much different when it came to the economy. Table 4 moreover suggests that many of the arguments advanced in Labour's manifesto were viewed more positively than its performance at the polls indicated. Thus, in regard to the relative merits of raising taxes or cutting spending and when to start reducing the debt, the public was evenly split—and a big majority thought government should become more involved in the economy instead of letting the market have a greater say. From this evidence, Labour had work to do but the public had not decisively discarded its economic agenda.

Even so, the party had good cause to reflect on the election and wonder in which direction it should travel. David Miliband claimed 'New Labour' should be abandoned, asserting that: 'What I'm interested in is next Labour'.[33] Mandelson, one of the architects of New Labour, accepted that the Miliband generation would stop using the term. However, he argued, 'the concept that New Labour represents should not be cast aside so easily' as that signified Labour's pursuit of 'a strong economy, social justice and high-quality public services' and

3. Party ratings

	Lab	Con	LibDem
Shares your values	31	35	22
For the right kind of change	25	38	28
Improving your standard of living	32	38	17
Keeping taxes at the right level for you	33	32	21
Trust to manage the economy	35	38	12
Right approach to immigration	22	37	23

Source: Greenberg Quinlan Rosner Research, UK Post-Election Frequency Questionnaire, 7–9 May 2010.

4. Reactions to policy statement pairs

Statement pairs	Agree (per cent)
This is a time for government to get more involved.	71
OR	
This is a time to depend more on markets.	22
To reduce the debt, we will need to make major cuts in spending and public services.	45
OR	
To reduce the debt, we must raise taxes broadly and do less cutting of spending and services.	46
We must start cutting the national debt right away.	49
OR	
We must wait to cut the debt until the economic recovery is underway.	48

Source: Greenberg Quinlan Rosner Research, UK Post-Election Frequency Questionnaire, 7–9 May 2010.

of it 'not being a party of class or sectional interest, but about being a broad-based party of conscience and reform'.[34]

There was little danger of 'New Labour' being abandoned—except in name, which it had been in effect some time before. Of the five candidates for the leadership, only one would have dissented from Mandelson's description of Labour's continuing purpose. For, as he argued 'New Labour' was the continuation of the party's revisionist tradition, which had set its strategic parameters for most of the post-war period.[35] Labour, however, had cause to put some distance between itself and at least some aspects of the government first elected in 1997 so it could reconnect with both swing and core voters. However, unlike Blair–who abolished the old clause four to symbolise New Labour's novelty—the party's new leader does not have a similarly redundant but prominent sacred cow to sacrifice. In charting the party's path back to power their task will be more nuanced and, by facing up to the conundrum that is the coalition government, much more tricky.

1   I would like to thank Declan McHugh and Paddy Tipping for their comments on an earlier draft of this work.
2   Steven Fielding, 'Labour's Campaign: Neither Forward Nor Back', in Andrew Geddes and Jonathan Tonge (eds), *Britain Decides. The UK General Election 2005*. Palgrave, 2005.
3   *Observer*, 19 August 2007.
4   Harold D. Clarke, David Sanders, Marianne C. Stewart and Paul Whiteley *Political Choice in Britain*, Oxford University Press, 2004.
5   Ana Inés Langer, 'A Historical Exploration of the Personalisation of Politics in the Print Media: The British Prime Ministers (1945–1999)', *Parliamentary Affairs*, 60, 2007, pp. 371–87.
6   Michael Foley, *The British Presidency*, Manchester University Press, 2000.
7   *Guardian*, 31 May 2010.
8   Peter Watt, *Inside Out*, Biteback, 2010, p. 170.
9   Andrew Rawnsley, *The End of the Party*, Penguin, 2010, pp. 532–41, 642–4.
10   *Sun*, 26 November 2008.
11   http://news.bbc.co.uk/1/hi/uk_politics/7751567.stm 21 February 2009.
12   Institute for Fiscal Studies, *Public Spending under Labour*, IFS, 2010; John Curtice, 'Back in contention? The Conservative's electoral prospects', *Political Quarterly* 80, 2009, 176–81.
13   John Hills, Tom Sefton and Kitty Stewart (eds), *Towards a More Equal Society*, Policy Press, 2009; Donald Hirsch, *Estimating the Costs of Child Poverty*, Joseph Rowntree Foundation, 2009.
14   *Guardian*, 19 April 2008.
15   *Guardian*, 18 July 2009.
16   *London Evening Standard*, 5 January 2010; *Financial Times*, 10 January 2010.
17   http://www.newstatesman.com/blogs/the-staggers/2010/03/spending-cuts-darling-thatcher   10   June 2010.
18   Ipsos MORI, *General Election 2010—An Overview*, Ipsos MORI, 2010, p. 38.
19   *Daily Telegraph*, 11 April 2010.
20   *Guardian*, 19 March 2010.
21   *Sunday Times*, 11 April 2010.
22   *Daily Telegraph*, 13 April 2010.
23   *Daily Telegraph*, 24 April 2010.
24   MORI, *Overview*, p. 23.
25   MORI, *Overview*, pp. 14, 18.
26   http://www.bbc.co.uk/blogs/nickrobinson/2010/04/brown_lib_lab.html 7 May 2010.
27   *Independent*, 5 March 2009.
28   *Independent*, 11 September 2009.
29   *Daily Telegraph*, 17 April 2010.
30   *Financial Times*, 15 April 2010.
31   *Independent*, 21 April 2010.
32   Greenberg Quinlan Rosner Research, 'The Change Election—What Voters Were Really Saying', paper presented at RSA, 17 May 2010.
33   *Times*, 17 May 2010.
34   *Times*, 3 June 2010.
35   As also argued in Steven Fielding, *The Labour Party. Continuity and Change in the Making of 'New' Labour*, Palgrave, 2003.

JANE GREEN

Strategic Recovery? The Conservatives Under David Cameron

In the final 36 hours of the 2010 election campaign, as David Cameron made his night and day sprint across the country to win last-minute votes, the Leader of the Opposition must have wondered why he was not walking into a comfortable and sizable victory. The preceding year had seen Conservative vote intentions reach the magic 40% level—enough to secure a firm majority—and Cameron had long been viewed as the answer to the Conservative party's opposition problems. He was campaigning against one of the most unpopular Prime Ministers in history, Gordon Brown, who had presided over the worst economic crisis since the Great Depression. This was arguably the Conservatives' best opportunity to form a government in a generation.

David Cameron increased the Conservative party's vote share by just 3.8% to 36.1%, between 2005 and 2010. This was only a 4.4% increase on the 31.7% share achieved by William Hague in 2001, in a much derided campaign. Winning 307 seats in parliament in 2010, David Cameron failed to reach the number of seats, 326, to obtain an overall majority. He achieved a much larger seat gain than his immediate predecessors, adding 97 Conservative MPs to the House of Commons, but instead of celebrating the arrival of an exclusively Conservative government following the first election victory for the party in 31 years, Conservative supporters looked on as their party formed a coalition with the Liberal Democrats—a party seen by many as bitter campaigning rivals.

This article offers an analysis of the Conservative party's successes, and failures, which precipitated the result on 7 May 2010. It traces the journey of David Cameron's Conservatives in opposition, highlighting the mixed picture of success achieved in the first two years, and then the latter three years of his opposition leadership. It offers two main observations to consider the electoral achievements, or otherwise, of

doi:10.1093/pa/gsq027

Cameron's Conservative party in opposition. (i) David Cameron increased the potential vote for the Conservative party but he did not enlarge the Conservative base. Roughly the same number of people expressed an affiliation for the Conservatives in 2010 as they did following the disastrous ERM crisis for the Conservatives in 1993. The number of voters on which David Cameron could count upon to vote Conservative in 2010 was not significantly larger than the number available to William Hague, Iain Duncan-Smith or Michael Howard. (ii) David Cameron's Conservative party was no longer viewed negatively, but neither was it viewed positively. The oft-cited strategy of decontaminating the Conservative brand had succeeded, to an extent, but the next step—of securing positive ratings on ideology, competence and leader qualities—had not been achieved. For voters undecided about their vote choice—of which there were many[1]—the 'utility differential' between the main political parties, failed to weigh strongly in the Conservatives' favour.

By the time of the 2010 campaign, many voters wanted a change, but could not yet put their faith in a government run by the Conservatives. The party needed a strong campaign to persuade potential voters, but in the event the campaign was a sideshow to the first-ever leadership debates, which derailed the Conservative strategy. These were all among the reasons that David Cameron stood holding a halibut at 6 a.m. on the eve of polling day in Grimsby, on the campaign trail in his last-dash to win a Conservative majority, but ultimately also the reasons why he was standing outside Downing Street on the morning of Tuesday 11 May 2010 with his Deputy Prime Minister, Nick Clegg, the leader of the Liberal Democrat party.

David Cameron: chosen one

All political parties learn lessons from defeat. The lesson the Conservative party learned from the general elections of 1997, 2001 and 2005, was that no matter how hard they tried, the electorate—and the media—would not give the party a fighting chance until its image had significantly improved. The now well-known observation—that voters rejected policies they would otherwise support when they were informed they were Conservative policies—motivated the strategy. This phenomenon, known simply as 'bias' (or the reverse effect, assimilation), reflects the endogenous nature of party evaluations and policy attitudes.[2] After eight years in opposition, by 2005, insufficient numbers of voters viewed the Conservative party as an acceptable self-identifying label. The party had failed to win back the large sections of support it lost in the 1992–1997 period—those voters who viewed the party as 'good for one class', but not 'good for all'.[3]

The negative image the Conservative party carried would not change, it was argued, so long as the party elected the same kind of leader and campaigned on the same kinds of issues—those issues which, ironically, the party was most trusted and most highly rated. The Conservative party needed a leader who could pull the image of the Conservative party into the centre ground, even if this centrist shift entailed relatively little policy change, and who would compel voters to adjust their perceptions of the Conservative party. In effect, David Cameron was to be the Conservatives' Clause IV moment—the symbolic change which signalled a new version of Conservatism.[4]

This was not a lesson the Conservative party learned particularly quickly or unanimously. The election contest of 2005, following the resignation of its leader Michael Howard, saw four candidates enter the race: Kenneth Clarke, Liam Fox, David Davis and David Cameron.[5] Two could be viewed broadly as coming from the right of the party, Liam Fox and David Davis, and two from the centre, Kenneth Clarke and David Cameron. However, the right and centre of the contemporary Conservative party, and its salient defining features, could quite easily be misunderstood.

In the midst of strategic difficulties there was a genuine split within the Conservative parliamentary party about the strategy the Conservative party should adopt, as well as, of course, individual differences in priorities and agendas. Few now argued that the Conservatives should simply wait for an economic downturn and for the issues of Europe, immigration and crime to come to the fore (those issues on which the Conservatives were most trusted). There was, however, a dilemma, characterised by whether parties win elections by giving emphasis to their core strengths on which they have a long-standing reputation—in this case taking a decentralising, family focused, tough on crime, pro-business, anti-immigration approach and maintaining a socially conservative commitment—or whether the Conservative party should simply move with the times, embracing social liberalism, rejecting some of its past, and actively avoid Conservative strengths to focus predominantly on issues traditionally 'owned'[6] by Labour; the NHS being the defining issue, and to a lesser extent an issue not owned by any party—the environment. The first strategy embraced the existing strengths of the party, believing that voters would come back to the Conservatives when they were disillusioned with Labour, with some broadening out in tone and emphasis. The second strategy was premised on the view that only by avoiding all issues on which Conservatives were usually associated, and by taking a strategy which challenged people's views of modern Conservatism—rather than confirming them—would voters believe that the Conservative party had changed. In this context the Conservative party held its leadership contest.

Kenneth Clarke, a known Europhile, promised experience and popularity. He did not define himself by the electoral strategy he would employ, but was by far the most popular leadership candidate in opinion polls—a fact the Conservative party could not easily ignore.

However, with keen memories of splits on Europe, and a euro-sceptic party, the argument that Clarke would divide the party tapped into a real concern, and Clarke was not helped by a reportedly 'lazy campaign'. These negatives left Clarke in fourth and last place in the first ballot on 18 October 2005 among Conservative MPs. Clarke received 38 votes, Fox 52, Davis 62 and Cameron 56.

Liam Fox and David Davis were both ostensibly candidates from the right. Liam Fox campaigned on the 'broken society', providing the right of the party with popular themes on marriage and the family, as well as on welfare, but also reassuring more centrist Conservatives that his focus would be on the poorest in society—rather than a traditional Conservative constituency. However, this strategy echoed the much misunderstood strategy of Iain Duncan-Smith, a feature which may have plausibly contributed to Dr Fox's unsuccessful ballot at the second round. He came third with 51 votes, to David Davis' 57 and David Cameron's 90; a result which took Davis and Cameron to the membership ballot.

David Davis was, then, the favourite candidate of the right and Cameron the candidate of the centre. Davis had been the frontrunner from the outset and had come first in the first parliamentary party ballot. He brought together experience with a straight talking electoral appeal, and emphasised the need for the Conservative party to 'maintain its traditional values'—a clear signal that his leadership would not entail a radical shift in style or emphasis. However, he had a reputation as a bully and stories circulated about an abrupt potential leadership style. Furthermore, when both candidates gave speeches at the party conference in September 2005, Davis' was lacklustre, lacking impact.

In the absence of Ken Clarke, David Cameron could command the support of the centre. This was a slightly surprising scenario. Cameron himself had not been a quintessential moderniser. He was an advisor to the John Major government, he had written the manifesto campaigned upon by Michael Howard, and was the preferred candidate of Howard during the leadership race. Cameron was also Eton and Oxbridge educated. In fact, he was to become the first Conservative leader in 40 years to come from a non-state education background. He was by far the least experienced. An MP for only four years, Cameron's leadership campaign had seemed unlikely, but his own leadership bid speech ('the one without notes') at Conservative party conference propelled him to pole position. Cameron distanced his strategy from those tried before and argued for a change and modernisation in the party's 'culture, attitudes and identity'.[7] Although he promised little in the way of specific policy change, he argued for a change in the relevance of the message, and a broader and less negatively toned response to the Labour government. This was to be the strategy pursued in the following years.

The two final candidates were polled in a postal ballot of all eligible Conservative members. Cameron beat David Davis by 134,446 votes to 64,398—a convincing victory, and he became leader of the Conservative party on 6 December 2005. This party, whose membership is traditionally composed of predominantly older voters, women, rural and suburban middle and upper middle class voters,[8] chose a leader who challenged the party's emphasis, moved the party onto the issue of the NHS, and diminished the party's focus on immigration and Europe. This was a vote-seeking and office-seeking grassroots party, eager for power.

A strategy for change

David Cameron benefited from a new electoral context: one in which the Labour party, and Tony Blair in particular, had lost credibility and trust over its action in Iraq,[9] and where the Labour party in government was beset by increasing unpopularity. William Hague, Iain Duncan-Smith and Michael Howard had all led the Conservative party when the Labour party was mostly significantly ahead in the polls. Despite various strategic efforts, and a plea for patience among colleagues, the leadership periods for Hague and Duncan-Smith were characterised by persistent dissent over strategy (whereas Howard organised the party effectively for the 2005 election). No matter what these earlier leaders did, it appeared to make no impact upon the electorate and ultimately saw no consistent and sizable improvement in the polls.

On 24 June 2007 Gordon Brown was crowned Labour party leader, and although he enjoyed an early period of popularity, his honeymoon period was short-lived. Not only were Labour's vote intention leads reduced by 2008, but so were Labour's ratings on the valence issues dominating the concerns of the electorate, such as public services and most damagingly, the economy. A new issue agenda was emerging based on security and immigration, on which Labour did not have a lead.[10] As long as the Conservatives were gaining in the polls, and Labour's issue advantages were narrowing, David Cameron could sustain support for a strategy of focusing on a new and broad issue agenda, in place of a narrower focus on issues of Conservative strength.

It would be incorrect, however, to describe the period as an overnight success. During the first two years of Cameron's leadership, the Conservatives did not look set to win the 2010 election, and the period was also characterised by questions over strategy, similar to those raised for leaders before him. Between December 2005 and December 2007, the Conservative poll rating was in the low thirties (an average 33.3% in this period). The Labour party maintained a consistent lead, and remained so until the autumn of 2008.

There was an early test of David Cameron's leadership, and strategy, in the Bromley and Chislehurst by-election, in June 2006. This by-election should have been a safe Conservative hold, a Conservative seat with a majority of 13,342 held by the late Eric Forth. The Conservative candidate Bob Neill won the seat with a majority of just 633, losing 11.1% in vote share compared with the 2005 election. This was a shock to the parliamentary party, as the first electoral test of the new leader who was supposed to deliver an electoral recovery. Cameron's popularity enabled him to quell these questions and he benefited from one key fact: there was no other potential leader to replace him. Any Conservatives disenchanted with Project Cameron knew they had, for the moment, little alternative.

The next high-profile test came in the form of European elections in 2009. The Conservatives 'won' these elections, gaining most seats and votes, but the party in second place was the UK Independence Party (UKIP). Although a disaster for Labour, such a surge in euro-sceptic support signalled the possibility that euro-sceptic voters were sufficiently numerous and willing to support UKIP over the Conservatives. It was the European elections, and the perceived success of the Conservative euro-sceptic campaign in 1999 which was argued to have pulled Hague onto a disproportionately euro focused general election campaign in 2001.[11] Cameron made no such reaction in focus, continuing to downplay the 'Europe issue' in the months and years ahead.

Cameron pushed ahead with a series of symbolic gestures, some which angered MPs in his party but all designed to signal 'change'. The four most noticeable were his policies on ruling out the revival of grammar schools, via a speech made by David Willetts; the commitment to environmentalism, which included opposition to a third runway at Heathrow; the claim to be the 'party of the NHS' and to downplay traditional Conservative issues, most strikingly the issue of immigration; and his European policy and decision to remove the Conservatives from the European People's Party (EPP).[12]

These initiatives saw mixed success. The first was seen as an opportunity to pick a fight with the party, with Cameron describing the resulting opposition to the policy as 'ideological self-indulgence'.[13] The policy changed to considering grammar schools where a pressing need existed, and the internal dissent, signalling a process of confrontation, may also have contributed to the view that the Conservative party (rather than its leadership) was still the same. The new focus on green issues was an affront to some of those who viewed the party as on the side of business. It is still a position on which many Conservative MPs remain unconvinced. Cameron's focus on the environment, reviving Hague's slogan 'Vote Blue, Go Green', was a clear attempt to focus on an issue seen as the preserve of the left, and was matched by the new Conservative tree logo—a statement of change. Cameron's focus on the NHS was the cause long argued for by arch Conservative modernisers, although by 2010, when Cameron announced the party's policies, Labour's rating on the issue, and its salience, had both descended. Cameron committed to increase spending on the NHS. He consistently refused to give prominence to the issue of immigration—an issue of clear Conservative strength, one on which both Hague and Howard had campaigned before him. His different issue agenda and more conciliatory tone were the clearest strategic differences in comparison to his predecessors. On one issue, Cameron moved to the right, although his euro-scepticism was matched by his party and to some degree, by the country, given a majority euro-sceptic position. Cameron's withdrawal of Conservative MEPs from the EPP (the centre-right grouping in Europe) led to his party's European representatives forming part of a new grouping of euro-sceptic European Conservatives. Although ideologically and institutionally significant, Cameron avoided focusing on the issue in his speeches or in his campaigns. The Conservative party moved to a more moderate centre on domestic policy, doing so in emphasis, if not obviously in position, but shifted ostensibly towards a more euro-sceptic institutional position.

The end result, it seemed, was some confusion. On policy, few voters seemed to understand what the Conservatives stood for. The change in emphasis and tone had not been matched by the unveiling of a clear philosophy, and many of the party's policies had been kept under wraps. Some policies, such as the 'Free Schools' policy, were better researched versions of existing ideas, but the Conservatives feared they would lose policies to Labour if they announced them too soon. Despite a new leader, a new logo, considerable attempts to select more women and minority candidates, an internal refocus onto social justice and the pursuit of a different issue agenda, many voters had not noticed much change. A survey for Politics Home, in October 2009 (during party conference) revealed that almost half of respondents thought the party had not 'changed significantly' and those who thought the party had changed were mostly prior Conservatives.[14]

Winning some minds but few hearts

In autumn 2007 Northern Rock announced its approach to the Bank of England for assistance and the financial crisis hit the UK. Opinion polls showed an initial Labour peak in the late summer of 2007, following the ascent of Gordon Brown, but more negative ratings by early 2008, after Brown eschewed an early election and when the force of the financial crisis had begun to hit home. From thereon the Conservative lead over the Labour party was almost constant. Between September 2008 and May 2010 the average Conservative vote intention was 36.5%, just above the 36.1% the party achieved in the May 6 general election poll. These poll leads were matched by more positive Conservative ratings on a range of policy issues, and emerging support for David Cameron as leader (see below). There appeared to be a direct and an indirect effect of the economic crisis on Labour's popularity, in favour of the Conservatives. The direct effect was a loss of Labour's opinion poll lead, almost immediately following the onset of the credit crunch. The indirect effect was a loss of general performance ratings on Labour leadership and on a range of issues—all of which gave the Conservatives a slight relative advantage. If voters turned towards the Conservatives, they appeared to do so as a judgment on the government. This does not equate, however, to a 'revival' attributable to the Cameron strategy, or a recovery in the popular support for the British Conservative party.

An alternative way of evaluating the relative success of the 2005–2010 years is to examine the 'normal vote'[15] of the party, alternatively defined as those voters who were willing to express a party identification.[16] Although party identification is used by some as a 'running tally'[17] of party performance and competence, the concept is used by others to define the expressive attachments held by voters for a party.[18] David Cameron stated a hope, in his 2005 leadership bid speech at the Conservative party conference: 'I want people to feel good about being a Conservative again'. It is possible that voters judging the Labour party responsible for the economy were willing to lend their support to the Conservatives, without an improvement in the size and popular support for the Conservatives in the form of 'feeling good' or expressing an identification. It was this identification support that was lost so dramatically between 1992 and 1997.[19] As either a running tally or an expressive identity, the proportion of people willing to identify with a party is a signal of that party's reliable vote.

Figure 1 (a and b) below suggests that on this criterion of support the Conservative party had not succeeded. Note that the time axis varies in the graphs, to provide a comparison of early British Election Study observations in the 1970s through 2000s, and the monthly Continuing Monitoring Survey (CMS) data between June 2008 and April 2010. The figures reveal that the Conservative party retained approximately the same proportion of 'identifiers' as it achieved in 1997 and never recovered to 1992 levels. Whereas vote intention increased under David Cameron, the proportion of identifiers with the party resembled the flat lining the party had been experiencing, but for vote intention, under Hague, Iain Duncan-Smith and Howard.[20]

Furthermore, comparing these patterns with those for the Labour party [Figure 2 (a and b), below], the Conservative recovery can be questioned further still. Notwithstanding a period of partisan dealignment,[21] in which we might evaluate a stable degree of partisanship as something of a success, the Labour party retained its 'base' support, in the form of those people still willing to express identification with Labour, despite significant setbacks. The Conservatives, meanwhile, failed to increase the size of the Conservative base over an 18 year period.

Figures 1 (a and b) and 2 (a and b) together suggest that there has been a decoupling of vote intention and party identification in the

Figure 1. (a) Conservative party identification and vote, 1974–2005 (BES data). (b) Conservative party identification and vote intention, July 2008–April 2010 (BES CMS data).

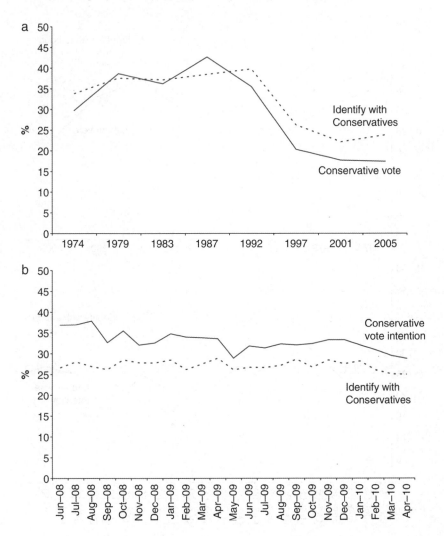

British electorate. Whereas party identification and vote intention have corresponded closely in Britain in the past, calling into question the application of the expressive concept of party identification in the British electorate,[22] Labour party identification has proved relatively robust to its declining popularity in vote intention over recent years. Conversely, whereas new voters became available to the Conservative party under David Cameron, these voters did not all view themselves as Conservatives. The Conservative party had succeeded in persuading new (or returning) voters to lend the party their support, but had not succeeded in making more voters 'feel good about being a

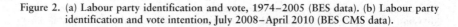

Figure 2. (a) Labour party identification and vote, 1974–2005 (BES data). (b) Labour party identification and vote intention, July 2008–April 2010 (BES CMS data).

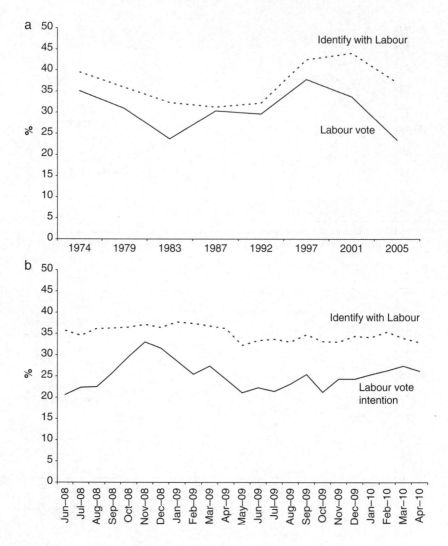

Conservative'—to the point of expressing a self-identification with the Conservatives.

An additional way of evaluating the strength of feeling towards Cameron's Conservatives, positive or negative, is via a comparison of thermometer scores in British Election Studies. These thermometer scales ask respondents to rate their feelings towards each main party, from 0 (strongly dislike) to 10 (strongly like). The table below provides the average score for the three main parties in the 2001 post-election BES, the 2005 pre-election BES and the 2010 pre-election BES.[23] Given the furore over MPs expenses, and distrust for politicians, it is relevant to compare these scores by party, since all may have become more unpopular. As the table shows, this was only partially the case (Table 1).

The strategy of broadening out the Conservative message, of adopting a less partisan tone, and modernising the party under a new leader did appear to shift voters' liking of the Conservative party to some degree. Prior to the 2010 campaign the Conservatives were the least disliked party. However, although the Conservative party was slightly more liked than it was in 2005, the jump from 2001 to 2005 was larger, and the 2010 ratings were not close to those of the Labour party under Tony Blair. Furthermore, the party was only slightly more liked than Labour under Gordon Brown and Nick Clegg's Liberal Democrats. These incremental improvements may have been due to the broader context. It would not be surprising if the expenses scandal damaged all parties' likeability (and failing to improve the ratings of the Liberal Democrats). On these expressive criteria of support, however, the Conservative strategy made limited progress. Under Cameron's leadership, identification with, and warmth towards, the Conservative party did not significantly increase. In the battle for hearts and minds, the Conservatives had won over some conditional support from some voters but had not yet convincingly won over their hearts.

Neutralising the negative, but not achieving the positive

The Conservative party achieved improvement on a range of 'valence' criteria—related to performance or competence. The Conservatives were no longer the least popular party in terms of leader approval, they no longer had overwhelmingly negative ratings on important valence issues such as health and education, and crucially, they were, at times, considered the best party on the economy. However, as shown here, the Conservative party no longer had negative ratings but neither were its ratings strongly positive. The party, under Cameron, had succeeded in neutralising the negatives, but had not received a positive lead in a range of important respects. The result was that both main parties entered the election almost neck and neck on many competence judgments, despite Gordon Brown's unpopularity and despite the financial crisis and recession.

David Cameron's leader ratings were more positive than his predecessors'. Cowley and Green[24] showed the net satisfaction–dissatisfaction scores collated by Ipsos-MORI for William Hague, Iain

1. Feelings towards the main parties: thermometer averages, 2001–2010 (British Election Study 2001, 2005 and 2010 election surveys; 0 strongly dislike; 10 strongly like)

	Conservative	Labour	Liberal Democrat
2001	3.6	5.7	5.0
2005	4.4	5.0	4.7
2010	4.9	4.6	4.7

Duncan-Smith and Michael Howard. For all three Conservative leaders, the net ratings showed far more dissatisfaction than satisfaction, albeit after a brief honeymoon period at the beginning of their leaderships. The ratings for Howard were similar to those for Iain Duncan-Smith. Evans and Andersen[25] argued that William Hague's ratings were strongly determined by those of the party (rather then vice versa), and for eight years it seemed that it was impossible to be a popular leader of such an unpopular party. As the figure below shows, David Cameron managed, for the most part, to buck this trend, although this was not evident towards the early part of his leadership. His relative popularity coincided with the mid-2008 period when Britain experienced the onset of the financial crisis and Gordon Brown's honeymoon period ended.

Figure 3 shows how David Cameron's leadership began with a similar honeymoon to those of his predecessors, and then his net-positive rating (satisfaction–dissatisfaction) declined, reaching its lowest point when Gordon Brown became Labour leader. However, from early 2008 those ratings remained net-positive throughout and even saw peaks of considerable popularity. On this net satisfaction criterion alone, we can surmise that David Cameron became a more popular electoral choice than Conservative leaders before him. Nevertheless, as the Conservatives neared the election, the positive ratings for Cameron only just outweighed the negatives. The gap between the same score for Gordon Brown and the score for David Cameron began to narrow,[26]

Figure 3. Net satisfaction–dissatisfaction for Conservative opposition leaders, 1997–2010 (Ipsos-MORI data).

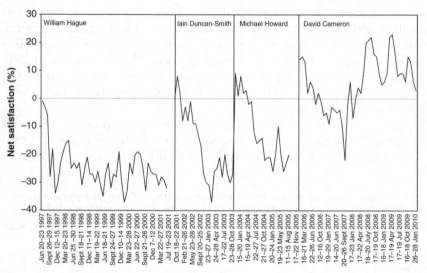

although Gordon Brown was still much more disliked than liked. On this basis, David Cameron had an advantage over Gordon Brown, but his satisfaction ratings were not sufficiently high to induce confidence that his leadership alone would deliver an overall majority for the Conservatives.

In addition to the importance of leader ratings, Clarke *et al.*[27] point to the importance of party ratings on the most important problem; a measure of trust and competence to deliver on the issues of concern to voters. As discussed earlier, the concept of competence or of 'ownership'[28] was central to the strategic dilemma defining the difficulties of the Conservatives in opposition. The party had been most trusted on issues commonly associated with 'the right': immigration, taxation, crime and euro-scepticism, but Labour had commanded much higher ratings on issues most important to voters: health, education and the economy.[29] As ratings of Labour's competence and trust began to decline, so did its relative advantage across the issue domain and David Cameron had a wider pallet of available issues. Cameron also sought to increase his own advantage on 'new' issues (health, the environment) by focusing on these, demonstrating commitment where unable to display handling in office.

The following table demonstrates the improvement made in 'best party on the most important problem', between 2001 and 2010 for the Conservatives on this important valence indicator. This summary measure does not distinguish by issue, and so relates to the overall rating of the party by respondents choosing different issues as their number one concern.

In Table 2 we see, once again, Conservative ratings were only just ahead prior to the 2010 election, comparing the Conservative lead with Labour, and the party failed to gain the proportions held by Labour in 2001 and 2005.[30] There is no doubting that a jump from 15 to 22.6% for the Conservatives is significant between 2001 and 2010, but 22.6% is a low value compared with Labour's ratings in 2001 and 2005. The highest proportion of respondents listed 'no party' or a 'do not know' response prior to the election in 2010, and this climbed as Labour lost its advantage on this measure, rather than translating directly to the Conservatives.

2. 'Best party on the most important problem' 2001–2010 (%) (British Election Study, 2001 post-election, 2005-election post and 2010 pre-election)

	2001	2005	2010
Conservative	15.0	20.1	22.6
Labour	38.5	35.8	21.2
Liberal Democrat	7.6	7.4	4.6
Other	3.5	4.9	5.3
None/do not know	26.8	31.8	46.2
Total (*n*)	2480	3980	1882

Under David Cameron, the numbers of issues which could be argued to be off limits in the saliency theory of Budge and Farlie[31]—those issues which, if campaigned upon, could only hand an advantage to an opponent—were significantly reduced. On all issues, the Labour advantage over the Conservatives had declined by 2010, and on most issues the Conservatives had a narrow lead,[32] including on the symbolic issue of the NHS. It is not clear whether the new issue handling advantage arose from a strategic emphasis on some issues over others, although this may be a contributing factor. It is much more likely that a general competence advantage—due to the declining popularity of the Labour government and some satisfaction with David Cameron—contributed to more positive ratings on all issues. What is clear was that by 2010, the advantages were not large, as indicated in Table 2. On the criterion of valence issues, we see that although the party's negative ratings had been neutralised, the party did not receive a positive endorsement of its potential handling of the issue agenda. On the issue where the Conservatives had a commanding advantage—immigration—the decision was taken not to place this issue in the long or the short campaign.[33]

Finally and crucially, the pattern also extended to the economy. It was highlighted above that the Conservatives' and David Cameron's fortunes improved when the financial crisis hit Britain in force, in the spring and summer of 2008. However, there was not a simple translation from concerns over the Labour government's handling of the country's finances and, by the time of the general election, the size of the deficit, towards trust in the Conservative government to solve the country's economic problems. Britain emerged from the recession in January 2010, and it was undoubtedly Gordon Brown's best hope that this would help shore up Labour's support. By February 2010 the British Election Study's Continuing Monitoring Survey (CMS) recorded a series of pre-election economic judgements. True, respondents had experienced financial losses (57% believed the national economy had got worse in the past year, and 45% said their own financial situation had worsened), but only 27% listed Gordon Brown as responsible and 40% the British government. There was also some anticipation that things would get better or at least not get worse. Sixty-two per cent thought their personal circumstances would improve or remain the same and 65% thought the country's economic situation would get better. The upshot of this was that with many voters believing things might improve, they were now undecided about who to trust. Thirty-one per cent thought that Labour had handled the crisis very or fairly well—a low figure, but only 24% thought this would be true for the Conservatives. As the election neared, a fascinating trend emerged, which is revealed in the following table of CMS responses to the 'which party is best on the economy' question, monthly during the year (May 2009–April 2010) prior to the 2010 general election.

Table 3 shows that the Conservative lead over Labour on this cri-terion narrowed as the parties neared the general election, and it did so as Britain emerged from the recession. Strikingly, in the April 2010, as Gordon Brown called the general election, Labour had even gained a lead over the Conservatives on this policy area.

Although the Conservative party had managed to undo a serious dis-advantage on economic ratings—an evaluation which had beset the party from the ERM crisis in 1992, and although the Conservatives had gained a lead on the economy in the midst of the recession, the incumbent Labour party went into the election with a narrow advan-tage over its main opponent, despite presiding over the most serious recession since the Great Depression.

The pre-campaign position of the Conservative party, relative to its opponents, was on a knife-edge. The party had been in opposition for 13 years, and had seen its potential vote reach figures which would assure the party a majority, but as the election neared, the party's ratings on a wide array of measures were not much better than Labour's. It is little wonder that large numbers of voters could not make up their minds prior to Election Day. In theories of party choice, voters are expected to maximise their utilities—the things they want—by choosing the party closest to their preferences.[34] This utility decision can be extended to the party who will best deliver or which is most competent, especially when parties offer voters similar policies.[35] If there is little to differentiate the choices on offer, voters will be indifferent between can-didates or parties—a factor which is known to reduce turnout[36] and which may prompt voters to look to minor or third parties. In 2010, the utility differential between Labour and the Conservatives was small. The Conservatives had a more popular leader than Labour, but the lead had narrowed (and Nick Clegg was slightly preferred to Cameron). There was a tiny gap between the best party on the economy and there was an equally small gap between the best party on the most important issue

3. 'Best party on the economy' May 2009–April 2010 (%) (BES Continuous Monitoring Survey)

	Conservatives	Labour	Conservative lead
May-2009	34.0	24.4	9.6
June-2009	34.1	26.7	7.4
July-2009	35.5	25.4	10.2
August-2009	35.6	25.9	9.7
September-2009	34.7	29.6	5.0
October-2009	36.2	26.7	9.5
November-2009	34.5	27.8	6.7
December-2009	33.5	29.4	4.2
January-2010	36.7	29.3	7.3
February-2010	34.4	31.7	2.7
March-2010	34.3	32.0	2.3
April-2010	34.7	35.9	−1.2

(which could, of course be the economy for many). The Conservative party was not much more liked than its rivals, and its committed base was no larger than before. In policy terms, voters may have been closer to the Conservatives on some salient issues, but ideologically there was little to distinguish the three main parties from each other,[37] particularly once Cameron had emphasised his position at the centre. Overall, by the time of the 2010 campaign, voters might have been largely indifferent or at least confused between choices. If the outcome of the general election showed no party with a clear majority, neither did either of the main parties have a clear and overwhelming lead on any criteria entering the election campaign. If either major contender was to make a break though, this needed to happen in the final four weeks of the election, during the short campaign.

Campaign strategy: what strategy?

David Cameron must have hoped to enter the 2010 general election campaign with a much more convincing set of strengths. However, it was still, in effect, his election to lose. This was a campaign which could, despite electoral bias, have secured a Conservative majority, albeit on a significant swing. It could also have secured a sufficient number of seats to make a minority Conservative government a much more plausible outcome than the result eventually achieved.

The campaign was a series of reactions, for two reasons. First, the Conservatives' main message had not been tested prior to its unveiling, and was quickly dropped once it became clear it was not working. Second, this was a campaign almost completely derailed by Nick Clegg's performance in the first of three leader debates. For these reasons the strategy is difficult to detect. The usual agenda-shaping nature of the campaign had changed in 2010. In previous elections, each party held a daily morning media briefing, and the campaign plan followed an issue-by-issue strategy designed to shape the agenda onto the issues the party wanted to focus upon each day. In 2010, the Conservative and Labour parties ditched these events in favour of schedules on media campaign buses and daily moving briefings. It is not clear whether this meant the parties relinquished control, but it is certainly true that their strategies appeared more fluid, reactive and much more difficult to discern.

It is an irony that the criticism made of two of the most derided political campaigns of the last 30 years—the election campaign run by William Hague in 2001 and the campaign run by Michael Foot in 1983—that opinion polls were not conducted, or rejected, was strangely true for the central platform of the Conservative campaign in 2010: the 'Big Society'. The 'Big Society' was intended to offer an inspirational call to participation and responsibility, to address (perhaps) the taint that there was 'no such thing as society',[38] and to contrast the Big Society with small government—a philosophy of decentralisation and lower taxation and of the cooperation of voluntary organisations and individuals in addressing 'the broken society'. The theme was given prominence at the start of the campaign, centre-stage at the launch of the manifesto. This manifesto was fronted with the words: 'Invitation to Join the Government of Britain' and the pre-launch teaser featured an image on Battersea Power Station, asking 'Who is the New Member of Cameron's Team?' with the answer being 'you'. The Conservatives hoped to inspire a sense of responsibility, of 'togetherness' and a defining philosophy which people could understand, providing a dividing line between the Conservative party and other parties. The result was confusion. This was a party offering a new governing philosophy five years after the previous election and with four weeks until polling day. It sounded ambitious, slightly strange and rather unrealistic. David Cameron attempted to define the agenda in his first leader debate. From that day the campaign theme which was to inspire the country to a Conservative majority was dropped quietly and quickly.

The decision of David Cameron to agree to the televised debates was a game changer. David Cameron's first performance, like Gordon Brown's, was eclipsed by the dramatic effect of the performance of Nick Clegg. Liberal Democrat polling support surged and the attention thereafter to the Liberal Democrat leader was unprecedented for a third party. Overnight, the traditional campaign dominance of the Conservative and Labour leaders became a thing of the past, and the Conservative assumption that it was their campaign to win, or lose, was proved wrong. The fact that the extent of apparent Liberal Democrat support was not translated into votes should by no means detract from the profound significance of 'Cleggmania' on the 2010 campaign. The Conservative message was largely lost, and while David Cameron continued in his cross-country visits and campaigns, visiting factories and other venues to signal his commitment to economic recovery (as did Gordon Brown), and whereas campaign posters continued to warn of Labour's 'job tax' and attempts to make voters identify with 'new' Conservative voters, the story was Nick Clegg and the Liberal Democrats. The Conservatives launched a knee-jerk campaign, warning of the 'Hung Parliament Party'. They switched focus from Conservative–Liberal Democrat marginals and asked voters for a 'decisive' majority, but in the end they failed to provide a clear message.

What would the campaign have looked like without the leader debates? It is hard to say, but it appeared that the Conservatives had 'left their powder dry' on a series of policy announcements before the campaign and that the campaign would be characterised by issue-by-issue announcements of a range of new Conservative policies. This would have addressed the problem that voters were not sure what the Conservatives stood for and the 'Big Society' could have made the party look different to Labour, offering an inspirational narrative. That this was a risky strategy so late in the electoral cycle was certain before the campaign, but in the event, it was eclipsed by the three-horse race that the campaign was to become. In the BES Campaign Panel Internet Survey, the Conservatives began the campaign on April 6 with 39% of electors intending to vote Conservative, but ended the campaign on May 5 with that figure at 36%.[39] Once again, the Conservative campaign resulted in a decline in support.

As Denver shows in this volume, the Conservative party failed to achieve a breakthrough in Scotland. The Conservative party of 2010 was still predominantly the party of England and still far stronger in its electoral support in the South. David Cameron had stated the goal in his 2005 leadership speech, 'We've got to recognise that we're in third place among under-35s, that we've lost support among women, that public servants no longer think we're on their side, that the people with aspirations who swept Margaret Thatcher to power have drifted away from our party'.[40] The Conservative goal under David Cameron was to reach out to those groups of voters.

The BES data shows that among under-35s the Conservatives moved from third to second place. In 2001, just 23.3% of under-35s reported a Conservative vote. This increased to 29.5% in 2010, whereas the proportion voting Liberal Democrat was 38.4%. The proportions of women expressing a Conservative vote saw little change, at 34.1% in 2005 and 35.2% in 2010, but the Conservatives gained a lead over Labour, who secured 27.9% of women's reported votes (post-election BES, internet survey).

The following table provides the average change in Conservative vote, between 2005 and 2010, among areas of the country with the highest and lowest proportions of electors from various demographics; those aged between 18 and 24, those from upper middle and middle classes, lower middle and skilled working class categories (A and B, C1 and C2 groups, respectively) and areas with high and low proportions of ethnic minorities.

The data in Table 4 confirms the problem the Conservatives had among the youngest eligible voters, with only a modest increase in their vote between 2005 and 2010 in areas with high concentrations of young voters. The table also reveals that the Conservative party suffered in areas with high concentrations of ethnic minorities. The evidence suggests that the Conservatives won support from C2 (skilled working class) voters, whilst also doing well in areas with the highest concentrations of AB voters. It appears that David Cameron succeeded in winning over the support of the 'people with aspirations' within the upper working class, also enjoying success among the upper middle and middle classes.

On a 36.1% share of the UK vote (36.9% of the Great Britain vote), the Conservatives are now governing with a higher vote share than achieved by Tony Blair in 2005 (35.3%), who won 356 seats in

4. Change in Conservative vote share, lower and upper quartile concentration by demographic, 2010 BBC exit poll

	Change in Conservative vote, 2005–2010
All areas (average)	3.8
% 18–24 age group	
Low	3.9
High	2.7
% A and B social class	
Low	3.2
High	5.7
% C1 social class	
Low	1.4
High	3.4
% C2 social class	
Low	2.9
High	5.0
% Ethnic minorities	
Low	3.8
High	2.5

parliament. At a final result of 307 seats, however, a 'supply and confidence' arrangement with the Liberal Democrats, and other parties, was ultimately too unstable. This calculation was informed by the relatively weak mandate the party was given and the lack of a decisive electoral recovery.

Conclusion

David Cameron entered Number 10 Downing Street as Prime Minister on Wednesday 12 May 2010. He was the first Conservative opposition leader in 13 years to significantly increase the numbers of Conservative MPs and he was the first in that period to secure a consistent poll lead over Labour. He was undoubtedly more popular than recent Conservative opposition leaders before him, and his strategy of modernisation and of a new issue agenda must be attributed with some of this success.

However, this article has also highlighted the limits of the 'strategic recovery' which could be attributed to the Cameron strategy. Despite a period of modernisation, considerable work on policy, advances in campaigning, more money, a new more popular leader, a longer time period from which the memory of Conservative government could be a hindrance, and of course, the unpopularity of the Labour Prime Minister Gordon Brown and a serious recession, Conservative recovery has been partial. Although numbers of new voters were willing to cast a vote for the Conservatives, the Conservative base has not increased, and although the Conservatives were the most trusted party on important valence issues, the lead over Labour was narrow. For undecided voters, it was not clear that a Cameron government would be so much more desirable than the government they knew. The utility differential—the ranking difference of the Conservatives over Labour—was minimal on a range of criteria. A vote for the Conservatives in 2010 was largely instrumental: it was not cast with a growing sense of identification or of expressive support.

It is not possible to test the reasons for these successes, and failures, in the Conservative electoral recovery. Some successes may be due to David Cameron, others to his strategy, and had it not been for the expenses scandal, the opposition party's message might have gained more ground. However, it also the case that the Conservative lead over Labour coincided with the onset of the financial crisis, and that David Cameron's ratings improved at the same time. The narrowing gap between the two main parties on the crucial issue of the economy occurred as Britain emerged from recession. At least part of the explanation for the changes in Conservative fortunes is likely to be due to Labour's ratings on a range of competence criteria which suffered in 2008, and which began to improve at the beginning of 2010. Therefore, we should be cautious in how much we credit electoral gains to the strategies of parties and leaders and cautious in assuming that a modest rise in Conservative vote represents a stable increase in Conservative electoral support. We should also look to the long-term nature of Conservative ratings before we attribute the lack of overall majority to the weakness of the short campaign.

Overall, there is a story of some electoral success, but the cost of government comes to all incumbents, and the Conservatives are not starting from the position they might have expected. The Conservative party entered government in an unenviable electoral position. It is difficult to predict the effects of coalition government on Conservative party support but it is likely to be a difficult period ahead. The necessary decision to enter a formal coalition with the Liberal Democrats can be seen in this context, and also in the context of the previous five years of Conservative opposition under David Cameron.

1 In the British Election Study pre-election in person survey (first beta release), 46% said they were still undecided who to vote for.

2 See B. Sárlvik and I. Crewe, *Decade of Dealignment: The Conservative Victory of 1979 and Electoral Trends in the 1970s*, Cambridge University Press, 1983; D. Granberg and S. Holmberg, *The Political System Matters: Social Psychology and Voting Behaviour in Sweden and the United States*, European Monographs in Social Psychology, Cambridge University Press, 1988.

3 G. Evans, 'Economics and Politics Revisited: Exploring the Decline in Conservative Support, 1992–1995', *Political Studies*, XLVII, 1999, 139–51.

4 Clause IV was the commitment in Labour's constitution to the common ownership of the means of production, which Tony Blair finally removed in 1994 in a symbolic expression of Labour's moderation and modernisation.

5 Sir Malcolm Rifkind and Alan Duncan both announced their intention to run, but withdrew before the ballot once it became clear they had insufficient support.

6 J. Petrocik, 'Issue Ownership in Presidential Elections, with a 1980 Case Study', *American Journal of Political Science*, 40, 1996, 825–50.

7   David Cameron 2005 Conservative Party Leadership Speech, accessed from http://www.guardian.co. uk/politics/2005/oct/04/conservatives2005.conservatives3.

8   P. Whiteley, J. Richardson and P. Seyd, *True Blues: The Politics of Conservative Party Membership*, Clarendon Press, 1994.

9   H. Clarke, D. Sanders, M. Stewart and P. Whiteley, *Performance Politics and the British Voter*, Cambridge University Press, 2009.

10 H. Clarke, D. Sanders, M. Stewart and P. Whiteley, *Performance Politics and the British Voter*, Cambridge University Press, 2009, Chapter 3.

11 D. Butler and D. Kavanagh, *The British General Election of 2001*, Palgrave, 2001.

12 There was one important mostly unseen change which built on the work done by Iain Duncan-Smith. The Conservative party adopted a far more social action oriented approach and philosophy in the years in opposition, with candidates and MPs getting involved in a broad range of hands-on projects, including projects overseas, as part of a commitment to international aid. The culture of the Conservative parliamentary party, in this respect, had certainly changed, and changed significantly.

13 David Cameron, *This Sterile Fixation with Grammar Schools is a Dead End*, Times 22 May 2007.

14 http://page.politicshome.com/uk/voters_expect_tory_government_to_raise_taxes.html.

15 P. Converse, 'The Concept of a Normal Vote', in A. Campbell, P. Converse, W. Miller and D. Stokes (eds), *Elections and the Political Order*, Wiley, 1966.

16 R. Johnston and C. Pattie, 'Representative Democracy and Electoral Geography', in J. Agnew, K. Mitchell, G. Thathail and G. Toal (eds), *A Companion to Political Geography*, Blackwell, 2003; G. Cox, Swing Voters, Core Voters and Distributive Politics. Paper presented at the Yale Conference on Representation and Popular Rule, 2006.

17 M. Fiorina, *Retrospective Voting in American National Elections*, Yale University Press, 1981.

18 See: Campbell, Angus, Philip E. Converse, Warren E. Miller and Donald E. Stokes, *The American Voter*, University of Chicago Press, 1976.

19 G. Evans, 'Economics and Politics Revisited: Exploring the Decline in Conservative Support, 1992–1995', *Political Studies*, XLVII, 1999, 139–51.

20 P. Cowley and J. Green, 'New Leaders, Same Problems: The Conservatives', in A. Geddes and J. Tonge (eds), *Britain Decides: The UK General Election 2005*, Palgrave Macmillan, 2005.

21 See D. Denver, *Elections and Voters in Britain*, Palgrave Macmillan, 2003.

22 D. Butler and D. Stokes, *Political Change in Britain: Forces Shaping Electoral Choice*, Macmillan, 1969.

23 The post-election average thermometer ratings, for the Conservative, Labour and Liberal Democrat parties were 4.5, 4.2 and 5.3, respectively (BES post-election internet survey), suggesting that the Conservatives were less liked following their 2010 campaign (those waves in which the question was asked. The 2010 pre-election BES was fielded before the leader debates).

24 P. Cowley and J. Green, 'New Leaders, Same Problems: The Conservatives', in A. Geddes and J. Tonge (eds), *Britain Decides: The UK General Election 2005*, Palgrave Macmillan, 2005. The satisfaction question is, 'Are you satisfied or dissatisfied with the way (David Cameron) is doing his job as Leader of the Opposition?'.

25 G. Evans and R. Andersen, 'Who Blairs Wins? Leadership and Voting in the 2001 General Election', *British Elections and Parties Review*, 13, 2003, 229–47.

26 As the election neared, Gordon Brown's net satisfaction–dissatisfaction score was −24, but this was an improvement on a low of −51 in July 2008 and it was trending upwards from May 2009 (−43).

27 H. Clarke, D. Sanders, M. Stewart and P. Whiteley, *Performance Politics and the British Voter*, Cambridge University Press, 2009.

28 J. Petrocik, 'Issue Ownership in Presidential Elections, with a 1980 Case Study', *American Journal of Political Science*, 40, 1996, 825–50.

29 See J. Green and S. Hobolt, 'Owning the Issue Agenda: Explaining Party Strategies in British General Election Campaigns', *Electoral Studies*, 27, 2008, 460–76.

30 Note that the proportion listing the Conservatives as the best party on the most important issue in the 2010 post-election British Election Study (internet) was 27.4% whereas for Labour the proportion was 21.7%. The proportions for the Liberal Democrats and 'no party' were 11.7 and 27.1%, respectively.

31 I. Budge and D. Farlie, *Voting and Party Competition: A Theoretical Critique and Synthesis Applied to Surveys from Ten Democracies*, Wiley, 1977.

32 See Ipsos-MORI data: http://www.ipsos-mori.com/researchspecialisms/socialresearch/specareas/ politics/trends.aspx.

33 This was motivated by two factors: first, to campaign on immigration risked positioning the Conservative party on the right—the very problem David Cameron wanted to avoid. Second, the

threat of a surge in British National Party support meant that all mainstream parties mostly avoided the issue.

34 A. Downs, *An Economic Theory of Democracy*, Harper & Row, 1957.

35 D. Stokes, 'Spatial Models of Party Competition' *The American Political Science Review* 57, 1963, 368–77; J. Green, Jane, 'When Voters and Parties Agree: Valence Issues and Party Competition', *Political Studies*, 55, 2007, 629–55; H. Clarke, D. Sanders, M. Stewart and P. Whiteley, *Performance Politics and the British Voter*, Cambridge University Press, 2009.

36 J. Enelow and M. Hinich, *The Spatial Theory of Voting: An Introduction*, Cambridge University Press, 1984, in Hinich, m. Melvin J. and Michael C. Munger (eds), *Analytical Politics*, Cambridge University Press, 1997.

37 In a question in the British Election Studies, 23.4% of survey respondents in 2005 agreed there was 'a great deal of difference between the main parties', whereas 84.6% agreed with the statement during Margaret Thatcher's leadership in 1987. These figures closely correspond with respondent placements of the two main parties on different policy scales.

38 The oft-cited quotation by Margaret Thatcher, argued to have been removed from context, *Woman's Own*, 23 September 1987.

39 Source: http://www.bes2009-10.org/.

40 David Cameron 2005 Conservative Party Leadership Speech, accessed from http://www.guardian.co.uk/politics/2005/oct/04/conservatives2005.conservatives3.

DAVID CUTTS, EDWARD FIELDHOUSE AND ANDREW RUSSELL

The Campaign That Changed Everything and Still Did Not Matter? The Liberal Democrat Campaign and Performance

From the party's inception in 1988 to the 2005 general election, the Liberal Democrats had grown almost exclusively at the expense of the Conservatives. In 2005, however, the Liberal Democrats benefited from hostility to the Labour government that enabled them to gain significantly at Labour's expense. The fact that success against Labour was offset by decline against the Conservatives in the south of the England mattered less than the Liberal Democrats' advance in terms of votes and seats in 2005.[1]

After the 2005 election, however, the Liberal Democrats found it harder to continue their momentum. Charles Kennedy was removed from his position as leader largely at the behest of a disaffected parliamentary party acting outside its constitutional remit.[2] Kennedy's replacement, Sir Menzies Campbell enjoyed a brief and unhappy time as leader. After Gordon Brown's failure to call a 2007 general election, Campbell decided to stand down and was in turn replaced by Nick Clegg (but only after an unexpectedly narrow victory over Chris Huhne). As leader Clegg struggled to impose himself on the British public's consciousness, the party's Shadow Chancellor, Vince Cable, had managed to find a niche in the public's mind as an economics guru and was widely credited with predicting the credit crunch and its impact on the British economy. However, Cable's popularity outstripped that of his party and the apparent failure to convert the 'Vince factor' to more general Liberal Democrat advantage had concerned the party's elite for a while.

Previous Liberal Democrat leaders have often managed to increase the party's (and their own) standing during an election campaign. In

doi:10.1093/pa/gsq025

2005, for instance, Charles Kennedy was shown to be the most popular (or the least unpopular) of all party leaders. Evidence from the British Election Survey (BES) continuous monitoring survey demonstrated that Nick Clegg too was well placed to make an impact with the British public—the thermometer scores for the Liberal Democrat leader were consistently warmer than those for the leaders of the Labour and Conservative parties. In January 2010, respondents to the BES continuous monitoring survey gave an average rating of 'feelings towards' Gordon Brown of 3.65, David Cameron's mean score was 4.74, while Nick Clegg's average was 4.80. Similarly, the Liberal Democrats were the best placed party—Labour's average score in January 2010 was 3.65 (out of a maximum of 10), the Conservatives' 4.65 and the Liberal Democrats' 4.91.

The problem with these scores is that they reflect indifference as much as positive endorsements. The Liberal Democrats and their leader appear to do well in the relative assessments of parties and leaders largely because the Liberal Democrats do not generate the level of hostility from opponents that the main parties do. The distribution of individual scores for the likeability from the BES continuous monitoring survey shows that while assessments of Labour (and Brown) and the Conservatives (and Cameron) were largely bi-modal, the spread of Liberal Democrat (and Clegg scores) was more normally distributed around the centre. Research has shown that the Liberal Democrats could cash-in on their relative popularity with the public if popular leaders, policies and programme could be matched by credibility—or an expectation that they might win locally at least.[3]

The campaign: great expectations, Cleggmania and a disappointing night

The Liberal Democrats entered the election year with low expectations. Nick Clegg had been leader of the party for nearly a year and a half but had failed to register an increase in the party's fortunes in the opinion polls. In all YouGov polls published between January 2008 and the first televised debate, most respondents felt that Clegg was not an electoral asset to his party. His approval rating was conspicuously low. The number of respondents who felt that Nick Clegg was the best choice as Prime Minister of Britain was never more than 13% (Figure 1).

With much conjecture on the apparent tightness of the forthcoming election, the Liberal Democrats must have been fearful of suffering classic third-party squeeze as voters were encouraged to choose between the viable single-party governments of the Conservative and Labour parties. However, all of this was to (apparently) change with the televised leaders' debates. Clegg's performance in the first debate (on 15 April) was a defining moment of the campaign. It electrified the party and allowed Clegg to emerge confidently from the shadow of the

Figure 1. Who would make the best Prime Minister? Ratings January 2008 to April 2010.
Source: YouGov: ukpollingreport.co.uk.

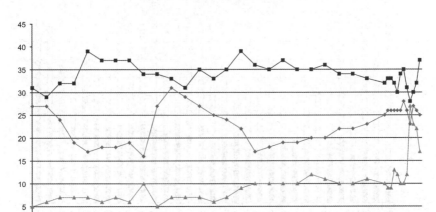

deputy leader and Shadow Chancellor Vince Cable as the party's most visible asset. This first debate was characterised by Clegg's confidence. His relaxed and assured television manner helped create a performance that was matched only by the reluctance of the other leaders to challenge him. Indeed far from confrontation, the other leaders seemed determined to ally themselves with the Liberal Democrat leader. Prime Minister Gordon Brown repeatedly told the watching millions that he 'agreed with Nick', seemingly in an attempt to isolate the Conservatives and create common cause with the Liberal Democrats with the type of progressive alliance familiar to students of the Blair-Ashdown era.[4] 'I agree with Nick' quickly became one of the more familiar slogans of the 2010 campaign as it was adopted by Liberal Democrat supporters up and down the country.

The effect of the debates on public opinion was dramatic, as shown in Figure 2. Clegg's approval rating which had been in the 40s since May 2009, rose to 77%. One newspaper famously reported that Clegg was now the most popular British politician since Winston Churchill's 83% approval rating in 1945—although its note that the Conservatives went on to a very heavy defeat in the 1945 election was less prominent.[5] Within hours of the first debate, Clegg's performance had apparently thrown the competition wide open, and the Liberal Democrats retained a prominent position in the polls for the rest of the campaign. Before the first debate Clegg had been identified as the 'best' available Prime Minister of around 10% of respondents. Thereafter, he was the choice of around one-quarter. From the outset of the campaign until

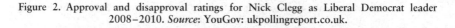

Figure 2. Approval and disapproval ratings for Nick Clegg as Liberal Democrat leader 2008–2010. *Source*: YouGov: ukpollingreport.co.uk.

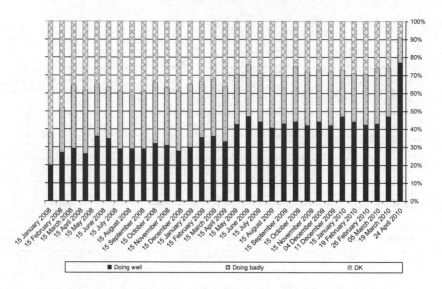

the first TV leadership debate, the Liberal Democrats reported vote intention in the polls averaged 19.9%; thereafter it averaged 28.7% of reported vote intention.

Public discourse too was affected by Cleggmania. If the expectation that the Liberal Democrats would significantly increase their numbers in parliament had turned out to be true, it would have significantly altered the dynamic within the parliamentary party—as for the first time many Liberal Democrat parliamentarians would owe their position not to their own pavement politics, but to the popularity of the leadership. In truth, the second and third leadership debates saw a much closer contest between the party leaders, but Clegg had established his own credibility—and that of his party—at the first debate.

As the campaign wore on, the Liberal Democrat bandwagon showed little sign of abating. Leading newspapers the *Guardian*, *Observer*, *Independent* and *Independent on Sunday* officially endorsed the Liberal Democrats while even the *Daily Mirror*—Labour's only national newspaper in 2010—suggested that its readers should vote tactically for the Liberal Democrats in Liberal Democrat/Conservative marginal seats. As might have been guessed by the defection of the *Guardian* to the Liberal Democrats, it seemed that the left were the most enamoured. On the eve of the election, Labour ministers Peter Hain and Ed Balls urged Labour supporters in hopeless seats to 'vote intelligently' against the Tories. The Labour party machine swiftly moved against such talk as it attempted to shore up its core vote at a time when Labour's second place in the popular vote seemed far from assured.

The electoral outcome

The scene was thus set for a significant Liberal Democrat surge at the 2010 general election. However, despite high poll ratings during the campaign and a general expectation that the Liberal Democrats would perform much better than in 2005, the final outcome proved to be an 'electoral disappointment' for the third party of British politics. In the early morning of 7 May, Nick Clegg conceded that his party had under-performed, acknowledging that: 'As for the national campaign, this has obviously been a disappointing result for the Liberal Democrats. We simply haven't achieved what we had hoped'.[6] At the final reckoning, the Liberal Democrats secured 23% of the UK national vote, a rise of 1% from 2005, and won 57 seats, a net loss of five seats from the general election in 2005. The Liberal Democrats did manage to increase their vote in 378 of the 629 seats they contested and were second in 242 seats (from 188 second places in the notional results from 2005). Moreover, the Liberal Democrats moved closer to the winner in many seats—on the 2005 notional calculations the party was within 10% of the 'winners' in 31 seats; in 2010, the party was within 10% of the winning candidate in 45 constituencies. Yet, like previous elections, the national electoral outcome obscures a fair amount of unevenness in the Liberal Democrats' performance.

Five years earlier, the Liberal Democrats' vote share was highest in the traditional Liberal heartlands on the 'celtic periphery' and the south coast of England. However, the patterns of change were some-what different: the largest increase had been in the North and in Scotland. In summary, 'the Liberal Democrats did better in Labour's regional heartlands and less well where the Conservatives were predo-minantly the main opposition'.[7] In 2010, there were once again distinct regional variations in the Liberal Democrats' performance. However, this time the party failed to advance further into Labour territory. While the geography of their vote share was broadly similar to 2005—winning most votes in the southwest, the southeast and east Anglia, the patterns of change were a mirror of 2005. The Liberal Democrat lost votes in Labour heartlands, especially Scotland, but its vote held up well in its largely southern battle with the Conservatives, even though it lost more seats than it won after failing to convert and hold on to a number of close marginal contests.

Perhaps due to the waning of the effect of the war in Iraq and the possibility of a Liberal Democrat-Conservative coalition, there were signs of a 'ceiling effect' in the Labour heartlands of the North West, North and parts of Greater London where the Liberal Democrats barely saw an increase in their vote from five years earlier. In 2005, the Liberal Democrats achieved above average increases in Scotland on the back of Kennedy's leadership and enhanced electoral credibility follow-ing their participation in the coalition in the Scottish Parliament.

However, in 2010, against a resilient Labour Party in Scotland, the Liberal Democrats saw their vote decline by around 4% as pre-election targets in Edinburgh and the by-election success in Dunfermline and West Fife were either held or returned to the Labour fold. Elsewhere, there were above average increases in Wales, despite a high profile loss in Montgomeryshire, and the South East, where the party had a net loss of two seats. The party also made above average improvements in their vote share in the Midlands and the Yorkshire and Humber region, although the Liberal Democrats started off from a much lower base than in the South of England.

In the past two general elections, there was growing evidence that the Liberal Democrats were experiencing something of a 'ceiling' effect in their southwest heartland.[8] Despite only moderate increases in their vote since 2001, with improvements gained largely at the expense of Labour than the Conservatives, the Liberal Democrats had continued to maintain a strong electoral presence in the region. There was clear evidence that they achieved recognition as the main alternative to the Conservatives in the region, boosting their prospects of tactical support from centre-left voters. In 2005, the Liberal Democrats achieved the lowest average increase in vote share of all the regions but still made a net gain of one seat. Five years later, the party saw its vote share increase by more than 2%, but once again this masked the unevenness of its performance as it generally fared worse where it was in two-party contests with the Conservatives (rather than Labour) leading to a net loss of three seats, with all losses to the Conservatives.

GAINS AND LOSSES. Like the regional shifts, the pattern of Liberal Democrat gains and losses, detailed in Table 1, reflects the revival of the Conservatives in the South where the Liberal Democrats lost a number of key seats, and their inability to make inroads into the Labour heartlands. In total, the Liberal Democrats made eight gains, five of which were from Labour and three from the Conservatives. Yet, the party lost 13 seats, with all except Chesterfield falling to the Conservatives.

The Liberal Democrats failed to win any additional seats in Scotland, losing the Dunfermline and West Fife by-election gain, and most spectacularly Lembit Opik managed to lose the Welsh Liberal heartland seat of Montgomeryshire to the Conservatives, only the second time in a century that the Liberals, in their various incarnations, had relinquished the constituency. Perhaps the biggest surprise among a patchy set of Liberal Democrat performances was the 20% swing to the party from Labour in Redcar, where local disillusionment over the closure of the Corus steel plant certainly contributed to the Liberal Democrats' victory. Elsewhere in the North the party took Bradford East from Labour and saw its vote increase in Westmorland and

1. 2010 Liberal Democrat gains and losses

	% Swing 2005–2010
2010 Liberal Democrat Gains	
Bradford East	7.6 Lab-LD
Brent Central	11.0 Lab-LD
Burnley	9.6 Lab-LD
Eastbourne	4.0 Con-LD
Norwich South	4.0 Lab-LD
Redcar	21.8 Lab-LD
Solihull[a]	0.3 Con-LD
Wells	3.6 Con-LD
2010 Liberal Democrat Losses	
Camborne & Redruth	5.2 LD-Con
Chesterfield	3.8 LD-Lab
Cornwall South East	9.1 LD-Con
Harrogate & Knaresborough	9.1 LD-Con
Hereford & Herefordshire South	3.8 LD-Con
Montgomeryshire	13.2 LD-Con
Newton Abbot	5.8 LD-Con
Oxford West & Abingdon	6.9 LD-Con
Richmond Park	7.0 LD-Con
Romsey & Southampton North	4.5 LD-Con
Truro & Falmouth	5.1 LD-Con
Winchester	9.1 LD-Con
York Outer	3.7 LD-Con

Note: [a]Solihull was notionally a Conservative seat in 2005 following redistricting. Dunfermline & West Fife was won by the Liberal Democrats in a by-election but was re-taken by Labour in 2010.

Lonsdale where it had won last time from the Conservatives. But despite a strong local presence in Durham and running the local council in Newcastle-upon-Tyne, a mobilised core Labour vote prevented any possibility of any Liberal Democrat gains. A similar story occurred in the North-West. The Liberal Democrats held the Manchester Withington seat from a strong Labour challenge and nearby Cheadle from the Conservatives thanks to personal support for the incumbent Liberal Democrat Mark Hunter, but failed to convert strong possibilities in both Oldham seats and Liverpool Wavertree despite apparently favourable local conditions. A 9.6% swing in Burnley saw the party win what was a three-way marginal from Labour, yet emblematically, it failed to win back Rochdale which had notionally become Labour since redistricting, despite the town being the scene of the 'bigotgate' drama. The party's defeat in Chesterfield, Labour's only gain from the Liberal Democrats, further illustrated the party's uneven performance against Labour in the Northern regions.

Further south, former Labour Home Secretary Charles Clarke lost his Norwich South seat to the Liberal Democrats, as the party polled well in East Anglia. In Greater London, the story against Labour was once again mixed. The Liberal Democrats held the Hornsey and Wood

Green seat won in 2005, but failed to win Islington South and Finsbury target for a second successive election as the Labour vote across the city largely held firm. One exception was Brent Central. Following redistricting, Sarah Teather had seen her Brent East seat abolished and therefore chose to fight the new Brent Central seat against the Labour incumbent Dawn Butler. This seat was notionally Labour, but in a local contest that bucked the national trend, Teather won the seat with an 11% swing to the Liberal Democrats. However, against Labour such local variations were largely the exception to the rule as the party failed to build on its promising position it fought so hard to obtain five years earlier.

Against the Conservatives, the Liberal Democrats found the going equally tough. However, the electoral mosaic was complex. While the Liberal Democrats were close enough in a number of constituencies to win seats from the Conservatives, they were also defending a number of seats with small majorities and were therefore exposed to any national Conservative revival. Conservative victories against Liberal Democrat incumbents defending wafer-thin majorities in York Outer and in Romsey and Southampton North were offset by the Liberal Democrats extending their margins of victory in similar scenarios in Cheltenham, Somerton and Frome, Eastleigh and in Westmoreland and Lonsdale. The Conservatives took Liberal Democrat scalps in Hereford and South Herefordshire, Richmond Park, Truro and Falmouth, Newton Abbot, Cornwall South East and in Camborne and Redruth but failed to take target seats such as Carshalton and Wallington, Taunton Deane, Chippenham, Torbay, Sutton and Cheam, Cornwall North, Cheadle, Portsmouth South, Southport, Leeds North West, Brecon and Radnorshire and Devon North from incumbent Liberal Democrats as they failed to secure a majority in the Commons. Ultimately, the Liberal Democrats successfully defended a number of key seats and won three Conservative held seats as their vote largely held up. In total, they suffered a net loss of nine seats to the Conservatives. Again local variations were common place with the Liberal Democrats holding, losing and winning seats for local as well as national reasons.

The Liberal Democrats lost four and gained one seat in the South West. Swings to the Conservatives of more than 5% in the new Truro and Falmouth and Camborne and Redruth seats led to two Liberal Democrat losses, with Julia Goldsworthy suffering defeat despite increasing her share of the vote. The Liberal Democrats also lost Cornwall South East, thereby halving their representation in Cornwall. In Devon, the Liberal Democrats fared little better, with large swings to the Conservatives across the county, apart from in the stronghold of Devon North. Richard Younger Ross, in Newton Abbot, was another Liberal Democrat casualty where local activists claimed the adverse effects of the expenses scandal contributed to defeat. The party fared better in Somerset, where it held Yeovil, Taunton Deane and the marginal Somerton and Frome, and won Wells with a 3.6% from the Conservatives following the incumbent candidates' high profile problems with parliamentary expenses. Elsewhere in the southwest region, the party rebuffed Conservative efforts in Chippenham and Torbay but failed to make any other gains. Across the south of England, the Liberal Democrats performance was uneven. While the party won Eastbourne from the Conservatives, it failed to win back Guildford from last time, despite an intensive local effort. With Sandra Gidley also falling foul of expenses in the new Romsey and Southampton North seat, nearby Winchester also fell to the Conservatives with a 9.1% swing. Yet, the party held Eastleigh, Lewes and Portsmouth South comfortably, despite the national Conservative revival.

Like Winchester, the defeat of the Liberal Democrats in Harrogate and Knaresborough was put down to the loss of high profile incumbents that had built up a local vote. Yet in 2010, the Liberal Democrats generally tended to fare better against the Conservatives when they were defending small majorities. It was the notionally safer Liberal Democrat seats that the Conservatives managed to capture. Other exceptional results occurred in Montgomeryshire, Oxford West and Abingdon .and Richmond Park. The 6.9% swing to the Conservatives in Oxford West and Abingdon was mainly due to local complacency, with an intense local effort to win the nearby Oxford East seat leading to the constituency becoming exposed. The defeat of Susan Kramer in Richmond Park was also put down to local circumstances, with nearby Twickenham, Carshalton and Wallington, Kingston and Surbiton and Sutton and Cheam remaining loyal to the Liberal Democrats. Opik's defeat in Montgomeryshire perhaps provides the ultimate evidence of the familiar mantra of party strategists; 'there is no such thing as a Liberal Democrat safe seat'.

CONSTITUENCY CONTESTS AND MARGINALITY. Despite the Liberal Democrat national vote increasing by around 1%, it is clear that the national picture obscures considerable local variation. In part, this reflects different patterns of party competition in different areas. Table 2 presents Liberal Democrat vote share, average change in vote share and swing, by seat types and vulnerability. The Liberal Democrats performed poorly regardless of whether it was defending the seat from either the Conservatives or Labour. In contests where Liberal Democrats were defending and the Conservatives were the main challengers, their average vote share declined (−0.36%), albeit from a relatively high base. The decline may have been much larger if the party had not gained support from some dissatisfied Labour voters. In seats where the main challengers were Labour, the average Liberal

2. Liberal Democrat performance: mean vote share; mean change in vote share 2005–2010; Lab-LD/Con-LD swing 2005–2010; by seat type, vulnerability/margin (%)

Seat type/margin	Mean 2010 LD %VS	±05–10 Mean LD %VS	Lab-Lib Dem swing	Con-Lib Dem swing
Seat type (N)				
LD-Con (45)	46	−0.36	2.15	−2.03
Con-LD (81)	30.77	0.45	3.64	−1.81
LD-Lab (16)	43.87	−0.9	0.5	−2.47
Lab-LD (107)	24.35	0.37	2.84	−1.32
LD-Nat (1)	50.03	13.51	9.9	7.2
Con-Lab (127)	20.82	3.29	6.49	−0.18
Lab-Con (213)	16.92	0.59	3.4	−1.97
Lab-Nat (26)	10.37	−2.93	−1.63	−2.08
Lab-Other (2)	11.55	1.08	−6.4	−0.45
Nat-Lab/Con (8)	11.42	−1.84	0.24	−3.19
Other-Lab/Con (3)	14.05	8.1	0.67	1.63
Vulnerability to LDs (N)				
Con seats[a]				
Vulnerable to LDs (17)	37.58	−0.7	2.5	−2.77
Non-vulnerable (191)	23.55	2.45	5.63	−0.64
Lab seats[b]				
Vulnerable to LDs (12)	32.5	−2.19	−0.82	−2.58
Non-vulnerable (336)	18.19	0.35	2.92	−1.74
LD Held[c]				
All marginal (28)	45.14	3.08	4.67	−0.01
LD-Con marginal (18)	46.28	3.35	5.01	0.26
LD-Lab marginal (9)	42.23	1.39	3.4	−1.34
Safe (34)	45.82	−3.04	−0.47	−3.63

Notes: 629 seats in total—excludes the current and former Speakers' seats (Buckingham and Glasgow North East) and Thirsk and Malton.
[a]Con seats: vulnerable to Liberal Democrats 0–9.9%; non-vulnerable 10%+.
[b]Labour seats: vulnerable to Liberal Democrats 0–9.9%; non-vulnerable 10%+.
[c]LD Held marginal 0–9.9%; safe 10%+.

Democrat vote change also fell (−0.90%), most likely because of voters switching back to the Conservatives.

Table 2 reveals the full extent of the party's toothless offensive performance in the most vulnerable seats held by either the Conservatives or Labour. In tight Conservative–Liberal Democrat contests, there was a small fall in Liberal Democrat vote share (−0.70%) for the second successive election. The swing from Liberal Democrats to the Conservatives in these seats largely offset any benefits the Liberal Democrats gained from squeezing the ever-dwindling Labour vote in these constituencies. Despite previously persuading large numbers of Labour voters in vulnerable Conservative seats to shift their support, the results provide circumstantial evidence that the Liberal Democrats failed to hold onto enough of their own voters, some of whom most likely switched back to the Conservatives. The Liberal Democrat performance in non-vulnerable Conservative seats was much better, although a large proportion of the party's vote share continues to stem from disgruntled Labour voters.

While making further inroads into Conservative support proved difficult, the Liberal Democrats found the going even tougher against Labour. In seats where Labour was the incumbent, the Liberal Democrat vote barely increased. This was mirrored in other seat types where Labour was the incumbent, and in Labour-Nationalist contests, the Liberal Democrat vote also fell. Not surprisingly, the party fell back in vulnerable Labour seats, with Labour's vote firming-up in these seats (0.8% swing to Labour) and Liberal Democrat voters switching to the Conservatives in greater numbers. The party's long-term strategy of gradually building support to position itself as the most credible opposition in Labour heartlands clearly took a backward step. The Liberal Democrats performed little better in non-vulnerable Labour seats where their average vote share remained around 18%. As in 2005, the party still remains too far behind in the majority of Labour seats to substantially benefit from any possible decline in the Labour vote.

Despite the toothless nature of its offensive performance, defensively the Liberal Democrats largely held their own, although they did fare better in marginal than safe seats. In the most marginal Liberal Democrat–Conservative contests, the Liberal Democrat vote increased to over 46% as the party saw their vote rise by more than 3%. Where Labour was a close second, the Liberal Democrats also saw their vote increase by 1.39% and subsequently held onto all their seats except for Chesterfield. As in 2005, the Liberal Democrat vote marginally declined in its safe seats from an average of 48.26%, suggesting that the party may have reached its ceiling with little scope to make much further progress.

In summary, the Liberal Democrats had the problem of 'tight targeting'— in other words, they had a number of seats to defend with small majorities while other held seats were not safe enough to neglect. At the same time, there were few potential seats that the party could gain (i.e. they were just too far behind in too many seats which restricted the possibility of them making large scale gains). Offensively, the party had little room for manoeuvre. Defensively, the party performed well against a revived Conservative party, although losses in notionally fairly safe seats cost the party dearly.

INCUMBENCY. The Liberal Democrats suffered a reversal in seats held before 1997 with major losses in Truro and Falmouth and the aforementioned Montgomeryshire. In the seats the party had won since 1997, the Liberal Democrat vote largely held steady (Table 3). However, the party lost 11 of these 46 seats. After winning seats at the expense of the Conservatives in 1997, the party then increased their support in these breakthrough seats at the 2001 election after targeting them heavily. While intensive targeting and local effort mattered,

3. Liberal Democrat performance and historical base, incumbency (seats) and new candidates

Historical base and incumbency	Mean % LD vote 2010	Mean % LD vote ± 05–10	Seats held	Gains	Losses	Total seats
Pre-1997 seats (16)	46.39	−0.65	14	–	2	14
Post-1997 seats (46)	45.20	−0.14	35	–	11	35
First-time incumbency[a] (17)	46.17	+4.34	15	–	2	15
LD incumbents (35)	46.56	−1.25	30	–	5	30
LD new (10)	40.71	−4.69	4	–	6	4
All LD seats (62)	45.5	−0.27	49	–	13	49
All non-LD seats (567)	20.76	+0.98	–	8	–	8

Notes: 629 seats in total—excludes the current and former Speakers' seats (Buckingham and Glasgow North East) and Thirsk and Malton.
[a]First-time incumbency does not include Lorely Burt in Solihull (notionally Conservative), although the candidate was an incumbent; Sarah Teather in Brent Central (fighting a new seat after Brent East abolished) or Paul Rowen in Rochdale (notionally Labour but incumbent candidate standing). If these are included—LD 2010 vote share (45.32%); 2005/2010 vote change +4.21%. They also gained two seats (Solihull and Brent Central).

electoral credibility was also important with voters more likely to support the Liberal Democrats if they felt they could win. Only by winning the constituency at a previous election could the Liberal Democrats fill this 'credibility gap' thereby ensuring they became a viable electoral option in the minds of the electors.[9] Yet, in 2005, such seats did not receive the same level of party support and become more vulnerable to a Conservative revival. In 2010, seats such as Winchester and Oxford West and Abingdon became high-profile casualties as the Conservatives reclaimed some of the seats they lost in 1997. However, a closer inspection suggests that other factors may have played a part.

The importance of first-time incumbency and new candidates should not be ignored. As in 2005, the Liberal Democrats benefited from a first time incumbency effect. The average increase in vote share for seats gained in 2005 where the same candidate stood again was 4.34%. Of the 15 seats, where a Liberal Democrat first time incumbent candidate stood, the party won 13 and lost two (Camborne and Redruth and Richmond Park). Elsewhere, first time incumbents in Sheffield Hallam, Eastleigh and Bristol West saw increases in their majorities. In 2010, the Liberal Democrats selected ten new candidates to stand in seats where they were the incumbent party. Not only did they lose six Liberal Democrat seats[10] to the Conservatives, but their average vote share since 2001 declined by -4.69%. The only Liberal Democrat successes were in Cambridge, Chippenham, Edinburgh West and St Austell and Newquay. Those who were neither new nor first time incumbents saw their vote share fall by 1.25%, with five incumbents losing their seats. Across all Liberal Democrat held seats, party performance only marginally declined, although an average vote share of 45.51% suggests that the Liberal Democrats have reached their high water mark. The party's performance in non-Liberal Democrat seats bucked the trend with a one percent increase from 2005.

Understanding unevenness: reassessing the impact of socio-demographics

Scholarly work has long pointed out that there is no clear social base of support for the Liberal Democrats.[11] Previous evidence suggested that, although it does better in more middle class areas, Liberal Democrat electoral success owed much to its targeting strategy, local government base and its emphasis on local campaigning.[12] Yet, in 2005, the Liberal Democrats' anti-war stance and opposition to tuition fees were widely believed to have influenced the Liberal Democrats electoral prospects, leading to an improved performance in seats with large Muslim and student populations.[13]

Five years later and the war in Afghanistan had now replaced the war in Iraq as a salient issue. Although the Liberal Democrats had become less vehement in their opposition to the Afghan war, partly because they came out in favour of it in 2001, they frequently reminded electors of their anti-Iraq war stance. Moreover, university tuition fees were now in place and the Liberal Democrats had modified outright rejection of fees to a less straightforward policy of their phasing out within six years. With the party actively targeting the under 30 votes and local candidates actively encouraged by the centre to tailor their campaigns to attract support from the Muslim community, was there any evidence that the Liberal Democrats benefited either from these continued targeted approaches or from a previous legacy of policy commitments in these areas?

Table 4 shows the 2010 Liberal Democrat performance in seats by the Muslim population in the constituency. Contrary to 2005, Liberal Democrat average vote share marginally deceased by nearly 0.3% from 2005 in the 39 seats with the highest Muslim population. Despite this decline, the party won 2 (Brent Central and Bradford East) of the 39 most populated Muslim seats, although it failed to win back Rochdale which was notionally Labour following redistricting. Elsewhere, there was evidence that the Liberal Democrats failed to recruit the Muslim vote. The party was beaten into third by Respect in Birmingham Hall Green and saw a swing against it in Birmingham Hodge Hill. It did beat Respect into third in Bethnal Green and Bow, although it easily lost the seat to Labour. The Liberal Democrats also failed to get any Muslim candidates elected or build on previous increases in support (Holborn & St Pancras, Bradford North and Birmingham Ladywood), and although it did win Burnley, from those seats where the Muslim population varied between 5 and 9.9%, it was apparent that any shift away from Labour towards the Liberal Democrats among Muslim voters had slowed down or reversed.

4. Liberal Democrat performance in Muslim seats, mean percentage vote share, mean change
in vote share 2005–2010, Lab-LD/Con-LD swing 2005–2010

Muslim population	Mean 2010 % LD vote share	Mean % LD vote share ± 2005–2010	Lab-LD swing	Con-LD swing	LD gains	LD losses
0–4.9% (528)	23.52	+1.03	+3.95	−1.43	5	13
5–9.9% (62)	22.02	+0.14	+1.97	−1.89	1	0
10%+ (39)	20.72	−0.32	+0.05	−1.47	2	0

Note: 629 seats in total—excludes the current and former Speakers' seats (Buckingham and
Glasgow North East) and Thirsk and Malton.

In contrast, Table 5 shows that the Liberal Democrats continued to
record average vote increases in those seats with more than 10% of students. However, closer inspection reveals that the party failed to
convert its popularity among students into seats. Indeed, it lost one
'university seat' (Oxford West and Abingdon) to the Conservatives.
However, many of the Liberal Democrat university seat gains from
2005 (Bristol West, Ceredigion, Leeds North West and Manchester
Withington) recorded higher majorities and increased swings from
Labour. As in 2005, the party narrowly failed to win Oxford East,
Newcastle upon Tyne Central and City of Durham. With the Labour
vote also remaining strong in Islington South and Finsbury and
Liverpool Wavertree, the party simply failed to make the impact that it
expected in these key target seats.

Of course, these university seats are not solely inhabited by students,
but often also contain large numbers of academic staff, young professionals with degrees and individuals working in education. In 2005,
the party performed well in these seats reflecting the fact that it was
not only students who caused the dramatic swings in university areas
but also university teaching staff (as well as further education and high
school teachers). However, despite increasing their vote in those 55
seats where more than 10% of the working population worked in education, the average vote change was actually very slightly lower than in
the rest of the country.

5. Liberal Democrat performance in full-time student seats: mean percentage vote share,
mean change in vote share 2005–2010, Lab-LD/Con-LD swing 2005–2010

Student population	Mean 2010 % LD vote share	Mean % LD vote share ± 2005–2010	Lab-LD swing	Con-LD swing	LD gains	LD losses
0–4.9% (476)	22.62	+0.91	+4.02	−1.51	5	8
5–9.9% (110)	22.71	+0.38	+1.89	−1.73	3	4
10%+ (43)	30.93	+1.45	+2.02	−0.40	0	1

Note: 629 seats in total—excludes the current and former Speakers' seats (Buckingham and
Glasgow North East) and Thirsk and Malton.

Overall, while there is some circumstantial evidence that the party had largely maintained its vote in those university seats it had won at the last election, the Liberal Democrats' 'electoral bonus' of seats attributable to educational workers especially in universities and the Muslim vote were largely the products of unique circumstances that existed in 2005. Despite the Liberal Democrats' efforts to target under 30-year old voters and build support in these 'new types' of areas, the evidence from the 2010 election suggests that such effort had little or no additional effect on existing support.

Conclusion: did the campaign matter?

The more things change, the more they stay the same: despite the seemingly cataclysmic events of the election campaign, the Liberal Democrats finished just 1% up in vote share and five seats down on the 2005 result. They dramatically lost some seemingly safe seats but equally surprisingly gained others. The story of the 2010 Liberal Democrat election was the remarkable similarity with 2005. Even the geographical variations are themselves part of a long tradition of local upsets reflecting local issues, campaigns and personalities. Overall, following what appeared to be a ground-breaking campaign, the Liberal Democrat performance in the 2010 election was—as Clegg acknowledged—disappointing for the party.

The reason for that disappointment is clear. As we have documented above, the televised leadership debates transformed the campaign for all three main parties, giving an equal platform for the Liberal Democrats, potentially, helping them overcome the 'credibility gap' and persuading voters there was a real alternative to the 'old parties' (as Clegg liked to call them). As the outsider, and with very low expectations from the outset, Clegg gained the most from the debates—and was able to give himself and his party a popularity boost from the first debate onwards. Nevertheless, any immediate sense of disappointment will have been tempered by two important and obvious factors. First, for the first time since the Second World War, the Liberals are a formal partner in a coalition government. Second, the source of this disappointment was the party's heightened expectations during the short campaign period. Six months before the 2010 election, fearful of being squeezed towards the periphery of politics in Britain altogether, the Liberal Democrats would have been delighted with a single point increase in their popular vote and the loss of only a handful of seats, not to mention a role in government and a referendum on voting reform. With David Cameron's Conservatives riding high in polls throughout 2009 the Liberal Democrats faced a real battle for their effective existence.

Notwithstanding this, why did the campaign success seem to make so little difference to the final result? Perhaps the Liberal Democrat surge failed to materialise in the actual poll due to late swing—perhaps

the Liberal Democrats failed tactically to convert enough Labour supporters with Clegg's promise to uphold the 'moral victor' of an election
(defined as the party with the most seats and most votes) and the
public distancing of Clegg from Brown after the 'I agree with Nick'
strategy of Labour's leadership failed to resonate with the Liberal
Democrat elite. Indeed, by expressing a preference for working with
whoever was the larger party (most likely the Conservatives) and for
not working with Brown, Clegg sent a signal to Labour voters that a
centre-left alliance was an unlikely result even if they tactically supported the Liberal Democrats. Despite the interventions of Ed Balls
and Peter Hain in support of tactical voting, this message was
re-enforced by the Labour hierarchy as the party sought to shore up its
core support and avoid electoral meltdown.

The result may have been to put-off soft-Labour or 'floating' voters
from the centre left, who have traditionally formed an important part
of the Liberal Democrat vote base. Indeed, it is telling that various
opinion polls showed that self declared Liberal Democrat voters were
more likely to see Labour rather than the Conservatives as their
second-choice party. For example, a TNS poll during the campaign
suggested 29% of Liberal Democrat voters selected Labour as their
second choice party compared with 22% for the Conservatives.[14]
Moreover, a substantial majority of voters in a YouGov poll placed the
Liberal Democrats ideologically closer to Labour than the
Conservatives.[15] These findings, which are consistent with a previous
scholarly research,[16] indicate an important centre-left axis which may
have been threatened by the party's electoral positioning in 2010, and
the subsequent coalition with the Tories. In the event, the Liberal
Democrat performance was relatively weak in Labour heartlands,
perhaps due to this positioning and the fear of Conservative cuts. A
senior strategist claimed that 'the fear tactics deployed by Labour over
welfare and benefits' were the main reason why 'many people went
back to Labour in the final days of the campaign and even on polling
day'. A simple correlation analysis of the change in Liberal Democrat
vote share by the previous vote share of the other parties shows that
the Liberal Democrats increased their vote precisely where the
Conservatives were stronger.[17] Unfortunately, for them in most cases,
this was insufficient to hold off the resurgent Tories, whereas in
Labour-held areas they were unable to make the necessary inroads into
the stubborn Labour support.

However, it would be wrong to suggest that the electoral calculus
clearly should have pointed the Liberal Democrats towards a radical
centre-left alignment. In order to make a breakthrough, the party had
to make substantial inroads in the South and in affluent areas in the
face of a rising tide of Conservative support. Moreover, in order to
defend the seats they held going into the election, they were much
more at threat from the Conservatives than from Labour. In 2005, it

was suggested that the 'radical' centre-left appearance of the Liberal Democrats may have contributed to some electors returning to the Conservative fold.[18] While the new leadership distanced itself from the 'left-of-Labour label' by ending its opposition to tuition fees (in the short term) and outlining fiscally prudent deficit reduction policies (no ring-fencing of departmental budgets), proposals such as the 'mansion tax', increasing the personal allowance for the lowest earners, advocating a 1p increase in national insurance and no nuclear deterrent, still left it tarnished with that label. This may have hampered the Liberal Democrats' offensive effort in southern seats, which in turn was unlikely to have been aided by the party's 'immigration amnesty' policy (which may also have proved unpopular in Labour areas).

Perhaps an even more crucial factor in the failure of the Liberal Democrats to defy the incoming tide of Conservative support lay in the electoral system. It seems that the suggested performance of the Liberal Democrats, in terms of reported vote intention during the campaign period, reflected what people might do if elections were unfettered by the complexities of local competition and history. When faced with the reality of the election, too many voters perhaps decided that, whatever their personal views of Nick Clegg or Liberal Democrat policies, the party simply could not win in their particular seat and the Liberal Democrat vote crumbled at the last gasp. This is a familiar feature of Liberal Democrat voting—the party needs to pass a credibility test at a local or national level to encourage people to vote for it. In other words, they were unable to surmount the age-old problem of electoral credibility created by the dynamics of the first-past-the-post voting system. In 2010, the party once more failed to break the mould of British politics because too many people either did not want a Liberal Democrat government or did not believe a Liberal Democrat could win the national or local constituency contest.

Yet, ironically, the outcome of the election (and the vagaries of the electoral system that has cost them so dear) may have finally delivered some of the credibility that the Liberal Democrat so badly need. The rainbow coalition of Labour, Liberal Democrats and other 'progressives' hardly seemed a viable option due to a lack of parliamentary numbers and uncertainty about its desirability among the Labour elite. By entering into a coalition with the Conservatives, Nick Clegg's party may be vulnerable to electoral blowback from Labour supporters unhappy with the new alliance—and those who now think they may as well vote Conservative. However, participation in coalition government does give the Liberal Democrats ammunition to tackle their most enduring obstacle. It provides the third party with the trappings of legitimacy. The real legacy of Clegg's performance in the campaign may not have been witnessed in the general election results but in the negotiations after the poll. Maybe Clegg's campaign performance (and the harsh electoral mathematics of a hung, if not perfectly balanced, parliament) gave him the credibility to be taken seriously within Westminster. He will hope that, as a viable coalition partner for the Conservatives and with his stint as Deputy Prime Minister, the Liberal Democrats will gain even more credibility in the next election.

1   A. Russell and E. Fieldhouse, *Neither Left Nor Right? The Liberal Democrats and the Electorate*, Manchester University Press, 2005; A. Russell 'The Liberal Democrat Campaign' in P. Norris and C. Wlezien (ds.) *Britain Votes 2005*, Oxford University Press, 2005.

2   A. Russell, D. Cutts and E. Fieldhouse, 'Local-Regional-National: the state of the Liberal Democrats in 2007', *British Politics*, 2, 2007, 191–214.

3   E. Fieldhouse, D. Cutts and A. Russell, 'Neither North Nor South: The Geography of Liberal Democrat Voting in 2005', *Journal of Elections and Public Opinion*, 16, 2006.

4   S. Fielding, *The Labour Party: Continuity and Change in the Making of New Labour*, Palgrave MacMillan, 2002.

5   *Sunday Times*, 'Nick Clegg Nearly as Popular as Churchill', 18 April, 2010.

6   *Guardian*, 'Nick Clegg Admits to Disappointing Election Results', 7 May 2010.

7   E. Fieldhouse and D. Cutts, 'Steady Progress or a Failure to Seize the Moment? The Liberal Democrats' 2005 General Election Performance', in A. Geddes and J. Tonge (eds), *Britain Decides: The UK General Election 2005*, Palgrave Macmillan, 2005.

8   Ibid., p. 75.

9   A. Russell and E. Fieldhouse, *Neither Left Nor Right? The Liberal Democrats and the Electorate*, Manchester University Press, 2005.

10 The Liberal Democrats lost Harrogate and Knaresborough, Winchester, York Outer, Truro and Falmouth, Cornwall South East, Hereford & Herefordshire South.

11 A. Russell and E. Fieldhouse, *Neither Left Nor Right? The Liberal Democrats and the Electorate*, Manchester University Press, 2005.

12 D. Cutts and N. Shryane, 'Did Local Activism Really Matter? Liberal Democrat Campaigning at the 2001 British General Election', *British Journal of Politics and International Relations*, 8, 2006, 427–44.

13 E. Fieldhouse, D. Cutts and A. Russell, 'Neither North Nor South: The Geography of Liberal Democrat Voting in 2005', *Journal of Elections and Public Opinion*, 16, 2006, 77–92.

14 http://www.tnsglobal.com/news/newsCC6A60116AC74225B5F27D156E2E4FDB.aspx 27 May 2010.

15 http://my.yougov.com/commentaries/peter-kellner/is-there-really-a-progressive-majority.aspx 14 May 2010.

16 E. Fieldhouse, D. Cutts and A. Russell, 'Neither North Nor South: The Geography of Liberal Democrat Voting in 2005', *Journal of Elections and Public Opinion*, 16, 2006, 77–92.

17 The correlation is +0.22 and is significant at the 95% level.

18 E. Fieldhouse and D. Cutts, 'Steady Progress or a Failure to Seize the Moment? The Liberal Democrats' 2005 General Election Performance', in A. Geddes and J. Tonge (eds), *Britain Decides: The UK General Election 2005*, Palgrave Macmillan, 2005.

JAMES MITCHELL AND ARNO VAN DER ZWET

A Catenaccio Game: the 2010 Election in Scotland

At the Scottish Conservative conference following the 1979 general election, Margaret Thatcher thanked the party for its contribution to victory. The Scottish Conservatives had won 31% of the vote, up almost 7% on the previous election. With 22 of Scotland's 71 seats, Mrs Thatcher commended the six new Tory MPs who had gained a seat for the party. But the new Prime Minister was conscious that her party had a long way to go to achieve the level of support it had won in England, 'Is it that our policies are not so popular in Scotland? Of course not', she asserted.[1] Being in government afforded the Conservatives with the opportunity to pursue popular policies that might allow them to close the gap between their support in Scotland and England.

However, 14 years later in her memoirs, Mrs Thatcher reflected that there had been 'no Tartan Thatcherite revolution... The balance sheet of Thatcherism in Scotland is a lopsided one: economically positive but politically negative'.[2] Over the 18 years in power, the Conservatives lost support in Scotland and ultimately lost all seats north of the border in 1997. The Conservative brand in Scotland had been seriously tarnished. Being in government had created more problems than opportunities. Whatever they did would be presented by opponents as anti-Scottish simply because the Conservatives had so little support in Scotland. Mrs Thatcher's style did not help. There is evidence that many Tory policies were popular in Scotland, most notably council house sales, but paid no electoral dividends.

The diagnosis of Conservative unpopularity in Scotland after 1979 was similar to that offered by a number of senior Tories for the Conservatives' defeat across Britain in 1997. The brand, rather than its policies, was the cause of its problems. In his speech to the Tory conference in 2005, Francis Maude noted that popular policies lost their appeal as soon as they were associated with the Conservative Party. In his booklet, *Smell the Coffee: A Wake-Up Call for the Conservative Party*, Michael Ashcroft argued that the 'Conservative label was

doi:10.1093/pa/gsq019

undermining its ability to sell its policies' and that many voters 'had such a negative view of the Conservative Party's brand that they would oppose a policy they actually agreed with rather than support a Tory proposal'.[3] David Cameron's challenge as leader was to detoxify the brand. He was aided in this in that the main competition's brand was also damaged. In less than five years, Cameron reached parts of the UK none of his predecessors since John Major had done.

However, the much vaunted 'Cameron effect' had no impact on Scotland. The Tories' brand problem ran deep north of the border. Annabel Goldie, the party's Holyrood leader, is popular, but has been unable to overcome the deep-rooted unpopularity of her party in Scotland. This problem goes further back than the difficulties Cameron confronted with his detoxification strategy across Britain. Over the 13 years in Opposition, the focus was on winning back the support lost in 1997, neglecting the longer term loss of support in Scotland. Back in government, the Conservatives' Scottish problems have become exposed once more. Whether being in government offers the Conservatives more opportunities than problems will be conditioned in part by the economic and fiscal contexts. The existence of a Scottish Parliament adds to the mix and might either become a means through which the Government is able to devolve penury, evading many difficult choices itself or becomes an authoritative voice of opposition to London government. With only one Scottish MP, coalition with the Liberal Democrats, with 11 MPs in Scotland, ensures that on this occasion opposition to the Conservatives will at least be more limited.

A Scottish result

Despite a very British campaign, the outcome of the election in Scotland was quite different from that elsewhere in Britain. No seats changed hands in Scotland (see Table 1).[4] Labour retained all 40 seats won in 2005, including winning back 2 seats lost in by-elections during the last Parliament. The Scottish Conservative Party held onto its solitary Scottish seat, but failed to win any of its 11 target seats.[5] Although Labour's vote fell by 6.5% in Wales and by 7.4% in England, it rose by 3.1% in Scotland, the first increase in Labour support in Scotland since its landslide in 1997. In contrast, the Conservatives increased their share of the vote by 4.7% in Wales, 3.8% in England and only 0.9% in Scotland. The Scottish National Party (SNP) vote was up 2.3%, although it failed to win any additional seats and fell well short of its target of 20 additional seats to make Westminster 'dance to a Scottish jig'.[6] The Liberal Democrats' vote fell by 3.7% and dropped behind the SNP to third place in share of the vote while in England the Liberal Democrat vote was up by 1.3%.

No party has governed Scotland with such a low share of the vote and only one seat. Coalition rather than minority government may

1. The 2010 election results in Scotland

	Seats won (change since 2005)	% share of vote (change since 2005)
Labour	41 (+1[a])	42.0 (+3.1)
SNP	6 (0)	19.9 (+2.3)
LibDem	11 (0)	18.9 (−3.7)
Conservative	1 (0)	16.7 (+0.9)
Others	0 (−1[a])	2.4 (−2.6)

[a]Speaker's seat.

have been David Cameron's preference, but it looks more like a necessity from a Scottish perspective, offering cover for its poor performance north of the border. But even the combined Conservative and Liberal Democrat share of the vote was 3.9% below that won by the Conservatives in England and 3.2% below the Labour's Scottish support. The coalition's 12 Scottish MPs represent predominantly Highland and rural constituencies, and East Dumbartonshire is the only seat held by the parties in west central Scotland where the bulk of the population resides. The Liberal Democrats do not offer the Conservatives much Scottish cover.

While the SNP replaced the Liberal Democrats as Scotland's second party in share of the vote, it remained firmly in third place in number of seats and failed to come close to challenging Labour's dominance of Westminster elections north of the border. The SNP's breakthrough three years before in elections to the Scottish Parliament had convinced many in the SNP that it could make a similar breakthrough at Westminster. But the SNP failed to take account of the electorate's willingness to behave differently at Westminster and Holyrood elections. Even in the heat of the election, the electorate's preferences continued to distinguish between Westminster and Holyrood elections. While Labour and SNP compete as largest party at Holyrood, Labour remains dominant at Westminster.

Though no seats changed hands, 15 new MPs were returned from Scotland, of whom 13 were Labour members. Alex Salmond was replaced as SNP MP for Banff and Buchan by Eilidh Whiteford and Mike Crockart replaced his Liberal Democrat colleagues John Barrett as MP for Edinburgh West. The number of women MPs rose from 9 (7%) in 2005 to 13 (13.2%) in 2010, including the youngest MP at 25 years of age. Mohammad Sarwar, Scotland's only Muslim and ethnic minority MP, was replaced by his son in Glasgow Central. While Alex Salmond stood down after 23 years as an MP, two Labour Members of the Scottish Parliament (MSPs) became dual members on election to the House of Commons and two Conservative MSPs stood unsuccessfully. With the elevation of former Labour First Minister Jack McConnell to the House of Lords, there are now two members of the Lords who are also MSPs (both Labour).

A *very British election*

The 2010 election was a very British affair. There has always been a Scottish dimension to UK general elections. Since 1959, the three main British parties have each produced Scottish manifestos, though these were often little more than the British manifestos with Scottish covers. The Scottish dimension manifested itself in debates on Scotland's constitutional status in elections up to 1997. However, there have been other distinguishing features of elections in Scotland, not the least of which have been the results. In 1979, when the Conservatives last returned to power following a period of Labour Government, the election in Scotland saw the 'temporary eclipse of the Scottish dimension'.[7] The 2010 election also appeared to be a very British election in which the Scottish dimension was eclipsed though the result bucked the British trend.

Three aspects of the campaign signified its Britishness: the British leaders' debates; the public policy debate with particular emphasis on the economy and public finances and the relative absence of much debate on Scotland's constitutional status. The focus on the British leaders' debates had the effect of marginalising any distinctive Scottish dimension. Styled by the BBC as 'Prime Ministerial Debates', the rules for the debates had been agreed between the three main parties and excluded the leaders of the smaller parties, including the SNP. The Prime Ministerial debates not only gave the impression that broadcasters had re-written the constitution to be a Presidential system, but a formula was required to deal with issues that were devolved.

Broadcasters had three responses in dealing with devolved issues. First, in hosting the three debates in England (Manchester, Bristol and Birmingham) the broadcasters side-stepped the difficulties of accommodating matters that were devolved by simply focusing on the election as it affected England. Secondly, each time a matter was raised that was devolved to Scotland, Wales or Northern Ireland, the debate moderator noted that the subject was devolved. Alastair Stewart, ITV moderator in the first debate, prefaced a question on law and order, for example, by simply stating that 'I need to point out that it is an area where powers are devolved to the parliament in Scotland and from this week, also the assembly in Northern Ireland'.[8] This was to be the standard operating procedure during debates for dealing with the broadcasters' equivalent of the West Lothian Question. None of the party leaders felt compelled to engage with the implications of Britain's territorial constitution during the debates. References to Scotland were almost non-existent. In answer to what he had done personally to tackle climate change, Gordon Brown mentioned the solar panel installed at his North Queensferry home in Scotland. Nick Clegg's nearest comment on Scotland was a reference to MPs who had 'flipped' properties getting away 'scot-free'. Scotland, Scottish and Scots never passed the lips of David Cameron in any of the debates. Thirdly, the broadcasters offered separate Scottish, Welsh and Northern Ireland debates at other times. In essence, the broadcasters' response to their own West Lothian Question has been much like successive UK Governments until now and to ignore it.

The Prime Ministerial debates attracted considerable public interest beyond England (Table 2). The first debate attracted high viewing figures across Britain and while there was a lower proportion of viewers in Scotland, the figures watching the three British party leaders' debates were much higher than any of the Scottish leaders' debates (Table 3). In addition, there was the usual coverage of the election that tended to marginalise the Scottish dimension and smaller parties, including interviews with the three British party leaders. The SNP objected and took their case to the Court of Session in Edinburgh in an attempt to stop the third (BBC) debate being broadcast in Scotland but failed to win its case.[9] The judge argued that impartiality was not the same as 'giving each and every political party an equal coverage' and that the SNP had not demonstrated that the BBC had failed to take account of the need for impartiality. She also noted that the SNP had failed to act earlier but had waited until the final debate before issuing its legal challenge and had failed to explain adequately what fairness entailed.[10]

Part of the SNP's case had been that the 'impact of the previous two debates on the media coverage of the General Election campaign as a whole, has been demonstrably the single largest factor in the current UK General Election campaign in terms of impact on the media profile, approval ratings of party leaders and overall intention to vote' and that the inclusion of Nick Clegg in the previous two debates 'greatly increased the coverage of that party in the media' and 'greatly improved the fortunes of that party in the opinion polls'.[11] Polls had indicated a 'Clegg bounce' following the first debate, though Scottish polls suggested that the Liberal Democrats only managed to climb back to the level of support won in 2005 (although up on how they had been doing prior to the debate). Evidence from a YouGov poll conducted before and after the first debate suggests that Liberal Democrat support jumped from 17 to 23% in Scotland and from 21 to 24% after the third poll (Table 4). The Liberal Democrats appeared to be fighting it out for third place with the Conservatives in Scotland at the start of the campaign with Labour pulling well ahead of the SNP in second place. The first debate gave the Liberal Democrats a boost, drawing ahead of the SNP and for much of the remainder of the campaign appeared likely to retain their position, won in 2005, as Scotland's second party at Westminster.

The dominance of the economy and public finances may have had distinctly Scottish dimensions but these did not feature in the main

2. Viewing figures for 'Prime Ministerial' debates and UK leader interviews: Scotland and the UK compared

Channel	Date	Start time	UK network 000s[a]	Network TVR %[b]	Share %[c]	Scotland 000s	Scotland TVR %	Scotland Share %
ITV1	15/4/10	20:32	9679	17	36	699	15	33
BBC News	22/4/10	20:00	1388	2	5	70	2	3
Sky News	22/4/10	20:00	2212	4	9	148	3	7
BBC1	29/4/10	20:30	7428	13	27	419	9	19
Programme	Date	Start time	Network 000s[a]	Network TVR[b]	Share[c]	Scotland 000s	Scotland TVR	Scotland Share
BBC1 Paxman interviews Clegg	12/4/10	20:30	2170	3.81	5	70	2	3
BBC1 Paxman interviews Cameron	23/4/10	20:30	2336	4.1	10.18	180	3.97	9.52
BBC1 Paxman interviews Brown	30/4/10	20:30	2574	4.52	11.19	194	4.28	11.07

[a]This is average audience across the programme. [b]This is the % of UK/Scotland population watching the debate—e.g. 17 TVR means 17% of UK population watched the first debate while it was 15% in Scotland. [c]This gives viewing share of all people watching television at the time of the debate, e.g. 36% of those watching television tuned into the first debate.

3. Viewing figures for Scottish party leaders' debates

Debate	Channel	Date	Start time	000s	TVR %	Share %
Scottish debates	ITV	22/4/10	21:00	251	6	13
Scottish leaders' debate	BBC1	2/5/10	21:58	199	4	9
SKY News Scotland debate	Sky	25/4/10	10.30	59	1.3	<5

debates. While the Scottish implications of the economic crisis and impact on Holyrood's finances were part of the debate in Scotland, the UK-wide dimension dominated as the economy and decisions on how much money Holyrood would have to spend are matters retained at Westminster. The Scottish dimension appeared to have been marginalised both by the focus on the Prime Ministerial debates but also by the policy concerns.

Even though many of the issues debated in UK elections have been the responsibility of the Scottish Parliament since its establishment in 1999, there was little effort to distinguish between matters that were devolved or retained. Indeed, it would have been difficult to mount a British-wide campaign without surrounding many commitments with devolution caveats. What was significant was that the Scottish manifestos and campaigns largely ignored the fact that MPs would have no direct say in devolved matters. Policies appeared in the Scottish manifestos which would have been more appropriate in manifestos for next year's Holyrood elections. Scottish Labour's manifesto, for example, stated, 'our goal is educational excellence for every child' and describes Labour's 'ambitious programme of school building' from its period in government in Scotland from 1999 to 2007.[12] Devolved matters were the subject of debates as if these were Holyrood elections. In essence, Holyrood and devolved matters were subsumed within this UK election. There was little effort on the part of the parties or media to attribute responsibility to reflect the constitutional realities.

Scotland's constitutional status hardly registered in the election despite the SNP Government's 'National Conversation', a Scottish Government-sponsored debate, on the subject. The SNP Government had proposed a referendum on independence, but lacks a Parliamentary majority at Holyrood. The opposition parties at Holyrood—Labour, Conservatives and Liberal Democrats—had established a commission under Sir Kenneth Calman to review devolution. The commission reported in June 2009, recommending minor changes in devolved powers and changes in how Holyrood would be financed. None of the SNP's opponents was keen to discuss the subject during the election and there was the appearance of cross-Unionist consensus around the proposals of the Calman Commission.[13] Calman had been set up in response to the SNP's electoral success at the Holyrood elections and its success was evident in removing Scotland's constitutional

4. Scottish opinion polls (% vote share)

Publication	Polling firm	Sample dates	Sample size	Labour	SNP	LibDem	Cons
2005 Election result				*39.5*	*17.6*	*22.6*	*15.8*
Scottish Daily Mail	YouGov	24–26 Aug 09	1078	33	25	16	19
Scottish Mail on Sunday	YouGov	26–28 Aug 09	1183	30	26	18	20
Herald	TNS-BMRB	28 Oct–3 Nov 09	983	39	25	12	18
Telegraph	YouGov	18 Nov–20 Nov 09	1141	39	24	12	18
Sunday Times	Ipsos MORI	19 Nov–23 Nov 09	1009	32	34	12	15
Herald	TNS-BMRB	27 Jan–4 Feb 10	1000	42	26	11	18
Sun	YouGov	15–17 Feb 10	562	34	24	15	21
Sun	YouGov	17–24 Feb 10	667	40	23	14	18
Scotsman	YouGov	24–26 Feb 10	1002	35	24	15	20
Scotland on Sunday	YouGov	24–26 Feb 10	1002	38	21	15	20
Times	Ipsos MORI	18 Feb–21 Feb 10	1006	34	32	12	17
Sun	YouGov	24 Feb–3 March 10	821	39	24	14	18
Sun	YouGov	3–10 March 10	720	39	26	12	18
Sun	YouGov	10–17 March 10	781	39	24	15	16
Sun	YouGov	17–24 March 10	885	36	23	13	21
Sun	YouGov	24–31 March 10	936	39	23	15	21
PoliticsHome	YouGov	4–11 April 10	1227	38	24	16	17
Scotsman	YouGov	14–16 April 10		40	20	19	16
Politics Home	YouGov	11–18 April 10	1227	39	20	20	17
STV	Ipsos MORI	14–17 April 10	1005	36	26	20	14
Sun	YouGov	14–21 April 10	1329	36	21	23	15
Sky	YouGov	21–23 April 10	1001	36	22	24	15
PoliticsHome	YouGov	18–25 April 10	1227	36	21	25	14
Times	Populus	23–26 April 10	1000	37	19	24	16
Sun	YouGov	21–28 April 10	1121	36	23	23	14
Scotland on Sunday	YouGov	28–30 April 10	1520	37	20	22	17
PoliticsHome	YouGov			37	25	22	14
Scottish Mail on Sunday	TNS BMRB	21–27 April 10	1029	44	23	16	13
Scotsman	YouGov	3–5 May 10	1507	37	21	22	17
2010 Election result				*42.0*	*19.9*	*18.8*	*16.4*

status from the political agenda. This left the SNP alone in struggling to raise the constitutional question.

The most pressing issues in Scotland as elsewhere during the election focused on the economy and public finances, crowding out discussion of Scotland's constitutional status. Although there was a Scottish dimension, the key issue of when spending cuts would occur dominated the debates. There was less debate on which services would be cut, given a fair degree of consensus across the three British parties, thereby making the question of where the cuts would be imposed, both in terms of services and territories, less controversial than might otherwise have been the case.

Leaders and leadership

There was even more focus on the party leaders in this election than in the past. However, this was complicated in Scotland, where Alex Salmond, the SNP's leader, is First Minister of the Scottish Government and was standing down as an MP. Angus Robertson, leader of the SNP group at Westminster, is hardly a household name in Scotland. A further complication was that Gordon Brown is a Scot and Scottish MP. Given that the Conservatives have suffered from an image as an anti-Scottish or at least English party, David Cameron's leadership might have been seen by many Scots as epitomising an upper class Englishman. Nick Clegg might also have been expected to suffer from a similar image problem north of the border given his background, not least compared with Charles Kennedy who had led the Liberal Democrats in 2005. However, polls suggest that Cameron and Clegg were more popular than their respective parties in Scotland, a situation that had also occurred when John Major had led the Conservatives.

Polls suggest that there was little evidence of a 'Cameron bounce' since his election as Conservative leader in December 2005 though considerable evidence of a Clegg effect after the first Prime Ministerial debate and a persistent positive Brown effect in Scotland. In February 2010, Clegg's ratings were low compared with the other party leaders though this was probably due to his low profile. The Prime Ministerial debates gave him a platform that raised his profile and ensured that his personal ratings soared (see Table 5) but it had far less impact on his party's support. As we saw earlier, Scottish Liberal Democrat support at the time of the third Prime Ministerial debate (29 April) was only around the same level that the party had won in 2005. There was also evidence that Alex Salmond polled well, but again this appears to have had little impact. In this case, the electorate may have decided that 2010 was not the year in which their judgment of the First Minister was relevant. Though David Cameron's poll ratings improved during the election in Scotland, his net ratings remained negative. Gordon Brown's ratings proved the mirror of Cameron's in Scotland but also mirrored his ratings in England. While a poll taken at the end of April showed Brown to have a net positive rating of 7 points, his ratings across Britain in a poll conducted around the same time showed a net negative rating of 19 points. Labour in Scotland was keen to make much of Gordon Brown's Scottish roots. As Douglas Alexander said during the campaign, 'I think people are proud of having a Scottish Prime Minister who knows where he is from and where he wants to take the country'.[14] This was a view given prominence in Labour-supporting media north of the border where there was often a backlash against harsh criticism of the Prime Minister from other media outlets.

5. Leaders' ratings in Scotland

Leader	Total		Date	Sample	Polling Firm
	Good	Bad			
Gordon Brown	43	35	24–26 Feb	1002	YouGov
Alex Salmond	36	38			
David Cameron	28	33			
Nick Clegg	26	23			
Gordon Brown	45	38	28–30 April (last election debate)	1628	YouGov
Alex Salmond	39	34			
David Cameron	32	35			
Nick Clegg	55	14			

Change under the surface

The extent of Labour's success in 2010 was evident in its ability to hold onto or increase its share of the vote across Scotland. Labour's share of the vote fell in only five Labour-held constituencies compared with 2005: Livingston, where Jim Devine, the former Labour MP, had been charged with expenses related crimes; Aberdeen South, a Liberal Democrat target seat; Dunfermline and West Fife, won by the Liberal Democrats at a by-election in 2006; Falkirk, where a former Labour MP came out in support of the SNP candidate; and Airdrie and Shotts, where former Home Secretary John Reid was standing down and there had been controversy surrounding proposals for an all-women short-list of Labour candidates. However, Labour's vote held up well in seats that might have been expected to record a significant swing against the party, including many marginal seats. Incumbents, who would have been likely to damage Labour due to embarrassing expenses claims, personal issues and peccadilloes were replaced by new candidates who staved off swings against the party.

Though no seats changed hands, other changes are discernible. As the Liberal Democrats slipped back, their position as second party in share of the vote across Scotland was lost to the SNP, while they held onto second place in number of seats. The SNP moved into second place in ten more seats, whereas Labour and the Conservatives moved into second place in one more seat each. These movements were all achieved at the expense of the Liberal Democrats except in Edinburgh West, held by the Liberal Democrats, where Labour moved ahead of the Conservatives to become second party. In only two of these seats—Edinburgh West and Gordon—is the new second party within less than 10% of the winning party, so that these changes are unlikely to affect who wins at the next election. The SNP has moved into second place in 29 constituencies and its share of the vote rose in 46 of Scotland's 59 constituencies, but it remains well behind Labour and still has a long way to go to have a chance of gaining seats. The Conservatives are in second place in 15 seats with Labour in second in 9 and Liberal Democrats in only 6.

While the SNP may have become the second party, its best hope of gaining an additional seat is Scotland's twelfth most marginal seat and would require a swing of 5.1%, even larger than was required after 2005. The Liberal Democrats are in second place in the two most marginal seats in Scotland, both in Edinburgh, but Labour is in second in the next two most marginal seats (Table 6). The picture that emerges is that Labour retains its pre-eminent position while the other three parties fight it out to become challenger. Labour not only holds 41 seats but does so comfortably. It would take a uniform swing of 10.8% and the loss of former Scottish Secretary Jim Murphy's Renfrewshire East seat before Labour lost its overall majority of seats in Scotland. The SNP would require a uniform swing of almost 10% to get into double figures in number of MPs and a uniform swing of just under 20% to reach the additional 20, the objective Alex Salmond set his party before 2005. The Conservatives would require a swing slightly less than this to get into double figures. Labour's continued dominance of Westminster elections in Scotland looks as assured as can be imagined.

A Catenaccio game

The 2010 election in Scotland appears to have been a defensive Catenaccio game though that may only be a retrospective impression rather than a strategy adopted by all or any party. At the Scotland-wide level, Labour was able to easily hold its own, but this also applied at individual constituency level. At the outset of the campaign, it was widely anticipated that the SNP would improve on its performance in 2005 and that a British-wide Conservative revival would pay dividends in Scotland. Labour and the Liberal Democrats were anticipated to be the main defenders.

The Scotland-wide pattern was evident in individual constituencies, with Labour's vote share up in 44 seats, the SNP's in 46, the Conservatives in 43 and Liberal Democrats in only 9 seats. Under the surface, however, there were some intriguing results and a different pattern is evident in target seats. The general tendency was that the incumbent party improved its position regardless of which party was challenging, with the exception of the Liberal Democrats who did less well in all but three seats where they were incumbents though, crucially, two of the three were their most marginal seats. In large measure, this is explained by the party's general decline, with its best chance of holding onto its share of the vote found in seats in which it was incumbent. David Mundell, the sole Tory incumbent, saw his majority increase. The SNP majority decreased in two of its six seats, the neighbouring seats of Moray and Banff & Buchan, the latter the seat vacated by Scottish First Minister Alex Salmond, where the

6. Constituencies by marginality

Rank 2005	Rank 2010	Constituency	Winning Party	Second place 2005	Swing 2005	Second place 2010	Swing 2010
1	1	Edinburgh South	Lab	Lib	0.47	Lib	0.36
2	3	Dundee East	SNP	Lab	0.48	Lab	2.245
3	12	Ochil and South Perthshire	Lab	SNP	0.74	SNP	5.14
4	6	Aberdeen South	Lab	Lib	1.62	Lib	4.07
5	10	Perth and North Perthshire	SNP	Con	1.66	Con	4.535
6	11	Dumfriesshire, Clydesdale and Tweeddale	Con	Lab	1.95	Lab	4.57
7	9	Angus	SNP	Con	2.10	Con	4.325
8	2	Edinburgh North and Leith	Lab	Lib	2.52	Lib	1.82
9	20	Dumfries and Galloway	Lab	Con	2.87	Con	7.135
10	4	Dunbartonshire East	Lib	Lab	4.35	Lab	2.28
11	25	Inverness, Nairn, Badenoch and Strathspey	Lib	Lab	4.69	Lab	9.31
12	16	Na h-Eileanan an Iar	SNP	Lab	5.21	Lab	6.405
13	23	Stirling	Lab	Con	5.46	Con	8.93
14	17	Glasgow North	Lab	Lib	5.98	Lib	6.58
15	15	Berwickshire, Roxburgh and Selkirk	Lib	Con	6.50	Con	5.785
16	5	Argyll and Bute	Lib	Con	6.52	Con	3.79
17	27	Renfrewshire East	Lab	Con	7.02	Con	10.175
18	26	Dundee West	Lab	SNP	7.28	SNP	9.805
19	18	Moray	SNP	Con	7.32	Con	6.82
20	33	Edinburgh East	Lab	Lib	7.81	SNP	11.515
21	24	Edinburgh South West	Lab	Con	8.24	Con	9.29
22	35	East Lothian	Lab	Lib	8.32	Con	12.47
23	7	Aberdeenshire West and Kincardine	Lib	Con	8.97	Con	4.08
24	30	Aberdeen North	Lab	Lib	9.27	SNP	11.09
25	36	Midlothian	Lab	Lib	9.63	SNP	13.185
26	37	Kilmarnock and Loudoun	Lab	SNP	9.80	SNP	13.295
27	29	Ayr, Carrick and Cumnock	Lab	Con	11.10	Con	10.8

28	34	Linlithgow and East Falkirk	Lab	SNP	12.07	SNP	12.2
29	38	Ayrshire Central	Lab	Con	12.16	Con	13.675
30	19	Gordon	Lib	Lab	12.41	SNP	6.915
31	28	Ayrshire North and Arran	Lab	Con	12.78	SNP	10.725
32	45	Paisley and Renfrewshire North	Lab	SNP	13.45	SNP	17.48
33	14	Dunfermline and West Fife	Lab	Lib	13.64	Lib	5.585
34	40	Lanark and Hamilton East	Lab	Lib	13.70	SNP	14.475
35	41	Glasgow South	Lab	Lib	14.09	SNP	15.785
36	50	Glenrothes	Lab	SNP	14.27	SNP	20.305
37	21	Falkirk	Lab	SNP	14.73	SNP	7.72
38	22	Caithness, Sutherland and Easter Ross	Lib	Lab	14.76	Lab	8.39
39	31	Livingston	Lab	SNP	14.77	SNP	11.265
40	42	Cumbernauld, Kilsyth and Kirkintilloch East	Lab	SNP	14.79	SNP	16.715
41	48	Glasgow North West	Lab	Lib	14.82	Lib	19.125
42	8	Edinburgh West	Lib	Con	15.02	Lab	4.095
43	51	Dunbartonshire West	Lab	SNP	15.09	SNP	20.595
44	43	Glasgow Central	Lab	Lib	15.21	SNP	17.25
45	39	East Kilbride, Strathaven and Lesmahagow	Lab	SNP	15.42	SNP	14.235
46	49	Inverclyde	Lab	SNP	15.60	SNP	19.235
47	13	Banff and Buchan	SNP	Con	15.90	Con	5.235
48	32	Fife North East	Lib	Con	16.30	Con	11.295
49	52	Paisley and Renfrewshire South	Lab	Lib	17.47	SNP	20.77
50	59	Glasgow North East	Lab	SNP	17.83	SNP	27.105
51	54	Rutherglen and Hamilton West	Lab	Lib	18.62	SNP	22.35
52	58	Orkney and Shetland	Lib	Lab	18.68	Lab	25.66
53	53	Motherwell and Wishaw	Lab	SNP	20.51	SNP	21.475
54	44	Airdrie and Shotts	Lab	SNP	21.24	SNP	17.305
55	57	Kirkcaldy and Cowdenbeath	Lab	SNP	21.79	SNP	25.12
56	46	Glasgow East	Lab	SNP	21.83	Lab	18.405
57	47	Ross, Skye and Lochaber	Lib	Lab	21.90	Lab	18.76
58	55	Glasgow South West	Lab	SNP	22.43	SNP	23.08
59	56	Coatbridge, Chryston and Bellshill	Lab	SNP	25.45	SNP	24.875

Parties in shading indicate changes in second place between 2005 and 2010.

7. Incumbents and challengers 2005–2010

Challenger/incumbent swing required to win/ lose % following 2005	Party challenging/incumbent (N) and change in swing 2005–2010			
	Labour (N)	SNP (N)	LibDem (N)	Cons (N)
Challenger				
0–4.99	−1.74 (4)	−4.4 (1)	−0.5 (3)	−2.8 (4)
5–9.99	−1.95 (5)	−3 (2)	−4.1 (12)	−0.4 (10)
10–19.99%	3.4 (8)	0 (39)	−3.5 (26)	0.2 (25)
20+	3.1 (1)	1.5 (11)	3.1 (7)	−1 (19)
Incumbent				
0–4.99	2.1 (5)	1.8 (1)	1.3 (2)	2.6 (1)
5–9.99	2.8 (10)	1.5 (4)	−2.8 (3)	(0)
10–19.99	1.3 (20)	−10.7 (1)	−4.2 (5)	(0)
20+	−0.5 (6)	(0)	−4.2 (5)	(0)
N	59	59	59	59

Conservative candidate was a local television celebrity. Banff & Buchan remains fairly solid SNP territory, but there was a swing to the Conservatives of 10.7%. But in each of its other four seats, the SNP increased its share of the vote.

In Table 7, we have classified seats according to the swing required to win or lose. In some cases, the party that is in third place may be better placed to win than one in second place if, for example, there is evidence of a national swing in favour of the third party while the party in second place is falling back. The top row indicates the average swing achieved in seats by each of the parties where less than 5% was required to win following the 2005 result. There was one seat, Ochil and South Perthshire, in which the SNP was challenging Labour and vulnerable to under a 5% swing following 2005. In that seat, there was a swing of 4.4% to Labour. There was also only one seat, Dundee East, in which the SNP was incumbent and vulnerable to a swing of less than 5% following 2005. In 2010, there was a swing to the SNP of 1.8%. The picture that emerges is of incumbents fighting off challenges and generally improving their position across the board. One consequence is that the Conservatives have an even greater challenge to win more seats than after 2005. After that election, 2 of the top 50 Conservative targets were in Scotland, requiring swings of 1.7 and 2.1%, but after 2010 the Conservatives' best prospect in Scotland is number 60, requiring a swing of 3.8%.

There is no obvious reason why this should have happened in Scotland. One possible explanation is that tactical voting generally favoured incumbency rather than favoured or undermined any particular party. It is, however, unclear why that should be the case unless the incumbent was a particularly well-known and appealing figure. However, in some cases, the incumbent candidate stood down and it was the incumbent party that was the beneficiary. In Edinburgh South, Labour held the seat with a new candidate against a strong challenge from the Liberal Democrats. The former Labour MP stood down following revelations about his private life. It would appear that replacing candidates who might have damaged the party's performance, due to personal peccadilloes or embarrassing expense claims, proved a successful strategy.

Implications of the result for Government

The coalition has given the governing parties one more Scottish MP than the Conservatives had in 1992 when they last won an election (though 20% of seats rather than 15% due to fewer Scottish seats than 18 years before). Although there is nothing unconstitutional in the Conservatives governing with only one Scottish seat, issues of legitimacy undermined Conservatives in the 1980s and 1990s and may well have returned had they attempted to govern without Liberal Democrat support.[15] The Conservatives were committed to keeping the Scotland Office while the Liberal Democrats wanted it scrapped. Both were committed to the implementation of the Calman Report and David Cameron had emphasised his 'respect agenda' by which he meant that Conservative Government would respect the devolved institutions. The agreement reached between the coalition partners and issued five days after the election included a commitment to implement Calman. Danny Alexander, Scottish Liberal Democrat MP and chief of staff to Nick Clegg, became Secretary of State for Scotland. Alexander became Chief Secretary to the Treasury following David Laws resignation and was replaced in his briefly-held job by Michael Moore, another Liberal Democrat MP. The Tories' sole Scottish MP became Under Secretary of State, having served as Shadow Scottish Secretary. The Liberal Democrats appeared to offer the Conservatives cover in governing Scotland.

As Margaret Thatcher hinted, the Conservative problem in Scotland was less to do with policies than with image. Governing with little support in Scotland created problems. Throughout the campaign and since David Cameron was elected leader, the Conservatives went to considerable lengths to convince voters that a Conservative Government would be sensitive to Scottish distinctiveness. Being in government affords the Conservatives an opportunity to demonstrate that they are sensitive to Scottish needs and aspirations, but the context of a major fiscal crisis and the need for cuts presents challenges, especially for a party about whom the electorate has deep suspicions. Coalition may limit accusations that they govern without a Scottish mandate, but also means that credit for popular policies will have to be shared with or may simply be accredited to the Liberal Democrats.

Implications of the result for 2011

After the SNP's victory in 2007, that party's hierarchy misread its increase in support as evidence that it would make a significant breakthrough at the UK general election. This misreading had been encouraged by the result of the Glasgow East by-election two months after the Holyrood elections in 2007, when the SNP vote rose by 26% and gave the Nationalists their first by-election victory at Westminster in over a decade. However, the Glenrothes by-election in November 2008 was a major setback for the SNP. In a seat that the SNP had high hopes of winning, having won the nearest equivalent seat in Holyrood 18 months before, the result was a major fillip for Gordon Brown, whose own seat lay adjacent to Glenrothes. In November 2009, Labour easily held another by-election, in Glasgow North East, after Michael Martin, former Labour MP and Speaker of the House of Commons, resigned. The Labour candidate won 59% of the vote and the SNP managed to win only 20%, increasing its share of the vote by only 2.3%. The SNP continued to do well in polls of Holyrood voting intentions, but it was struggling to have an equivalent impact on Westminster voting intentions.

However, until a few months before the 2010 election, polls suggested that the SNP would increase its share of the vote significantly, if struggle to translate this into seats given how far behind it was in 2005. But the polls and profile of the SNP Government in Edinburgh contributed to a sense that the Nationalists would advance. The SNP failed to take account of accumulating evidence that the Scottish electorate distinguishes its electoral preferences in Holyrood and Westminster elections. Following the 2010 election, Labour may be tempted to make the same mistake and assume that its success in a Westminster election will translate into easy success in the Holyrood elections in 2011.

During the course of the election, some pollsters not only asked Scottish electors how they would vote on May 6th pending but also how they would vote in a Holyrood election. The context in which the polling took place seems likely to favour Labour over the SNP. Nonetheless, the SNP could take comfort from the Holyrood preferences expressed in these polls. Labour's 20-point lead over the SNP almost disappeared in both constituency and list voting intentions. A YouGov poll that showed Labour having a 15-point lead over the SNP a few days before election day found the SNP three points ahead of Labour in constituency preferences for Holyrood and Labour one point ahead of the SNP in the Holyrood regional vote.[16] Other polls taken during the election showed similar results.

While there is evidence that voters distinguish between Westminster and Holyrood elections, the outcome of Westminster elections is likely to have a greater impact on Holyrood elections more than vice versa.

The UK election result means that Labour are able to contest next year's Scottish elections as an unambiguous opposition party, without having to defend a record of public spending cuts that would have been near inevitable had Labour won the UK election. Labour's task of linking the SNP in government in Holyrood with the Conservatives (and Liberal Democrats) in government in London is made easier simply because each of Labour's opponents are in government and having to make unpopular decisions. Scottish Labour has also had a major morale boost and while the party lost the election in 2010 across Britain, it performed better than many commentators had expected and it did very well in Scotland. Consequently, it is less likely to suffer from the insularity that often comes with defeat.

Conclusion

The 2010 election was remarkable in Scotland in that no seats changed hands while the Conservatives gained 90 seats in England and 5 in Wales. Labour's position strengthened. Part of the explanation lies in the enduring unpopularity of the Conservatives in Scotland. Voters may well have supported Labour so strongly as a consequence of the real prospect of a Conservative Government. The SNP looked less relevant in a contest that was more focused on the main Westminster parties than in recent years. The paradox of a more distinctively Scottish result following a more uniformly British campaign might therefore be explained by the hostility to the Conservatives north of the border.

The four-party system at Holyrood looks more like a one and three party system at Westminster. Scottish Labour is in the enviable position of having no clear challenger at Westminster. Despite a poor election, the Liberal Democrats held onto all their seats and remain challengers in a few key marginals. The Conservatives remain the outsiders—fourth in terms of share of the vote and number of seats. The key difference from previous occasions when a Conservative Prime Minister has been in power is that there is a coalition in government at Westminster and the key Scottish Ministerial office is held by a Liberal Democrat. Other differences are the existence of a Scottish Parliament and the difficult economic and fiscal contexts. However, the real test of David Cameron's premiership from a Scottish perspective is what his respect agenda amounts to in practice and how it is perceived north of the border. Cameron returned his party to the centre ground across Britain, detoxifying the brand. A more deep-rooted toxic brand of Conservatism in Scotland remains. The Prime Minister's challenge lies in altering that brand in the more challenging context of government.

1   D. Torrance, *We in Scotland: Thatcherism in a cold climate*, Birlinn, 2009, p. 39.
2   M. Thatcher, *The Downing Street Years*, HarperCollins, 1993, pp. 618, 623.

3   M. Ashcroft, *Smell the Coffee: a Wake-up Call for the Conservative Party*, Michael Ashcroft, 2005: 52.

4   Technically, one seat changed hands compared with 2005.   Glasgow North East had been the Speaker's seat in 2005 and was won by Labour in 2010, but this was a traditionally safe Labour seat and Michael Martin, the former Speaker, had been a Labour MP.

5   Tory Scottish target seats were Dumfriesshire, Clydesdale and Tweeddale; West Aberdeenshire and Kincardine; Angus; Argyll and Bute; Berwickshire, Roxburgh and Selkirk; Dumfries and Galloway; Edinburgh South; Edinburgh South West; Perth and North Perthshire; East Renfrewshire; and Stirling. http://news.scotsman.com/politics/SNP-39irrelevant39-at-Westminster.5907453.jp?

6   *Scotsman*, 21 April 2008.

7   William Miller, *The End of British Politics?* Clarendon Press, 1981, p. 254.

8   http://news.bbc.co.uk/1/shared/bsp/hi/pdfs/16_04_10_firstdebate.pdf, p. 6.

9   http://www.scotcourts.gov.uk/opinions/2010CSOH56.html.

10   Ibid.

11   Ibid.

12   *A future fair for all*, Scottish Labour Manifesto 2010, Scottish Labour Party, 2010: 3:3.

13   http://www.commissiononscottishdevolution.org.uk/.

14   BBC News, 24 April 2010.

15   J. Mitchell, 'The Unfinished Business of Devolution', *Political Quarterly*, 77, 2007, 465–74.

16   http://www.today.yougov.co.uk/sites/today.yougov.co.uk/files/YG-Archives-Pol-ScottishScotsman-100504.pdf.

JONATHAN BRADBURY

Wales and the 2010 General Election

Party electoral performance in Wales has long been distinctive from broader patterns in Great Britain. Labour dominance in the post-Second World War period was such as to lead to discussion of Wales in terms of Labour one-partyism rather than the two-party Conservative–Labour British-wide system.[1] Labour commonly polled over 40% of the vote in UK general elections and took a majority of the seats. In 1997 Labour won a crushing 54.7% of the votes and 34 of 40 seats. In contrast, in 1997 the Conservatives polled fewer than 20% of the votes and won no seats in Wales at all. The party system has been further differentiated by the development of Plaid Cymru (Party of Wales) as an electoral force. Plaid Cymru in the 1997 general election were nearly on a par with the Liberal Democrats in vote share and in winning four seats won more than both the Conservatives and Liberal Democrats in Wales. In recent memory the outlier election result was that of 1983, when Labour fell to 37.5% of the vote, the Conservatives polled 31% and won 14 seats and the Liberal–SDP alliance won 23.2% of the vote. While Labour still held a narrow majority of the seats 1983 represented a vision of what Welsh politics could look like if Labour were weakened, the Conservatives were buoyed by British-wide success and third party politics had fresh momentum.

From 1997, of course, the Labour Party held office at the UK level for three terms for the first time in its history. Up to 2005 Labour did remarkably well in Wales in sustaining party representation despite being a governing party. In 2001 Labour's vote share was down on 1997 but they retained 34 seats. In 2005 Labour's vote share fell again and this time they lost five seats, three of which went to the Conservatives, one to the Liberal Democrats and one to an independent candidate in Blaenau Gwent. Yet, the other parties were not able to land serious blows on Labour. Plaid Cymru also lost vote share in 2005 and surprisingly lost Ceredigion to the Liberal Democrats. Both

doi:10.1093/pa/gsq029

the Conservatives and Liberal Democrats increased their vote share in 2005, but won only seats that were very marginal from Labour. Labour's superiority in Welsh representation, with still over 40% of the vote and 29 of 40 seats, was basically retained.[2] The question in 2010 was whether Labour dominance, though much reduced from the high watermark of 1997, could now withstand the long period in which the party under Gordon Brown as Prime Minister had trailed heavily in the polls. Would Wales see a result akin to the nadir of 1983 and correspondingly a breakthrough for multi-party politics? How would the other parties organise to maximise their performance in Wales; and correspondingly, what strategies would the Labour Party pursue to defend its electoral fortress?

An added dimension in the analysis of the UK general election in Wales is political devolution. The National Assembly for Wales, created in 1999, has now seen three sets of elections, in which the operation of a mixed member electoral system has resulted in patterns of differential voting. Labour has done significantly worse than in UK elections and Plaid Cymru significantly better, resulting in a hung Assembly throughout its short history, except for Labour's technical majority between 2003 and 2005.[3] Since 2007 Labour and Plaid Cymru have formed the Welsh Assembly Government (WAG) on the basis of their One Wales coalition agreement. The key question here was what implications the 2010 election might have for these patterns of multi-level electoral politics.

Devolution has also raised challenges for party strategies at general elections. Key public services such as health and education are devolved issues and therefore the setting of priorities in these areas is principally a matter for the National Assembly for Wales. Equally, British-wide party strategies have been characterised by some differentiation at the Welsh level. For example, Labour in Wales has adopted a clear red water position to differentiate its socialist credentials from the more centrist politics of British New Labour.[4] Nevertheless, the British-wide parties fought both the 2001 and 2005 UK general elections in Wales largely as devolution-blind events; with campaign strategies ignoring whether policy issues were devolved or not, as well as the differences between their British and Welsh party units. The question in 2010 was whether this would continue to be the case. In addition, of course, UK general elections have been significant for revealing the commitment of British-wide party units to the development of Welsh devolution more broadly. This was of particular relevance in 2010 as at the devolved level all of the parties had supported the 2009 All Wales Convention report in favour of holding a referendum on further powers for the Assembly.[5] The Holtham Commission also suggested in 2009–2010 that the base level of UK Government funding to the Assembly should be protected and the method for funding distribution should be reformed to make it more based on needs.[6]

To examine these issues this article addresses first the election results and party performance in the 2010 election, and how they can be assessed in terms of both recent UK and multi-level politics. Then secondly, it examines party strategies, assessing approaches to policy debate and campaigning and how each took account of devolution. The conclusion addresses the implications of the results in 2010 for future party fortunes and strategies in the context of both UK and devolved Welsh politics.

Election results and party performance

In 2010 Labour did indeed see a marked decline by 6.5% in their vote share to 36.2% across Wales, with reduced vote shares in 39 of 40 constituencies (see Table 1). The party lost four seats, all to the Conservatives: Cardiff North, Vale of Glamorgan, Carmarthen West and Pembrokeshire South and the newly created seat of Aberconwy. The main excitement occurred in Cardiff North where, after a recount, the Conservative majority was 194 and the former MEP, Jonathan Evans ousted Julie Morgan. At the same time though Labour won Blaenau Gwent, re-establishing a majority of over 10,000, meaning that Labour lost a net three seats on 2005. Plaid Cymru also again marginally lost ground as their vote share fell by 1.3%. They won with reduced majorities in Meirionnydd and Carmarthen East and Dinefwr; the latter a seat where the colourful Adam Price had stood down ahead of an expected career in the Assembly. Nevertheless, Plaid Cymru retained overall its three-seat share won in 2005. The Liberal Democrats did actually gain in their share of the vote across Wales by 1.7%. Nevertheless, in terms of seats they were also losers. While they were delighted to consolidate their hold on Ceredigion, they lost Montgomeryshire. The flamboyant MP, Lembit Opik, sitting on a majority of over 7000, lost to Glyn Davies, a local farmer and former Conservative list member in the National Assembly. They held on to their other two seats in Brecon and Radnorshire and Cardiff Central with static or slightly reduced majorities. In this context, the only clear winners in the election in Wales were the Conservatives. They increased their share of the vote across Wales by 4.7%, as well as in every constituency except for Ceredigion, Merthyr Tydfil and Newport East. They increased their seat haul by five, from three to eight, and the four victories over Labour and one over the Liberal Democrats enabled them to become clearly Wales' second party.

In evaluating the significance of these results, it is clear that the result was in very important ways a bad one for the Labour Party. Labour's vote share was worse than 1983, and represented the party's worst vote share performance in a UK election in Wales since 1918. Such a result underlines Labour's long-term vulnerability as a party able to represent both class and nation in Wales. The strains of being in office had seen a decline in the party's vote share in Wales of 18.5%

1. UK general election in Wales, 1979–2010

	Conservative	Labour	Liberal Democrats (formerly Lib and Lib–SDP)	Plaid Cymru	Others
1979					
Vote share (%)	32.2	47.0	10.6	8.1	2.2
Seats	11	21	1	2	1
1983					
Vote share (%)	31.0	37.5	23.2	7.8	0.4
Seats	14	20	2	2	0
1987					
Vote share (%)	29.5	45.1	17.9	7.3	0.2
Seats	8	24	3	3	0
1992					
Vote share (%)	28.6	49.5	12.4	8.8	0.7
Seats	6	27	1	4	0
1997					
Vote share (%)	19.6	54.7	12.4	9.9	3.4
Seats	0	34	2	4	0
2001					
Vote share (%)	21.0	48.6	13.8	14.3	2.3
Seats	0	34	2	4	0
2005					
Vote share (%)	21.4	42.7	18.4	12.6	4.9
Seats	3	29	4	3	1
2010					
Vote share (%)	26.1	36.2	20.1	11.3	6.2
Seats	8	26	3	3	0

Turnout: 1979, 79.4%; 1983, 76.1%; 1987, 78.9%; 1992, 79.7%; 1997, 73.6%; 2001, 60.6%; 2005, 62.4%; 2010, 64.9%.

between the great optimism of 1997 and the sense of decline and defeat in the air in 2010. Nevertheless, in many ways the Labour Party in Wales judged the election a relative success. Labour had suffered a string of electoral reverses: in the 2007 Assembly election the party had won only 32.2% on the constituency vote (and just 29.6% on the list vote); at the 2008 local elections Labour lost control in a number of councils and in the 2009 European elections the Conservatives had actually topped the poll. Given this very difficult backdrop the party held up remarkably well on seat share in still winning 26 of 40 seats.

Labour lost only its most marginal seats; in all of the seats that Labour lost to the Conservatives they were defending a real or notional majority of between only 2.53 and 5.32%. Labour also held seats they were expected to lose to the Liberal Democrats: winning in Swansea West by 504 votes and Newport East by 1650. Labour clearly went to the edge of the abyss in this election: winning 10 of their 26 seats with a majority of less than 3000 votes. But despite reduced majorities right across Wales, Labour had a sense of holding on in many seats that they might have lost. They even had the bonus of winning back Blaenau

Gwent. Overall, despite the historic collapse in overall vote share akin to the disaster of 1983, Labour retained a share of the Welsh seats comparable to the performances achieved in the more normal elections of 1987, 1992 and indeed even 1979. As in 2005 rather than Labour suffering catastrophic losses they lost only further seats on the outer edge of its electoral fortress. Labour retained a heavy dominance in its strongholds of South and North-East Wales.

A corresponding assessment of the other main parties is that 2010 again accentuated a trend while Labour was in office of them increasing their vote share. The Conservatives achieved their best performance since 1992 and the Liberal Democrats their best since the Liberal–SDP performance in 1983. Plaid Cymru still achieved their third best performance ever in terms of vote share in a UK election. Nevertheless, no party was able to decisively harness voter disillusionment with the Labour Party in terms of winning seats. Although they saw some progress, the Conservatives failed to breakthrough in a clutch of seats which on their most confident pre-election prognoses they might have won: seats such as Vale of Clwyd, Clwyd South and Delyn in the North, and Gower, Newport West and Bridgend in the South. All of these Labour had held with majorities of between 14 and 20% in 2005, but the Conservatives considered them potentially winnable. The Liberal Democrat majority of 10.18% in Brecon and Radnorshire had also been considered potentially vulnerable to a Tory win. During the campaign even seats such as Cardiff South and Cardiff West, where the Labour majorities in 2005 had been over 20%, were strongly contested. In Cardiff South, Alun Michael faced specific criticisms from his Liberal Democrat and Conservative opponents of his expenses record and, beyond his constituency, via his association with anti-hunting legislation. In Cardiff West, Labour Party canvassing indicated a move to the Conservatives early in the campaign which led to a high-profile media campaign by a clearly rattled Kevin Brennan.

Equally, the Liberal Democrats were utterly aghast at Lembit Opik losing Montgomeryshire, but also were disappointed at failing to progress in those constituencies where the local pavement politics strategy of winning council seats ahead of winning Westminster and/or Assembly constituency seats was perceived as due for success. This related most to Swansea West and Newport East, but it also underpinned a strong effort in Wrexham where the party had had significant successes in council elections in 2004 and 2008. Plaid Cymru in turn was thwarted in its attempts to re-take Ceredigion where the Liberal Democrats consolidated their hold on the seat by increasing their majority from 218 to over 8000. But Plaid Cymru was also further disappointed again not to take Ynys Mon, a seat held in the Assembly by the party's leader Ieuan Wyn Jones, from Labour. In other target seats they performed woefully. In Llanelli they came second to Labour trailing by nearly 5000 votes. In both Aberconwy and Carmarthen West and South Pembrokeshire the party came fourth.

Overall, in the context of a simple plurality electoral system the Labour Party was able, even in the adverse circumstances of 2010, to dig in and eke out victories in individual constituency contests to gain a seat share very much at the upper end of its expectations. Labour was able to achieve a remarkable efficiency in the distribution of its vote that outweighed its broader problem of declining overall vote share. To put this more critically, Labour dominance was sustained on the basis of an ever more stark disproportionality in its representation. Labour won 65% of the seats in Wales on 36.2% of the votes. Meanwhile, all the other main parties were deeply frustrated at near misses on expected seat hauls that would have put the Conservatives at least in to double figures, the Liberal Democrats up to around six seats and Plaid Cymru up to between four and seven. Instead of achieving decisive breaks into Labour's strong holds in the more densely populated southern and North-East belts, the other parties' representation was scattered. The Conservatives had seats in predominantly rural/ small town seats in the south, south-west, mid-Wales and north; the Liberal Democrats in heavily University-based seats in Cardiff and Ceredigion (Aberystwyth) as well as rural mid-Wales and Plaid Cymru in the Welsh-speaking North-West and South-West. The UK election map of Wales shifted slightly, but not at all decisively.

When one considers the 2010 general election result in terms of multi-level electoral politics, it again produced clear evidence of differential voting patterns between UK and Welsh elections. However, there were indications that the manner in which these patterns affect individual parties may be about to change, potentially again confirming Labour resilience. In comparing the 1997–1999, 2001–2003 and 2005–2007 elections, there was a relatively clear pattern of Plaid Cymru performing considerably better in Assembly elections, and Labour considerably better in Westminster elections (see Tables 1 and 2). The Liberal Democrats performed slightly better in Westminster elections, while the Conservatives received more or less similar vote shares at both levels. The 2010 general election resulted again in Plaid Cymru performing at around 10% below their Assembly vote share in Westminster elections, but on this occasion much of that vote share at the UK level was net taken by the Conservatives and to a lesser extent the Liberal Democrats.

From this point it is reasonable to hypothesise that with Labour now out of power at the UK level, the expected rise in the Plaid Cymru vote at the next Assembly elections in 2011 may correspondingly come more at the expense of the Conservatives and the Liberal Democrats than Labour. A second reasonable hypothesis is that Labour may also now be able to compete with Plaid Cymru to be the main beneficiary of multi-level voting at the expense of the Conservatives and Liberal

2. Distribution of votes and seats in National Assembly for Wales, 1999–2007

	Constituency		Regional lists		Total seats
	Vote share (%)	Seats won	Vote share (%)	Seats won	
1999					
Conservative	15.9	1	16.5	8	9
Labour	37.6	27	35.5	1	28
Liberal Democrats	13.5	3	12.5	3	6
Plaid Cymru	28.4	9	30.5	8	17
Others	4.7	0	5.1	0	0
2003					
Conservative	19.9	1	19.2	10	11
Labour	40.0	30	36.6	0	30
Liberal Democrats	14.1	3	12.7	3	6
Plaid Cymru	21.2	5	19.7	7	12
Others	4.8	1	11.8	0	1
2007					
Conservative	22.4	5	21.5	7	12
Labour	32.2	24	29.6	2	26
Liberal Democrats	14.8	3	11.7	3	6
Plaid Cymru	22.4	7	21.0	8	15
Others	8.3	1	16.2	0	1

Democrats as the UK governing parties. The data from a YouGov poll conducted in Wales immediately following the election appeared to confirm the potential for these hypotheses. When asked how they would vote if an Assembly election had been held in June 2010, 35.8% of voters chose Labour for their constituency vote (−0.4% on the 2010 UK general election), 17.3% Plaid Cymru (+ 6.0%), 19.3% Conservative (−6.8%), 15.7% Liberal Democrat (−4.4%) and 11.9% other parties (+5.7%).[7] This suggests that Plaid Cymru and others would benefit at the expense of the Conservatives and Liberal Democrats; and Labour could now at the very least bottom out in its vote share across the levels and indeed gain an improvement on its 2007 Assembly result. This points to Labour being again the largest party after the 2011 elections, but potentially a majority in the Assembly now also is a viable goal if the Plaid Cymru vote also slightly recedes at the Assembly level. The very fact of a Conservative–Liberal Democrat coalition at Westminster and the logic for both Plaid Cymru and Labour to campaign against it in the 2011 elections further limits the potential for an alternative set of coalition arrangements involving Plaid Cymru with the Conservatives and the Liberal Democrats.

When one turns to other features of the election results in Wales, there were a number of characteristics that were consistent with British-wide trends. Turnout at 64.9% was very close to, but slightly below, the UK average. The highest turnouts were seen in the existing Conservative seat of Monmouth (74.1%); the Conservative gains of Cardiff North (72.7%) and Carmarthen West and South

Pembrokeshire (70.4%); the Liberal Democrat hold of Brecon and Radnor (72.5%); and the Plaid Cymru hold of Carmarthen East and Dinefwr (72.56%). Meanwhile the safe Labour seat of Swansea East once again had the lowest turnout, this time of 54.6%. The average swing from Labour to Conservative in Wales was 5.6%, compared with the UK average of 5%. But patterns of turnout generally confirmed the British-wide experience that many more Conservative votes than Labour votes are wasted in their parties' respective safe seats and that it takes more votes to get a Conservative elected. Overall, the election saw a 27.5% turnover in MPs; among the experienced Labour MPs standing down were Kim Howells in Pontypridd and Don Touhig in Torfaen, as well as former father of the house, Alun Williams in Swansea West. The number of women MPs went down one to seven (17.5%), basic continuity in representation being principally the product of Labour's continued readiness to use all women shortlists. Perhaps most distinctive in terms of issues of descriptive representation was the fact that even though black and ethnic minorities constitute a rising section of the Welsh population there was still no MP drawn from their ranks elected in Wales in 2010.

However, a novel feature of the election, judged in terms of Wales's long-term electoral patterns, is the gradual rise in the vote for others. This was below 1% until the 1997 election, but since then other parties have gained a foothold in Welsh electoral politics, collectively amassing 11.8% in the 2007 Assembly constituency vote and 16.2% in the regional list vote, and in this 2010 UK general election it crept up to 6.2% of the vote. This includes the emergence of the UK Independence Party (UKIP), which took 2.4% of the vote, and the British National Party (BNP), which achieved 1.6%. In the vast majority of seats in Wales in the 2010 election the four main parties took the first four places, but in 19 seats UKIP came fifth and in 14 the BNP came fifth, generally amassing around 1000 votes each time. The BNP beat Plaid Cymru in Newport East to come fourth, and in Newport West both the BNP and UKIP beat Plaid Cymru to come fourth and fifth respectively.

This vote reflects one aspect of a continued British identity politics in Wales. It is still the case that if forced to make a choice around one-third of people would say they were British rather than Welsh. Equally, there is still a reasonably significant minority of people of between 15 and 20% who would rather not have devolution. More specifically, it represents some support for an explicit politics that focuses on concerns about immigration and/or European integration.[8] This support for parties that could be generally defined as British nationalist is not yet of great significance and should not be seen as anything like on a par with the position of Plaid Cymru, but it does indicate that Welsh voters are at least joining in the trend seen in England towards giving a platform for UKIP and the BNP to express

British nationalist opinion in challenging the three main British-wide parties.

At the same time though, the more immediate challenge from independent and People's Voice candidates in the South Wales valleys, who composed most of the rest of the others, appears to have receded. This movement emerged during the early 2000s from a politics that was of the labour movement, but not of the Labour Party, hostile to Labour's apparent drift towards centralisation. Independents in Wales in this election still took 1.7% of the vote. However, Dai Davies' capture of Blaenau Gwent was reversed, and independents in Rhondda, Merthyr and Islwyn managed no better than fourth place. In this important respect, therefore, fragmentation of the party system was contained. It reflected a broader truth concerning the election in Wales that while much of what happened suggested a politics in flux, underlying continuities in Welsh electoral politics remained strong, and at the root of that was the continued pull of and support for Labour power.

Party strategies and the election campaign

Given the backdrop of election results and opinion poll returns since 2007, it is not surprising that the campaign in Wales in this election was framed differently from previous ones in 2001 and 2005. In practice, the campaign developed on a novel basis for two reasons. First, in 2001 and 2005 the expectation had been that Labour would win and so the campaign debate developed as a Labour versus the rest battle. In 2010 the assumption was that the Conservatives were ahead across the UK; Labour this time was very much fighting a rearguard action in Wales as elsewhere. Second, the British leadership debates, which were accompanied by televised Welsh leadership debates, also stimulated a major surge for the Liberal Democrats in the opinion polls, which was felt also in Wales. A YouGov poll on 19 April put the Liberal Democrats in Wales on 29%, just 4% behind Labour on 33% and ahead of the Conservatives on 23% and Plaid Cymru on 9%.[9] Both the Conservatives and the Liberal Democrats were felt to be on the ascendant. Plaid Cymru, excluded from the British-wide leadership debates, felt unfairly marginalised, but behaved all the more as the occupier of the high moral ground as a result of this repeatedly emphasised sleight. In contrast, Labour was very much on the back foot in seeking to combat the apparent rise in popularity of its rivals.

In this context, the Conservative Party campaigned in Wales with an air of a party seeking not to blow its UK-wide lead. The Welsh dimension to its campaign revolved around trying to detoxify the Conservatives as a perceived right-wing and anti-devolution party. Their Welsh manifesto pledged to end Labour's poverty of ambition for Wales, and made commitments to revive the Welsh economy by investing in the electrification of the rail link to South Wales, a universal broadband network and new jobs, focused on carbon capture industries. The party pledged to hold a referendum on further powers for the National Assembly for Wales.[10] Cheryl Gillan, the Conservative shadow secretary of state for Wales, also committed the party to working closely and co-operatively with the WAG; contrasting its open door approach with an alleged detached and remote relationship between UK Government and the WAG under Labour. At the same time though the Conservatives shied away from clarifying the nature of the referendum question on more powers and from giving support to reforming the system of central government finance of the Assembly, which may have given it more funding.

David Cameron himself launched the Welsh manifesto in Prestatyn in North Wales and the Party clearly had expectations of gaining a number of seats in Wales. No one knows exactly which seats had campaign assistance from the support given by Lord Ashcroft. But there were reports of extensive under the radar canvassing in Cardiff North and the Vale of Glamorgan. Further high-profile visits were made during the campaign by Cameron, George Osborne and Kenneth Clarke. The central messages of the British-wide campaign were re-iterated and always in response to specifically Wales-related questions Cameron sought to calm fears of any return to the type of Conservative approach to the governing of Wales associated with John Redwood's very Thatcherite tenure of the Welsh Office in 1992–1994, while decrying Labour's failures in Wales.

Meanwhile the Welsh Liberal Democrats, despite being the only territorially federal party in the UK, simply echoed the British leadership's promotion of fairness. The Welsh manifesto focused on the key aims of fair taxes, a fair chance for children, a fair economy and a fair way of dealing with cleaning up politics. It committed the party to increasing the budget for the National Assembly by £125 million.[11] Kirsty Williams, the leader of the party in the National Assembly, led the campaign in Wales, arguing strongly for the need to rebalance the economy. Nick Clegg made several campaign visits, stressing how Labour had shamefully let Wales down and that disillusioned progressive voters should not move to Plaid Cymru, which he dismissed as an 'irrelevant, two-bit party'.[12]

Plaid Cymru had perhaps the most distinctive platform for campaigning in the election. Having joined forces with the Scottish National Party (SNP), Plaid Cymru hoped for a hung Parliament at Westminster; in this context the two parties would act as Celtic champions of their countries interests to prevent them being treated unfairly by government cuts or economic reform. Plaid Cymru's manifesto specifically itemised seven concessions that it would seek in the context of a hung parliament, chief among which were the protection of the National Assembly budget, a rise in the basic state pension and improved care for armed forces veterans as well as the guarantee of their much cherished desire for a referendum on further devolution.[13]

Against these strategies for advancement, the Labour Party in Wales had a number of positive policy platforms. It laid out a vision in particular for bringing new jobs to Wales based on high-technology industries, green technologies and the digital economy. Labour also promised a fairer funding guarantee for the Assembly. Overwhelmingly though Labour positioned itself as seeking to stoutly defend the economic recovery, public sector jobs and services and the interests of Wales more generally from a Conservative Government.[14] Peter Hain, the secretary of State for Wales, sought to make a vote for the Labour Party the repository of all anti-Tory sentiment. He asked voters who might otherwise vote Green, Plaid Cymru or Liberal Democrat to lend their vote to the Labour candidate. This was a message that he repeated assiduously throughout the campaign. In the Sky News Welsh leaders debate he added some civility to this request by stating that if there was a hung parliament then Labour would work with other parties on a national recovery plan for the economy.[15] Labour drew up a list of key seats which they focused their resources on in an effort to minimise the losses, and campaigning was supported by a series of constituency visits by key party figures in Wales such as Neil Kinnock and leading cabinet ministers such as Alan Johnson.[16] In the run up to polling day, there were already signs of the Liberal Democrat bubble bursting and the Labour vote returning. A poll published on the weekend before the election put Labour on 37.5%, the Conservatives on 23.5%, the Liberal Democrats on 21.0% and Plaid Cymru on 10.8%.[17]

How effectively did each of the party's play their hands? The Conservatives undoubtedly suffered some presentational problems. In the first Sky News Welsh leaders debate on 18 April Cheryl Gillan appeared to talk as though Rhodri Morgan was still the First Minister of Wales, a fact gleefully seized upon by Peter Hain and widely reported in the Welsh media in the following days.[18] Gillan was duly replaced by Nick Bourne, the Conservative leader in the Assembly for the final BBC Welsh leaders' debate on 2 May and it was reported that she was regarded as 'one of four plodders in the shadow cabinet whose performance was not highly rated by the leader'.[19] But there were no further gaffes, and the electoral performance was greeted after the election with apparent calm and celebration.

In contrast, the post-mortem in the Liberal Democrats started as soon as the election was over. Lord Carlisle, who had originally won Montgomeryshire for the Liberals in 1983, called for the party's policies on immigration and nuclear defence to be reopened. In his view the party needed to reorganise itself internally to ditch policies that plainly were losing the party votes. Peter Black, a regional list Assembly Member in South Wales West, decried the over-confidence that had gripped the party. In his view Cleggmania had led to a belief that the party would win seats as a result of national appeal and therefore it widened its ambitions and spread its resources too thinly across seats. The result had shown that the party had got ahead of itself; it still needed to have a major focus on localist pavement politics campaigning, supported in a targeted way by national party resources, to gradually accrue seats.[20]

In certain respects Plaid Cymru could be held to not have done much wrong. Indeed in the Welsh television debates in which he was allowed to take part, Ieuan Wyn Jones was widely estimated to have been the most popular leader with the viewing audience. Ieuan Wyn Jones excused his party's performance more generally by the fact of being excluded from the British-wide televised debates. However, within the party there was open criticism after the election of the crudeness of the Celtic champions' policy and the complaint about exclusion from the UK leadership debates. Both policies made Plaid Cymru look anti-British in a UK election and therefore unlikely to amass support outside of their core strongly Welsh identifying constituency. There was a feeling that organisationally the campaign was not as well run as in the 2007 Assembly election, since which time there had been a change in the party's chief executive. Jonathan Edwards, the party's new MP in Carmarthen East, suggested that it had been a mistake to target national party resources on target seats, as it had been both unsuccessful and had led to a reduced Plaid Cymru majority in his own seat.[21]

Of all the parties, Labour came out of the campaign in the most upbeat mood in Wales. In some ways, as we have seen, it had no right to do so, given the historically low vote share. But relative to previous performances and expectations, party leaders were delighted to keep the number of seat losses so low. There was a widespread perception that Hain's request to anti-Conservative voters to vote tactically as well as a number of strong local campaign efforts had yielded results. Peter Hain responded to journalists that he had 'a sense that Labour has turned the corner in Wales'. Nevertheless, there was an acceptance that Labour had little alternative but to go into opposition at the UK level. Immediately after the election Rhodri Morgan, the former Labour First Minister, recalled the experience of trying to go into coalition in the WAG with the Welsh Liberal Democrats in 2007. He remembered that 'there was an anyone-but-Labour movement, led by Mike German, and an anyone-but-Conservative group, led by the new leader Kirsty Williams. That's what made it very difficult to do a deal with the Liberals and ... which is why we did a deal with Plaid'.[22] He was suitably prophetic about the calculations that led in the particular circumstances of 2010 to Labour at the British level choosing opposition rather than trying to stitch together a coalition with the Liberal Democrats. This was not though before, in recognising that Gordon Brown was in any case an obstacle to Liberal Democrat interest in a coalition, Morgan suggested that 'Gordon did the Scott of the

Antarctic thing...it might make it much easier if he threw himself on the barbed wire like Captain Oates'.[23]

In contesting the Welsh dimension of the election, the parties in Wales in some ways did campaign in a less devolution-blind spirit than in 2005. In part this was because the election was fought much less on specific issues to do with how any one party would develop services such as health or education with new initiatives, and much more on how parties would approach the general issue of public spending cuts and how this would feed through into grant settlements for the National Assembly. The televised leadership debates also made both the politicians and the public more conscious of what were devolved issues, as it was a requirement of the broadcaster to state when the three leaders were debating matters that in Scotland, Wales and/or Northern Ireland were devolved issues.

On the other hand, the dividing line between Westminster and Assembly issues remained very blurred. For example, Labour's focus on specific pledges to defend services such as Sure Start missed the fact that in Wales a similar though not identical programme went by the different name of Flying Start. The televised Welsh leaders' debates revealed that the parties also still paid little respect to the fact of devolution in deciding who to put forward as the leaders of their campaigns in Wales. Only the Labour Party consistently fielded their British-level figurehead in Peter Hain. Indeed, Carwyn Jones, Rhodri Morgan's successor as Welsh Labour leader, featured very little in the campaign. The Conservatives, as already revealed, started with their British-level shadow secretary of state, Cheryl Gillan, but switched to Assembly leader, Nick Bourne half way through. In the Liberal Democrats, leader of the party in the House of Commons, Roger Williams, was entirely kept in the background in favour of fielding the Assembly leader, Kirsty Williams. The same occurred with Plaid Cymru, with House of Commons leader, Elfyn Lloyd, making way for Ieuan Wyn Jones. The expediency of televisual impact and party power overrode the significance of whether a politician was actually standing in the election.

Overall, it is hard to ascribe causal linkages between campaign efforts and party results. But a focus on party strategies does reveal the manner in which the parties fought the election in Wales, what they expected and why they interpreted the result they got in the way that they did. In policy terms there were Welsh-specific strategies, not least in Welsh Labour's lend us your vote pitch to play on the particular animosity towards the Conservatives in Wales. There was also great care taken to indicate party positions in relation to the future constitutional development of the Assembly. But much of party campaign strategy took its cue in the British-wide parties from their British leaderships, and there was, for example, no discernible easing of competition between Labour and Plaid Cymru, despite the fact that they were in coalition in the WAG. In promoting what they considered to be their most attractive policies and fielding the politicians who they considered to be the most persuasive all the parties appeared entirely pragmatic in drawing either from the British-level or Welsh levels of the party. In territorial party politics as in all party politics, a key objective remains that of simply maximising the vote.

Conclusion

In the period before the 2010 general election, it was possible to predict that a transformation of the Welsh political landscape was about to unfold. National Assembly politics, with the usage of a mixed member proportional electoral system, had to some extent broken the mould of Labour one-partyism.[24] The month-long deliberations after the 2007 National Assembly elections in which Labour had to find and woo a coalition partner, ultimately Plaid Cymru, to stay in office exposed the vulnerability of the Labour Party. When the leaders of Plaid Cymru, the Conservatives and the Liberal Democrats sat together and offered the so-called rainbow coalition, Labour was reminded very starkly of the possibility of being removed from office. In the context of a UK general election analysts could very reasonably ponder whether 2010 might be the occasion when the mould was broken and the Conservative Party made a significant breakthrough. Plainly this did not happen. Labour went to the edge of the electoral abyss but it still dominated representation. The Conservatives increased their representation but they were not able to establish any clear mandate for change in respect of the governance of Wales. Nor did the Conservative–Liberal Democrat combined vote clear the 50% threshold, also undermining claims the parties might have had for setting a new agenda for the politics of Wales.

Overall, Welsh politics has been changed by the fact of Labour actually having been the government party at the UK level and because of devolution. Over the whole 13-year period 1997–2010, this gave Labour unprecedented levels of power to do things for Wales instead of simply representing the politics of a territorial heartland. But with power came vulnerabilities to criticism and opportunities for other parties to exploit disillusionment, and seize the values and aspirations of a changing political culture. To some extent party fortunes did change, reflected in the rise in support for Plaid Cymru in the National Assembly and for the Conservatives and the Liberal Democrats at a UK level. But arguably the other parties did not seize the opportunities fully, allowing Labour to maintain ascendancy.[25]

Meanwhile, Welsh Labour was far from complacent. Party insiders were well aware that whilst Labour's 2007 National Assembly election performance could be attributed in part to anti-Iraq war votes it should not hide them from the fact that the Welsh Labour campaign was strategically complacent and poorly run. There was an attempt to renew and broaden Welsh Labour's appeal beyond the purely core vote appeal of clear red water. This was somewhat arrested during the period in which Rhodri Morgan continued to be leader, but the election of Carwyn Jones in December 2009, provided a manifest opportunity for cautious modernisation.[26] The Conservative–Liberal Democrat coalition may go on to become very popular in Wales; Plaid Cymru may decisively challenge Labour as the party of Wales. Labour remain vulnerable. In 2010 the Labour Party survived when arguably it was there for the taking. But survive it did in political circumstances that are not likely to be as advantageous to its political opponents for some time. In the immediate aftermath of the 2010 election, it felt more like Labour's 13-year sojourn as a party of UK Government had stretched the elastic of popular Welsh support for Labour, but never broken it. It would be a brave person who suggested now that Labour's dominance in Wales was about to be broken any time soon.

1   I. MacAllister, 'The Dynamics of One-partyism', *Llafur: The Journal of Welsh Labour History*, 3, 1980, 79–89.

2   See J. Bradbury, 'Wales: The Second Post-devolution General Election', in A. Geddes and J. Tonge (eds), *Britain Decides, The UK General Election 2005*, Palgrave, 2005, pp. 113–27.

3   R. Scully and R. Wyn Jones, 'Devolution and Electoral Politics in Scotland and Wales', *Publius: The Journal of Federalism*, 36, 2006, 115–34.

4   J. Hopkin and J. Bradbury, 'British Statewide Parties and Multi-level Politics', *Publius: The Journal of Federalism*, 36, 2006, 135–52.

5   All Wales Convention, Report, Welsh Assembly Government, 2009.

6   Independent Commission on Funding and Finance for Wales, *Funding Devolved Government in Wales: Barnett and Beyond*, Welsh Assembly Government, 2009.

7   R. Wyn Jones and R. Scully, 'What Happened in the 2010 Election?' Wales Governance Centre, Cardiff University and Institute of Welsh Politics, Aberystwyth University, Briefing, 26 May 2010.

8   J. Bradbury and R. Andrews, 'State Devolution and National Identity: Continuity and Change in the Politics of Welshness and Britishness in Wales', *Parliamentary Affairs*, 63, 2010, 229–49.

9   *Western Mail*, 20 April 2010.

10 Welsh Conservatives, *Invitation to Join the Government of Britain*, Conservative Party, 2010.

11 Welsh Liberal Democrats, *Manifesto of Fairness for Wales*, Welsh Liberal Democrats, 2010.

12 *Western Mail*, 10 April 2010.

13 Plaid Cymru, *Think Different, Think Plaid*, Plaid Cymru, 2010.

14 Welsh Labour, *A Future Fair for All*, Welsh Labour, 2010.

15 *Western Mail*, 19 April 2010.

16 *Wales on Sunday*, 18 April 2010.

17 *Western Mail*, 1 May 2010.

18 *Western Mail*, 19 April 2010.

19 *Western Mail*, 4 May 2010.

20 *Western Mail*, 8 May 2010.

21 *Western Mail*, 8 May 2010.

22 *Western Mail*, 8 May 2010.

23 *Western Mail*, 8 May 2010.

24 R. Scully and R. Wyn Jones, 'The End of One-partyism? Party Politics in Wales in the Second Decade of Devolution', *Contemporary Wales*, 21, 2008, 207–17.

25 J. Bradbury, 'British Political Parties and Devolution: Adapting to Multi-level Politics in Scotland and Wales', in D. Hough and C. Jeffery (eds), *Devolution and Electoral Politics*, Manchester University Press, 2006, pp. 214–47; J. Bradbury, 'Devolution in Wales', in J. Bradbury (ed.), *Devolution, Regionalism and Regional Development: The UK Experience*, Routledge, 2008, pp. 45–66.

26 J. Bradbury and R. Andrews, 'State Devolution and National Identity: Continuity and Change in the Politics of Welshness and Britishness in Wales', *Parliamentary Affairs*, 63, 2010, 229–49.

Northern Ireland: Unionism Loses More Leaders

The election in Northern Ireland was more sedate than the previous Westminster contest in the region, yet still witnessed personal and political drama. In 2005, the Ulster Unionist Party (UUP) has suffered a catastrophic result, losing four of its five seats, including that of the party leader, David Trimble, to the Democratic Unionist Party (DUP). Much of the DUP's success was attributable to continuing Unionist unease over the terms of the 1998 Good Friday power-sharing agreement, with the DUP then in the vanguard of opposition. In eclipsing its Unionist opponent, the DUP had highlighted the problematic aspects of the Agreement, most notably the requirement for Unionists to share power with Republicans while the Provisional IRA remained in being and Sinn Fein did not support the Police Service of Northern Ireland (PSNI).

By 2010, the political position had been transformed. The Provisional IRA had disbanded and decommissioned its arsenal in 2005. Following a re-negotiation of some of the terms of the Good Friday Agreement in the 2006 St. Andrews Agreement, Sinn Fein declared its support for policing in 2007. Elections to the Northern Ireland Assembly, an institution suspended since 2002, took place shortly afterwards, confirming the hegemonic position of the DUP and Sinn Fein within their respective ethnic blocs. Headed by a DUP First Minister and a Sinn Fein Deputy First Minister, the power-sharing Executive and Assembly were restored. Given the history of both parties, this political marriage of convenience was astounding, acidly labelled the 'Molotov-Ribbentrop' pact by one detractor.[1] Nonetheless, the mandatory power sharing coalition proceeded apace, acquiring, amid some political grandstanding, some control over policing and justice in the run-up to the election, completing the devolution process.

While ethnic bloc voting would again dominate the 2010 contest, there was perhaps less focus than usual upon the old constitutional issues during the campaign. Northern Ireland featured more broadly in UK-wide analyses in three respects. Firstly, there was intrigue over

© The Author [2010]. Published by Oxford University Press on behalf of the Hansard Society
doi:10.1093/pa/gsq020

whether the new alliance between the Conservative Party and the UUP would reap electoral reward. Secondly, there was speculation over whether the Conservatives might also attempt a deal with the DUP after the election, if falling just short of an overall majority. Thirdly, Northern Ireland attracted attention when, halfway through the campaign, the Conservative leader, David Cameron, highlighted the region as 'the first one I'd pick out' as an example of where the public sector had grown too large.[2] Almost one-in-three jobs in Northern Ireland are based in the public sector, compared with one-in-five across the UK.[3] In opposing the cuts hinted at by Cameron, the outgoing Secretary of State for Northern Ireland, Shaun Woodward, abandoned bipartisanship for electioneering, claiming that widespread spending reductions in the province would be a 'substantial risk to the peace process'.[4]

Locally, the affair with a teenage lover of Iris Robinson, MP for Strangford and wife of the DUP leader Peter Robinson, had provoked astonishment, but it was the financial issues surrounding the family's wealth, including the employment of several members as researchers and assistants, which potentially was more damaging, attracting the derogatory 'Swish Family Robinson' tag. Of greater long-term significance for Unionism would be the utility of the UUP-Conservative alliance, under the banner of the Ulster Conservatives and Unionists New Force (UCUNF). The election would also indicate the extent to which the Traditional Unionist Voice (TUV) party, opposed to mandatory coalition with Sinn Fein, could split the Unionist vote, with implications for the 2011 Northern Ireland Assembly election. Sinn Fein had its eye on the prize of becoming the largest Assembly party at that election, thus providing the First Minister. The Westminster contest might indicate whether this was attainable. Beyond the electoral arena, the 'noises off' were provided by a 'dissident' republican campaign of violence, evident since the Good Friday Agreement, but recently revived.

The results: electoral deep freeze?

Table 1 provides an overall summary of the results, while Table 2 offers a breakdown according to constituency.

Amid a largely static picture in terms of seats won, one result stood out; the ousting of the DUP leader, Peter Robinson, in East Belfast, where he had been MP since winning the seat from Vanguard's William Craig in 1979. Robinson's ousting had high UK visibility, an early result as Northern Ireland embarked on a first-ever election night count. This was the second successive Westminster election in which a unionist party leader had lost his seat. Beyond East Belfast, the DUP comfortably held its seats, but in Robinson's constituency the DUP's vote share fell by almost 20% and the Progressive Unionist Party did not stand, allowing the avowedly non-sectarian Alliance Party to take its first ever Westminster seat. Alliance's successful candidate, Naomi Long, is a prominent Assembly member who fought an impressive

Britain Votes 2010

1. Party vote shares and seats

	Votes	%	Change from 2005	Seats	Change from 2005
DUP	168,216	25.0	−8.7	8	−1
SF	171,942	25.5	+1.2	5	0
SDLP	110,970	16.5	−1.0	3	0
UCUNF*	102,361	15.2	−2.6	0	−1
Alliance	42,762	6.3	+2.4	1	+1
TUV**	26,300	3.9	N/A**	0	N/A**
Others	51,320	7.6	+5.2	1	+1

*Contested seats as the UUP in 2005.
**Was formed in 2007.

campaign, delivering a vote share for her party more than double that of Alliance's second best performance, in South Belfast.

Long successfully steered anti-Robinson sentiment away from the alternative potential repository of the UCUNF and towards Alliance, a party more associated with a middle class support base (and membership) than with backing from a predominantly working-class unionist community such as that in East Belfast.[5] Cognisant of her new support base, Long declined to take the whip of her party's sister organisation, the Liberal Democrats, following its coalition arrangement with the Conservative Party. Long was one of four women to be elected as MPs, a record number for the province and possibly a modicum of compensation for the fact that, at 17%, the representation of women in the Northern Ireland Assembly is by some distance the lowest of the devolved institutions.

Alliance enjoyed greater prominence than normal during the election campaign after its leader, David Ford, was elected Justice Minister (with DUP and Sinn Fein support), following the transfer of powers of policing and justice to the devolved assembly in April 2010. Notwithstanding the exceptional result in East Belfast, the more important development was the continued growth, albeit at a much more modest pace than evident during the previous decade, of Sinn Fein's vote share. As in the 2009 European election, the party obtained the most votes, potentially placing it in position to win the most seats at the 2011 Assembly election. The final leg of the advancement of the party's Martin McGuinness, from former IRA commander to First Minister of Northern Ireland, would be impaired if Unionists agreed electoral pacts.

At the 2010 election, Sinn Fein continued to trail the DUP in Westminster seats mainly due to two factors: the Social Democratic and Labour Party's (SDLP) resilience in the two seats it was defending, where the swing to Sinn Fein was negligible (Sinn Fein did not contest the SDLP's South Belfast seat) and the disproportionality of the DUP's vote share relative to seats, the DUP holding 44% of constituencies on 25% of the vote. Sinn Fein's most notable triumph came in Fermanagh

2. Percentage party support, result and turnout by constituency (winning percentage shown in bold)

Constituency	SF	SDLP	DUP	UCUNF	Alliance	Independent (Unionist)	TUV	Turnout	Turnout change	Result
BELFAST E	2.4	1.1	32.8	21.1	**37.2**	–	5.4	58.4	–0.3	ALLIANCE gain
BELFAST N	34.0	12.3	**40.0**	7.7	4.9	–	–	56.5	–1.1	DUP hold
BELFAST W	**71.1**	16.4	7.6	3.1	1.9	–	–	54.0	–13.5	SF hold
BELFAST S	–	**41.0**	23.7	17.3	15.0	–	–	57.4	–5.1	SDLP hold
ANTRIM S	13.9	8.7	**33.9**	30.4	7.7	–	–	53.9	–8.2	DUP hold
ANTRIM N	12.4	8.8	**46.4**	10.9	3.2	–	16.8	57.8	–7.3	DUP hold
ANTRIM E	6.8	6.6	**45.9**	23.7	11.1	–	6.0	50.7	–6.6	DUP hold
DOWN N	0.7	2.0	–	20.4	5.6	**63.3**	4.9	52.2	–1.1	IND gain
DOWN S	28.7	**48.5**	8.6	7.3	1.3	–	3.5	60.2	–8.5	SDLP hold
STRANGFORD	3.6	6.7	**45.9**	27.8	8.7	–	5.6	53.7	–3.4	DUP hold
LAGAN VALLEY	4.0	5.0	**49.8**	21.1	11.4	–	8.6	56.0	–6.6	DUP hold
FOYLE	31.9	**44.7**	11.8	3.2	0.6	–	–	57.5	–12.5	SDLP hold
FERMANAGH & S TYRONE	**45.5**	7.6	–	–	0.9	45.5	–	68.9	–6.9	SF hold
TYRONE W	**48.4**	14.0	19.8	14.2	2.3	–	–	61.0	–14.2	SF hold
NEWRY & ARMAGH	**42.0**	23.4	12.8	19.1	5.2	–	–	60.4	–13.3	SF hold
LDERRY E	19.3	15.4	**34.6**	17.8	5.5	–	7.4	55.3	–8.4	DUP hold
MID ULSTER	**52.0**	14.3	14.4	11.0	1.0	–	7.3	63.2	–12.3	SF hold
UPPER BANN	24.7	12.7	**33.8**	25.7	3.0	–	–	55.4	–9.2	DUP hold

and South Tyrone, the Agriculture Minister, Michelle Gildernew, holding her seat by four votes, despite the constituency being contested by two nationalist candidates against a solitary Unionist unity candidate. Sinn Fein's Gerry Adams, Party President since 1983, was unaffected by controversies over issues relating to his past and family, re-confirming West Belfast as the safest seat in the UK. Whereas the party's growth in the Irish Republic appears to have stalled, Sinn Fein can conceivably target future parliamentary constituency gains in North Belfast and Upper Bann, although the party has struggled to make further inroads into the SDLP seats of South Down and Foyle.

For the UCUNF, the results were a major disappointment, with the lack of utility of the link between the UUP and the Conservative Party exposed. The formal alliance had led to the resignation of the UUP's only MP, Lady Sylvia Hermon, who, to compound the UUP's embarrassment, retained her North Down seat in 2010 with a huge majority, standing as an Independent. As another indication of the unsatisfactory nature of the link, the UUP had ignored requests from the Conservative Party leadership (and even the former US President, George Bush) to vote in favour of the devolution of policing and justice in the run-up to the election. Following the election result, the UCUNF leader, Sir Reg Empey, announced his intention to resign. Empey had failed to be elected in South Antrim, having been adopted as candidate there belatedly after the original UCUNF candidate was dropped for comments made about the undesirability of gay guests at his bed-and-breakfast establishment (the topic later resurfaced as an issue for the Conservative Party leadership). While Empey's departure was inevitable, the inability of the link between his party and the Conservatives to achieve anything also asked questions of the judgement of the Conservative leader and of the new Secretary of State for Northern Ireland, Owen Patterson, given their public enthusiasm for the partnership.

Amid continuing problems for the UUP in its new guise, the DUP was also heartened by the weak performance of the TUV, under Jim Allister. During the previous year, Allister had gathered 14% of the vote in the 2009 European elections, with the DUP's share falling by an identical amount. In taking on Ian Paisley Junior in the North Antrim seat held by Paisley Senior for 40 years, Allister polled a respectable 17% of the vote. Given the 14% vote share quota required to gain an Assembly seat, using the same constituencies, he remained on course for election to the devolved institution. However, the moderate showing of his party colleagues, averaging only 6% of the vote in the eight other contested constituencies, suggested Allister might be attending in isolation, even allowing for the dangers in extrapolating possible Assembly election results (under proportional representation) from Westminster contests. While the TUV was not entirely 'decimated', as claimed by the DUP leader, its constant portrayal of the DUP as quislings doing business with the 'Sinn Fein/IRA' bogeyman appeared to be already wearing thin.[6] Sinn Fein's leaders had become increasingly distant from their old associations for a new generation (16 years had elapsed since the first Provisional IRA ceasefire) while their condemnation of republican 'dissidents' and 'militarists' had been unequivocal.

Continuing communal voting

Overall, what was striking was the strong correlation between the 2005 and 2010 election votes for the main parties, the former being a good predictor of the latter, as Table 3 indicates. For three of the main four parties, the fit is almost perfect, with the vote variation across constituencies in 2010 consistent with that in 2005, while for the UCUNF the fit is quite good, but with greater variation. As expected given the rigid sectarian base, there is a massive correlation between 2005 and 2010 Sinn Fein vote: 0.956 (p < 0.001). In mainly Catholic constituencies, there is a negative correlation between the change in Sinn Fein's vote and the SDLP vote, i.e. where Sinn Fein did better, the SDLP did worse. For the DUP, there was an even stronger correlation between its 2005 and 2010 votes, of 0.967 (p < 0.001).

As well as illustrating across-time stability in party support, Table 3 also shows a clear association between bloc votes. Of course, the strength of association between moderate and supposedly more 'hardline' parties in each bloc is lower than the across-time stability for each individual party, but there is no mistaking the negative association between either of the parties belonging to one bloc and their counterparts across the divide, and with stronger negative correlation between moderate and 'hardline' in both directions.

Those hoping for the arrival of an electoral 'Spring' and a thawing of Northern Ireland's communal voting patterns were disappointed. A first-past-the-post Westminster election is not ideal for encouraging (or

3. Correlations between party votes at constituency level, 2005–2010

Party 2010		DUP vote 2005	UUP vote 2005	SDLP vote 2005	SF vote 2005
SF	Pearson corr.	−0.802	−0.731	0.491	0.956
	Sig. (two-tailed)	0.000	0.001	0.045	0.000
	n 17				
SDLP	Pearson corr.	−0.623	−0.492	0.879	0.391
	Sig. (two-tailed)	0.006	0.038	0.000	0.108
	n 18				
DUP	Pearson corr.	0.967	0.611	−0.653	−0.825
	Sig. (two-tailed)	0.000	0.012	0.006	0.000
	n 16				
UCUNF	Pearson corr.	0.571	0.733	−0.528	−0.740
	Sig. (two-tailed)	0.017	0.001	0.029	0.001
	n 17				

judging) the melting of the region's ethnic bloc glaciers, whereas the Single Transferable Vote contests utilised at all other times potentially allows lower preference vote traffic across the divide. Regardless of the system used, the electoral chasm over which elite level consociational power sharing rests has not markedly diminished. The shift of Unionist votes to the non-aligned centre party in East Belfast was highly untypical and situational, rather than ideological. Elsewhere, the correlation between the Roman Catholic population in each constituency and the combined nationalist Sinn Fein and SDLP vote remained acutely strong, while the same pattern was evident regarding the size of the Protestant population and the combined votes for DUP, UCUNF, TUV and Independent Unionists (Figure 1). Table 4 provides the figures for combined votes and Protestant and Catholic populations, while these figures are plotted and compared with the 2005 election in the figures (5 and 6). Figure 2 indicates how the extraordinary result in East Belfast provided a significant outlier, where few Unionists were mobilised. Other than in this case, however, the religious affiliation and ethnic bloc vote link remains rock-solid.

Electoral traffic across the divide has been modest in PR-STV elections, confined almost exclusively to UUP-SDLP and SDLP-UUP terminal vote transfers. Given this, it was highly unlikely that single votes in a Westminster election would stray beyond the bloc. It was nonetheless common for victorious candidates to claim support from all sections of the community. For example, Sinn Fein's Michelle Gildernew insisted that 'Catholic, Protestant and Dissenter came out to vote for me' in

Figure 1. Nationalist vote (Sinn Fein+SDLP) by Catholic population in each constituency, 2005–2010
[2005 correlation: r = 0.975 (p < 0.001) 2010 correlation: r = 0.987 (p < 0.001).]

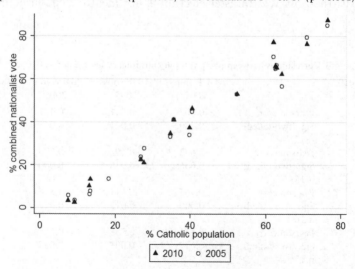

4. Ethnic bloc votes and religious composition of constituencies

Constituency	RCs	RCs (%)	Combined SF+SDLP vote	Combined SF SDLP (%)	PROTS	PROTS (%)	Combined DUP, UCUNF, TUV/IND Unionist vote	Combined DUP, UUP, TUV/IND Unionist (%)
BELFAST E	5935	7.4	1182	3.5	55,968	70.6	20,467	59.4
BELFAST N	34,880	40.5	17,132	46.3	37,786	44.0	17,649	47.7
BELFAST W	66,986	76.4	28,101	87.5	11,673	3.1	3436	10.7
BELFAST S	33,845	35.6	14,026	41.0	40,332	42.4	14,010	41.0
ANTRIM S	26,785	26.8	7684	22.6	55,478	55.6	23,778	69.7
ANTRIM N	28,077	27.6	9899	21.2	61,000	60.1	31,420	74.1
ANTRIM E	11,190	13.3	4083	13.4	56,056	66.7	23,042	75.6
DOWN N[a]	7911	9.1	930	2.7	56,575	65.8	29,632[a]	88.6[a]
DOWN S	64,879	62.0	32,884	77.2	28,581	27.3	8244	19.4
STRANGFORD	12,854	13.0	3325	10.3	65,770	67.0	25,790	79.3
LAGAN VALLEY	18,467	18.1	3300	9.0	65,543	64.4	29,066	79.5
FOYLE	74,483	70.9	29,020	76.4	21,808	20.1	5710	15.0
FERMANAGH[a] & S TYRONE	47,673	52.4	24,878	53.1	35,721	39.1	21,300[a]	45.5[a]
TYRONE W	55,347	64.2	23,262	62.4	24,423	28.3	12,646	34.0
NEWRY & ARMAGH	63,413	62.8	29,383	65.4	28,911	28.6	14,978	33.4
LDERRY E	30,826	34.7	12,141	34.7	45,763	51.6	20,887	59.8
MID ULSTER	54,090	62.5	27,065	66.3	26,838	31.0	13,380	32.7
UPPER BANN	40,938	39.8	15,513	37.4	49,698	48.3	24,639	59.5

Source: www.nisranew.nisra.gov.uk/Census/Census2001Output/KeyStatistics/keystats.html#.
[a]The candidate attracting the bulk of Unionist votes stood on an Independent label but was demonstrably Unionist.

Fermanagh and South Tyrone.[7] The combined Sinn Fein and SDLP vote share varied by only 0.7% from the percentage of Catholics in the constituency. Of course, aggregate data may mask cross-cutting under-currents of voting for candidates from the 'other' community. It is con-ceivable, for example, that the SDLP's Margaret Ritchie benefitted from tactical voting by some Unionists in South Down, to keep out Sinn Fein's Catriona Ruane. However, the very strong constituency cor-relations between the number of identifiers with a particular religion and the total Unionist or Nationalist votes suggest that, if cross-community voting is occurring it is happening with remarkable symmetry, with the numbers cancelling each other out; a possible but unlikely scenario.

In contrast to the trend across the water, turnout fell in Northern Ireland, by an average of 7.7% per constituency, to an overall figure of 57.6%, the first time it had dropped below the UK-wide average since 1997. The mean fall was higher in Nationalist held seats, at 10.8% with Sinn Fein claiming that this highlighted the disconnect between Westminster and nationalist voters, given the transfer of many powers onto the island of Ireland and lack of interest in, or hostility to, British politics.[8] However, turnout in nationalist seats remained higher, 60.3%, than in Unionist-held seats, at 54.6%, with turnout falling by 5.8% from the already-lower base in Unionist areas.

The correlation between turnout and Sinn Fein's vote in 2005 was 0.779 ($p < 0.001$) but this has dropped now to 0.511 ($p = 0.04$) and

Figure 2. Unionist vote (DUP+UUP+TUV+Independent Unionist) by Protestant population, 2005–2010
[2005 correlation: r = 0.974 (p < 0.001) 2010 correlation: r = 0.943 (p < 0.001).]

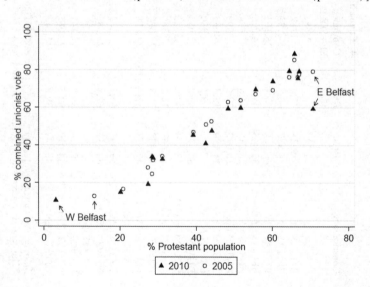

only just reaches significance, as Sinn Fein's almost mystical powers of voter mobilization begin to wane. Although there is still evidence that Sinn Fein does well in constituencies with high turnout, that relationship has weakened as turnout has declined. The SDLP's weakly positive relationship between turnout and vote (0.497, p = 0.04) in 2005 has now disappeared. The DUP's vote remains negatively correlated to turnout: −0.698 (p < 0.001) although this is less negative than in 2005, when the DUP performed particularly well in Protestant areas of low turnout. The (weaker) negative relationship between the UUP and turnout in 2005 disappeared in 2010. The weakening of the negative relationship between DUP vote and turnout is not because DUP supporters are suddenly heading to the polls en masse. The average vote for the DUP dropped, from 34.7% in 2005 to 28.9% in 2010, with the drop almost identical across constituencies, irrespective of the majority religion.

The unionist campaign

Within unionism, the run-up to the election campaign had been marked by discussions over whether Unionist electoral, or even political, unity was possible. Two sets of talks, both initially secret, were held between the DUP and the UUP, one brokered by the Orange Order (which also involved the TUV) in December 2009; the other, more startlingly, given the Conservative alliance with the UUP, hosted by the then Shadow Secretary of State, Owen Patterson, in January 2010. In attempting to unite differing strands of unionism, the Orange Order was fulfilling its traditional self-ascribed role as a vehicle to bring together the political, religious and cultural strands of unionism.[9] Although aligned for a century to the UUP, the severing of that alliance in 2005, the transfer of the political allegiances of members to the DUP[10] and the internecine fighting for Unionism were concerns for the Orange Order's leadership, which advocates a united Unionist party.

The Conservatives' brokering of talks hinted that the party might favour a broader Conservative-Unionist alliance beyond the UUP linkage, a move excoriated even in a sympathetic newspaper as a manifestation of 'Orange Cameron...jeopardising the neutral status as honest broker which it is important that the British prime minister remains'.[11] Ultimately, only one Unionist unity candidate emerged, narrowly unsuccessful against Sinn Fein in Fermanagh and South Tyrone, but electoral and/or political Unionist unity loomed as a distinct possibility for the 2011 Assembly election. Elsewhere across the province, the UCUNF trumpeted its alliance via 'Conservative and Unionist' posters, displayed even in working-class loyalist areas such as Belfast's Sandy Row. It was buoyed by the visit of David Cameron on the Monday prior to polling day, a highly unusual foray by a British party leader during a General Election campaign.

Beyond the tactical, the political aspects of the campaign covered the defence of services and the appropriate response to 'dissident' republicans. Differences on the appropriate security measures elicited some sharp exchanges in the second of the two televised Northern Ireland party leader debates.[12] For the UCUNF, Sir Reg Empey argued that the British Army might usefully be re-deployed in certain areas of the province to combat the Real and Continuity IRAs. Although associated with repeated demands for tougher security policies throughout the Troubles, the DUP's Peter Robinson rejected Empey's plea, arguing that policing and security matters were issues for the Chief Constable to address, a line closer to that offered by Sinn Fein's President, Gerry Adams, than that of his Unionist counterpart.

Following the Conservative leader's highlighting of the region's economic dependency, the DUP placed advertisements in Northern Ireland's Unionist newspaper, the *Newsletter*, warning that 'Cameron and Empey target Ulster for cuts' and claiming: 'Cameron's mask has slipped. He treated Northern Ireland with contempt by comparing us to a communist country and targeting us for Tory cuts'.[13] Empey accepted the need for immediate reductions in the government deficit, but stressed the need for Unionists to 'vote for candidates who will form part of the Government of the United Kingdom', a plea which appeared to elevate UCUNF vote-seekers to government office in the event of victory.[14]

Despite the politicking, there was little difference between the economic policies of the DUP and UCUNF, with cross-party agreement on the need to reduce corporation tax to 12.5% and create enterprise zone status for the region, in order to stimulate Northern Ireland's small private sector. There was also cross-party Unionist consensus over support for selective grammar schools (at odds with Conservative Party policy in Great Britain) and over the need to reduce the number of departments within the Northern Ireland Executive. The DUP trumpeted its role in ring-fencing all-island economic bodies and pledged commitment to a voluntary coalition eventually replacing the mandatory version at Stormont. Communal designations for Assembly members (Unionist, Nationalist or Other) would be abolished, with decisions to be taken by weighted majority voting based upon a 65% consensus.[15]

The TUV's manifesto lambasted the main Unionist parties for 'the ignominy and failure of terrorist inclusive government', highlighting how the TUV would be 'opposing Sinn Fein 24/7'.[16] In particular, the 'toxic veto' allowed to Sinn Fein via mandatory coalition was attacked, with the manifesto, which read like a pre-2007 DUP document, asserting: 'Sinn Fein is not fit for government. We believe terrorists should be in jail, not government'.[17] The party proposed to introduce legislation barring anyone with a terrorist conviction from holding government office.

The nationalist campaign

Within nationalism the unwillingness of the SDLP to step aside and allow Sinn Fein a free run at Fermanagh and South Tyrone caused considerable argument, the SDLP leader dismissing the idea as 'sectarian and tribal'.[18] Although ultimately inconsequential, the decision enraged Sinn Fein, which accused the SDLP of 'insulting the electorate' insisting that 'for the SDLP to have cooperated with Sinn Fein, a party committed to equality and democratic rights for all, would be anti-sectarian'.[19] Yet Adams should not have been surprised. Other than in the exceptional period of the IRA hunger strikes when the SDLP withdrew from the electoral field, the SDLP has carefully guarded its independence. It has refused not merely electoral pacts, but has also rejected overtures from parties in the Irish Republic regarding formal alliances or mergers, the Irish Labour Party being a potential suitor of the 1990s and Fianna Fail in more recent times.

Sinn Fein again based its campaign upon an 'equality agenda', defending its record within the community and the Executive and pledging to somehow defend jobs and services. Despite these emphases, Sinn Fein continued to highlight the need for Irish unity, arguing that 'the partition of Ireland, with the denial of rights and all the distortions it brings with it, IS a real issue and a defining one in many people's minds'.[20] The party's manifesto claimed that the 'work of the peace process has brought Irish unity and national reconciliation closer than ever before'.[21] This arguably conflated two items, the Good Friday Agreement having *removed* the Irish government's constitutional claim to unity and enshrined a consent principle within Northern Ireland, while achieving 'reconciliation' in terms of all-island backing for these measures. Optimistically calling on the British government to act as persuaders for Irish unity, Sinn Fein's manifesto claimed that 'the British government is signed up' to Irish unity, 'should a majority in Ireland wish it'.[22] This was an incorrect reading of the Good Friday Agreement, which makes clear that Northern Ireland's constitutional status will not change without majority consent in Northern Ireland, even if there was a 100% majority in favour of unity in the Irish Republic. Sinn Fein's highly detailed manifesto offered a detailed record of its role in the government of a state(let) in the UK it wishes to end, presented by Martin McGuinness, who defined himself as 'one of the leaders of government on the island of Ireland'.[23]

The party's attacks on the SDLP followed a familiar theme; that the more moderate nationalist party does not fight sufficiently hard for nationalists. Thus Gerry Adams noted how the SDLP had, variously, supported the Sunningdale Agreement during the 1970s when that deal was bereft of the term 'equality'; campaigned against the MacBride fair employment principles during the 1980s; supported the PSNI prematurely, with Sinn Fein securing more concessions and briefly labelled itself 'a "post-nationalist" party before reverting to being a united Ireland party when it realised how unpopular that was'.[24]

As the perceived stouter defender of nationalist interests, Sinn Fein's movement towards becoming a 'catch-all' party within its own ethnic bloc has been apparent since the mid-1990s. Its election campaign reflected this, the old hardline militarism long expunged and the socialist agenda of the party greatly diluted. Electoral growth has occurred across all social classes and its support within the salariat has risen from a negligible base, pre-IRA ceasefires, to become a frequent nationalist party choice amid the modern respectability of the party.[25] Indeed, the rise of Catholic 'new money', prepared to support a once-ghettoised party, has been a defining feature of the peace and political processes.[26]

For the SDLP's new leader, Margaret Ritchie, the task was to convince voters that the party's vision had not already been realised via the agreed Ireland of the Good Friday Agreement and the creation of shared northern and all-island institutions. Given this, the emphasis upon what was to come was strong, reflected in the party's manifesto title, *For your Future*.[27] Ritchie highlighted how her party had 'secured civil rights and equality; got the IRA to see the futility of its campaign and ... got everyone to see that a power sharing government was essential'.[28] According to Ritchie, the SDLP 'believes in a united Ireland, unambiguously', but the argument for unity needed to be credible; the party would 'not promise something unrealistic like Irish unity by 2016 simply because it is the anniversary of the Easter Rising'.[29] The SDLP's agenda argued for greater economic independence from Britain, including control of taxation and welfare regimes, although given the level of subvention and reliance upon the public sector, these issues remained problematical. Greater North–South integration, with the first move the establishment of an all-Ireland environment agency, was also advocated. The Executive's current plan for limited reintegration of Northern Irish society was dismissed by the party leader as the 'worst policy document she has ever seen', vague and lacking substance.[30]

Sinn Fein's abstention from Westminster also proved a divisive issue. In an era where much of what appeared to be republican principle has been reduced to tactic,[31] the refusal of Sinn Fein's elected representatives to swear an oath of allegiance to a British monarch remains non-negotiable. While the SDLP argued that it was pointless for nationalists to elect non-participants to Westminster, Sinn Fein defended its policy of 'active abstentionism' on the grounds that the interests of constituents could still be represented via dealings with (British) ministers. The allowances and expenses accruing to Sinn Fein are also of obvious benefit to the party. Sinn Fein also highlighted the low level of voting at Westminster undertaken by SDLP MPs, with an average absentee rate of over 80% in divisions during the 2009 parliamentary session.

The 'dissident' republican threat

After several false starts, power-sharing finally began to embed in Northern Ireland after 2007, the peace and political processes seemingly irreversible. Nonetheless, in the 12 years following the Good Friday Agreement, 'dissident' republicans killed 38 people. From 2003 to 2009, these 'dissidents', mainly in the Real and Continuity IRAs, were responsible for 288 shootings and assaults.[32] During the same period, there were 413 bombing incidents in Northern Ireland.[33] By the end of the first decade following the Good Friday Agreement, 57 'dissident' republican prisoners were in jail in Northern Ireland for their actions[34] with a larger number imprisoned in the Irish Republic. Almost 500 persons had been arrested under anti-terrorism legislation by the PSNI since the restoration of devolution.[35] Between April 2009 and March 2010, there were 127 casualties of dissident shootings and assaults, more than double the total of 61 during the previous 12 months; 1264 sectarian crimes were recorded, an increase of 24% on the previous year and almost 35,000 rounds of ammunition found by the PSNI.[36] The level of incidents provoked the startling comment by the Irish Minister for Justice, Dermot Ahern, that 'the threat is as strong as it was at any time during the Troubles'.[37]

The start of the election campaign coincided with the transfer of policing and justice powers, an opportunity for the 'dissidents' to display their threat. Within 20 minutes of powers being devolved, a Real IRA car bomb was detonated outside the headquarters of MI5 in Northern Ireland, an attempt to show that certain policing powers, those dealing mainly with republican subversives, remained under British control with little local accountability. The election campaign concluded with disruption to election counts in Foyle and Londonderry East due to bomb alerts.

Bereft of electoral support, republican dissidents declined to contest the election, having managed to obtain a mere 3% of the nationalist vote in the 2007 Assembly elections. Their 2007 failure followed a prominent campaign of support from hundreds of former and serving republican prisoners, angered at Sinn Fein's perceived 'sell-out' in supporting the PSNI, an organisation obviously committed to arresting those republicans who continued the same type of operations executed by Sinn Fein's comrades in the Provisional IRA for 25 years. Sinn Fein argued that the context was entirely different, as there was now a political route to achieve equality then unification. The Sinn Fein Deputy First Minister, Martin McGuinness, denounced the 'dissidents' as 'traitors to Ireland' after they killed two British Army soldiers and a police officer in 2009.

Republican ultras argued that Sinn Fein's acceptance of the Good Friday Agreement, their working of the institutions of Northern Ireland and support for a 'British' police force, all betrayed republican principles. While a number of notable defections from Sinn Fein have been evident in recent years, including the party's former Director of Elections in Northern Ireland in 2005, the inability of the 'dissidents', an eclectic collection of organisations and individuals, to unite around a common programme has impaired the development of a coherent republican alternative. The 'dissidents' used the election to campaign for political status for their prisoners, although there was little sign of the broad mobilization of the nationalist population which had been evident in the campaign for such status over three decades earlier. The counter-narrative of the outgoing Secretary of State, that dissidents were 'common criminals... who just like killing people'[38] nonetheless perhaps needed refinement. Common criminals tend not to target MI5 Headquarters, or the Army and police, in their activities and a more useful narrative would stress the futility of armed actions and the political isolation of the 'dissidents'.

Northern Ireland's Chief Constable, Matt Baggott, described the dissident threat as severe and, under pressure from Unionists of various hues before and during the election campaign, delayed plans to scrap the full-time police reserve. The Chief Constable also announced his intention to move on from policing the past, promising to abolish the PSNI's Historical Enquiries Team, established to investigate aspects of the Troubles, in 2013, despite 1360 unsolved killings. Amid the devolution of policing and justice responsibilities to the Executive and enhanced accountability mechanisms, mainly via the continuing development of local Policing Boards, the Chief Constable would retain operational autonomy for policing matters, while control of several criminal justice agencies, including MI5, will remain in London.

Conclusion

Considerable electoral prizes await a party capable of attracting sizeable cross-community support across Northern Ireland, but that prospect remains distant. Beyond the particular circumstances adversely afflicting the DUP leader, the communal pillar electoral model remained intact, despite much chatter to the contrary and amid a greater focus on non-constitutional issues. Electoral integration, under which the main British political parties contest Northern Ireland seats, might dislodge such pillars, but appears unlikely (the Conservative-UUP link aside) and might polarise division if countered by parties in the Irish Republic standing in Northern Ireland. Fianna Fail has established branches in the province, but it remains doubtful whether electoral intervention will follow. While the 60% of the electorate who voted remain predominantly positioned within their ethnic pillars, the level of non-voting appears to be growing. Turnout has fallen at the council (2005) Assembly (2007) European (2009) and now Westminster elections in Northern Ireland and the old constitutional or sectarian impulses which motivated electors to cast votes may be in retreat. Among the 40% who do not vote in contemporary Northern Ireland elections, one might expect to find a sizeable proportion of the 30% of the electorate who eschew the label Unionist or Nationalist in a persistent finding of the Northern Ireland Life and Times Survey. Increasingly, elections in the region may be contests of the 'true believers'.

Academics and journalists agreed that the difficulties for Unionist politics evident throughout the election were far removed from a crisis for the Union, which appeared secure.[39] Despite intra-Unionist rivalry, the emergence of a single, united Unionist Party is now a possibility, Given their respective strengths, such a move might appear to be a takeover of the UUP by the DUP and electoral alliances seem more likely than full merger at this stage. The political difficulties for Unionists included another poor turnout of Protestants, falling from an already low base; intra-bloc division over power-sharing, although this was greatly diminished by the TUV's poor showing; credibility issues for the DUP leader and confusion over the purpose of the UUP-Conservative Party link, which had failed to place Northern Ireland at the heart of the UK or boost UUP fortunes, whatever the rhetoric, and may not survive.

During a campaign in which Northern Ireland appeared, as ever, to be peripheral to the main electoral battles, David Cameron repeated his strong support for the Union, a rhetorical, if not actual, shift from the 'no selfish strategic interest' position which characterised pronouncements during the peace process. Reliant upon Liberal Democrat rather than Unionist parliamentary assistance however, the likely selfish and strategic interest of the Conservative-led administration lies in reducing the colossal public sector dependence of Northern Ireland's failed economy. It is unclear how Northern Ireland's politicians can resist such forces, beyond the year's grace which, post-election, the Conservative-Liberal Democrat coalition indicated could be offered. Beyond such economic challenges, the broad issues confronting local politicians within the power-sharing institutions lay in how to construct a shared future; re-integrate civil society in Northern Ireland; develop credible legislation on marches and parades and utilise the limited new powers over policing and justice.

Sinn Fein challenges the interpretation that the Union is secure in perpetuity, but the lack of extensive support within Northern Ireland for constitutional change and continuing electoral polarisation ensured that good election results bolstered party morale but achieved little else. Within the Executive, Sinn Fein stresses its 'equality agenda', making 'the North' work better but not necessarily moving any closer to reunification of the two polities. Continuing commitment to Irish reunification has arguably kept the issue alive, played well with Sinn Fein's northern support base and helped the party mobilise sections of the Irish diaspora. Sinn Fein's focus was less upon seats they would not take at Westminster and more upon the possibility of winning the next attainable prize, that of First Minister of Northern Ireland, if they can capture the largest number of seats in the 2011 Assembly contest. Meanwhile, armed republican dissident groups, denounced by the former IRA leader-cum-potential First Minister, Martin McGuinness, continued a low-level campaign, a reminder of the refusal of diehard republicans to believe that an onward electoral march by Sinn Fein, no matter how strong, is sufficient to achieve a united independent Ireland.

1   D. Godson, 'The real lessons of Ulster', *Prospect*, 140, 6–12.
2   Interview with Jeremy Paxman, BBC1, 23 April 2010.
3   http://www.dfpni.gov.uk/2009-10_pay_and_workforce_technical_annex.pdfth, 9, (accessed 23/05/2010).
4   (*Belfast Telegraph*, 3 May 2010).
5   J. Evans and J. Tonge, 'The Future of the Radical Centre in Northern Ireland after the Good Friday Agreement', *Political Studies*, 51, 2003, 26–50.
6   (*Belfast Telegraph*, 12 May 2010, p. 5).
7   (*Belfast Telegraph*, 7 May 2010, p. 6).
8   (*An Phoblacht*, 13 May 2010, p. 6).
9   See E. Kaufmann, *The Orange Order: A Contemporary Northern Irish History*, Oxford University Press, 2007; H. Patterson and E. Kaufmann, *Unionism and Orangeism in Northern Ireland since 1945: The Decline of the Loyal Family*, Manchester University Press, 2007.
10 J. Evans, R. Jeffrey, J, Tonge J. and McAuley, J. 'New Order: Political Change and the Protestant Orange Tradition in Northern Ireland', *British Journal of Politics and International Relations*, 12, 2010, 42–62.
11 (*Times*, 12 February 2010, p. 2).
12 BBC Northern Ireland, 2 May 2010.
13 (*Newsletter*, 29 April 2010, p. 4).
14 (*Belfast Telegraph*, 28 April 2010, p. 4).
15 Democratic Unionist Party, *Let's keep Northern Ireland moving forward: Westminster election manifesto*, DUP, 2010.
16 Traditional Unionist Voice, *Putting it Right: Westminster Election Manifesto*, TUV, 2010, p. 1
17 Ibid., pp. 20–2.
18 (*Belfast Telegraph*, 14 April 2010, p. 6).
19 (*An Phoblacht*, 13 May 2010, p. 6).
20 Ibid., p. 9.
21 Sinn Fein, *Peace, Equality, Jobs, Unity: Westminster Election Manifesto*, Sinn Fein, 2010, p. 4.
22 Ibid., p. 50.
23 Ibid., p. 12.
24 *An Phoblacht*, 13 April 2010, p. 9.
25 J. Evans and J. Tonge, 'Social Class and Party Choice in Northern Ireland's Ethnic Blocs', *West European Politics*, 32, 2009, 1012–30.
26 K. Bean, *The New Politics of Sinn Fein*, Liverpool University Press.
27 Social Democratic and Labour Party, *For your Future: Westminster Election Manifesto*, SDLP, 2010.
28 (*Irish News*, 14 April 2010, p. 6).
29 Ibid.
30 Ibid.
31 See e.g. M. Frampton, *The Long March: The Political Strategy of Sinn Fein 1981–2007*, Palgrave Macmillan, 2008; A. Maillot, *New Sinn Fein*, Routledge, 2004.; G. Murray and J. Tonge, *Sinn Fein and the SDLP*, Hurst, 2005.
32 Independent Monitoring Commission, *Twenty Second Report*, IMC, 2010.
33 Police Service of Northern Ireland, Security Situation Statistics, www.psni.police.uk/index/updates/updates_statistics/updates_security_situation_and_public_order_statistics.htm,
34 *Hansard*, 12 October 2009.

35 www.psni.police.uk/index/updates/updates_statistics/
    updates_security_situation_and_public_order_statistics.htm
36 Ibid: (*Newsletter*, 12 May 10).
37 (*Irish Times*, 15 April 2010, p. 10).
38 Shaun Woodward, BBC2 Newsnight, 28 October 2009.
39 e.g. L. Clarke, 'Why a Crisis for Unionist Politics Doesn't Mean a Crisis for the Union', *Newsletter*,
    (11 May 2010); P. Shirlow, 'Politics is about more than Counting Heads', (*Belfast Telegraph*, 19 May
    2010).

'Wags', 'Wives' and 'Mothers'... But what about Women Politicians?

Cartoon by Jacky Flemming*

2010 should have been a critical election for women; all the main parties were publicly committed to selecting greater numbers of women MPs. On the policy front, Labour was confident of its legislative record on women's concerns and if the Liberal Democrats had had the most women friendly manifesto in 2005, the Conservatives looked to have successfully played the politics of 'catch up', with a host of new policies for women this time around. Portends looked good one year out, at least in terms of policy, if less so in respect of political recruitment. With all seeking the women's vote, the parties were keen to compete over maternity pay, flexible working and the gender pay gap. Six months prior it still looked like 2010 would be an explicitly feminised election, albeit now a 'Mumsnet' one, with the parties and the media focused on women as mothers. But the 2010 short campaign eclipsed even this: not only did the party leaders and their wives trump women politicians, who were all but absent from the TV screens and newspapers, but family and work/life balance issues, despite being a significant part of each of the three manifestos, got lost as the

doi:10.1093/pa/gsq022

campaign became reduced to leaders' personalities. Sure, the election saw an unprecedented number of women elected—142—but this was only a tiny increase—just 14 more women—on 2005, and significant party differences in women's representation remain in Labour's favour. And then, when the negotiations to form a coalition government began, the leaders' lieutenants were all male. The message of 2010 was clear, high politics is the realm of men; it was left to women politicians and political journalists to lament their marginalisation—and even this generated a backlash.[1]

The long and short campaigns: women as mothers

The 2010 general election was all set to be the 'mumsnet election': it 'would be decided at the School gate'. Ubiquitous in the long campaign, newspapers, the TV and the internet heralded the importance of middle income mothers—43 articles making a direct reference to mumsnet after its first use in 2009 (*Times*, 17 November 2009).[2] And Gordon Brown, David Cameron and Nick Clegg all participated—at their own requests—in web-chats on the Mumsnet website,[3] as all three parties sought to capture women voters who are more likely to be undecided in their vote choice than men. In the words of Labour's election campaign coordinator, Douglas Alexander: 'Labour needs to win back middle-income female voters with children in marginal seats" (*Guardian*, 19 February 2010).

Across the three main parties' manifestos it was, indeed, as mothers (and parents) that women were mostly frequently represented. There were, unlike the 1990s manifestos, no women's sections, although both Labour and the Conservatives had designated women's web-pages.[4] On these, however, much of the policy was, again mostly about, and for, families.[5] All parties did make pledges on women and development, not least in prioritising women's health and education[6] and all addressed violence against women: more rape crisis centres with longer term funding, and action to address trafficking (Conservative); maintaining the DNA database and expanding services (Labour); more diverse elected police authorities, and permitting buses to drop off mid-stop (Liberal Democrat). Labour also had unique policies on teenage pregnancy, lap-dancing clubs,[7] political representation at Westminster, the ending of male primacy in the Royal Family and equality opportunities. The Liberal Democrats advocated citizen's pensions and confirmed their support for the Human Rights Act. The Conservatives sought single-sex hospital accommodation; more free votes for conscience issues;[8] and the recognition of marriage and civil partnerships in the tax system.

The key manifesto battleground was women's work/life balance and other measures to help families. There was wide agreement across the 2010 manifestos that women suffer from a gender pay gap and that government has a role in preventing and ameliorating this. Ditto flexible working—now a cross-party 'good'. Greater flexibility in maternity and paternity leave and pay were also supported by all three parties. Inter-party differences were not, crucially, always in the direction one might expect—in Labour and/or the Liberal Democrats' favour. Pay audits were to be voluntary (Labour); mandatory for companies found guilty of sex discrimination (Conservative); or limited to those larger than 100 employees (Liberal Democrat). The transfer of maternity/paternity leave/pay was set at six months (Labour); whenever parents choose (Liberal Democrat and, apparently, the Conservatives, who elsewhere state after 14 weeks); and paid leave might be for 18 months (a Liberal Democrat aspiration) or 12 months (Labour's aspiration). The right to request flexible working was for parents with children aged 16 (Labour), or 18 (Conservative), for older people, i.e., grandparents (all three), for all those in the public sector and in time, and subject to business consultation, for all (Conservative).

Party differences were evident too regarding who provides support and services and who should be in receipt of them, as Table 1 outlines.[9] Of particular note is the contrast between Labour's universalism (Sure Start and the £4 'toddler tax credit', for example), and Conservative selective benefits (Sure Start targets poor and needy families; tax credits are for those with incomes <50K). The Conservatives also seek diversity in providers of childcare services.

The final notable policy difference relates to the marriage tax break—a policy that is best described as 'Cameron's baby'. Labour was critical of the Conservatives apparent privileging of marriage: their pledge to recognise marriage in the tax system was considered 'divisive' and 'unfair' and likely to 'stigmatise' children with unmarried parents. The Conservative counter charge contends that Labour had penalised couples by making them better off by living apart. The issue garnered significant media coverage during the long campaign. If the Tory manifesto maintained it would 'send an important signal that we value couples and the commitment that people make when they get married', the tax break was decried by Harriet Harman as 'back to basics with an open-necked shirt and converse trainers'; a policy thought up by a group of 'Mad Men' (*à la* US hit TV show). It did not look to have played out well with some women, providing the Conservative front bencher, David Willetts, with prolonged discomfort during an interview for Mumsnet (Feb 2010) and forcing Theresa May to publicly state her support for the policy (May 2010). And the policy appears, at least to some women, as a tax on the abandoned wife and first family—the 'golden hello' to the younger model: '... we can't all be smiley Daves and Sams. There is little in a tax benefit that makes a single woman in my position—middle-aged wife abandoned for a much younger woman.' (woman commentator, *Spectator* on line).

1. Manifesto pledges for families, by party

Party	Policies
Labour	Expansion of free nursery places for two year olds and 15 h a week of flexible free nursery education for three and four year olds
	New national under-fives service
	'One-stop shops' open to all families
	Expand number of free early learning places for disadvantaged two year olds
	Long-term goal of universal free childcare for two year olds; more flexibility over hours/days
	Retain childcare vouchers
	Raise childcare standards by a more qualified workforce
	Greater diversity in providers of Sure Start Children's Centres
	Toddler tax credit of £4 a week from 2012 . . . to all parents of young children (whether stay home or not)
	Where parents, especially mothers, want to stay at home or work part-time we will do more to help families with younger children
	Reform Job Centre Plus to provide extra help to lone parents, with childcare, training and support to find family-friendly work
	Require those with children aged three to take steps to prepare for work and actively to seek employment once their youngest child is seven years old;
	Ensure that work always pays for hard-working lone parents
	Greater support for maternity services
Conservative	Support families in the tax and benefits system
	End couples penalty
	Tax credits no longer justified for 'households earning more than £50K
	Freeze council tax
	Free nursery care with a diverse range of providers
	Stable, long-term funding for relationship support; increase the use of mediation
	Sure start [taken] back to its original purpose of early intervention for the neediest families
	4, 200 Sure Start health visitors
	Newly created Early Years support team
	Help reverse the commercialisation of childhood
	End closure of local maternity hospitals
Liberal Democrat	Ending government payments into child trust funds
	Protect existing childcare support arrangements until the nation's finances can support a longer term solution
	Move to 20 hour free childcare for every child, from the age of 18 months
	Introduce a Default Contact Arrangement—dividing child's time between their two parents in the event of family breakdown, if there is no threat to the safety of the child
	Regulating airbrushing in adverts
	End the closure of local maternity hospitals

J.K. Rowling—perhaps the UK's most well-known ex-single mother— took umbrage too, accusing David Cameron of being completely 'ignorant of' single parent poverty. She asked, given the emphasis on the symbolism of the tax recognition, whether it would have been 'more cost-effective, more personal, to send all lower income married people flowers?' (*Times*, 14 April 2010).

The new—and welcome—emphasis by all three main parties on the family/work nexus arguably reflects British society in which women are more likely to work than ever before, irrespective of whether this is out of personal choice or necessity; it is also acknowledgement of the needs of the UK economy. The Conservatives' new found focus reflects efforts to modernise its women's policy under the political leadership of May, as shadow spokeswoman for Women and Equality (*Guardian*, 29 April 2010).[10] Their manifesto—addressing issues that were notably absent from its 2005 manifesto—no longer stands out compared with the other two.[11] Collectively, the parties' approach, even whilst mostly leaving non-mothers and elderly women on the margins, might be politically astute, given Labour's past success in capturing middle income mothers' votes; it may also be a good thing that the parties are talking to parents, in the sense that responsibility for families is constituted as both a women's and a men's concern. Yet, and key to any substantive judgement between the three parties offerings to women at the 2010 general election, is acknowledgement that none of the parties, in either their main or web manifestos, address the Fawcett Society's—the UK's leading women's equality civil society group—question of how the current economic situation, and each of the parties' policies on tax and spending, will affect women.

Gender and voting in the 2010 British General Election

With no gender gap in voter turnout—women are as likely as men to vote—and given what is known about gender and voting behaviour in the UK, there is a rationale behind parties targeting middle- and high-income mothers. Historically women's voting patterns tended to favour the Conservative party—the traditional gender gap. In 1997 the Labour party won the votes of more women born since 1945 than men; although the reverse was true amongst older women and men—a gender generation gap.[12] One potential explanation for this was that New Labour had secured the support of the middle- and high-income mothers.[13] In 2010 all parties explicitly wanted these votes and, unlike in the US, they have the ideological space to compete for women's vote on this terrain. A focus on Mumsnetters, accordingly, looks logical: for Labour, in terms of trying to maintain its advantage amongst these women; for the Conservatives, in trying to win them back, conceiving them as natural Conservative supporters; and for the Liberal Democrats, who argue this is their territory too.

This close to the election, analysis of women and men's voting is limited to early released data. On the basis of the British Election Study's continuous monitoring survey, Figures 1 and 2 provide an overview of men and women's self-reported vote intentions prior to the short campaign.[14] In this there was little difference in the way men and women responded to the long campaign. Women were more likely than men to say that they did not know who to vote for, and men were slightly more likely than women to say that they intended to vote for one of the smaller parties or for the Labour party.[15] These trends are in keeping with the wider literature[16] and do not suggest that women have realigned themselves to the Labour party at an aggregate level—which would be necessary to establish the presence of a UK modern gender gap (that is, where women are more likely than men to vote for left of centre parties) (Figure 2).

BES data collected during the short campaign (after 6 April) shows a small traditional gender gap with 39.7% of women and 35.1% of men stating that they intended to vote Conservative but there was little sex difference in support for the other two main parties, with approximately 28% of men and 27% women intending to vote Labour, and 25% of men and women intending to vote Liberal Democrat. Turning to the 'Mumsnet' phenomena Table 2 shows there is no statistically significant difference in the vote intention of men and women who are carers for children aged under 15 (a surrogate for parenthood). This suggests that Labour might well have lost its recent electoral advantage amongst mothers, as all the main parties compete over women's issues and offered policies 'for mothers'.

Figure 1. Vote intention for the three main parties. *Source*: British Election Study CMS.

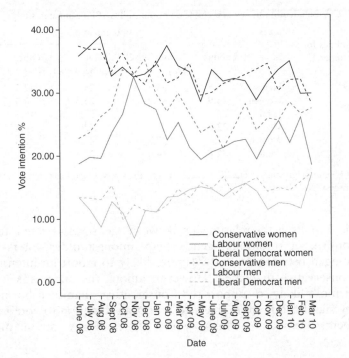

Figure 2. Vote intention for other parties and undecided voters. *Source*: BES CMS.

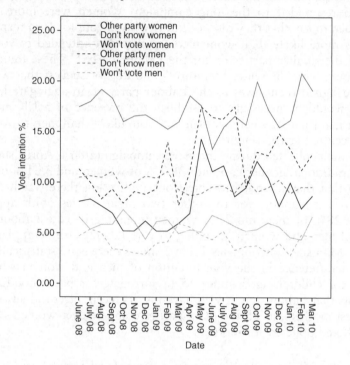

2. Vote intention by sex and childcare responsibility (BES campaign study)

Caring responsibilities for children under 15	Sex	Vote intention				
		Labour (%)	Conservative (%)	Liberal Democrat (%)	Other (%)	Total (%)
Not carer[a]	Men	26.9	35.3	25.3	12.5	100.0
	Women	25.9	40.2	25.5	8.4	100.0
	Total	26.4	37.7	25.4	10.5	100.0
Carer	Men	32.7	34.4	22.6	10.4	100.0
	Women	32.6	37.7	22.4	7.3	100.0
	Total	32.6	36.0	22.5	8.9	100.0

Source: BES campaign study. [a]The difference between the sexes is significant at the 0.00 level, chi square test, $N = 9941$.

Table 3 looks at the relationship between age, sex and vote intention and confirms a traditional gender gap amongst older voters—with women aged between 45 and 74 more likely to report an intention to vote Conservative than men. However, among the under 45s women are not more likely to support the Conservatives than men but neither are they significantly more likely to report an intention to vote Labour or Liberal Democrat—which would be necessary for a modern gender gap.

3. Vote intention by sex and age group (BES campaign study)

Age group	Sex	Vote intention (%)				
		Labour	Conservative	Liberal Democrat	Other	Total
18–24	Men	26.4	27.0	38.0	8.6	100.0
	Women	24.5	25.8	44.3	5.3	100.0
	Total	25.6	26.4	40.8	7.1	100.0
25–34	Men	27.4	35.8	31.1	5.8	100.0
	Women	26.6	34.9	32.7	5.7	100.0
	Total	27.0	35.4	31.9	5.8	100.0
35–44	Men	30.9	33.5	24.3	11.3	100.0
	Women	33.1	34.1	24.8	8.0	100.0
	Total	31.9	33.8	24.5	9.8	100.0
45–54[a]	Men	37.0	29.7	21.6	11.8	100.0
	Women	30.0	37.8	23.1	9.1	100.0
	Total	33.6	33.6	22.3	10.5	100.0
55–64[a]	Men	24.4	35.5	23.3	16.8	100.0
	Women	24.9	43.8	21.4	9.9	100.0
	Total	24.6	40.0	22.3	13.1	100.0
65–74[a]	Men	20.1	45.5	20.3	14.1	100.0
	Women	24.2	49.9	18.1	7.8	100.0
	Total	22.1	47.7	19.2	11.0	100.0
75–84	Men	26.4	42.8	16.4	14.5	100.0
	Women	24.2	49.5	18.2	8.1	100.0
	Total	25.6	45.3	17.1	12.0	100.0
85+	Men	26.7	33.3	26.7	13.3	100.0
	Women	14.3	42.9	28.6	14.3	100.0
	Total	22.7	36.4	27.3	13.6	100.0

Source: BES campaign study. [a]Difference between the sexes significant at the 0.001 level, chi square test, $N = 9920$.

Should the lack of difference between women and men voters, and between mothers and everyone else be supported by the post-election British Election Study face-to-face survey then it would invite two readings. The first is that gender is not a crucial factor in vote intention at the 2010 general election. The second is that the parties, and particularly the Conservative party's, attempts to attract back women voters has undermined Labour's recent advantage amongst younger women and middle- and high-income mothers. It is too soon to call unquestionably but if further data backs this story up then it might well be that 2010 should be viewed as a success for the Conservatives in winning back these women voters.

A few more women MPs but an unfulfilled promise[17]

Eighteen months out from the election it was not looking good for women's descriptive representation. With opinion polls forecasting a clear Conservative victory, the attendant swing against Labour was likely to see an overall decline in the number of women MPs. If this reflected the historic asymmetry in Labour's favour, most notable since 1997, it also reflected the failure of the Conservatives, as the main opposition party, to select sufficient women in its winnable and vacant held seats. The parliamentary expenses scandal of summer 2009 significantly changed the prospects as many more MPs retired from Westminster than was usual—nearly 150. This 'freed' up precisely those seats that will, all other things being equal, return a party's selected candidate to Parliament. If women were selected in equal numbers in these, then a party might just achieve sex parity amongst its newly elected MPs, and a larger increase in the numbers of women MPs overall. Unfortunately this did not happen.

The key to understanding the patterns of women's political recruitment in 2010 is party demand. This is not to say that there should not be concern about the overall numbers and diversity of women seeking parliamentary selection (supply).[18] However, immediate and significant improvement in the sex composition at Westminster requires translating parties' aspirant women candidates into candidates selected for a party's held and winnable seats. Of the three main equality strategies available to political parties—equality rhetoric, equality promotion and equality guarantees—the most efficient is the latter.[19] Measures that 'facilitate' or 'encourage' or 'expect' the greater *selection* of women, or rules that set a minimum quota at the nominating or short-listing stages simply cannot *require* an increase in the number or proportion of particular parliamentarians; they do not make a particular social characteristic *a necessary qualification* for office.[20]

All Women Shortlists (AWS) remained central to Labour's candidate selection strategy for 2010, as in 1997 and 2005, and were used in more than half of the party's retirement seats. The Party again sought their voluntary adoption although it was more conscious this time of the need to manage central-local relations.[21] Some antipathy remained, but to little public effect (*Times*, 8 May 2009). Given that Liberal Democrats overwhelmingly perceive their problem as one of insufficient supply, their efforts focused mostly on encouraging more women to seek selection. The key equality promotion measure was a sex short-listing rule: shortlists of three or four must require at least one applicant of each sex; shortlists of five, at least two. The Conservatives have, since 2005, implemented a series of reforms to their selection procedures. The central plank of the first set of reforms was the creation of a priority ('A') list of candidates (50% would be female). The second reforms strongly advocated the use of primaries and in their absence, that Local Associations' Executive Committees, not the members at large, would make the final decision. The third set permitted Local Associations to choose from the full list of approved candidates with a 50% sex quota at each stage. Primaries were again pushed. The fourth reforms involved six candidates ideally going before a Special General Meeting or Open Primary. 'By-Election' rules—a choice of three candidates—would kick in from January 2010. To much surprise, Cameron's deposition to the Speaker's Conference included a further provision: 'some' of these would be AWS. In practice, neither was. And in any case, Conservative AWS—had there been any—would not have constituted equality guarantees. Rather, in a particular seat the 'best' three candidates would simply have been women; happenstance.

The 'good news' story of the 2010 general election for women—the return of an historically unprecedented number of women MPs, up 14 on the 128 in 2005—is more apparent than real. To be sure, Westminster is now 21.9% female; the Conservatives more than doubled their number—from 17 in 2005 to 48 women in 2010; and the percentage of Labour women MPs increased at a general election where they lost a large number of MPs, to a high of 31%. There were also a number of women's 'firsts': the first Muslim women MPs (three Labour); the first BME and first 'out' Lesbian Conservative women MPs; and the first Green party MP was a woman too. In Northern Ireland, women MPs represent Sinn Fein, the SDLP, the Alliance party as well as one Independent. Nevertheless, the overall increase in the numbers of women is very small—a net gain of only 2.5%. The *Observer's* claim for a 'dramatic increase over the past few decades', whilst factually accurate should invite scorn: the post-war average until the mid-1980s was roughly 4%, but the increase from 1997 to 2010 is from 120 to 142 women MPs, a difference of just 4 percentage points (from 18 to 22%). At the Executive level, the Conservative/Liberal Democrat coalition Cabinet includes just four women (17%, and the same number as Brown's last Cabinet), all Conservative. May's appointment as the second woman Home Secretary is the high point, and Sayeeda Warsi sits as the first Muslim woman Cabinet Minister, albeit from the Lords. In total there are just 14 women of 95 government ministers (15%).

The 2010 general election results have, then, to be regarded as a missed opportunity—this was, in short, no breakthrough election. And this is despite 2010 constituting a favourable moment: all the parties were publicly committed to increase the diversity of representation and some had expended considerable political capital on introducing and implementing measures to that end and there were, as noted above, many more party-held vacant seats. The swing against Labour saw a decline of 17 Labour women MPs, including the ex-Home Secretary Jacqui Smith and the then Solicitor General Vera Baird.[22] The Liberal Democrats' worse than expected result saw their number decline, from 10 to 7, and the exit of two senior MPs, Susan Kramer and Sandra Gidley. The Liberal Democrat male MP, Evan Harris, one of the House's most vocal pro-choice champions, also lost his seat. Conservative efforts fell short of their expectation of some 60 women—which prevents agreement with the *Telegraph* (10 May 2010) that the party had made 'huge strides'; and some high profile 'A-list' women candidates, such as Philippa Stroud and Joanne Cash, failed to be elected. The number and percentage of Conservative women MPs continues to compare unfavourably with the Parliamentary Labour Party (48 versus 81 women MPs and 16% compared to 31%). At an election where it gained nearly 100 seats, women constitute less than 20% of all Conservative MPs and only 22% of its newly elected ones. In contrast, at a general election where it lost nearly 100 seats Labour actually increased the percentage of its women MPs and it continues to have more women MPs than all the other parties added together.

The reason for the ongoing inter-party asymmetry in the 2010 Parliament lies, as it has before, in the different attitudes towards, and adoption of, measures designed to increase the selection of women for seats where a party has a good chance of winning. The three tables show the selection of women candidates, with regard to the 'safety' of the seat in 2005 (Table 4) and 2010 (Table 5), and in terms of the 2010 'retirement' seats (Table 6). Four main observations stand out: (1) Labour and the Conservatives selected more women candidates overall in 2010 than they did in 2005 whilst the Liberal Democrats selected fewer women in both absolute and percentage terms; (2) the only party whose overall percentage of women candidates matches or exceeds its percentage of women MPs is the Labour party, at 31% MPs and 30% candidates—the other parties have smaller percentages of women MPs than they do candidates, suggesting that their women were less likely to win than their male equivalents; (3) the distribution by seat safety shows that Labour was alone in distributing women candidates disproportionately in its held seats—30% compared to 15% for the Conservatives and 19% for the Liberal Democrats. (Note that Labour was expecting a swing against it at the election.) The Conservatives, in contrast, placed most of its women candidates in percentage terms (30%) in its unwinnable seats. They unexpectedly benefited from six gains in this seat category. The Liberal Democrat party placed more women candidates in seats they expected to gain, yet too many of these failed to translate into MPs on the night; and (4) looking at the retirement seats, both Labour and the Liberal Democrats (on smaller numbers) selected women in more than half of the retirement seats. The percentage for the Conservative party was just 26%— this was the Tories missed opportunity.

Prospects for the future enhancement of women's descriptive representation at Westminster look, on the basis of the 2010 results, to point to the necessity for the wider adoption of equality guarantees. The Equality Act 2010 permits their use until 2030. Given their established effectiveness since 1997 there is every reason for Labour to continue using AWS until sex parity in the PLP is secured; with women constituting less than 20% of its parliamentary party the Conservatives must not be tempted to walk away from further reforms to its selection procedures—any future commitment to AWS should be stronger than 'happenstance'; and finally, following the decline in the number of women candidates and MPs in 2010, a

4. Women candidates and MPs by type of seat 2005 (men)

	Seats won 2001		Winnable[30] 5%		Winnable 10%		Unwinnable		Total	
	Candidates	MPs	Candidates	MPs	Candidates	MPs	Candidates	MPs	Candidates	MPs
Labour	115 (288) 9% 26%	98 (257) 28%	2 (6) 25%	0 (0)	2 (19) 10%	0 (0)	47 (149) 24%	0 (0)	166 (462) 26%	98 (257) 28%
Conservatives	14 (150) 9%	14 (146) 9%	4 (26) 13%	1 (17) 6%	7 (32) 18%	1 (11) 8%	93 (296) 24%	1 (7) 14%	118 (504) 19%	17 (181) 9%
Liberal Democrat	4 (46) 8%	4 (41) 9%	2 (7) 22%	1 (2) 33%	5 (8) 38%	1 (3) 25%	131 (423) 24%	4 (6) 40%	142 (484) 23%	10 (52) 16%

5. Women candidates and MPs by type of seat 2010 (men)

	Seats won 2005		Winnable 5%		Winnable 10%		Unwinnable		Total	
	Candidates	MPs	Candidates	MPs	Candidates	MPs	Candidates	MPs	Candidates	MPs
Labour	118 (231) 30%	80 (175) 27%	20 (12) 63%	0 (1) 0%	5 (8) 39%	0 (1) 0%	48 (188) 20%	0 (1) 0%	191 (439) 30%	81 (177) 31%
Conservatives	27 (181) 15%	26 (179) 14%	12 (32) 27%	9 (25) 27%	12 (36) 25%	7 (27) 21%	98 (232) 30%	6 (26) 19%	149 (481) 24%	48 (257) 16%
Liberal Democrat	12 (50) 19%	4 (45) 8%	7 (9) 44%	1 (1) 50%	3(11) 21%	1(1) 50%	112 (425) 21%	1(3) 25%	134 (495) 21%	7 (50) 12%

6. Retirees and replacements at the 2010 general election, by main parties

	Retirements, all[31]	Women retirements	Women replacements
Labour	102	24 (23.5%)	52 (53%)[32]
Conservative	38	5 (13.1%)	10 (26.3%)
Liberal Democrat	7	0	4 (57.1%)
Others	2	0	1
Total	149	29 (19.4%)	67 (46.2%)

series of poor returns for women over the last few elections, and Nick Clegg's rhetorical commitment to increasing women's presence, not least at the Speaker's Conference, the Liberal Democrats must revisit the debate about AWS—a debate which has caused deep internal divisions and has prevented the party addressing the issue in an objective manner.[23]

One of the Speaker's Conference recommendations is, moreover, for Parliament to consider *prescriptive* rather than permissive quotas should the parties 'fail to make significant progress' at the 2010 general election.[24] No such progress was made in 2010. But in the absence of a Labour Government that looks most unlikely unless and until the Conservatives and Liberal Democrats embrace the logic of equality guarantees.[25] In the meantime, other Speaker's Conference recommendations should ensure that all parties' selection measures and outcomes are reported to Parliament and are made available to the public. Party activists and civil society groups can and should mobilise around these and, in so doing, contest interpretations of merit that critics hold against AWS and equality guarantees in general.

Conclusion

The 2010 general election was a largely unfulfilled promise for both dimensions of feminisation: the integration of women and the integration of women's concerns. To be sure, women voters, or rather, the UK's mothers were much sought after creatures at the 2010 general election. The main parties proffered them considerable wares—a smorgasboard of issues relating to women's work/life balance. Yet it is unlikely that many voters, male or female, actually read the party manifestos. Those watching the news or reading the newspapers would instead have seen a presidential electoral campaign with policies for women and women politicians pushed to the sidelines. Harman and May, the two main parties leading women MPs were effectively silenced. The media's emphasis on the three party leaders, and 'all male preening' (*IOS*, 9 May 2010) TV debates, of course left little space for any other politician, male or female in 2010, but women's role in British politics became further marginalised by representations of the leaders' wives—unelected women who had simply married political men. They were unsurprisingly and un-inspiringly dubbed the 'Wags'. The almost continuous media coverage took two main forms:

first, discussions of their fashion nous and secondly, and more substantively, evaluations of their contribution to their husbands' election campaigns. We learnt, for example, that pregnant Samantha Cameron's peeped toe wedge shoes were from Zara; Sarah Brown's 'double belt' from Jigsaw; and Miriam Gonzalez Durantez's trench coat a classic beige. We could go on, *ad nauseum*. As ciphers for their husbands, the sassy Mrs Cameron and wholesome Mrs Brown especially, were seen to signal that neither man was out of touch with the voters—either for reasons of class (Cameron) or personality failings (Gordon). Sure, both men were untidy and messy (*Guardian*, 28 April 2010), but this apparently made them normal husbands and, in any case, did not detract from being good potential Prime Ministers.

Amongst all this highly gendered copy, some feminist journalists were not backward in their criticism. 'Implicit and patronising assumptions' that women voters would be swayed by the leaders' 'loveableness'[26] were ridiculed: 'always, at times, such as these, the female vote (the Mumsnet factor) is discussed as if it were pink, fluffy silly thing—with women needing to be courted, flattered and directed' (*Observer*, 2 May 2010). Campaign strategies that explicitly courted mothers, but not fathers, and ignored the 'one-fifth of women' who do not have children was questioned—alongside criticism of the various monikers thought up by 'male wonks who go red when a lady speaks' (*Guardian*, 21 April 2010 and 7 April 2010; *Observer*, 9 May 2010). There were fears of a 2015 'leaders' wives debate' chaired by Myleen Klass' (*Guardian*, 7 April 2010). Questions were raised for the future: what precisely does the public want from the spouse?' What happens if one has a 'mumsy appendage'? (*Guardian* 28 April 2010; *Observer* 11 April 2010) And where does all this leave the female aspirant leader? Are women perceived to be capable of performing well in the 'televised combat' that is the leadership election debate? (*Observer*, 9 May 2010)[27]

Of course, women politicians were present, campaigning on the ground. And the general election did produce a Parliament that has more women MPs than the 2005 one. But the welcome increase to 142 must be seen as only a very small, and most importantly, an insufficient advance. Women MPs are far from parity and this was at an election where the parties expressed explicit motivation and had many more opportunities—Cameron had made it central to his party's modernisation. But only in the Labour party does women's presence breakthrough the 30% barrier. What this Westminster election proves, yet again, is the importance of all parties adopting equality guarantees, in addition to employing equality rhetoric and promotion. In 2010, just like in 1997 and 2005, Labour's AWS efficiently delivered women MPs to the House. The other two parties have much more to do. Ensuring that none takes their eye off the 'women's descriptive representation' ball remains an immediate political project. Despite claims that the coalition will hold for five years, there could well be a second general election before then; any reduction in the number of parliamentary seats, for which there are already legislative plans, will see sitting MPs fighting it out for selection and election. The outcome of these contests must not disproportionately affect women. If the debate over electoral reform widens then questions arise about the best PR system for women, and any particular measures that might be used to enhance women's (s)election. It is also important that women succeed in government too. Cameron's aspiration for one-third women in his Government requires monitoring.

One does not need accept a straightforward link between women's descriptive and substantive representation ('being' a woman and 'acting for' women) to hold expectations that the 2010 women MPs might, in some way, re-gender politics. Evidence from the 1997 to 2005 Parliaments is highly suggestive; Labour's women MPs and Ministers pushed women's concerns up the political agenda.[28] For feminists the end of the New Labour government—and the exit of some key feminist women MPs associated with acting for women—will be worrying (*Guardian*, 7 May 2010). Yet, the Conservatives come into government, alongside the Liberal Democrats, with their most detailed and thorough manifesto commitments for women and there is suggestive evidence that the party is more favourably disposed to acting for women, with key women MPs like May, the author of many of its policies for women in the Cabinet and retaining her responsibility for Women and Equalities. Yet, the coalition negotiations and programme do not necessarily augur well.[29] Commitments to flexible working, shared parental leave and the gender pay gap remain, and are complemented with commitments to promote gender equality on company boards. However, on sexual violence the funding of new rape crisis centres looks less secure—a shift in language from delivery to consideration. Finally, and despite the Liberal Democrats being allowed to abstain in any parliamentary vote, the Conservatives have retained their policy of recognising marriage and civil partnerships in the tax system, which they could—had they wanted to—given up. The extent to which, and how, women's concerns are addressed in the coming months and years remains, admittedly, to be seen. In this immediate post-election period what can be concluded is that, whilst, from the election of Cameron as leader of the Conservative party in 2005 to the start of the short campaign, it seemed as though the 2010 British general election might turn out to be a critical gender election, in the end, it was not to be.

*Permission granted by the artist.

1   See Janet Street Porter, *Independent on Sunday*, 9 May 2010; Catherine Bennett *Observer*, 9 May 2010; *Guardian*, 6 April 2010.

2   Mumsnetters are deemed well-educated, middle-class mothers (Mumsnet cofounder, Justine Roberts).
3   Mumsnet cofounder, Carrie Longton.
4   S. Childs, P. Webb and S. Marthaler, 'Constituting and Substantively Representing Women', forthcoming, *Politics and Gender*.
5   The Fawcett Society sought the parties' positions on: the economy; work/family life; crime and justice; democracy and political reform; attitudes; media and culture; equality and human rights.
6   The Liberal Democrats spoke of women's gender equality; Labour supported the UN Women's Agency.
7   Stated in terms of the impact on neighborhoods not women.
8   NB, Conservative MPs are less pro-choice (P. Cowley and Stuart, 'Party Rules Ok', *Parliamentary Affairs*, 63, 2010, 173–81.
9   Labour and Liberal Democrats agree that childcare provision should be expanded; Labour specifically targets lone parents with policies to support them back into work.
10 S. Childs and P. Webb, *Gender and the Conservative Party*, Palgrave, forthcoming. The Conservatives' 'women's' webpage, at only half a page long belies detailed policy work.
11 S. Childs, 'Feminizing British Politics' in A. Geddes and J. Tonge, *Britain Decides: The UK General Election 2005*, Manchester University Press, 2005, pp. 150–67.
12 P. Norris, 'Gender: A Gender-Generation Gap?', in P. Norris and G. Evans, *Critical Elections*, Sage, 1999, pp. 148–163.
13 R. Campbell, *Gender and the Vote in Britain*, 2006, ECPR Press.
14 The British Election Study 2010, funded by the ESRC, is run by Harold Clarke, David Sanders, Marianne Stewart and Paul Whiteley (http://www.bes2009-10.org/). The CMS is an innovative monthly electronic poll, conducted by YouGov, of approximately 1000 respondents. The pooled data set (July 2008 to March 2010) contains some 24 655 respondents (weighted data).
15 Women's greater representation in the 'don't know' category is common in political surveys and is usually partially related to their relatively lower levels of interest in party politics (R. Campbell and K. Winters, 'Understanding Men and Women's Political Interest', *JEPOP*, 2008, 18, pp. 53–74.
16 R. Campbell, *Gender and Vote in Great Britain*, ECPR, 2006.
17 J. Ashe *et al.*, 'A Missed Opportunity: Women and the 2010 General Election', *British Politics*, forthcoming.
18 The narrowing of the political class to graduate, professional politicians has been widely noted.
19 J. Lovenduski, *Feminizing Politics*, 2005, Polity.
20 Op cit, with emphasis added.
21 D. Cutts, E. Fieldhouse and S. Childs, 'This is What Happens When You Don't Listen', *Party Politics*, 14, 2008, 575–95.
22 Baird lost on a swing of 25% reflecting the closure of a steel works in her constituency; Smith was embroiled in the expenses scandal.
23 Gaby Hinsliff, *Grazia* April 2010.
24 Andrew Rawnsley, admittedly, does not gender his comment that no party will elect a leader without considering how well they will fare in such a contest.
25 R. Campbell, J. Lovenduski, and S. Childs, 'Do Women Need Women MPs?', *The British Journal of Political Science*, 40, 2010, pp. 171–94; S. Childs, *Women and British Party Politics*, 2008, Routledge.
26 HM Government, *The Coalition: Our Programme for Government*, 2010.
27 Winnable seats are where the party came second in 2001 and the majority was less than 5 and 10%.
28 This excludes ex-Conservative Andrew Pelling MP who re-stood as an Independent. Labour's Clare Short and Bob Wareing are included; Conservatives Quentin Davies, Derek Conway and Bob Spink are included.
29 Four labour seats were abolished.
30 E. Evans, 'Supply or Demand?', *BJPIR*, 10, 2008, 590–606; L. Harrison, 'Selecting Women Candidates', *Journal of Liberal History*, 2009, 62, 36–52.
31 House of Commons, *Speaker's Conference (on Parliamentary Representation)*, HC239-1, 2010, TSO.
32 R. Campbell, S. Childs and J. Lovenduski, 'Equality Guarantees and the Conservative party', *Political Quarterly*, 2006, 7, 18–26.

JUSTIN FISHER

Party Finance: Normal Service Resumed?

Introduction

The periods between elections since 1997 had seemingly produced a significant change in British party politics—Labour had become established as 'the wealthy party', suggesting that political success was influencing financial success. Yet, the period between the 2005 and 2010 election—especially the final 18 months of the Parliament—suggested that normal service may have been resumed, with the Conservatives again emerging as the well-endowed party financially. This had a significant bearing on the levels of campaign expenditure. While the Conservatives could easily spend up to the campaign limit (£18.9 million), Labour could only raise enough to spend barely half that sum and the Liberal Democrats, as usual, could spend even less. In sum, whereas in the previous two elections, Labour and Conservative national spending had been fairly evenly matched, this election was about one party's financial domination. The success of the Conservatives and the relative failure of the Labour Party in raising money meant that there was not only significant disparity in terms of the amounts spent, but also in terms of the type of campaign techniques that were utilised. Yet, the significant financial disparities were not neatly reflected in disparities in electoral performance. And all this after a Parliament where the issue of party finance and party finance reform had never been far from the agenda.

Long-term trends in income and expenditure

The period from the mid-1990s to the mid-2000s was a lean time for the Conservative Party. Not only did the party lose three general elections in a row, it also consistently generated less income than its main rival. As Figure 1 shows, from effectively soon after the time that Tony Blair became leader, Labour enjoyed a fairly significant financial advantage.[1] After the 2005 election, however, the situation began to change, with the Conservatives becoming the wealthier party. At the time of writing (May 2010), the latest full year accounts

doi:10.1093/pa/gsq033

available are for the year-ending 2008. Notwithstanding, the picture is clear—Conservative income caught up with that of Labour, and in some years after 2005, overtook it.

This change in the financial pecking order is particularly well-illustrated if we calculate Labour income as a percentage of that of the Conservatives (Figure 2) or use 'smoothed' data (Figure 3). In Figure 2, a data point above the reference line indicates greater Labour income compared with that of the Conservatives, and *vice versa*. The 'smoothed data' used in Figure 3 (and in subsequent figures) 'smoothes' out the peaks and troughs in the time series to produce a rather clearer impression of trends over time. Both Figures 2 and 3 neatly illustrate how Labour's financial advantage grew from the mid-1990s, but also how significant the Conservatives' financial recovery was following the last election.

What Figures 1 and 3 also illustrate is that despite the introduction of the *Political Parties, Elections and Referendums Act* in 2001, whereby campaign spending limits were introduced—ostensibly to

Figure 1. Central party income 1989–2008.

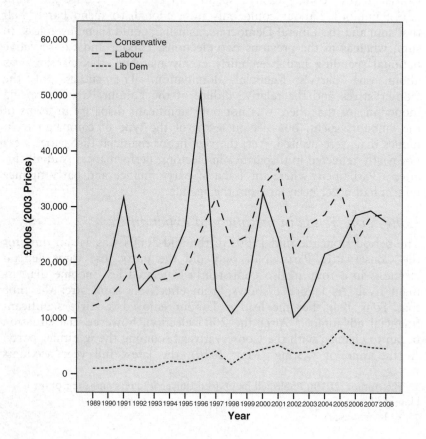

Figure 2. Labour income as a percentage of Conservative income 1989–2008.

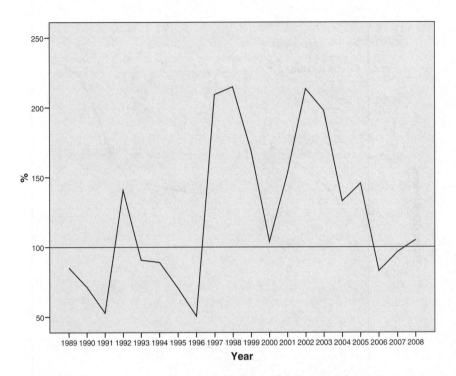

suppress the need for income—the income gap between the Liberal Democrats and the other parties has barely changed, although the income levels of the Liberal Democrats have been rising fairly continuously (if slowly) over the years.

The changes in the larger two parties' fortunes in respect of income have also been reflected in levels of expenditure. Again, from the mid-1990s onwards, Labour enjoyed a fairly significant advantage—reflecting greater success in generating income. After 2005, however, the picture changed quite dramatically, with Conservative expenditure easily outstripping that of Labour (Figure 4). Although party spending (and indeed income) peaks around the time of general elections, Conservative spending did not fall away nearly as much as Labour's in the years following the 2005 election. This turnaround in fortunes is particularly well-illustrated by Figure 5, which uses 'smoothed' data. Here, we can see very clearly how Conservative spending grew, while that of Labour declined after 2005. Liberal Democrat expenditure—like their income—has risen slowly, but is still way below that of the two larger parties.

Part of the reason for the Conservatives' recent dominance in terms of expenditure can be demonstrated using Figure 6, which shows parties' annual expenditure as a percentage of their annual income. Here, data

Figure 3. Central party income 1989–2008 (smoothed).

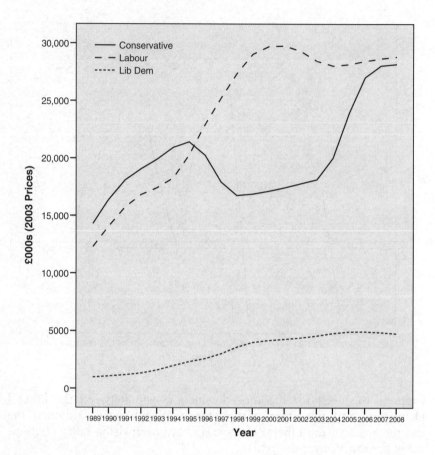

points above the reference line indicate greater spending relative to income and *vice versa*. As is evident for Labour and the Conservatives, and to a lesser extent for the Liberal Democrats, spending tends to outstrip income in general election years and as far as possible, parties attempt to lower their spending in between. And, as Figure 6 illustrates, the peaks of 'overspending'[2] tend to be highest for the Conservatives. However, Figure 6 also shows that while Conservative spending as a proportion of income had been rising since 2006, Labour had been spending less of its income ever since 2005. The Liberal Democrats, by way of contrast, had been uncharacteristically profligate.

The party finance parliament: loans, honours, Hayden Phillips and new legislation

In the run-up to the 2005 election, the first significant strains appeared in the party finance legislation introduced in 2001 with the

Figure 4. Central party expenditure 1989–2008.

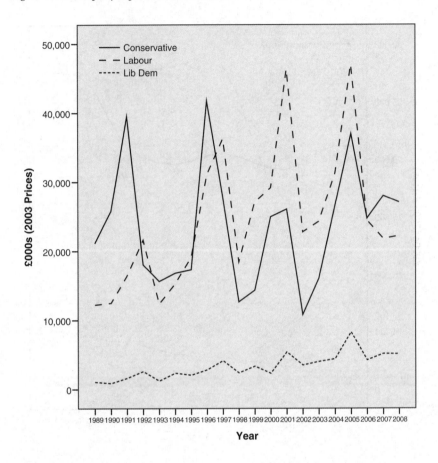

Conservatives and the Liberal Democrats appearing to challenge the spirit of the new legislation.[3] The Conservatives had been accepting loans (which did not require declaration) rather than donations, while the Liberal Democrats had received donations in excess of £2.4 m from 5th Avenue Partners Ltd, a company whose registered address was in London and from whom no accounts had at the time been filed. No breach of the law had occurred, yet the benefactor was actually resident in Majorca, thus again challenging a principle laid down in the *Political Parties, Elections and Referendums Act*—the ban on overseas donations. The benefactor was subsequently found guilty of fraudulent activity (*in absentia* on the grounds that he had absconded), yet following an investigation, the Electoral Commission eventually accepted that the Liberal Democrats had made appropriate steps to check on the legitimacy of the donation and were permitted to keep the money (or more accurately, not repay it).

Figure 5. Central party expenditure 1989–2008 (smoothed).

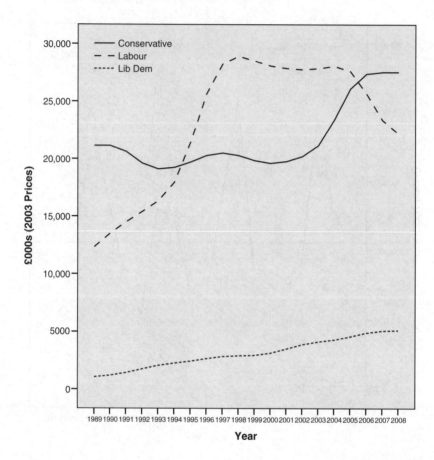

Then came the events of Spring 2006. It emerged that Labour had also sought loans rather than donations, and that a number of those making them had subsequently been nominated for political honours. In fact, all nominations were rejected by the House of Lords Appointments Commission, but the whole issue escalated rapidly following a complaint by a Scottish National Party MP to the Metropolitan Police that the Labour Party had breached both the *Honours (Prevention of Abuses) Act* (by allegedly trading honours in return for loans) and the *Political Parties, Elections and Referendums Act* (by allegedly securing loans at non-commercial rates, but not reporting them to the Electoral Commission). This process led to the Prime Minister being interviewed by police and a number of arrests of other individuals. Ultimately, however, no charges were brought. In many ways, while extremely damaging politically, the complaint and police investigation was of debateable value given that the chances of any prosecutions being brought were extremely slim. First, there was

Figure 6. Expenditure as a percentage of income 1989–2008.

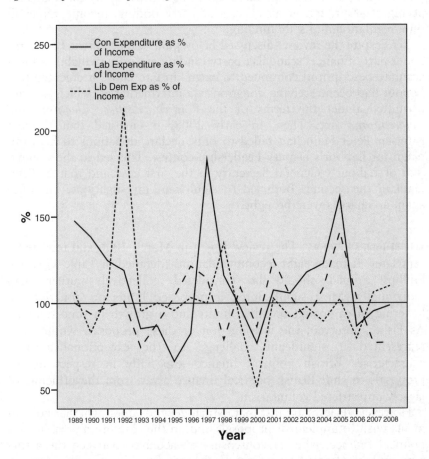

no legal definition of a loan on *commercial terms*, which would have rendered any ruling on a breach of the *Political Parties, Elections and Referendums Act* open to significant challenge. Second, any attempted alleged wrong-doing in respect of the honours system was arguably prevented by the effective working of the House of Lords Appointment Commission. Moreover, the failure to declare loans (as opposed to donations) by those nominated for honours was more a fault of the nomination process than the individuals concerned, since the process did not require any such declaration. Nonetheless, the whole episode contributed to the view that there was a need to 'clean-up politics'.

Although the government acted swiftly to close the loans loophole by tagging a provision onto the *Electoral Administration Act*, which came into force in the autumn of 2006, the loans episode threw the whole issue of party funding into sharp focus. The result was that the then Prime Minister (Tony Blair) asked Sir Hayden Phillips, a retired senior civil servant, to review the whole basis of party funding—

looking not just at the immediate concerns thrown up by the 'loans for peerages' affair, but at all aspects of party finding: income, expenditure, regulation and state funding.

Yet despite the review (discussed below) and the heightened concerns about party finance 'scandals', party funding episodes (which is a more accurate description) continued to occur. In late 2007, it emerged that Labour had been receiving donations via intermediaries, which was not permitted under the terms of the *Political Parties, Elections and Referendums Act*. Then, in early 2008, it emerged that Cabinet Minister Peter Hain had failed to fully declare donations to his campaign for Labour's Deputy Leadership contest. This led to the resignation of Labour's General Secretary in the first case and that of Peter Hain in the second. Both led to significant investigations, but once again no charges were brought.

THE PHILLIPS REVIEW. The review began in March 2006 and reported a year later. It made eight recommendations (detailed in Table 1) which Phillips argued should be considered collectively rather than individually. Most significantly, it proposed limits on donations, a lowering of campaign spending limits and a growth in state funding. As Fisher observed, the introduction of these proposals would have represented a significant challenge to the exceptionalism that characterises British political finance—especially in respect of the proposals to shift British political finance away from the principle of largely unrestricted voluntarism.[4]

However, reviews are just that. Much depends upon whether governments wish to implement proposals and, in the case of an area such as political finance, whether consensus can achieved between the actors who will be affected by proposed changes (in this case, the parties). The proposals of the Neill Committee[5] both enjoyed the political will to see them succeed, together with broad cross-party consensus. The result was the *Political Parties, Elections and Referendums Act*. In the case of the Phillips proposals, the same conditions were not present—especially in respect of consensus. Labour opposed limits on donations as it argued that this would threaten its constitutional link with affiliated trade unions, while the Conservatives opposed a significant extension of the period of spending regulations at constituency level on the grounds that such a move would constitute an unreasonable burden on volunteer election agents.[6] The result was a White Paper, outlining the government's response, which ruled out any limits on donations or increases in state funding (and therefore any challenge to British exceptionalism in the form of a challenge of voluntarism rather than state support as the principal means of funding parties[7])—and the subsequent legislation (the *Political Parties and Elections Act*). Of the eight substantive recommendations made by Philips, the Act introduced

1. Recommendations of the Phillips review

1 The status quo, in which there are no caps on donations, is unsustainable and therefore donations to parties should be limited
2 Restrictions on donations should be buttressed by measures to prevent breaches of the new regulations
3 Expenditure on general election campaigns has progressively grown and should now be reduced
4 Controls on expenditure by all third parties should be strengthened
5 The price of a fairer, more stable system of party political financing may be some increase in public funding of political parties
6 Any increase in public funding should be linked to a recognised measure, or measures, of popular support, and should encourage greater democratic engagement
7 The public should have access to better, clearer information on the sources of party income
8 A new funding settlement will present the regulator with fresh challenges. The Electoral Commission must have the powers, the capacity and the practical experience needed to fulfil its new role

Source: Phillips, 2007.

only greater powers for the Electoral Commission, some increases in the transparency in respect of donations, and the introduction of a rather complex new way of regulating candidate spending in Parliaments that run for five years.

THE POLITICAL PARTIES AND ELECTIONS ACT 2009. Although large parts of the provisions in the Act led to at least some of consensus between the major political parties, it was nevertheless widely criticized in its scope. Most poignant was the criticism that there was much in the Phillips review that did not feature in the original Bill, and that the Bill did not in fact address many of the pressing problems in party finance adequately. Liberal Democrat MP, David Heath, for example, described it as a 'pathetic little mouse of a Bill',[8] while Conservative MP Andrew Tyrie, who had fronted the Conservatives' stance on party finance during the Phillips review, argued that it was 'a tiny Bill that is designed to deal with major problems, but... does not address them'.[9]

In terms of party finance, the key new provisions were concerned with greater transparency in respect of donations, and further regulation of candidate spending at constituency level. First, following the case at the end of 2007 when it was revealed that some donations to the Labour Party had been made through an intermediary, the legislation now required anyone making a donation (direct or 'in-kind') to a registered party (at any level—national or local) in excess of £7500, to make a declaration that the donation is from that person, rather than a third party. Second, and following up the requirements introduced by the *Political Parties, Elections and Referendums Act* such that donations made by individuals must be registered to vote in the

UK, the new act introduced the requirement that persons making a cash or 'in-kind' donations in excess of £7500, or a series of donations in excess of £7500 in one calendar year, must now declare that they are resident, ordinarily resident and domiciled in the UK for income tax purposes in the tax year in which the donation is made. This section of legislation proved to be particularly controversial having been introduced very late following amendments proposed by Labour backbenchers. It appeared to be specifically targeted at donations to the Conservative Party by Lord Ashcroft, whose tax status was, at the time, unclear (but who was subsequently revealed to have had non-domiciled tax status). The government initially wished to resist the move, but backbench pressure led to its late inclusion.

Third, the act introduced greater transparency in respect of donations made by unincorporated associations.[10] This area of political finance had proved to be very controversial with a significant growth in donations from unincorporated associations, especially—but not exclusively—to the Conservatives. The concern with unincorporated associations was that while any donation from the association to a political party was transparent (provided that it was above the minimum declaration threshold); there was no transparency in respect of donations to the unincorporated association. Thus, there were concerns that some unincorporated associations could, in effect, be 'front' organisations. As a result, the new act stipulated that unincorporated associations making donations (cash or 'in-kind') or loans in excess of £25,000 in any calendar year to any political parties must now declare donations and loans received in the period before during and after that year to the Electoral Commission.

Fourth, the act raised the minimum reporting thresholds for cash donations, in-kind donations, loans or regulated transactions to parties, to reduce the legal and administrative burden on parties. Specifically the reporting threshold made at constituency level increased from £1000 to £1500; and the reporting threshold made at national level increased from £5000 to £7500. Both increases represented above average inflation rises.

The most significant change in terms of party finance, however, was the new provision in respect of candidate spending. The changes followed criticisms of the growth of campaign spending in constituencies—particularly in target seats—before the official campaign period began. Johnston and Pattie showed that this was particularly the case in respect of the Conservative Party[11] and coupled with broader evidence of longer-term pre-campaign activity,[12] there was a good case to be made that the regulated campaign period (effectively standardised by the *Political Parties, Elections and Referendums Act* as from the point of dissolution) was not capturing significant activity which could influence the electoral result.

As a consequence, the government originally proposed a return to 'triggering'—the system that had been in place prior to the *Political*

Parties, Elections and Referendums Act—to better capture such activity.[13] However, it became clear that this proposal was unworkable and in its place, the Act introduced a new system of regulating candidate expenditure. The key change was the introduction of two campaign periods: the first covered prospective candidates for the period from 1 January 2010 and ended on the day that Parliament was dissolved (the 'long' campaign); the second covered the period from adoption to polling day (the 'short' campaign)—it effect, from dissolution. Importantly, however, the new regulations applied only in cases where a Parliament runs for over 55 months before it dissolves.[14]

Under the new rules, spending limits for the 'long' campaign could vary, depending upon the date of the election relative to the 55th month. The maximum spend became £25,000 plus 5p per Parliamentary elector in a borough/burg constituency and 7p per Parliamentary elector in a county constituency—the differentiation in rates per elector being long established and reflecting the differing costs associated with urban and rural campaigns. The variation of maximum spend for the long campaign was now such that 100 per cent of the maximum could be spent if dissolution was in the 60th month of Parliament (e.g. after 10 April 2010), 90 per cent in the 59th (e.g. between 11 March and 10 April 2010), 80 per cent in the 58th, 70 per cent in the 57th, and 60 per cent in the 56th. Spending limits for the 'short' campaign remained fixed: £7140 plus 5p per Parliamentary elector in a borough/burg constituency and 7p per Parliamentary elector in a county constituency. Most significantly for this election, it created some very generous spending limits overall. Given that Parliament was dissolved after April 10th, a candidate could spend around £40,000 from January 1st until polling day. Previously, regulated candidate spending had been limited to around £12,500 (although of course, this only covered the period following dissolution).

Party donations 2005–2010

While the overall levels of income illustrated a growing Conservative strength up until the end of 2008 (for when the latest data are available), data on declared donations are available over the whole period (Figure 7).[15] What is apparent is that the Conservatives periodically received considerable boosts in terms of the amounts donated, and after the end of 2008 enjoyed a significant and growing advantage over Labour. The two previous 'peaks' were likely to be reactions both to the election of David Cameron as leader and to the possibility of a snap election in late 2007. However, after 2008, the Conservatives were consistently generating more money than Labour in each quarter. And in the period from the Autumn of 2009, the gap became extremely large. To put this in some perspective, the Conservatives raised more than £20 million in declared donations in quarter four of 2009 and quarter one of 2010—more than the maximum permissible spend in the election (£18.9 million). Indeed, the £10,659,521 raised in quarter one of 2010 was the largest ever recorded since the *Political Parties, Elections and Referendums Act* was introduced (quarter four of 2009 was the second largest).

By way of contrast, the level of Labour donations over the inter-election period was hit by two particular problems. First, following the 'cash for peerages' episode, donations fell, partly in response to the negative publicity that surrounded any donations to the governing party at the time. Second, following a mini-recovery that followed Gordon Brown's election as leader, donations fell again following 'the election that never was' in the Autumn of 2007. After that, despite a boost in mid-to-late 2008 (which included a donation of over £2.5 million from Lord Sainsbury and one of £1,000,000 from the author, J.K. Rowling), donations did not recover to the levels necessary to fight a general election on the same financial footing as the Conservatives. Of particular note was the fall in the value of donations

Figure 7. Registered cash donations 2005–2010.

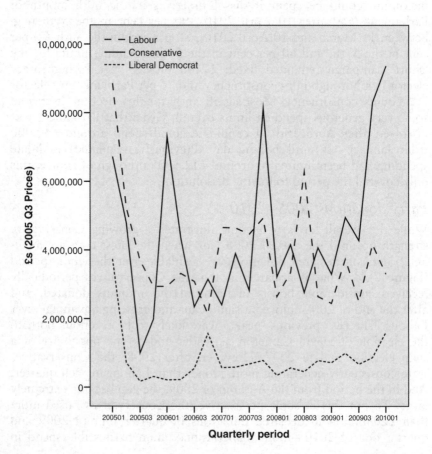

in the first quarter of 2010, compared with rises for both the Conservatives and Liberal Democrats.

As with the previous cycle, Labour continued to receive far fewer donations from individuals compared with the Conservatives and Liberal Democrats (Figure 8), compounding the party's problems. And although Labour (£23,012,698) received more than three times that of the Liberal Democrats (£7,302,715) from individuals, the Conservatives received nearly two and a half times that of Labour (£56,917,290), including 332 donations totalling £6,932,799 in the first quarter of 2010 alone. There was a similar story with corporate donations. Labour received £2,856,847 compared with £25,140,074 for the Conservatives, with 143 donations totalling £3,303,138 received in the final quarter of the cycle. Indeed, in terms of corporate donations, the Liberal Democrats received nearly twice that of Labour (£5,186,531). Trade unions provided much more significant sums for Labour—£44,554,722 over the inter-election period.

Finally, it is worth looking at the value of 'non-cash donations' over the inter-election period (Figure 9). As in the period 2001–2005, the Conservatives were the main beneficiaries. However, the gap between the levels of donations received between 2005 and 2010 was significantly wider. During this period, the Conservatives received £12,224,458 (including £3,643,268 from Lord Ashcroft's company, Bearwood Corporate Services Ltd[16]), compared with Labour's total of £2,752,180. Indeed, the Conservatives received £1,646,940 in the first quarter of 2010 alone—some £320,211 more than the Liberal Democrats received over the entire inter-election period.

Overall, the Conservatives entered the short campaign in rude financial health, attracting very high levels of both cash and non-cash donations—particularly in the last six months or so before the election. Labour, by way of contrast, was far less healthy financially, even recording a fall in the amount donated in the first quarter of the election year. Thus, while the period under Blair had been one of notable financial strength relative to other parties, under Brown, Labour fell back well behind its principal opponent. In terms of party finance, normal service was resumed, such that the Conservatives were the wealthy party once more.

Election period donations

During a general election period, donations are reported weekly following the *Political Parties, Elections and Referendums Act*. Although the introduction of more regular reporting was well-intentioned, these data tell us less about any potential impact of money on elections than the donations received in the previous two quarters. It is that money (and that which is generated earlier) that helps fund the infrastructure required to fight modern elections such as call centres and direct mail operations. Nevertheless, the election period donations were notable

Figure 8. Number of individual donations 2005–2010.

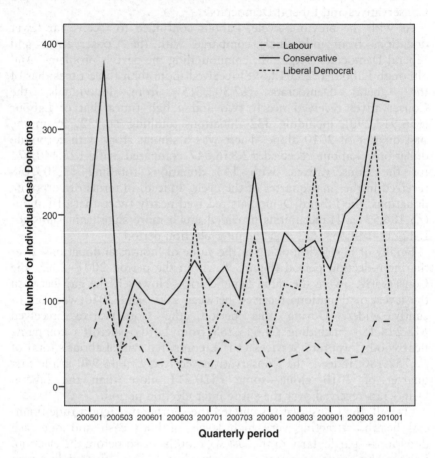

for their high volume. In 2005, the Conservatives raised just over £2 million in declared donations, and Labour just over £2.6 million.[17] These figures themselves represented significant growth compared with 2001.[18] However, the growth in election period declared donations in 2010 was particularly high (Table 2). The Conservatives received nearly £7 million in declared cash donations, while Labour received nearly £5.3 million. Indeed, the comparison with 2005 might be even more stark when one takes into account that all central party donations were declared for sums of £5000 and over in 2005, while in 2010, the threshold was £7500. The Liberal Democrats also received significantly more—£710,000 compared with just under £200,000 in 2005.

In terms of patterns, the Conservatives raised significant sums throughout the campaign (with the exception of Week 3—and even that was very close to the total raised by the Liberal Democrats through the whole campaign). Labour was also successful in attracting

Figure 9. Value of non-cash donations 2005–2010.

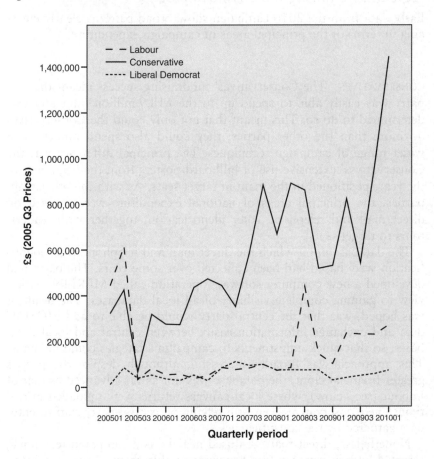

money throughout (although attracted fewer donors overall and received much of its money from trade unions). By way of contrast, the volume of Liberal Democrat fundraising was more uneven, not really reflecting the party's momentum generated during the campaign. In the fourth week, they did attract £500,000, but £350,000 originated from one source—the Joseph Rowntree Reform Trust. Overall, the Conservatives dominated once again—they received more donations from individuals than Labour's total number of donations, and were by some margin, the principal recipients of the corporate donations received during the election campaign period. Coupled with that, the Conservatives also had a significant advantage in terms of non-cash donations, raising over four times as much as Labour. This included nearly £22,000 from Bearwood Corporate Services Ltd as well as 17 other non-cash donations. Labour, by way of contrast, received only one non-cash donation for £76,304 for staff, travel accommodation and website design, made by one Anthony Blair (Table 3).

Expenditure during the 2010 campaign

Early data from the 2010 campaign show broad patterns clearly emerging in terms of the principal areas of campaign expenditure.

CONSERVATIVES. The Conservatives' fundraising success meant that the party was easily able to spend up to the £18.9 million limit and was determined to do so. This meant that not only could the Conservatives do more than the other parties; they could also spend money on a wider range of campaign techniques. The principal difference was the Conservatives' extensive use of billboard posters from the beginning of the year, positioned in the main in target seats. As with the other main parties, the principal areas of national expenditure were focused on direct mail and telephone voter identification, together with leaders' tours to target seats.

The database upon which the direct mail and telephone voter identification were based had been collected over some years. The party had developed a new computer software operation called MERLIN, with a view to gaining complete visibility of all local databases. The result, it was hoped, was that the central party would be able to add MOSIAC data and exchange information easily between central and local databases, so that quick adjustments to campaign strategies could be made. This approach was broadly successful, although despite the party's greater financial clout, the database was not as far advanced as that of Labour (see below), where local canvass returns were uploaded in real time. The Conservatives were still relying on central party staff to enter data gathered by the constituencies.

Nonetheless, direct mail was used heavily as a campaign technique, targeted both in key seats and key voters within them—'using a sniper's rifle rather than a shotgun'. Importantly, the advances in the party's use of its database meant that it could shift the focus of its activity relatively quickly during the campaign. For example, after the television debates when the Liberal Democrat poll rating soared and Labour's fell well below 30 per cent, a shift was made in the Conservatives' national direct mail strategy away from marginals being fought with the Liberal Democrats towards seats where the Conservatives were fighting Labour, but where the party had previously felt it had less chance of winning.

The use of direct mail was supported nationally by extensive telephone voter identification. The party had a call centre in its Millbank headquarters of around 40 lines which had operated from the beginning of the year. In addition, it had regional call centres in Coleshill and Bradford, and encouraged volunteers from marginal seats to also make use of these facilities.

Unlike the other two main parties, the Conservatives were able to spend extensively on billboard posters. The first significant campaign

2. Weekly declared donations (cash and non-cash) reported during the election period, 6th April–6th May 2010

Party	Week 1 (6/4/10–12/4/10)		Week 2 (13/4/10–19/4/10)		Week 3 (20/4/10–26/4/10)		Week 4 (27/4/10–3/5/10)		Week 5 (4/5/10–6/5/10)		Total (6/4/10–6/5/10)		Mean donation
	(£)	No.	(£)	No.	(£)	No.	(£)	No.	(£)	No.	(£)	No.	(£)
Con	1,455,812	33	2,221,341	47	645,250	22	1,375,189	34	1,620,010	35	7,317,602	171	42,793
Lab	783,159	7	1,490,000	14	1,416,863	8	475,000	3	1,118,177	6	5,283,199	38	139,032
Lib Dem	20,000	2	120,000	3	64,000	5	500,000	9	20,000	1	724,000	20	36,200

Source: Electoral Commission.

3. Source of election period declared cash donations and levels of declared non-cash donations

	Conservative		Labour		Lib Dems		Total	
	(£)	No.	(£)	No.	(£)	No.	(£)	No.
Individual	5,220,999	123	1,236,867	19	225,000	14	6,682,866	156
Company	1,727,500	28	630,000	4	485,000	5	2,842,500	37
Trade Union	n/a	n/a	3,324,528	13	n/a	n/a	3,324,528	13
Unincorporated Associations	33,281	2	n/a	n/a	n/a	n/a	33,281	2
Limited Liability Partnership	n/a	n/a	15,500	1	n/a	n/a	15,500	1
Total Cash Donations	6,981,780	153	5,206,895	37	710,000	19	12,898,675	209
Total Non-Cash Donations	335,822	18	76,304	1	14,000	1	426,126	20
Total All Donations	7,317,602	171	5,283,199	38	724,000	20	12,840,286	229

Source: Electoral Commission.

began at the turn of the year, featuring a personalised message from David Cameron—'We can't go on like his. I'll cut the deficit, not the NHS' and was followed by a series of posters aimed at electors who had not voted Conservative previously. In this respect, the impact of new media in the election campaign was quite evident, although not in ways that the Conservatives would have hoped—the first poster was digitally altered and lampooned on a new website—MyDavidCameron.Com—and this created significant publicity such that this and subsequent posters were also subject to such treatment, with readers sending in their own designs. It is not at all clear whether this was damaging to the Conservative campaign (although the site reported 252,641 unique visitors in its first six weeks), but it was the case that as the campaign went on, the level of spending on billboard advertising was scaled back and more national expenditure was devoted to the use of direct mail.

A further area where the Conservatives had a significant advantage over the other two main parties was the greater ability of the central party to support local parties in the lead-up to the campaign. For example, although the Conservatives have traditionally been able to employ more full-time than other parties, it has often been the case that full-time agents were based in wealthy local constituency associations, which were typically safe seats. For this election, the central party was able to make grants available to local parties in target seats to help employ agents if the local association was unable to fund the position itself. From around 30 months before the election, local associations in target seats were required to submit a campaign plan which included a bid to fund specific activities. If the bids were successful, the national party would then allocate ring-fenced money to fund activities such as local surveys, newsletters and communications, local direct mail and database building. The result was that local associations in target seats would ideally be much better prepared for the election campaign.

In terms of new media, there was not a huge investment in the campaign, in part because the national party had a relatively limited database of email addresses and mobile telephone numbers. Social media sites such as Facebook were used, but were generally organised locally. The national party did, however, seek as far as possible to monitor local Facebook activity to ensure that no inappropriate pledges were being made.

Overall, despite the Conservatives' far healthier financial position, its campaign was focused very much on direct mail and telephone voter identification. Although billboards were used heavily at first, direct mail became a more significant area of expenditure. Equally, although the party made some use of press advertisements, they were used far less in both national and regional media than in previous elections. The critical difference for the Conservatives, compared with other parties was that, posters aside, they were able to support local associations in target seats relatively actively in the build-up to the election and were able to spend very significant sums on direct mail and telephone voter identification.

LABOUR. The less favourable financial position in which Labour found itself was—not surprisingly—reflected in its campaign expenditure strategies. Whereas the party had spent nearly £18 million in 2005 (95.4 per cent of the permitted maximum), initial estimates suggest that spending in 2010 amounted to between £10 and £12 million (between 53 per cent and 63 per cent of the permitted maximum), which included around £8 million spent during the short campaign. This comparatively low level of spending (compared both with that of the Conservatives and with previous Labour campaigns) had a number of significant implications. First, the national party was operating with a staffing level that was around a third of its 2005 level. Second, it meant that far fewer campaign organisers were in place on the ground, and that they took up their positions far later. Whereas in 2005 it was more common to have special organisers in place some two years before the election, in 2010, many were only appointed—either on short-term contracts or by secondment from the national office—at the beginning of 2010.

Third, it meant that some familiar campaigning techniques were not used. There was no billboard poster campaign, for example. Where posters were used, they were very few in number and were used on poster vans. More commonly, the 'posters' were created electronically in an attempt to generate news stories. Neither were there any newspaper advertisements in either the national or the regional press—again, for reasons of cost. Both of these changes marked the 2010 campaign as being very different from that of 2005, where extensive use was made of billboards and newspaper advertisements—especially in the regional press. Instead, Labour's campaign and expenditure in 2010 focused on direct mail, telephone banks, campaign organisers, new media and Party Election Broadcasts.

Much of Labour's reduced campaign expenditure was based around its Contact Creator database system. Built by Experian, it contains the whole of the electoral register together with MOSIAC demographic data. The key development for this campaign was the ability for all local parties to upload canvass returns and contact details in real time. This allowed the national party to produce daily reports on how each individual campaign was performing. By way of contrast, in the 2005 campaign, the national party had only one snapshot of canvass returns, produced when all the local parties had submitted their returns on disk. The use of this Contract Creator database allowed the party to fine tune where direct mail was sent, who received telephone calls etc. on a daily basis, and shift the emphasis of the campaigns accordingly.

More significantly, it allowed the party to plan and focus its target strategy more accurately. Following the June 2009 elections, all local parties were reassessed in respect of their work rate and contacts made (using the Contact Creator database), and target seats were then identified using propensity modelling. This technique applied four criteria: the level of activity in the local party, the electoral performance in various elections since 2005, the notional majority and the existence of any particular political circumstances (such as hospital closures or expenses). All criteria were given a score with the model then predicting the result. The innovation, here, was that there was far less emphasis on the notional majority in producing target seats, and that the local performance was captured by the database.

What flowed from this was that three key areas of Labour's national expenditure (direct mail, telephone voter identification and campaign organisers) were determined to a significant extent by the propensity modelling—all three of the expenditure areas being focused almost exclusively on target seats such that in the period after January 1st, some 8–10 million pieces of direct mail were sent—the strategy being that the national party would be responsible for sending out literature, freeing the local parties to concentrate on face to face contacts. Notwithstanding, the party's financial position still meant that these activities were curtailed somewhat. For example, Labour's national telephone bank in Gosforth employed far fewer callers (around 50) than was previously the case (there were around 200 in 2001). Nevertheless, the integrated database meant that more use could be made of 'late money'—donations made during the campaign. Hitherto, the lead time of campaigning techniques had meant that 'late money' had tended to be used for items such as newspaper advertisements. However, the sophistication of this database—reporting contacts in real time—meant that money could be utilised within two days to send direct mail and use telephone voter identification.

Labour also devoted some of its expenditure to campaigning through new media. Text messaging, for example was used to contact both Labour members and prospective Labour voters. This had followed a lengthy collection of mobile phone number over previous years (such as sending a text to receive a Labour beer mat) and resulted in prospective Labour voters being texted twice on polling day. Twitter was used within the party and also as a means of passing on information, while on Facebook, the national party created single-issue causes (such as 'Back the Ban', in reference to foxhunting) whereby it was hoped that this would draw in supporters to the Labour cause.

Overall, Labour's campaign expenditure was driven in part by its relatively poor financial position. However, the lack of resources inevitably concentrated minds upon which were the best campaigning strategies such that were more money to have been available, it would have much more likely to have been spent on campaign organisers and direct mail, rather than the more traditional forms of campaigning such as billboards or newspaper advertisements.

THE LIBERAL DEMOCRATS. Like Labour, the Liberal Democrats' campaign expenditure strategy was determined in part by their more modest financial position—the party was able to spend around £5 million in total. And again, like Labour, a considerable proportion of the party's campaign expenditure was devoted to direct mail. This was sent to all the party's key seats and this centralised mailing was the largest expenditure item in the national campaign. In support of the direct mail, regional phone banks were established across the country. A large phone bank in East Anglia had been set up in 2009 and others followed. These phone banks principally made calls to target seats.

As in 2005, tours by the party leader were another significant item of campaign expenditure. However, whereas the 2005 tour had been based principally around Charles Kennedy,[19] in 2010, there was an interlocking series of tours featuring Nick Clegg; Vince Cable and Chris Huhne. In addition, former leaders Charles Kennedy, Paddy Ashdown and Menzies Campbell were also involved in visiting key constituencies.

As with Labour, there was also a move away from more traditional forms of campaign expenditure. In 2005, the Liberal Democrats made extensive use of billboard posters and newspaper advertisements in both the national and regional press following a sizeable donation made shortly before the campaign.[20] In 2010, however, no billboard posters were used at all. Instead, poster vans were used sparingly and always in front of cameras. Equally, only one national press advertisement appeared. It was placed in *The Times* during the final week of the campaign and urged voters to act responsibly for the good of the country—a point which Nick Clegg then used after the election when he announced that he would first try and form a coalition with the party that had gained the most votes and seats. This advert effectively enabled him to say that his position had not changed.

In terms of new media, Twitter and Facebook were used heavily. The national party encouraged candidates to have a presence on Twitter and Facebook, but also offered advice and training on what not to put in Tweets or in Facebook updates. Nationally, the party's 'Rage against the Election' site had 160,000 'friends'.

Overall, despite the Liberal Democrats uncharacteristic overspending in the preceding years (Figure 6), the election campaign effectively broke even. Some campaign expenditure was made based on the expectation of donations being made during the campaign, and that gamble paid off with far more in the way of donations being made during the campaign compared with 2005.

Conclusions

The end of the Blair years also coincided with the Conservatives resuming their traditional financial pre-eminence. Yet the change was such that in 2010, it was not so much the case that there were two reasonably evenly matched parties in financial terms, with one slightly better off. Rather, the 2010 election was characterised by one party financial domination. It was also characterised by financial constraints helping to determine what campaigning techniques were funded. This has always been the case for the Liberal Democrats, but since the introduction of national spending limits, the opportunity costs of choosing one technique over another have been the principal drivers in determining how the larger parties spent their campaign funds. This remained true for the Conservatives, but not this time for Labour on account of its far weaker financial position.

Notwithstanding, the significant financial disparities were not reflected neatly in electoral performance. Put bluntly, given the Conservatives' significant financial advantage, one might have expected them to perform much better electorally, and Labour rather worse. Yet, what this reveals (or rather, confirms) is that there is a much more complex relationship between party expenditure and electoral performance. As Fisher has shown at both national and local levels, the relationship between spending and votes is anything but perfect—it is not what you spend that matters, but how you spend it.[21] And the experience of the 2010 election would appear to confirm that many debates about the raw impact of money on the vote are often over-simplified. Of course, elections cannot be fought without significant sums being spent. But the notion that *x* pounds equals *y* votes is actually a much more complex phenomenon than many contemporary debates would suggest.

A final thought focuses on how the parties spent their campaign funds. Despite the disparities in wealth, all three spent the bulk on direct mail and telephone voter identification alongside other techniques focused on marginal seats. Only the Conservatives made significant use of billboards, while press advertising was at a very low level. Campaigning through new media was particularly attractive to Labour and the Liberal Democrats not least because it is relatively inexpensive. But it was still direct mail and telephone contact that dominated for all three parties. Of course, the leadership debates dominated the conduct of the campaign, but the principal ways in which parties spent money suggests that the national campaign as we traditionally understand it may be slipping in importance behind efforts focused on target seats and supporting local constituency campaigns.

1   Exact year on year comparisons are complicated a little since until 2002, Labour and the Conservatives employed different accounting year ends—Labour 31st December, the Conservatives, 31st March. For comparability, therefore, Conservative accounts are counted here for the year in which there are most months, e.g. Year end 31st March 1997, would be counted as 1996.

2   Technically, this may not represent 'overspending' as such, since parties may well have some reserves that can be utilised in an election year.

3   J. Fisher 'Campaign Finance', in A. Geddes and J. Tonge (eds), *Britain Decides: The General Election of 2005*, Palgrave, 2005, pp. 180–1.

4   J. Fisher, 'Hayden Phillips and Jack Straw: The Continuation of British Exceptionalism in British Political Finance?' *Parliamentary Affairs*, 62, 2009, 298–317.

5   Committee on Standards in Public Life, *The Funding of Political Parties in the United Kingdom*, HMSO, 1998.

6   J. Fisher, 'Party Funding: Back to square one (and a half) or every cloud has a silver lining?' *Political Quarterly*, 79, 2008, 119–25.

7   See Fisher 2009, *op. cit.*

8   HC Deb 20 October 2008 c42.

9   HC Deb 20 October 2008 c105.

10 An unincorporated association is a voluntary organisation whereby a group of individuals voluntarily enter into an agreement to form a body (or organisation) to accomplish a purpose. It is not, in itself, a legal entity.

11 R. Johnston and C. Pattie, 'Funding Local Political Parties in England and Wales: Donations and Constituency Campaigns' *British Journal of Politics & International Relations*, 9, 2007, 365–95.

12 J. Fisher and D. Denver 'From Foot-Slogging to Call Centres and Direct Mail: A Framework for Analysing the Development of District-Level Campaigning' *European Journal of Political Research*, 47, 2008, 794–826.

13 Fisher, 2009, *op. cit.*

14 11th December 2009 marked the end of 55 months of the Parliament. However, the legislation came into force on 1 January 2010.

15 Declared donations are those over a particularly threshold declared to the Electoral Commission. For all donations until quarter 1 of 2010, the declaration threshold was £5000 to the national party and £1000 to a constituency party. Following the *Political Parties and Elections Act 2009*, those

thresholds were increased to £7500 and £1500, respectively. These new thresholds were employed for reporting on the donations during the election period.

16 These included items such as research, consultancy, focus groups, opinion research and printing.
17 Although as we now know, both parties were also in receipt of loans, which were only subsequently declared as donations.
18 Fisher, 2005, p. 177.
19 Fisher, 2005, p. 184.
20 Fisher, 2005, pp.174–5, 184.
21 J. Fisher, 'Party Expenditure and Electoral Prospects: A National Level Analysis of Britain' *Electoral Studies* 18, 1999, 519–32; J. Fisher, 'Political Finance and Local Party Activity in Britain' in K. Ewing, J.-C. Tham and J. Rowbottom (eds), *The Funding of Political Parties*, Routledge, 2010.

The Media and the 2010 Campaign: the Television Election?

It is something of a cliché to say that the media play a major role in modern general elections but this was particularly the case during the 2010 campaign. From the broadcasting perspective, interest focused on what influence the first televised leaders debates might have on the fortunes of the parties and the campaign generally—how far would this result in a further presidentialisation of campaigning and would any particular party/leader benefit? In relation to the oldest news medium—the press—interest centred on whether endorsement of the Conservatives by the *Sun* would make any difference and, more generally, whether newspapers were of declining significance in a multimedia age? At the outset of the election, much speculation centred on the Internet, notably how prominent and important would social networking tools, such as Twitter and Facebook, be in the course of the campaign. Commentators drew on the American experience, where Obama's campaign was seen to have extensively deployed new technologies to great effect, to ask whether the same techniques would be used here.

In the event, it was television and the leaders' debates that dominated the media agenda and became the centrepiece of the campaign. The significant rise in popularity of Nick Clegg following the first debate but the subsequent failure of the Liberal Democrats to turn this into votes and seats raises questions about how much difference the debates really made to the final outcome. Similarly, television also provided the other stand out moment of the campaign—the so-called 'Duffygate' incident—with Gordon Brown being recorded making derogatory remarks about a voter he had just met. Again, whilst this created a media storm, how much difference it really made is open to question.

Cleggmania: the impact of the leaders' debates

Contrary to pre-election hype this election campaign turned out to be quite traditional in many respects. Despite falling audiences the established news media still continued to inform most voters. Television, in particular, contributed much because, for the first time, the three main leaders appeared together in prime time 'Prime Ministerial Debates'. Each edition attracted a mass audience, a rarity for any current affairs programming. The ITV debate opened the series and was seen by 9.68 million, placing it second only to the channel's top rated Britain's Got Talent and just above EastEnders and Coronation Street that week.[1] The by-now lack of novelty together with the non-terrestrial platform contributed to only 2.21 m seeing the second instalment on Sky News together with an additional 1.39 m watching the simultaneous broadcast on BBC News 24. The viewing figure recovered to 7.43 m for the final encounter on BBC1. Cumulatively these represented huge, unprecedented audiences for general election-related broadcasting of any kind; during this period the most popular television news bulletin attracted 5.56 m viewers.

The debates were a major innovation for a British general election although they are commonplace in other democracies. Previous incumbents and/or challengers had rejected the format for fear of providing their opponents with added momentum and copious negotiations prior to past elections had failed to assuage these doubts. There were still extensive discussions prior to this campaign over the debates' format and 76 rules for the contests agreed. The 2010 general election was to be different because it would be fought by three politicians experiencing their first campaign as leader and who each calculated they could gain something from the debates. Gordon Brown had been installed unopposed as Labour leader in June 2007 and shortly after Labour's poll ratings began to plummet. Given this decline was partly caused by the economic downturn, the debates provided Brown with an ideal opportunity to justify and explain his response to the ensuing financial crisis. From the outset the Prime Minister attempted to position himself as the leader of most substance when, during the first encounter, he acknowledged 'if it is all about style and PR, then count me out' in an obvious criticism of his principal opponent David Cameron (if not predecessor Tony Blair). Cameron had been elected to lead the Conservatives in 2005 partly because of his presentational skills and, despite his party's longstanding lead in the polls, he also agreed to the debates because he evidently relished the opportunity to confront the less polished Prime Minister. For Liberal Democrat leader Nick Clegg the calculation was even more straightforward: the debates guaranteed him further exposure.

The debates had long been resisted by various politicians because they claimed such events were better suited to a presidential rather than parliamentary system. The decision to hold them has long-term ramifications because if judged solely in terms of their success in attracting sizeable audiences it seems very likely that they will play a significant role in future campaigns.[2] That they happened this time was in part due to the threat by Sky to invite the three major leaders to jointly participate in a live programme and then broadcast whichever of them turned up on the night. The more immediate short-term impact of the programmes was to turn the focus of this campaign ever more on the characters of the main leaders. This extended to their families and most especially their partners. Gordon Brown had initially got to know his wife Sarah when she was working as a public relations adviser to Labour and she subsequently played a major role in helping to 'humanise' him by accompanying him before and during the campaign and giving interviews to attest to his personal qualities. Similarly Samantha Cameron featured prominently, talking openly about her husband to ITV journalist Sir Trevor MacDonald and frequently accompanying him during the campaign.[3] *Private Eye* satirised the appearance of the 'leaders' wives' in recognition that there had been something of a departure from previous elections in which partners had been seen but remained largely silent.[4] Nick Clegg's partner Miriam Gonzalez made a virtue of continuing to work during the campaign although she too did give interviews. In the early stages of the election Clegg was more likely to be seen with a political partner, his deputy Vince Cable. Cable's image was emblazoned alongside his leader's on the Liberal Democrat battlebus in a move that underlined his perceived importance to the party going into the campaign although his presence markedly declined once the race got underway.

David Cameron had entered the campaign claiming he was the change candidate. Consequently the success of the rival opposition leader in the first debate proved especially unsettling for the Conservatives. Following the election several influential Tory commentators including donor and Vice-Chairman Lord Ashcroft and blogger Tim Montgomerie were particularly critical of the leadership for having agreed to participate in an untried format when the party had comfortably been ahead in the polls.[5] During the initial debate both of Clegg's opponents had sought to find common ground with him so as to appear reasonable but also as a precursor to negotiations in a hung parliament scenario. Brown's repeated utterance of the phrase 'I agree with Nick' was subsequently adopted by the Liberal Democrats as a campaign slogan. Some media pundits appeared surprised by what many now termed 'Cleggmania' although veteran commentator Robert Harris correctly anticipated heightened exposure during the campaign would enhance the Liberal Democrat appeal. Clegg's impact was further magnified because of his hitherto relatively low profile. Paddy Ashdown had supported his successor's leadership bid because of his 'extraordinary ability to communicate' but, having won the position,

Clegg appeared overshadowed by fellow party MPs such as the ubiquitous Lembit Opik and Vince Cable, the economist whose forensic yet accessible analysis of the 2008 crisis generated considerable media interest.[6] Consequently Clegg's lack of media visibility together with his presentational skill conspired to transform his public persona during and after the first debate. This was compounded by a format that afforded him equal billing despite the chance of him becoming Prime Minister being remote.

Elections have long favoured the third party and their forebears because of the broadcasters' desire to ensure greater parity between the rival contenders' share of coverage during the campaign period.[7] This was particularly the case in a close race with a strong likelihood of a hung parliament result in which the Liberal Democrats would be 'kingmakers'. But Clegg's performance in the debates added to this and the tenor of much of his party's coverage perceptibly changed and was no longer perfunctory as was often the case in past campaigns. This was growing recognition of the seriousness of the Liberal Democrats' bid for at least a share of power. An eve of first debate poll from Ipsos MORI poll reported 53% of voters expected Cameron to do best as opposed to 20% for Brown and 12% for Clegg. The outcome was, however, very different. Populus reported 61% of their respondents agreeing that Clegg had won as opposed to 21% for Cameron and 17% for Brown. The subsequent debates provided less dramatic postmortems with the Conservative leader vying with the Liberal Democrat for the opinion poll accolade of 'winner' in instant polls of dubious reliability with ITV actually mistakenly broadcasting the raw data from one survey provided to the station by its market researchers. Overall, the serious and exhaustive follow-up analysis, which featured assorted politicians, journalists and spin-doctors, promoted the 'horse race' election-as-game aspect of the campaign coverage. The BBC reinforced this by devoting considerable airtime to reporting the so-called 'worms' produced on screen when a tiny unrepresentative sample of three dozen undecided people turned electronic dials in positive/negative response to the leaders during each of the live debates. Rather than rely on these kinds of gimmicks, a series of ITV post-debate specials hosted by Jonathan Dimbleby proved more informative because they enabled floating voters to speak for themselves.[8]

It is questionable how and whether the debates contributed to the final election outcome. Following Clegg's opening performance media speculation focused on whether it might provide the catalyst for his party to overtake Labour. And although this was reflected in some of the mid-election polls, this apparent surge in support failed to materialise at the ballot box. This is perhaps not surprising given research on the US experience indicates that earlier debates tend to have the most impact and their influence is less on voting behaviour and more in terms of helping to inform the electorate about issues, candidates and their policies.[9] Arguably the key influence of the debates in the 2010 campaign was to transform the narrative of the campaign which had hitherto been preoccupied as to whether the Conservatives would win an outright majority. Clegg challenged this by highlighting his rival candidacy to those many undecided voters seeking change in government. This in turn encouraged a bifurcation in the right's message be this from the official Conservative campaign or its print media supporters.

Yes we Cam: the revival of the Tory press

In contrast to the three elections Tony Blair won, Labour faced a more hostile press going into this campaign. The circulation of its only reliable supporter, the *Mirror*, was slight when compared with that of the pro-Conservative newspapers. The latter group had been inconsistent in their support for Cameron but they proved willing allies during the actual campaign. The best selling *Sun* had formally abandoned its Labour allegiance during the party's 2009 conference, but had become a vocal critic of Gordon Brown's government sometime before.[10] The redtop's change of allegiance saw it rejoin the Tory press alongside the *Mail*, *Express* and *Telegraph* and together these titles launched robust attacks on Brown's character and his record (see Table 1). The other defectors to the Conservatives, *The Times* and *Financial Times*, were far more circumspect in their endorsement although their loss was a psychological blow to Labour. Interestingly the *Star*, despite its populist attacks on welfare 'scroungers', immigrants and such like, did not realign itself with the Conservatives, preferring to maintain its officially non-partisan stance.

Perhaps inevitably Cleggmania proved a defining moment for the press in this campaign. Some of the subsequent reaction was positive. *The Independent* once again backed the Liberal Democrats and this was followed by similar pledges of support from the *Guardian* and its Sunday sister the *Observer*. Their typically qualified endorsements provided a stark contrast to the more negative attention grabbing

1. Editorial declarations and circulations (in millions) of the national newspapers[11]

	2010	Circulation	2005	Circulation
The Guardian	Moderate Lib Dem	0.29	Weak Labour	0.34
The Independent	Moderate Lib Dem	0.19	Moderate Lib Dem	0.23
The Times	Weak Conservative	0.51	Weak Labour	0.65
The Telegraph	Moderate Conservative	0.68	Strong Conservative	0.87
The Financial Times	Very Weak Conservative	0.39	Very Weak Labour	0.38
The Daily Express	Very Strong Conservative	0.67	Strong Conservative	0.87
The Daily Mail	Strong Conservative	2.10	Strong Conservative	2.30
The Sun	Strong Conservative	3.00	Weak Labour	3.26
The Mirror/Record	Strong Labour	1.57	Strong Labour	2.29
The Star	No Preference	0.82	No Preference	0.85

responses in the Tory press. On the eve of the second debate there was a concerted newspaper attack on the Liberal Democrat leader and his policies. The *Daily Telegraph* published a story suggesting Clegg had improperly received payments from assorted party donors.[12] He denied the claims which appeared designed to compromise his integrity through reviving memories of the MPs' expenses controversy. The *Telegraph* had been the paper that first broke the scandal during the preceding parliament. Clegg's personal expenses briefly surfaced in the second televised debate when Sky's moderator Adam Boulton controversially raised the matter in an apparent contravention of the extensive rules governing the format.

On the same day the *Telegraph* revelations appeared, the *Express* bitterly attacked the Liberal Democrat's 'crazy' immigration policy whilst the previous day the *Sun* had mocked Clegg over his pre-debate preparations.[13] But the most audacious front page was the *Mail's* 'Clegg's Nazi slur on Britain', a reference to a 2002 *Guardian* article in which the then MEP had suggested the Germans had come to terms with the Second World War in a way the British had not.[14] Clegg rebuffed the coverage by joking that his public standing had gone from the level of 'Churchill to Nazi' within a week. The scale and severity of the press attacks even led to Labour's Chair of Electoral Strategy Peter Mandelson denouncing 'disgusting and classic smears… straight out of the Tory party', he ascribed to Conservative director of communications Andy Coulson, the former *News of the World* editor, and the 'Tory party dirty tricks manual'.[15]

The decline of newspaper sales implies press influence, such as it ever was, has diminished from the 1980s when the debate over their impact was at its most intense. However, some politicians still subscribe to the thesis that reporting can and does make a difference during elections. In the speech conceding her defeat Conservative Joanne Cash claimed: 'in Westminster North the media played an incredibly powerful role, and we have to beg the question what their role is going to be going forward—are they going to tell the truth or are they going to trash people and lie about their families?'[16] This had followed allegations relating to Cash's apparently fractious relationship with local activists published by the *Mail* and other newspapers who were critical of her and other so-called 'A-List' candidates whose selection had in part come about following an attempt by the leadership to bring greater diversity to the parliamentary Conservative party in terms of gender, ethnicity and sexuality. Some of those promoted in this way were subsequently dismissed by right-wing media commentators as so-called 'Cameron cuties' following their appearances in photo-shoots for glossy magazines such as *Vanity Fair* and *Grazia*, the latter of which also featured rival slates of glamorous representatives from the other major parties.[17]

Unlike broadcasters, the primary restrictions on what is permissible for a newspaper to publish relate to the general laws covering libel. At election times, the press routinely exercise their right to pontificate on the choices available and hence the interest in gauging whether or not this still matters. Most shifts in readership opinion between 2005 and 2010 were broadly in keeping with the 5% national 'swing' from Conservative to Labour (Table 2). Some of this may have been linked to declining sales or else demographic trends relating to changing gender, age, regional and class profiles of the differing titles' consumers. Nevertheless it is intriguing to note that there was a decisive 'swing' of 13.5% from Labour to Conservatives amongst *Sun* readers and within this evidence of a loss of support from the government to both of the main opposition parties. This marked shift may have been related to similarly disproportional changes of allegiance within some of those groups traditionally associated with this newspaper, notably the skilled working class, males of various ages and those living in certain regions. However, these demographic factors alone may not account for the scale of such change. Intriguingly, this was a campaign in which the *Sun* revived the kind of strongly partisan stance it had not adopted since 1992, the election in which it had last endorsed the Conservatives. During the intervening years the paper's support for Blair had been uncharacteristically nuanced and more about the leader than his party: it had been a prominent part of the 'Tony' press.[18] 2010 saw something of a revival in the more strident Tory press of the kind last seen in the early 1990s. One particular aspect of this was the *Sun's* negative portrayal of Gordon Brown. It was partly in response to such coverage that the Prime Minister decided to take his message directly to the public in an attempt to reconnect with the electorate. This strategy would present its own risks.

One day… in Rochdale: 'Duffygate' and other awkward moments

Human interest stories have long dominated news coverage and this reflects the belief of various theorists from Graham Wallas to Drew Westen, writing a century apart, that mass politics is guided by

2. Readership allegiances of newspapers 2010 (and 2005)[19]

	Lab	Cons	Lib Dem	Swing (Lab-Con)
Result	29 (35)	36 (32)	23 (22)	5
The Guardian	46 (43)	9 (7)	37 (41)	3.5 (Lib Dem-Lab)
The Independent	32 (34)	14 (13)	44 (44)	1.5
The Times	22 (27)	49 (38)	24 (26)	8
The Telegraph	7 (13)	70 (65)	18 (17)	5.5
The Star	35 (54)	21 (22)	20 (15)	10
The Daily Express	19 (28)	53 (48)	18 (18)	7
The Daily Mail	16 (22)	59 (57)	16 (14)	4
The Sun	28 (45)	43 (33)	18 (12)	13.5
The Mirror	59 (67)	16 (11)	17 (17)	6.5

emotion and not just reason.[20] Consequently more abstract topics can appear marginal to the election and/or media agendas. In response to this Channel 4 devoted a whole discussion to the issues it felt were being sidelined despite the extensive campaign coverage. The programme was particularly interested in the widely acknowledged debt problem afflicting the nation's economy.[21] And whilst others, notably the Institute for Fiscal Studies, attempted to press leaders on the issue, the scale and detail of the problem appeared beyond the comprehension or failed to attract the attention it arguably merited from many media outlets. This in part reflected the evasiveness of many politicians as to the level of the debt problem and how they proposed to tackle it.

A perception that the leaders were trying to avoid public scrutiny over the budgetary crisis, not to mention other issues, led to several apparently spontaneous interventions by assorted citizens. Some of them were reminiscent of Sharron Storrer who memorably confronted Tony Blair over the state of the NHS during the 2001 election. The media proved more than receptive to covering events of this kind because when voters were normally granted access to politicians there was a suspicion the former were party activists masquerading as ordinary members of the public. The cordon around politicians was symbolised in the way numerous leaders' campaign speeches were accompanied by a backdrop made up of often youthful supporters providing telegenic support to the visitor. The controlled nature of these kinds of event led one protestor to confront Gordon Brown during a meeting in the North East because the Prime Minister 'needs to see real electors, not just hand-picked people'.[22]

Brown's campaign tour of the country was periodically interrupted by citizens with varied grievances such as a disillusioned publican, a parent angry about the lack of school places and an anti-nuclear activist who invaded the stage during the leader's final major speech. Cameron too faced close questioning by members of the public including an anxious father concerned about his disabled son's educational provision. But there was nothing to match Brown's most memorable and excruciating meeting with Gillian Duffy on what had started as a routine campaign visit to Rochdale. The encounter with the disillusioned Labour supporting Mrs Duffy had ended warmly. But when Brown returned to the privacy of his car having failed to return his wireless microphone to the Sky News team following him his subsequent conversation with an aide was recorded and broadcast without either of them being aware that they were still being monitored. Brown's dismissal of 'that woman' with her 'bigoted' views dominated subsequent news bulletins with even the most populist Channel 5 programme devoting 10 minutes to the gaffe despite having largely avoided trailing the election as a lead item.

A recurrent feature of the 'Duffygate' coverage was Brown's seemingly despairing, head in hands, reaction to hearing the recorded conversation as a guest on BBC Radio 2's Jeremy Vine. Mrs Duffy's shocked reaction was also broadcast together with her objection to being labelled 'that woman'. Brown's campaign plans were effectively derailed as he opted to visit Mrs Duffy at her home, which was now besieged by reporters, to personally apologise for his comments. The voter eventually broke her silence in a *Mail on Sunday* interview in which she confirmed her intention to abstain in the election.[22] The gaffe was damaging to Brown but could have been worse as was noted by one of his most notable media critics Andrew Rawnsley of the *Observer*. Rawnsley, who featured prominently in the extensive journalistic analysis of Duffygate (which was also known as 'Bigotgate'), argued the incident was comparatively mild in contrast to some of the examples of the Prime Minister's allegedly dysfunctional behaviour discussed in his recent book.[24]

The first internet election... (again)

Just like the previous three elections, 2010 was once again dubbed the first Internet election or *the* Internet election.[25] In the early stages of the campaign, journalists and some political figures were falling over themselves to talk up the potential of the Internet. The *Daily Telegraph* excitedly proclaimed that Facebook and Twitter would have unprecedented impact and stated that 'many are predicting... that David Cameron will be swept into No. 10 on the crest of a digital wave as victor in Britain's first Internet election'.[26] The *Guardian* reported that former Labour chief strategist Lord Gould:

has suggested that the internet would be a giant autonomous force in the general election campaign and probably hold even more sway than in the US presidential campaign... likening the Internet to an army of the night that moves on its own and no one will be able to control its influence.[27]

Just three weeks later the Internet was being comprehensively rubbished, or at least talked down, as commentators discovered, seemingly to their surprise, that television was more influential and that the online stuff was merely a side show. Amongst others, Iain Dale, the leading Conservative blogger declared 'far from being an important player the internet has become all but an irrelevance'.[28] Similarly, Pat Kane in the *Glasgow Herald* summed up many column inches:

despite all the cyber predictions, from YouTube this to Twitter that, 2010 has become not the internet election but the Television election (and maybe even the Newspaper Election).[29]

Perhaps the first question to ask is what was meant by 'the Internet election' and why such excitement, (fake or otherwise), was generated in the first place. The hype prior to the election, predicting the Internet election combined several elements.

- The Internet would potentially dominate the news agenda and the parties would be unable to control the campaign agenda. Stories in the mainstream media would emerge from the web or blogosphere. Furthermore, in the age of the mobile phone camera there was an expectation that gaffes might be prominent amongst such stories.

- The parties and candidates would use social media and other tools extensively in their campaigns, with the result that the style of campaigning would potentially be more open, interactive and decentralised.

- As a consequence of some combination of the first two factors, the Internet would somehow then prove decisive in shifting voters' opinions or mobilising support for the parties, especially amongst the traditionally hard to reach younger voters.

The reasons for such excitement stemmed, as they had in 2005, from a mixture of political and technological factors. Many commentators again looked enthusiastically to the US and focused on the apparent success of Obama's online campaign in terms of fundraising and mobilisation of supporters.[30]

The expectation of a significant role for the Internet was also built on the growth and increasing appeal of the technology itself. Since the previous campaign, the Internet's reach had extended to a mass audience of around 70% of the British public. The political blogosphere, which was in its infancy in 2005, had become a central fixture of the Westminster landscape. Blog sites such as Conservative Home, Iain Dale, Labour List, Guido Fawkes and Lib Dem Voice, whilst not reaching mass audience, have become increasingly influential in terms of internal party debates.[31] What excited most attention, however, was the explosion of social media tools, notably Facebook and Twitter. Just prior to the election it was estimated that there were around 25 million Facebook accounts in the UK. The growth of public interest in online social networking was also mirrored by UK politicians, by summer 2009, around one-third of MPs had a Facebook site and over 10% had a Twitter account.[32]

Internet and mainstream media agendas

In the event, stories broken from the Internet did not dominate the mainstream media, although there were a handful of online gaffes that made the news. Labour's so-called 'Twitter Tsar' Kerry McCarthy found herself under police investigation after she revealed the results of postal votes prior to polling day on her Twitter feed. Similarly, an obscure Labour candidate Stuart MacLennan was 'sacked' following obscene postings on his Twitter account that were subsequently published in newspapers, but these were the exceptions. If anything, the new media tended to respond reactively to the old media. As a result, the Internet formed the backdrop to mainstream media coverage in several ways. It tended to act as a partisan echo chamber to events on television or in the newspapers. The key partisan blogs did little to rock the party boat and acted more as cheerleaders and mobilisers for their respective parties. In fact, in many respects, leading bloggers such as Iain Dale and Tim Montgomerie (Conservative Home) have become part of the mainstream media anyway through regular media appearances.

The net also provided broadcasters, journalists and party campaigners with instant feedback on the campaign. During, and immediately following, the leadership debates, Twitter, social network sites and online polls were used by journalists to gauge public opinion and then shape the subsequent debate about who had won. Interestingly, the parties, through prominent figures such as Eric Pickles and Alastair Campbell, tried to influence the Twitter agenda during the debates although arguably to little effect. Twitter, even if its direct reach was limited, proved largely uncontrollable.

Finally, debate on the Internet also acted to counter and sometimes ridicule newspaper coverage. When the tabloids launched their attack on Nick Clegg it was met by a wave of ironic responses from social networkers who launched the satirical nickcleggsfault hashtag on Twitter where people blamed Clegg for all the world's ills. Whilst the effect of such activities might be limited, the Internet could be seen as chipping away at the mainstream media as the authoritative voice on the campaign. Yet, perhaps the main message of from the election, in terms of the relationship between the Internet and traditional media, is that it makes little sense any more to separate them. They are now fundamentally intertwined.

E-campaigning

Much of the focus of media coverage of the e-campaign centred on the interactivity and mobilisation possibilities of web 2.0 technology (blogs and social network sites). At a superficial level, the main parties did utilise a full range e-campaign tools and had already created official YouTube channels and Facebook pages, well before the election. Parties also adopted some of the features of Obama's e-campaign toolkit most notably through the Conservatives MyCon site, which was a clear nod to Obama's MyBO web portal. However, most critics argued that whilst the technology was being deployed, there was still a high degree of risk adversity surrounding their e-campaigns. Parties were accused of failing to engage in a dialogue with voters and acting largely in old-fashioned broadcast mode merely transmitting their messages top-down to the electorate.[33] Yet, as Coleman pointed out after the 2001 election, campaigns are rarely the time for engaging in conversation since the main objective is to communicate the message clearly to voters.[34]

Whilst the interest of academics and commentators has often been on the public face of the web campaign, arguably, some of the more significant developments are the private face of Internet-based campaigning. Two elements of this more hidden type of campaigning are worth noting. Firstly, the use of the Internet to mobilise and inform activists and core supporters via closed areas. Labour's operation allowed activists to communicate with one another, discuss issues, promote groups and events and was integrated with social network tools. Secondly, Internet-based technology was used to gather information about voters, build databases and improve direct mail and marketing tactics. The Conservatives, in keeping with their marketing-led strategy, used a software system that theoretically allowed candidates to identify key groups of voters within their constituency merely by typing in local postcodes. The system also allowed candidates to feedback locally gathered information about voter concerns to party headquarters. The idea then was that the party could deliver a segmented marketing approach with specifically tailored direct mail messages to groups of voters in local constituencies.[35] However, how successful this was is more questionable. There were several reports of the system not working properly and not being deployed early enough to iron-out glitches.

Although the growth of marketing approaches suggests a continuation of trends in the professionalisation of campaigns since the 1980s, others have noted that the Internet possibly challenges the top-down, centralised command and control model of the TV era.[36] In particular, it has been suggested that the Internet might erode party campaign control or at least fragment campaign messages. New media have been seen as providing more opportunities for individual candidates to personalise their message. Web 2.0 tools, in particular, also allow activists and interested supporters more scope to create their own campaigns and network with one another without having to go through party HQ or even become members of party.[37] Certainly, early evidence suggests that in 2010 there was again a significant increase in the number of candidates with an online presence. In England, amongst six main parties contesting elections (Cons, Lab, Lib Dem, UKIP, BNP and Greens) some 47% of candidates had a web presence (with nearly two-thirds of the big three parties having a website). Strikingly, in marginal English seats, a sizeable minority of party candidates used the full range of web 2.0 tools—(42% had Facebook sites, 35% ran blogs, 34% had Twitter accounts and a third also used YouTube). How far this truly represents a departure from centralised campaigns is more questionable, since the parties have countered some of the individualising possibilities by providing templated websites and content and around 16% of candidate websites followed such a template format (over a fifth amongst the big three parties).[38]

One area where parties did lose control of the message was in terms of their campaign posters. Nearly all the traditional campaign posters were heavily spoofed and satirised online. Within minutes of being launched, posters would be subverted by altering the images or changing the slogans. These would then be spread virally across the web. One of the most successful spoof poster sites was the mydavidcameron.com site that allowed people to modify a series of Conservative posters. The site gained over a quarter of million unique visitors in its first six weeks and some of the spoof posters ended up in several newspapers. This continual online defacing of posters had led Alastair Campbell, amongst others, to declare that the campaign poster was dead as a means of communicating the party message.[39] Whilst this maybe an exaggeration, there's no doubt that party slogans and messages are more open to challenge though the Internet. Nor was it simply official posters that were challenged; unofficial videos and social network groups also offered alternative means of involvement in the campaign. The YouTube video using Pulp's hit, 'Common People', satirising David Cameron's privileged background was viewed by more people than many of the official campaign videos. Similarly, one unofficial Facebook group 'We got Rage Against the Machine to #1, we can get the Lib Dems into office!' ended up with twice as many supporters as the party had members (over 150,000 by the end of the campaign).[40] On the eve of polling day Facebook users declaring their affinity to the major political parties numbered: Conservatives 83,987, Liberal Democrats 83,441 and, trailing in third place, Labour 38,034. In small ways, therefore, the Internet is beginning to break down the boundaries between official and unofficial campaigns.

Voter engagement online

Compared to 2005, the 2010 campaign appears to have seen a significant growth in the number of people looking for election information online. Post-election survey data suggests that the numbers of voters looking for information online more than doubled to around a third of the population.[41] This increase was seen across a range of destinations and the Internet was the fastest growing source of information especially amongst the younger age cohorts, although, it is still considerably less popular and less trusted than the traditional media. Whilst mainstream media websites were still the most prominent, the official sites of parties/candidates saw even more significant rises. Around 15% of voters claimed to have visited them up from just 3 or 4% in 2005. It seems plausible to suggest that some of the increase may be as a result of the closer election race and the TV leader debates. Traffic data from the company Hitwise indicates, not surprisingly, that searches for election information and party website visits saw significant spikes of activity following television leaders debates especially for the Liberal Democrats.[42] How far the party campaigns reached beyond the usual suspects is more difficult to judge though. Around 5% of voters signed up to register as official supporters though only around 3% could remember being contacted directly by the parties online (compared with about 47% offline).

Across the board, the younger age cohorts, most notably the 18–24 years old group, were significantly more likely to have engaged with online information. Over two-thirds of 18–24 year olds claimed to have accessed MSM sites and 43% visited official party sites. The youngest age cohort was also strikingly much more likely to have used social networking sites and online video material—16% suggested they had joined or started an election-related group on a social network site and over a quarter claimed to have viewed unofficial video material. Of course, the problem from the party perspective is that the voters most likely to access election information online are also the least likely age category to vote. Nevertheless, the early data suggests that there is a shift towards online information and communication amongst younger voters that is likely to become more prominent the next election.

It is worth remembering though that simply looking at crude numbers of people accessing information online alone may actually understate the influence and reach of the net. Previous studies have detected the possibility of a classic indirect effects model, where the net activates activists to go campaign offline and reach out to those who are less interested in politics.[43] Moreover, whilst the parties' online reach may be somewhat limited, other organisations campaigning in the election claimed they had used web tools to good effect. The Hope not Hate campaign, seeking to mobilise anti-BNP support in areas such as Dagenham and Barking, suggested that web tools, especially email alerts, were extremely useful in attracting volunteers to take action on the ground.[44]

Conclusions

Despite the hype surrounding the idea of the Internet election, it was the traditional platform of broadcasting that dominated the campaign. The leadership debates, whilst not necessarily influencing the outcome of the election, certainly helped shape the narrative of the campaign by elevating the status of the Liberal Democrat leader. The outburst of so-called Cleggmania triggered a strong response from Conservative supporting newspapers. How successful this reporting was is more questionable, since the long-term decline in press sales has arguably seen a diminution of their collective hold on the news not to mention the British psyche. This was revealed in the almost mocking reaction of other media commentators when there was a simultaneous but hardly spontaneous burst of criticism levelled at Nick Clegg by the Tory press. Their belated enthusiasm for attacking opponents of the Conservatives was something of a departure from their previously studied indifference towards the third party.

The idea that it was going to be the Internet election was always flawed. Despite its increasing ubiquity, in political terms, the Internet is still a medium for partisan elites and activists. Equally, expecting American campaign experiences to be repeated here ignores the realities of a very different political and media environment. Nevertheless, whilst it may not have been the Internet election, there are signs that the online world is beginning to become routinised into campaigns and intertwined with mainstream media. For younger voters especially the Internet is simply part of everyday life. Overall, the 2010 general election may well turn out to be rather unique in media terms. The novelty factor of the leadership debates and the emergence of social media are unlikely to be viewed as quite so new next time around.

1　Figures from Broadcasting Audience Research Board. There were also other debates featuring various senior frontbench politicians debating their particular issues mainly on BBC during the election. There was also a Chancellors' debate on Channel 4 just prior to the formal campaign.

2　The 2010 Labour leadership election has been in part framed by considerations as to how the five contenders might fare in a live debate situation.

3　Trevor MacDonald meets David Cameron, ITV, 15 March 2010.

4　*Private Eye*, 13 April 2010.

5　Conservativehome.blogs.com/generalelectionreview.

6　*Guardian* 18 October 2007. Opik lost his seat in this election, a shock result in part attributed to his personal celebrity.

7　J. Blumler, and D. McQuail, *Television in Politics*, Faber & Faber, 1968.

8　Campaign 2010 with Jonathan Dimbleby, ITV 15 April 2010.

9　The authors are very grateful to fellow contributor Jane Green for guidance on the impact of debates and for suggesting the following review of the literature, W.L. Beniot *et al.*, A Meta-analysis of the Effects of Viewing US Presidential Debates, *Communication Monographs*, 70, 4, 2003, 335–50.

10　*Sun*, 30 September 2009.

11　The partisanships of the given newspapers are determined by the statement declaring their allegiance normally published on or near polling day. For more on this see David Deacon and Dominic Wring, 'Patterns of Press Partisanship in the 2010 General Election', *British Politics*, forthcoming.

12　*Daily Telegraph* 22 April 2010.

13　*Daily Express*, 22 April 2010 and *Sun*, 21 April 2010.

14　*Daily Mail*, 22 April 2010.

15　*Guardian*, 23 April 2010.

16　www.timesonline.co.uk, 7 May 2010.

17　*Daily Mail*, 14 April 2010.

18　D. Deacon and D. Wring, 'Partisan Dealignment and the British Press' in J. Bartle *et al.* (eds), *Political Communications: the British General Election of 2001*, Frank Cass, 2002.

19　Figures from Ipsos Mori—the authors are grateful to Helen Coombs for supplying them.

20　G. Wallas, *Human Nature in Politics*, Constable, 1908; D. Westen, *The Political Brain*, Public Affairs, 2007.

21　Election Uncovered, Channel 4, 2 May 2010.

22　*Daily Telegraph*, 2 May 2010.

23　*Mail on Sunday*, 2 May 2010.

24　A. Rawnsley, *The End of the Party*, Viking, 2010. Interestingly despite 'Duffygate' Labour still managed to win the highly marginal Rochdale seat.

25　S.J. Ward and R.K. Gibson (1998) 'The First Internet Election? UK Political Parties and Campaigning in Cyberspace' in I. Crewe, B. Gosschalk and J. Bartle (eds), *Political Communications: How Labour Won the 1997 General Election*. Frank Cass, pp. 93–112; S. Coleman (ed.) Cyberspace Odyssey: Elections in the Age of the Internet, Hansard Society, 2001; S.J. Ward, 'The Internet and 2005

Election: Virtually Irrelevant?' in A. Geddes and J. Tonge (eds), *The Nation Decides: The 2005 General Election*. Basingstoke, 2005, pp. 188–206.

26 *Daily Telegraph*, 7 April 2010.
27 *Guardian*, 1 April 2010.
28 *Guardian*, 27 April 2010.
29 *Glasgow Herald*, 2 May 2010.
30 A.A. Haynes and B. Pitts, 'Making an Impression: New Media in the 2008 Presidential Nomination Campaigns', *PS: Political Science & Politics*, 42, 2009, 53–58.
31 M. Francoli and S.J. Ward, '21st Century Soapboxes? MPs and their Blogs' *Information Polity*, 13, 2008, 21–39; R.K. Gibson, F. Greffet and S.J. Ward (2009) 'Party Organisational Change and ICTs: The Growth of a Virtual Grassroots?' Paper presented at the 2009 Annual meeting of the American Political Science Association, Toronto.
32 A. Williamson, L. Miller and F. Fallon, *Behind the Digital Campaign: An Exploration of the Use, Impact and Regulation of Digital Campaigning*, Hansard Society, 2010.
33 Ibid.
34 S. Coleman, 'Online Campaigning', *Parliamentary Affairs*, 54, 2001, 679–88.
35 J. Crabtree, 'David Cameron's battle to connect', *Wired Magazine*, March 2010.
36 P. Norris, *A Virtuous Circle*, Cambridge University Press, 2000.
37 R.K. Gibson and S.J. Ward (forthcoming), 'Political Organizations and Online Campaigning' in H.A. Semetko and M. Scammell (eds), *Sage Handbook of Political Communication*, Sage.
38 The authors would like to thank Roslynd Southern at the University of Manchester for supplying the data regarding candidates.
39 *The Times*, 22 February 2010.
40 Thanks to Mark Pack for drawing our attention to this.
41 The authors would like to thank Rachel Gibson and Martja Cantjoch at the University of Manchester for supplying the data in this section. The survey conducted by the polling organisation BRMB was a face-to-face survey in the week following the election.
42 For details see http://www.weblogs.hitwise.com/robin-goad/2010/05/election_traffic_final_week.html
43 P. Norris and J. Curtice,'Getting the Message Out: A Two-step Model of the Role of the Internet in Campaign Communication Flows During the 2005 British General Election', *The Journal of Information Technology and Politics*, 4, 2008, 3–13; S. Vissers, 'From Preaching to the Converted to Preaching through the Converted', paper presented to ECPR Joint Research Workshops, Lisbon, 14–19 April 2009.
44 See M. McGregor, 'People Not Technology Are What Wins Elections', *Tribunemagazine.co.uk*, 23 April 2010.

MARTIN J. SMITH

From Big Government to Big Society: Changing the State–Society Balance

At the 2005 general election the economy was largely absent from debate largely as a consequence of Labour apparent competence in economic management.[1] Following a sustained period of economic growth, low inflation and unemployment and rising income, Labour appeared to have eliminated the economics of boom and bust that had characterised post-war economic policy. It also seemed that Britain was in a new period of economic consensus with Labour committed to a fiscal responsibility and market capitalism closely reminiscent of Thatcherism. Indeed, Labour's policy of encouraging enterprise and low levels of taxation was based on an explicit policy of using capitalist enterprise and innovation as the motor of growth. However, the events of the Autumn of 2008 revealed that Labour's economic success was not based on Brown's proclaimed economic prudence but in fact a combination of private, corporate and government debt. As politicians often repeated, by 2010 Britain was in the worst recession for 60 years with rising debt and the welfare expansion of Labour's renewed social democracy facing the prospect of a long period of cuts. New Labour's *raison d'être* had been to distinguish itself from the profligacy of previous Labour government and to demonstrate that the economy was safe in its hands. However, the economic crisis revealed that Labour had spent the income of the boom years and not saved for a recession; Gordon Brown had not followed his own golden rule of keeping the public finances in balance over the medium term.

Yet what was perhaps most surprising about the general election was that despite the extent of the economic crisis and the problems facing which ever party was elected, the economic debate was rather muted. None of the parties had an economic solution to the crisis Britain faced. The only real economic option placed before the electorate was the need to cut the deficit and so the economic options presented in the

Hansard Society
doi:10.1093/pa/gsq023

election revolved almost solely around plans to reduce Britain's borrowing. Indeed, the arguments were more an issue of the timing of cuts rather than substantive policy differences. However, what was revealed was a different conception of the relationship between the state and society. Much of Labour's period in government since 1997 had been based on reforming and expanding Britain's welfare state. Both education and health had been subject to considerable largesse in the 13 years of Labour government. However whilst the Conservatives, and to a degree the Liberal Democrats, supported the welfare state, this was on the basis of a re-conception of the role of the state. The recession opened up an ideological chasm over the nature of the state and its role in the economy and society. The political campaign focused not on substantive economic policies but differing conceptions of the relationship between the state and the market. This paper will start by reviewing Labour's economic record in government and then examining the nature of the economic campaign and how the parties presented very different conceptions of what government should do.

Labour in government

Gordon Brown's central campaign claim was, as he declared in the second leaders' debate, 'I do know how to run the economy in good times and bad'. The creation of New Labour had been about establishing Labour's credentials for running the economy and breaking from the alleged profligacy of previous post-war Labour governments. As Chancellor, Brown was very keen to establish a reputation for prudence and he claimed that he had broken the British cycle of boom and bust and through the 'golden rule' of ensuring that the budget was balanced in the medium he was following a prudent economic policy.[2] Indeed, it seems that between 1997 and 2008 Labour economic policy was highly successful. The period saw consistent economic growth, increases in real income, low levels of inflation (see Figure 1) and relatively low unemployment. In addition, there was a considerable increase in public expenditure (see Figure 2). In real terms public expenditure increased by a third from £400 billion a year in 1996/7 to £600 billion in 2009/10 and much of the increase was focused on Labour's priority areas of health and education.

The original vision of New Labour was a state that was relatively small building on a combination of Thatcherite retrenchment and the idea of the enabling state. Labour wanted to distinguish its conception of government from old Labour's welfare state, which appeared to have been undermined by the economic crisis of the 1970s. Despite New Labour's original small state aspirations, the reality of 12 years of Labour government was a considerable expansion in the size and functions of the state. Indeed, like the classic social democracy of Anthony Crosland, under the Governments of Blair and Brown the fruits of economic growth were reinvested in welfare. Not only did Labour

Figure 1. Inflation under Labour RPI 1997–2010. *Source*: ONS/Guardian, 15 June 2010.

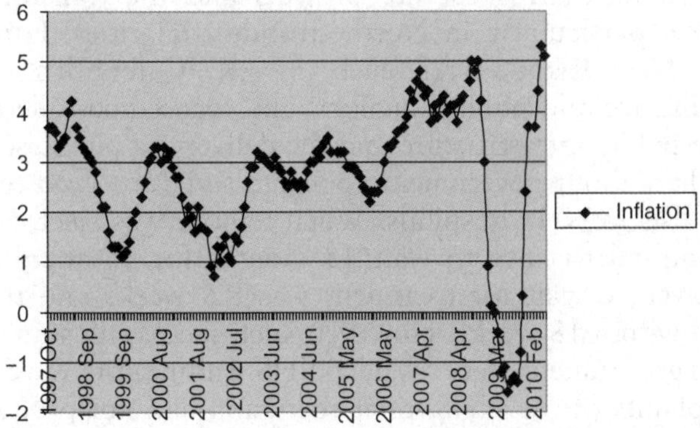

Figure 2. Public expenditure in real terms 1996/7 to 2009/10.

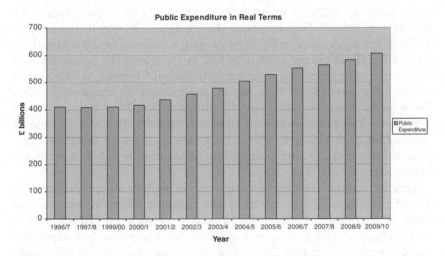

increase expenditure on welfare but a considerable number of policies were developed such as Sure Start, preventative health, housing, support for education which considerably expanded the role and the reach of the state. Indeed the number of state employee increased by over a million from 5.2 million in 1997 to 6.1 million by the end of 2009. As Lord Myners reported to the House of Lords:

The total increase in public sector employment since 1997 includes 116,000 more teaching assistants, 41,000 more teachers, 66,000 more nurses and 14,000 more police officers. These are important supports for our community and are consistent with our advocacy and support of good public service.[3]

The expansion of expenditure and employees was a reflection of a change in the nature of government in Britain. After years of decline in the public sector, the period of Labour government saw a raft of new hospitals, schools, infrastructure projects and the transformation of public space; particularly in Northern industrial cities. Labour abandoned the New Right's preference, in J.K. Galbraith's phrase, for 'private affluence and public squalor'[4] and focused considerable attention on the public infrastructure and the delivery of public services. For example, the Labour government appeared to have solved the problem of waiting lists in NHS hospitals. When Labour was elected in 1997 it was not unusual to have to wait 18 months for an appointment. By 2009 the average wait for treatment was 8.6 weeks and treatment is guaranteed within 18 weeks. However, such success illustrates the difficulties that governments face. Whilst NHS waiting lists were one of the great complaints of the NHS, their reduction had not produced acclamation; it is of course no longer a salient issue. If anything Labour has been criticised for the distortions of their target-driven approach and suffered from the short memories of voters.

A second central area of Labour's welfare strategy was the reduction of poverty; a commitment made by both Blair and Brown. Again the results were mixed. Under Labour there was a reduction in the number of children living in poverty by over half a million. In 2008/09, there were 2.8 million children living in UK households with below 60% of contemporary median net disposable household income, a decrease of 0.6 million from 1998/99. However, the number of adults in childless households in poverty increased by 800,000 by 2008.[5] Labour's child tax credit had been successful in terms of increasing the income of households with children. However, Labour's focus on ensuring taxation did not become a disincentive for innovation resulted in increased inequality.

Despite Labour's strong commitment to social justice and tackling poverty, its record was mixed. New Labour's electoral success was built on a coalition between traditional working class Labour voters, reclaiming the skilled workers and clerical workers that had supported the Conservatives in the 1980s, and significant elements of the middle class. It was this coalition that saw Labour win swathes of seats in the South in 1997. However, the coalition created a weakness in Labour's governing strategy because it meant expanding the welfare state (and particularly those elements that were used by the C2s and middle classes) but at the same time limiting tax increases so as not to frighten-off the same elements. Hence welfare spending was focused on the most widely used elements—health and education—and not on services used by core voters—poverty alleviation. At the same time, basing increased spending on economic growth rather than taxation meant that at time of economic slowdown the deficit grew quickly. Indeed it seems that Labour had a structural deficit of about 5% of GDP before the economic crisis as spending plans were not matched with rising revenue.

Labour was constrained by the limits of its electoral coalition. It needed to ensure it was not a threat to the middle class through demonstrating its economic competence and limiting its tax increases. However, both Labour's reputation and policy direction were damaged by the financial crisis that erupted in September 2008. These were most starkly illustrated by the events surrounding the bank, Northern Rock, in early 2008. As a consequence of the sub-prime mortgage crisis in the USA (stemming from low-income borrowers' inability to meet repayment obligations on lending), Northern Rock encountered problems of liquidity, reports of which prompted a 'run' on the bank. However, these problems merely presaged the major economic and political problems that were to face the Labour government towards the end of 2008 and into 2009. It was soon apparent that the measures that the Labour government had taken in relation to the banks could not prevent, in the context of a world-wide downturn, recession in Britain. By early 2009 economists agreed that Britain was facing one of the worst recessions for many years—much worse than in the 1980s and 1990s—and one which according to expert would last well into 2010. In the first quarter of 2009 the economy contracted by 2.4% with a further 0.9% reduction in the second quarter. Consequently, by the summer of 2009 unemployment reached 2.5 million and was continuing to rise. The Bank of England attempted to counteract the recession with a reduction of base rate to 0.5%. With no realistic prospect of reducing interest rates further, the Bank adopted a policy of 'quantitative easing' or, in other words, printing money. However, the impact of these measures was limited by the unwillingness of consumers to spend. With high levels of unemployment, continued credit restrictions and rises in certain commodity prices (despite declining inflation overall), the tendency of consumers was to save rather than spend. The extra money pumped into the economy was remaining in bank accounts.

The economic crisis essentially undermined Labour's strategy. Whilst tax receipts declined, expenditure increased exacerbating the structural deficit within Labour's programme. As the IFS has demonstrated, Labour's spending was greater than income from 2001. Labour had been gradually increasing the extent of borrowing and so when the economy was still growing the deficit was £40 billion by 2007.[6] However, by 2010 the size of the debt was £70 billion and projected to increase until 2011 (see Figure 3). Hence unlike 2005 it seemed that the economy would be a crucial element in the campaign.

The economy and the campaign: big government vs. big society

The context of the 2010 election campaign in terms of the economy was that Britain was in the midst of the 'worst recession for 60 years'.

The level of public borrowing partly reflected the recession and partly reflected a structural deficit produced by Labour's governing strategy. Labour electoral dilemma (how to expand the welfare state without frightening the middle classes) had produced a sustained period of government spending outstripping government revenue. As a result it would be expected that the economy would be the central issue of the campaign. Indeed, according to IPOS Mori, management of the economy was the most important issue in terms of how people would vote. The parties took this perception seriously and to a large extent campaigned around the issue of who was best positioned to lead Britain out of recession. Yet, what was similar to the 2005 campaign is that there were few fundamental differences between the parties over the tools of economic policy. Ostensibly all parties supported the continuation of the sound money market-led fiscal conservatism that had predominated since the 1980s. Where they differed was on the extent and timing of public expenditure cuts and the long-term implication that these potential cuts had for the nature of the state and its relationship with society. Yet, as we will see, the response to the crisis reflected a profound division over the conceptions of the role of the state between Labour and Conservative parties.

Labour's election campaign was based around a difficult premise considering the extent of the economic crisis facing Britain. It was that Labour had successfully run the economy for 12 years and was best placed to see Britain out of recession. Labour's central claim was that Britain was on the road to recovery and that it had undertaken a number of measures to ease Britain out of the recession. These included:

- Bailing out the banks. The Labour government was quick to spot the need to prevent the banking crisis spreading and to ensure the

Figure 3. Britain surplus/debt as a percentage of GDP.

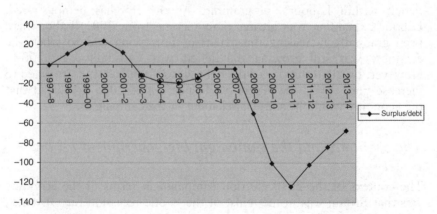

maintenance of confidence in the banking system. In addition, Labour was concerned to ensure that despite the banks getting their fingers burnt through lending, the banks continued to provide liquidity for businesses (although there is some evidence that they have not been particularly good at doing so). As a critical commentator said, Brown 'deserves credit for taking the correct decisions when the severity of the financial crisis at last became evident in the last quarter of 2008'.[7]

- Maintaining public expenditure (with an attempt to overcome the structural deficit once economic growth was well established). As Table 1 indicates Labour were committed, despite the deficit, to increasing public expenditure in 2010–2011; demonstrating a traditional Keynesian maintenance of demand in times of recession. They also retained their social democratic commitments to sustaining the key pillars of welfare policy: health and education.

- Inflation targeting—one of Labour's key innovations in 1997 was granting independence to the Bank of England. The control that the Chancellor had over the monetary policy committee in terms of setting interest rates was the inflation target that the Monetary Policy Committee (MPC) had to meet. The government's target was set at 2.5%, which was relatively high. This, intentionally or not, became a key element in Labour's strategy to end the recession. By setting a high inflation target the MPC has had to keep interest rates low and indeed inject more liquidity into the economy through quantitative easing. Labour were keen to avoid the fate of Japan whose recession became a sustained period of low inflation and low growth allowing the economy to stagnate. Brown believed that if there were inflation in the system, the economy would grow and therefore sustain demand in the economy. It is clear that there were tensions between Darling and Brown over the degree of the recession and the extent to which voters should know the truth.[8]

- Investment in technological industries—Labour never returned to the interventionist economic policy of the 1970s. However, Peter Mandelson did pursue an activist innovation policy. The 2009 White Paper, *Building Britain's Future*, outlined a distinctive industrial strategy:

We will pursue a new, more active industrial policy to drive growth and create the high value jobs of the future. We will invest to ensure that Britain can lead in the new industries of the global economy, ensuring broadband access for all by 2012 and working towards a nationwide high-speed broadband network by 2016. We will ensure that Britain's economy is underpinned by a world class modern infrastructure and that we have world-leading capabilities in the 'network' industries of the future—low carbon, biotechnology, life sciences, digital, advanced manufacturing and financial services. To support the key technology based sectors of the future we will establish a new £150 million Innovation Fund which will over time lever in up to £1 billion of private sector funding.[9]

The Government also undertook specific measures such as the car scrappage scheme and a temporary reduction in VAT in order to encourage economic growth.

Hence, Labour followed a highly traditional social democratic and Keynesian response to the economic recession. The aim was to use state resources to stimulate demand at a time when the private sector was reducing investment. The government's goal from the time of the banking crisis was to ensure that the economy kept moving and to prevent a long-term loss of consumer confidence. Despite criticisms from the opposition parties, commentators and economists, it seems

1. Labour's public expenditures and plans 2005–6 to 2010–11 £million

	2005–6	2006–7	2007–8	2008–9	2009–10	2010–11
Children, schools and families	14,326	42,098	44,904	46,848	49,232	51,302
Health	76,372	80,428	88,408	92,455	99,897	104,025
Of which: NHS England	74,168	78,468	86,402	90,940	98,217	102,272
Transport	6076	6921	6794	6546	6398	6371
Innovation, universities and skills	13,595	14,088	15,459	16,666	17,224	17,905
CLG communities	3476	3630	4224	4274	4545	4459
CLG local government	46,244	22,541	22,751	24,647	25,596	26,296
Home office	8296	8334	8552	8926	9354	9474
Justice	8018	8366	8932	9283	9465	9382
Law officers' departments	688	698	736	733	732	703
Defence	33,494	33,490	35,723	37,889	38,582	36,718
Foreign and commonwealth office	1879	1837	1878	2025	2029	1600
International development	4107	4247	4478	4835	5440	6231
Energy and climate change	709	1031	649	1016	1106	1142
Business, Enterprise and Regulatory Reform	1384	1373	1792	1594	1774	1331
Environment, food and rural affairs	2608	2884	2704	2654	2709	2682
Culture, media and sport	1438	1544	1595	1633	1681	1733
Work and pensions	8022	7876	8086	8059	9051	9929
Scotland	20,791	22,354	23,805	24,599	25,421	26,129
Wales	10,987	11,677	12,331	12,970	13,556	13,990
Northern Ireland executive	6799	7210	7596	8117	8389	8659
Northern Ireland office	1176	1252	1343	1342	1186	1174
Chancellor's departments	4782	4951	4716	4826	4637	4516
Cabinet office	1578	1724	1795	2049	2260	2411
Independent bodies	848	748	761	806	906	950
Total resource DEL	277,693	291,300	310,012	324,192	342,100	352,300

Source: HM Treasury (2009) *Public Expenditure Statistical Analysis*, CM 7630, London, Stationary Office, p. 29.

2. Debt and economic growth in selected European countries

	Economic growth 2010 (%)	Economic growth 2011 (%)	National debt as % of GDP	Budget deficit as % of GDP
UK	1.2	2.1	62.1	10.4
Ireland	−0.9	3	77.3	14.7
Portugal	0.5	0.7	85.8	8.0
Spain	−0.4	0.8	64.9	10.1
Germany	1.2	1.6	78.8	5
Hungary	0	2.8	78.9	4.1
Italy	0.8	1.4	118.2	5.3
Greece	−3	−0.5	124.9	12.2

Source: The *Guardian*, 12 June 2010.

that there is some evidence that Labour's handling of the economy and particularly the crisis was relatively effective. As Table 2 demonstrates, Britain appeared to be returning to economic growth more successfully than many other European economies and, significantly, whilst Britain's deficit is relatively large, the overall level of national debt is lower than in most other European countries. Indeed, Britain's national debt is lower than all the countries in Table 2. Brown's long-term and low key campaign to ensure that Sterling remained outside of the Euro has maintained economic sovereignty at a time of crises and not left Britain in the position of Spain and Greece of being unable to devalue their currencies at a time of economic difficulty. Comparatively, then, the British economy is in a relatively strong position (despite Conservative scares about the threat to the country's 'AAA' credit rating during the campaign) and in a comparative context it is difficult to see Labour having created a crisis that is particular to the UK. If anything Labour's economic management enabled the British economy to survive a global economic crisis in a better state than many other countries.

Despite, Labour's apparent steady handling of economic crisis from the start of the banking crisis through the recession, the rhetoric of the opposition throughout the election campaign was that Labour had bankrupted the economy through economic mismanagement. This view was reinforced by the message left by Liam Byrne, the outgoing Chief Secretary to the Treasury, to his successor: 'Good luck. There is no money left'. The Conservative response to what they defined as Labour's profligacy was in many ways a traditional Conservative response of promising to reduce spending in order to allow the private sector to thrive and to reassure the markets.

However, despite major differences between the parties on the economy and society—as we will see below—all three parties were aiming for very similar places. They were all committed to a significant fiscal tightening with a £70 billion reduction in spending by 2016/17 and a return of public expenditure to 40% of GDP by 2031/32.[10]

Emerson indicates this requires significant public expenditure cuts, although both Labour and Conservatives were vague about how these were to be delivered as both parties had considerable spending commitments in their programmes. However behind these shared goals was a very different vision. The Conservatives promised that the cuts would start immediately whilst both Labour and the Liberal Democrats were planning to delay cuts until 11/12. The other major difference was in how the cut in borrowing was to be facilitated. For Labour the ratio of cuts in spending to increase in taxes was planned at 2 to 1, for the Liberal Democrats it was 2.5 to 1 and for the Conservatives 4 to 1.[11] This highlights a significant ideological difference between Labour (and Liberal Democrats) in term of the welfare state and spending. All three parties recognised the need to cut public spending but both Labour and Liberal Democrats wanted to pay for more of the deficit reduction through taxation, thus protecting the welfare state. The Conservatives on the other hand were implicitly aiming to recast the welfare state with the aim of reducing taxations. Conservative welfare reforms were presented under the vision of 'The Big Society'.

What is interesting about the Cameron campaign in 2010 is that he was appealing to traditional Conservative prudence and presenting the party to the electorate as a party that could be trusted with the economy. Yet the Conservatives were keen to reassure the electorate that they would not damage the public services and in particular promised to maintain Labour's NHS spending plans. Cameron's claim was that his party was the only one that promised to increase Health expenditure. Cameron NHS commitment was an attempt to separate himself and the party from the Thatcherite scepticism of the 1980s by setting out his own personal commitment to free health care.

The commitment to the NHS was a watering down of a broader pledge made early in Cameron's leadership. In the first years of their leadership, Osborne and Cameron had followed Labour's strategy in 1997 and made a commitment to maintaining Labour's spending plans overall in order to quell the idea that they would cut the public services. This was a replication of the Blairite approach of building a broad electoral alliance and so developing an electoral strategy based on not frightening traditional Labour voters. However, in the context of deteriorating public finances and a desire for some cuts, they moved away from this pledge.[12] This change of policy reflects a ubiquitous tension within Conservative strategy and policy between a desire to pursue economic prudence with the prospect of potential tax cuts and a concern not to be seen to be following a Thatcherite approach to dismantling key elements of welfare. Labour had undoubtedly succeeded in securing education and health as services that the electorate wanted to retain as free at the point in the delivery. Consequently, both the Conservatives and the Liberal Democrats were prepared to sustain a high level of commitment to the core aspects of the welfare state.

Of course, these are the public services focused on all voters and not just the poor. Good health care and education provided by the state has broad electoral support. Nevertheless, both Liberal Democrats and Conservatives demonstrated scepticism of some of the middle class welfare subsidies such as tax credits and child bonds. However, the Liberal Democrat commitment to scrap university fees demonstrates a lack of consistency in terms of the flow of transfer payments.

The Liberal Democrats were more committed to Labour's welfarism than the Conservatives. In their manifesto they claimed:

We will provide a fair start for all children by giving schools the extra money they need to cut class sizes and provide additional one-to-one teaching, and by setting schools free to give all children the best possible education. We will scrap unfair university tuition fees so everyone has the chance to get a degree, regardless of their parents' income. We will help the NHS work better with the money it has by using the savings we have found to protect front-line services, such as cancer treatment, mental health care, maternity services, dementia care and preventive medicine.[13]

Like the Conservatives they were aware of the way that Labour's period in government had embedded the welfare state within the consciousness of the voters but their welfare policy was based on the chimera of paying for improved services through the holy grail of efficiency savings.

In order to try to reconcile the tension of reducing spending and maintaining welfare, the Conservatives attempted to develop an alternative vision to Labour's expanded welfare state through the idea of the Big Society: According to Cameron:

Big society – that's not just two words. It is a guiding philosophy – a society where the leading force for progress is social responsibility, not state control. It includes a whole set of unifying approaches – breaking state monopolies, allowing charities, social enterprises and companies to provide public services, devolving power down to neighbourhoods, making government more accountable. And it's the thread that runs consistently through our whole policy programme — our plans to reform public services, mend our broken society, and rebuild trust in politics. They are all part of our big society agenda.[14]

The Conservatives attempted to develop a narrative to support their complex, and what some may say, contradictory, economic/welfare policy. The Conservatives case was that because of the economic situation created by Labour, there was little choice but to cut public spending. However the public good and public services could be maintained through looking to non-state providers. For Cameron both social enterprises and the private sector could provide public services in order to develop the 'post-bureaucratic society'. Whilst the big society is presented as a new idea—and one legitimised in Cameron's early election campaign speech by reference to two-left-of centre US presidents, Obama and Kennedy—it is in many ways a development of welfare reform under Labour. Labour's public service reform programme had been focused on pluralising service delivery (and often bringing in third sector and private sector suppliers) and increasing choice for users. It was also a return to the complex patterns of welfare provision that occurred before the establishment of the welfare state in the 1940s. The big society is seen as a way of reforming the public sector through greater voluntarism and mix of providers as in the case of education policy where a range of providers will be allowed to set up Academies with much greater control over how they organise and deliver services.

However, it is not clear how successful the big society programme was at reassuring voters. For many voters, commentators and Conservative candidates there was a feeling that the big society was not sufficiently clear or distinct in terms of underpinning the Conservative electoral strategy. There were criticisms about how the concept was introduced and Cameron admitted in an interview in the *Evening Standard* that the idea was complicated and difficult to sell on the door step.[15] In many ways it was a return to traditional conservative ideas of public service and duty and it provided a distinct approach to public services to Labour's increasingly traditional social democratic vision. Indeed a Mori Poll for *The Economist* after the election demonstrated that there was still ambiguity amongst voters about the 'big society'. Whilst over 50% of those interviewed believed that government did too much, a majority were worried that government would not do enough in the future and 81% believed that NHS services should be the same everywhere and even on the issue of recycling 70% wanted uniform services, questioning the public commitment to localism.[16]

The 'big society' concept was part of the Conservatives' overall economic strategy. It was a way of trying to ensure the public good whilst reducing the size of the state. The Conservatives stressed a commitment to reducing the role of the state and expanding the private sector. As the Manifesto promised: 'We will increase the private sector's share of the economy in all regions of the country, especially outside London and the South East'.[17] Cameron made it clear during the campaign that he thought that some parts of the country were too dependent on the public sector in terms of employment and economic activity. As the manifesto states: 'Public sector productivity has fallen under Labour, acting as a drag on growth and reducing the quality of our public services'; implicitly referring back to arguments made by Bacon and Eltis in the 1970s that the public sector was crowding out private investment.[18] For Labour the public sector had been a mechanism for social interventions and a motor of economic growth. The Conservatives see public spending as a drag on private sector productivity.

The Big Society speaks to a Tory tradition of public duty and the social responsibility of the well off to the disadvantaged. It sits within the idea of welfare being provided by an organic civil society rather than the state and the role of the woman's institute, the roundtable and other voluntary organisations that 'do good'. People do not need the state but can organise themselves for the public good through a tradition of voluntarism. However, this is a difficult concept to reconcile with the Thatcherite, new right concept of individuals as rational actors concerned only with utility maximisation. Cameron's emphasis on there being such a thing as society contrasts both with Labour's emphasis on the public sector and the Thatcherite emphasis on the market. Cameron sees the collective action problem being resolved by a sense of duty. However much of the manifesto is underpinned by an apparent rational choice ontology. This means that the manifesto is thin on the transition from Labour's welfarism and Thatcherite individualism to Cameron's voluntary activists and also has contradictory understandings of the motivations for human behaviour throughout. The market approach to the economy relies on utility maximisation while a strong element of welfarism remains in the commitments to the NHS and education. Moreover, a big question is whether the 'big society' can develop without considerable state support and oversight.

The election campaign was thus based on big similarities and big differences. All parties were committed to cutting the deficit and maintaining welfare. Labour's preference was to maintain its welfare expansion through increased taxation whilst the Conservatives were focused on the creation of the big society. This underpins a significance difference. Before the coalition between the Conservatives and Liberals there was some considerable overlap between the two parties on economic policy. Both were committed to tax cuts, although in slightly different ways. The Liberal Democrats made a commitment to 'fair tax' and promised to raise the income tax threshold to £10,000. As we saw above both parties were committed to reducing the deficit. But here the Liberal Democrats were between Labour and Conservative with a strong commitment to deficit reduction but also agreeing with the need to delay cuts for a year. Conservatives and Liberal Democrats were focused on recalibrating the state in order to reduce the baseline of public spending. Vince Cable supported the Conservative notion of zero-based budgets—with departments having to defend all aspects of their spending and public sector reform based on increased efficiency.

All three parties whilst committed to reducing the deficit, focused on the need to rebalance the economy in the face of the banking crisis. This on one side meant a promise to encourage a growth in manufacturing and on the other to rethinking the regulation of the banks. All three parties promised a levy on banking transactions, much stronger regulation of the banks and mechanisms for controlling bank bonuses. Labour had illustrated its commitment to cracking down on bonuses announcing in the 2010 budget a 'supertax' on bank bonuses. Perhaps what was most surprising about the election was that although the banking crisis was in many ways the prelude to the economic crisis still affecting Britain there was relatively little discussion of it in the election campaign and little real difference between the parties. All wanted stronger regulation with Labour promising to strengthen the existing Financial Services Authority and the Conservatives promising to abolish it and to give stronger powers to the Bank of England.

However whilst the Conservatives wanted to rebalance the economy through cutting the public sector, Labour was focused on a much more interventionist approach. Labour's period in office saw a significant shift from a free market to increasing industrial intervention. Considerable funding was spent through regional development agencies to encourage regional economic growth. Lord Mandelson explicitly stated:

If markets fail or don't work efficiently, government has a role to play—as we saw in the financial markets. The Government's job is not to substitute for markets or displace the private sector. We are not into bailing out the past, but removing the barriers to investing in the future.[19]

Whilst this was not a return to previous Labour governments' economic intervention, the Government was committed to promoting industrial development in Britain through ensuring finance for industrial investment (such as the controversial £80 million loan to Forgemasters in Sheffield, subsequently scrapped by the coalition government) and using Government procurement to support domestic industry. In many ways both the Conservatives and Liberal Democrats shared this commitment to rebalancing the economy but they did so on the basis of market mechanisms and private financing rather than Labour's state-led industrial policy. However, the Liberal Democrats had a very clear commitment to state leadership on the development of a green and sustainable economy. Again activism in industrial policy illustrated the ways Labour and Conservatives were developing very different ideological positions.

Conclusion

The economic crisis which began in September 2008 has had a more dramatic effect on British politics than perhaps first appeared to be the case. For many years it has been assumed that the neo-liberal consensus had become hegemonic and effectively eliminated debate on economic policy (as was seen in the 2005 election). New Labour was characterised by its acceptance of free market economics. At the same time Cameron's political strategy was based on the need to rebuild a broader electoral coalition by stressing the Conservative commitment to the welfare state and, most particularly, the NHS. It seemed therefore that Labour had shifted to the right on economic policy and the Conservatives to the left on welfare policy thus creating a new Blairite consensus. However, the way that the parties have responded to economic crisis has illustrated significant ideological differences between Labour and Conservative. As we have seen, Labour's period in office has produced a consistent social democratic approach to welfare by using the fruits of economic growth to boost public expenditure. This policy was to some degree undermined by the economic crisis which cut off the supply of funds. The problem was made worse by Labour's caution in offsetting lost revenue through tax increases. Labour's response to the crises thus became increasingly Keynesian using deficit spending to counteract the effects of recession and ensure economic growth. To some degree this policy was effective in that the impact of the recession was less in the UK than in some other European economies. Nevertheless, it was a policy that left a growing deficit.

So whilst Labour's vision of state market relations was beset by the contradiction of increasing expenditure but failing to increase revenue, the Conservatives focused their response around the desire aiming to reduce the deficit rapidly through reducing the role of the state. The Conservative leadership appealed to the Thatcherite desire for small government and an expanded private sector role. Yet, unlike Thatcher the Conservatives were beset by their own contradiction; a commitment to key elements of welfarism in health and welfare. Their attempt to square this circle was based on the notion of the big society but what is yet to be seen is whether a big society can replace the welfare functions of the public sector whilst maintaining quality of service and social justice.

With the benefit of hindsight, it appears that the Liberal Democrats played a canny game with the prospect of coalition bargaining. With their policies fitting relatively neatly between the Conservative and Labour positions, they could work with the Conservatives on cutting taxes and reducing the deficit through better use of public money but at the same time they shared Labour's commitment to social justice and not imposing cuts that would damage economic recovery. However, what is clear is that both Conservative and Liberal Democrats wanted to recalibrate the baseline of public expenditure and so reverse core elements of Labour's expansionist welfarism. Hence what we saw developing before, during and after the election campaigns are profound differences in the parties over the relationship between the state and society with Labour reaffirming its commitment to a large publically funded welfare state and the Conservatives and Liberal Democrats advocating a smaller public sector and a lesser role for big government.

---

1   M.J. Smith, 'Its Not the Economy Stupid! The Disappearance of the Economy from the 2005 Campaign' in A. Geddes and J. Tonge (eds) *Britain Decides: The UK General Election 2005*, Palgrave Macmillan, 2005.

2   M. Watson, 'The Split Personality of Prudence in the Unfolding Political Economy of New Labour' *Political Quarterly*, 79, October–December 2008.
3   House of Lords Debates, 7 December 2009, column 890.
4   J.K. Galbraith, *The Affluent Society*, Penguin, 1962.
5   Department of Work and Pensions, 'Households Below Average Incomes', 2010 http://research.dwp.gov.uk/asd/hbai.asp).
6   L. Elliot, 'What caused the deficit?' *Guardian*, 7 June 2010.
7   Wolf 'The economic legacy of Mr Brown' *Financial Times*, 13 May 2010.
8   See Fielding article in this volume.
9   HM Government (2009) *Building Britain's Future*, CM7654, Stationary Office, pp.14–15.
10 Emerson, C., *Filling the Hole: How Do the Three Main UK Parties Plan to Repair the Public Finances?*, Institute for Fiscal Studies, 2010.
11 Emerson, op. cit.
12 F. Elliot, 'Tories will ditch plans to match Labour spending', *The Times*, 9 September 2008.
13 Liberal Democratic Party, *Our Manifesto*, Liberal Democratic Party, 2010, p. 33. http://www.network.libdems.org.uk/manifesto2010/libdem_manifesto_2010.pdf.
14 Cameron, D. 'Our Big Society Plan', 2010. http://www.conservatives.com/news/speeches/2010/03/david_cameron_our_big_society_plan.aspx.
15 *Evening Standard*, 29 April 2010.
16 Mori (2010) 'Is the Coalition Government Bringing the Public with It?' http://www.ipsos-mori.com/researchpublications/researcharchive/poll.aspx?oItemId=2616
17 Conservative Party (2010) *An Invitation to Join the Government of Britain*. http://media.conservatives.s3.amazonaws.com/manifesto/cpmanifesto2010_lowres.pdf
18 R. Bacon and W. Eltis, *Britain's Economic Problem: Too Few Producers*, Macmillan, 1976.
19 A. Grice, 'Labour's industrial revolution', *The Independent*, 20 April 2010.

RICHARD G. WHITMAN

The Calm After the Storm? Foreign and Security Policy from Blair to Brown

If discontent over foreign policy and more particularly the decision to go to war in Iraq was the leitmotif of the second half of Blair's premiership, Brown's administration was marked by the need to deal with the global financial crisis. Distinctions can be drawn between the respective foreign policy approaches of the Blair and Brown administrations. The differences were, however, those of style and emphasis, rather than substantive differences in the direction and objectives of the UK's foreign policy. The period from the 2005 General Election until the 2010 election can be characterised as one in which New Labour attempted to 'normalise' foreign and security policy by reducing its salience as an area of widespread public political concern, but then found itself struggling to respond to an unprecedented challenge to the global political economy.

The fire-fighting response to the emerging global financial crisis became a predominant concern for Brown in the final two years of his premiership, overriding longer standing commitments to reform the governance of the political economy to distribute its benefits more widely and to more effectively tackle climate change. There is a curious coincidence in Blair's and Brown's periods as Prime Minister in that both became the hostage of external events that they had initially sought to channel and direct. In both cases—the Iraq War and the global financial crisis—the two British Prime Ministers also sought to play a primary supporting role to that of the USA. Both Prime Ministers were strong transatlanticists, each seeking to act as advocate for the uses of US power for purposes that they sought to shape and influence.

A new labour foreign policy highpoint: the G8 presidency

The period immediately following the election of May 2005 was characterised by a high degree of continuity in the key foreign and

doi:10.1093/pa/gsq028

security challenges confronting the UK. This is to be expected as the UK's broad foreign and security priorities had been established in the first two terms of the New Labour government and the strategic reorientation of external relations was not a platform on which the 2005 election was fought. Furthermore, as the timetable for the withdrawal of British troops from Iraq was as yet to be defined, Iraq remained a key focus of political and military resources and its replacement by Afghanistan as the main theatre of operations for UK forces was yet to be initiated.

The year of the 2005 General Election was also one in which the UK enjoyed a high international profile. The UK chaired the G8 and held the Presidency of the EU for the second half of the year. The chairmanship of the G8 provided the government with the opportunity to further two of its long-standing foreign policy ambitions: to focus attention on mitigating climate change and to focus on the lack of African economic development. The government sought to use the G8 presidency as the locus for the mobilisation of publics within and without the UK to support these issues by its active encouragement of the Make Poverty History campaign and the worldwide Live 8 concerts, thereby putting pressure on the G8 members to commit to substantial poor-country debt-relief.

Year 2005 was a high point of the creative aspects of the Blair–Brown partnership on international policy.[1] Brown concentrated for weeks on the details of a debt elimination package for the 18 most indebted countries for which he gained the approval of the G8 finance ministers at their meeting in June in London. Blair appeared to deliver on the leaders of the G8 committing to fully realise the Millennium Development Goals and gaining George W. Bush's acceptance that climate change required attention with the potential for the G8 to play a leading future role.

The centrepiece of the G8 presidency was the Gleneagles summit held from 6 to 8 July. Blair's attendance was interrupted by the London bombings that took place on the second day of the summit. The summit could be read as a metaphor for New Labour's foreign policy: its aspirations were for the UK to provide active leadership to tackle some of the most intractable global development problems, but instead the government's attention was diverted by the 'war on terror'.

Brown's foreign policy doctrine: continuity over change?

When he became Prime Minister the totality of Gordon Brown's foreign policy aspirations were not entirely clear. As Chancellor of Exchequer Brown had sought to define Britain's foreign economic policy and had established a clear set of positions on development policy and climate change and the manner in which international financial institutions should be reformed to fit with his interests in dealing with global poverty. This vision for global governance could be expressed as the desire for a global new deal through a modern Marshall Plan.[2] In other areas of foreign policy the assumption was that he had not demurred from the major foreign and security policy choices made by Blair as this was a not an area of active contestation between the government's two protagonists. Once in office Prime Minister Brown broadened the range of foreign policy issues with which he was actively engaged and also sought to differentiate the position of his administration from that of his predecessor, whilst also maintaining the line that Blair's major foreign policy initiatives had been broadly correct. This position was unavoidable, in that as one of the central figures in the New Labour government, Brown was complicit in the key foreign policy decisions of Blair's tenure as Prime Minister. Consequently, Brown sought to introduce nuances into the philosophy underpinning the government's foreign policy alongside the presentational changes that came about through his different demeanour from that of his predecessor.

The first few weeks of the Brown administration did, however, appear to represent a change in tone and emphasis. This was most notable in the shift from an emphasis on the 'war on terror' to a more careful and nuanced choice of language. Furthermore, Brown's first meeting with President Bush at Camp David on 27 June 2007 was marked not by the protestations of the importance of the transatlantic relationship (which were duly made), but rather by the careful attention that was given to stressing the intention to make the Brown–Bush relationship businesslike, rather than the intimate understanding between Blair and Bush.

Transatlanticism was as central for Brown as it was for Blair, but the difference was that for the new Prime Minister there was a clear grand strategy: to harness US power and influence to his ambition to restore and renew the institutions of global governance to allow for a more effective management of global capitalism which would drive the development of the poorest economies.[3] The expectation was that President Obama would be a willing partner in this agenda. The Brown government showed the same neurotic preoccupation with the health of the transatlantic relationship as all of Britain's post-World War II administrations. The change of President from Bush to Obama was viewed as an opportunity to renew the partnership after the public unpopularity of the Bush–Blair relationship. From the onset of the Obama administration close attention was given to how the UK ranked in the relative pecking order of European states. Brown's position as the first European leader to travel to the White House and his invitation to address a joint session of Congress, acted to sooth initial anxieties.

A key challenge confronting Brown was to restore the reputational damage caused by the Iraq war. However, substantive structural changes in the direction of foreign policy were impossible with the UK locked into its existing overseas military commitments and with no major boost envisioned for Britain's wider diplomatic and foreign policy infrastructure. Furthermore, Brown continued Blair's policy of using the European Union to amplify Britain's wider foreign policy objective to remain a globally significant power rather than using Europe as the primary vehicle, or conduit, for British foreign and security policy.

As a heavyweight politician with over a decade in government Brown already had a well-defined political philosophy. Furthermore, in a series of interviews and speeches whilst still Chancellor in late 2006 and early 2007 three broad political priorities were stressed, with climate change and security reiterated, alongside economic reform.[4]

The importance for the UK in leading the world effort in responding to the challenge of climate change was also a recurrent theme in Brown's pre-Prime Ministerial speeches and statements.[5] Illustrative of this priority was his commissioning of the Stern Report whilst at the Treasury, and his welcoming of its conclusions. The 2006 Queen's Speech also reported that the government would be publishing a bill on climate change as part of its policy to protect the environment (and, indeed, the 2008 Climate Change Act set clear targets for carbon emissions and saw the introduction of the independent Climate Change Committee). Brown's perspective on climate change was that it was perceived through the prism of development, emphasising the impact that it will have on the world's poorest countries and arguing that the rich countries should put their financial resources at the service of the poor. This emphasis on developing countries was also highlighted at Brown's 2006 Labour party leadership coronation conference speech, in which he stated: 'I make this promise: tackling climate change must not be the excuse for rich countries to impose a new environmental colonialism: sheltering an unsustainable prosperity at the expense of the development of the poor'.[6]

Brown's Lord Mayor's Banquet speech in November 2007 and his Kennedy Memorial Lecture in April 2008 were two further attempts early in his premiership to outline a distinctive foreign policy philosophy.[7] The Lord Mayor's speech was well-received and noted both for its strident emphasis on the importance of transatlanticism and its warning to Iran on nuclear proliferation. Less remarked at the time— but to become of more substantive importance subsequently—was the stress on the need for the reform and renewal of the UN, G8, World Bank and the IMF. The Kennedy Memorial Lecture on Foreign Policy struck a different note as it was delivered as the credit crunch was unfolding and focused on the need to create new rules and institutions for the new global political economy.[8] Climate change and the need to deal with failed and rogue states were the other two main strands of the speech. The speech knits its three strands together through a central theme of the need for reform and renewal of the arrangements of global governance.

The publication of the British Government's first national security strategy in March 2008 was Brown's attempt to map the full spectrum of threats to UK security and the appropriate policy responses.[9] The document attempted to chart a distinctive approach to security and counter-terrorism in the 'post-9/11' context. The security strategy reinforced the linkage between domestic and international threats to national security and most especially in the area of terrorism. It was updated a year later with stress put on the results achieved since the preceding year and a greater emphasis on the need to counter the domestic terrorist threat with its origins in Afghanistan and the border areas of Pakistan.[10]

Changes at the Foreign and Commonwealth Office

The hallmark of Blair's premiership was the creation of a foreign policy making process that drained direction and authority for foreign policy away from the Foreign and Commonwealth Office (FCO).[11] The strengthening of the role of the Prime Minister in foreign policy making had been identified under previous prime ministers. However, Blair took this approach to a new level, with Downing Street driving key bilateral relationships. This was marked not just in UK–USA relations but also in the 'promiscuous bilateralism' pursued with continental European states.[12]

Across the period of the New Labour government the FCO was seen to lose, in terms of influence and budget, to the Department for International Development (DFID). This was the Chancellor of Exchequer using his powers of resource allocation to see his conception of the appropriate foreign policy aspirations for the UK realised.[13]

Blair's long-standing foreign secretary Jack Straw, who had provided the Prime Minister with the political support of the FCO for the decision to go to war in Iraq, was moved by Blair as part of his cabinet reshuffle after the local government elections in 2006. Straw's replacement by Margaret Beckett was met with a mixed reaction. The initial reaction was of the unexpected nature of her appointment and interest as the first female Foreign Secretary, and only the second woman (after Margaret Thatcher) to hold one of the great offices of state.[14] For the FCO, bruised by its divisions over the war with Iraq, there was a guarded welcome to the appointment.

Beckett's appointment as foreign secretary offered the possibility of refocusing public and media attention away from Iraq. However, Beckett had a short honeymoon period with the media, which grew much more hostile as her tenure progressed, particularly over the UK response to the Israeli invasion of Lebanon in July 2006 and the perceived lack of UK pressure upon Israel to end hostilities. The failure of the Prime Minister to respond to requests from Beckett to argue more forcefully with the USA for an Israeli ceasefire caused divisions with the Cabinet.

Beckett's successor as Foreign Secretary was one of the more eye catching aspects of Brown's cabinet reshuffle on 28 June 2007. The appointment of David Miliband as Foreign Secretary introduced a dynamism to the FCO through his attempts to alter the terms of debate on British foreign policy, which were redolent of Robin Cook's early period as Foreign Secretary.

Miliband sought to re-focus the main priorities of the FCO and to reinvigorate the UK's foreign policy by making a case for new thinking about the UK's position in international relations and asserting the need for the UK to be an active internationalist. Miliband set out a New Strategic Framework from which the FCO was to order the priorities of its operation.[15] Furthermore, he introduced the notion of 'Bringing Foreign Policy Home' by initiating a programme whereby the FCO gave greater attention to explaining the UK's foreign policy within Britain. Miliband used speeches to set out a post-Blair foreign policy and positioned himself as 'big thinker' on contemporary international relations. Notable was his attempt to re-establish the basis by which the UK should intervene in third countries. This was advanced in a lecture delivered in Oxford in February 2008 entitled 'The Democratic Imperative' in which he made the case of a continuing moral imperative to intervene to help spread democracy.[16] Miliband did not, however, enjoy complete latitude to reconceptualise British foreign policy single-handedly. Gordon Brown's intervention to force last minute changes to a speech on the European Union in November 2007 was an indication that the Foreign Secretary's revisionism had its limits.[17]

Foreign policy: issues and events

A hallmark of Blair's tenure as Prime Minister was the extent to which to it became consumed by foreign policy issues—and particularly by the issue of the use of armed force by the UK overseas. Of the five wars to which the New Labour government committed during its period in power two of these were still being waged when it was re-elected in 2005. The retreat from Iraq and the deepening of the UK's commitments in Afghanistan were the two major foreign policy preoccupations for the government between 2005 and 2010. There is a clear distinction between these two conflicts in that the military involvement was pursued in Afghanistan on the basis of a cross party support in contrast to party political divisions on Iraq.

IRAQ. The UK's role in Iraq underwent a transformation in the course of the Parliamentary term. UK combat operations (under the auspices of Operation Telic since the invasion in 2003) were declared completed on 30 April 2009 and all combat troops were withdrawn from the country by the deadline of 31 July agreed by the British and Iraqi governments. One hundred and seventy-eight service personnel were killed during the deployment.

A precise timetable for the withdrawal of troops from Iraq was resisted by the government in the early days of the Parliament. Elections in Iraq in January and December in 2005 paved the way for the formation of an Iraq government in March 2006 and the progressive handing over of responsibility for security to the Iraq army. During 2006 and 2007 the areas of the south east of the country, for which the UK had responsibility since the invasion in its role as head of the Multi-National Division (South East), were handed over to Iraqi control. By the time of the change of Prime Minister in May 2007 British troops had been reduced to a contingent of 5500. The government was reluctant to describe the force redeployments as withdrawals, but when the Four Rifles Battle Group withdrew to Basra Airport from their base in Basra City on 2 September the local population viewed this as a victory for the Madhi Army militias based in the city.[18] In the summer months of 2008 the four remaining provinces for which the UK had responsibility for security were handed over to Iraq forces and Basra airport came under Iraqi control on 1 January 2009 and following the expiry of UNSCR 1790 the continuing presence of UK troops was on the basis of bilateral agreements with the Iraq government. The UK retains a residual military presence in Iraq on the basis of the bilateral defence Training and Maritime Support Agreement with the Government of Iraq concluded in June 2009, under which UK forces train the Iraqi Navy and Royal Navy have a role protecting Iraq's offshore oil platforms.

The rather ignominious final stages of the UK's military deployment in Iraq ensured that Iraq remained an issue of active political controversy beyond the original decision to go to war. As indicated above the Brown government was keen to develop a new foreign policy narrative, but the ongoing security situation in Iraq and the political instability of the country (even though the humanitarian situation improved) created an ongoing and uncomfortable reminder of the foreign policy controversy of the Blair era.

The Iraq Inquiry (often referred to as the Chilcot Inquiry after its chairman Sir John Chilcot) announced by Brown in a statement to Parliament on 15 June 2009 was an attempt to satisfy public and media desire for a political catharsis on the decision to go to war in Iraq. Brown was quickly forced to go back on his original announcement that Inquiry proceedings would take place in private, following heavy Parliamentary and media criticism. The composition of the Inquiry, a committee of Privy Counsellors established by the Prime Minister under the agreement of the House of Commons, offered an opportunity to remove the Iraq war from Parliamentary politics in the run-up to the General Election. The remit of the Inquiry was broad, covering the period from the summer of 2001 to the end of July 2009 and so encompassing the run-up to the conflict, the military campaign, and its aftermath.[19]

Brown's appeared before the Inquiry on 5 March 2010 for four hours of testimony. Following the earlier appearance by Blair on 29 January, the public appearance reinforced the impression that the war was inextricably linked with the successive Prime Ministers. Brown was trenchant in his support for the decision to go to war. There was controversy over Brown's evidence on the financing of the war, and his assertion that all the necessary financial resources had been provided to conduct the war contradicted the evidence of earlier witnesses, including Sir Kevin Tebbit, the former Permanent Secretary at the MoD. Brown wrote to the Inquiry following his appearance to correct what were construed as misleading statements in his oral evidence on levels of defence expenditure.

AFGHANISTAN. Although the deepening of the UK's involvement in Afghanistan did not initially create the same degree of political controversy for the government as the Iraq war it has become an issue of active political debate and public disquiet throughout the course of the Parliament.

Over the last five years the security situation in the country has remained precarious, with the Taliban apparently not being weakened as a military opponent and showing a remarkable ability for tactical and strategic adaptation. The re-election of President Karzai in the Presidential election in the autumn of 2009 through a flawed and corrupt process put the UK government in a difficult position in which it appeared to be sustaining a corrupt regime incapable of reforming itself and developing the country. This was despite the UK increasing its modest troop deployment in the country to the most sustained military engagement since the Korean War of the 1950s.[20]

The lack of substantive political and economic progress in Afghanistan during the period in which the UK has increased its military involvement has increased the public unpopularity of the UK's participation, especially in the course of 2009. By late 2009 polling was consistently recording substantial majorities in favour of a UK military withdrawal.[21]

The decision to redirect the UK's major overseas military commitment from Iraq to Afghanistan served a number of domestic and foreign policy purposes for the government. It allowed the establishment of a much clearer link between the terrorist threat faced by the UK and the actions of the UK military. It also allowed the UK to compensate for the military withdrawal from Iraq by bolstering the US-led NATO military mission in Afghanistan.

However, the government faced criticism not only for its resourcing of the military commitment (outlined below), but also because the political and security situation in Afghanistan appeared to fluctuate rather than improve. Rising casualty figures acted as grim measure of the difficulty environment in which British forces were operating. British casualties increased from a total of five personnel killed between 2001 and 2005, climbing year-on-year to a total of 284 by the date of the General Election in 2010. No end date for the campaign has yet been set.

The UK's involvement in Afghanistan went through a key change in April 2006 with the expansion of the International Security Assistance Force (ISAF) operation into southern Afghanistan and the redeployment of a substantially increased British troop presence in Afghanistan to assume responsibility for the security of Helmand Province. Helmand was considered to be a lawless territory and the main location of Afghanistan's opium production but had not been the location of major fighting since the fall of the Taliban. The British involvement in the province is on the basis of a cross-Departmental plan devised by the MoD, DFID and the FCO to improve living conditions and governance in an area around the provincial capital Lashkar Gar designated as an Afghan Development Zone.

The British military presence is to provide the secure environment within which the work would take place. Commentators are divided on whether the rising British casualties demonstrate that these tactics and strategy are correct and if sufficient resources have been made available for the campaign[22] Politically, the government's handling of the war in Afghanistan was not assisted by a ministerial revolving door at the Ministry of Defence with four different Secretaries of State during the Parliamentary term (John Reid, Des Browne, John Hutton and Bob Ainsworth). Des Browne was subject to particular criticism as a 'part-time' Secretary of State for Defence as he combined his role with that of Secretary of State for Scotland under Gordon Brown from June 2007.

THE MIDDLE EAST. The Middle East created additional problems for the government during 2005–2010. Prime Minister Blair's handling of the Israeli military assault on Lebanon in July–August 2006 caused divisions within the cabinet (noted above) and did nothing for the UK's standing with the Arab countries of the Middle East.

David Miliband did attempt a 'reset' on the UK's relations with the Arab world after the Iraq war and the UK's response to the Israeli invasion of Lebanon. However, this was complicated by Hamas's takeover of Gaza in June 2007 and the subsequent Israeli military offensive in Gaza in the winter of 2008–2009. Britain, alongside other EU member states, followed the US policy of seeking to isolate Hamas by withholding recognition and seeking to bolster the position of Mahmoud Abbas in the West Bank.

The UK's contribution to the diplomacy on the Middle East peace process was pursued at one remove, through the EU's membership of the Quartet. However, in the absence of any serious peace initiative for the Middle East the situation remained largely unchanged during the course of the Parliament. The Quartet's appointment of Tony Blair as its envoy in June 2007, only hours after he stood down as Prime Minister, was something of a mixed blessing for Britain's profile in region in that it secured a high profile position for the UK but through a figure attracting divided views in the Middle East.

Britain's bilateral relations with states in the wider Middle East were also complicated by a series of political controversies. UK–Iranian bilateral relations, already poor because of accusations that Iran was supplying the material for improvised explosive devices being used against British troops in Iraq, were further complicated by the seizure and detention of 15 British sailors for 12 days in the waters off Iran in March–April 2007. Sections of the British media described the detained Royal Navy personnel as 'hostages' and accusations and counter-accusations were traded between Britain and Iran. The detainees were publicly released by President Ahmadinejad with live television coverage. Domestic controversy was stoked by the decision by the MoD to allow the detainees to sell their stories to UK newspapers; a move which was strongly criticised in Parliament, although the government's diplomatic handling of the crisis was spared substantive criticism.[23]

However, the biggest expected foreign policy crisis in the Middle East did not occur. Iran's continuing nuclear enrichment activity and the international diplomacy intended to halt the process, continued throughout the Blair–Brown period. The prospect of the use of military force against Iran either by Israel or by the USA was a frequently mooted prospect. Being challenged to contribute to political or military support for any such undertaking would have generated a domestic political controversy close on the heels of the Iraq controversy. The UK remained actively involved in a search for a diplomatic solution alongside France and Germany as a member of the EU3 diplomatic dialogue with Iraq, and through its membership of the UN Security Council.

RUSSIA. The UK's most difficult bilateral relationship between 2005 and 2010 was with Russia. Russia's new foreign policy assertiveness under President Putin, buoyed by rising oil and gas prices, made for deteriorating relations between the West and Russia in general. East–West relations took an event deeper downturn following the Russian military intervention in Georgia in August 2008. The UK's response to these events was largely coordinated through the EU which sought to mediate in the conflict through the French Presidency. For the UK this was further evidence of the unpredictability of the Russian government which the UK had already experienced through the harassment of the British Council's staff in Russia and the demand for it to close its offices outside Moscow.

The UK had already been the subject of continuing criticism from Russia as a favoured destination for Russian exiles and for its unwillingness to meet requests for extradition of business figures such as Boris Berezovsky. Matters came to a head with the poisoning of a British citizen Alexander Litvinenko by the radioactive substance Polonium 210. Enquires revealed that this was most likely administered during a meeting at a London hotel with a Russian Parliamentarian Andrei Lugovi whom the Russian government refused to extradite to allow for questioning. In July 2007 David Miliband announced the expulsion of four Russian diplomats from the Federation's London embassy.

Defence expenditure and the strategic defence review

Political controversy over levels of UK defence expenditure and more particularly the distribution of resources was a regular feature of the 2005–2010 government. Recurrent stories in the media about under-resourced British troops in Afghanistan, given an extra poignancy by losses of life being attributed to shortages of appropriate personnel protection equipment and suitable blast resistant troop transportation, and an inadequate supply of helicopters in-theatre were a recurrent theme. Despite the government's attempts to hasten procurement and to supply additional financial resources it found it difficult to persuade the media that it had given these issues appropriate priority.

The final stages of the 2005–2010 Parliament were marked by a consensus between the three political parties on the need to hold a Strategic Defence Review—the first since 1998. It was notable that none of the parties gave a commitment in their General Election manifestos to preserve defence expenditure at its current annual level of £40bn. On the overseas aid budget—the second largest aspect of Britain's foreign and security expenditure—all three main political parties backed the target of raising expenditure to 0.7% of GDP by 2013 from its current level of 0.4%.

In the context of the global financial crisis, and with the UK facing a budget deficit of £170bn, or 11% of national income, the review will take on a different complexion. Reductions in defence expenditure will be a crucial consideration in determining foreign policy priorities and the manner in which the UK is able to address security threats. Large procurement programmes that were initiated under New Labour—and that include orders for aircraft carriers, future tranches of the Eurofighter advanced European interceptor aircraft and the US Joint

Strike Fighter—are all identified as areas of cuts by the three main parties.

One of Blair's final actions as Prime Minister impacting on UK defence was to seek approval by the House of Commons for the decision to renew Britain's strategic nuclear deterrent by initiating the process of planning and procurement for the Trident nuclear missile system. The Commons' six hour debate and vote on 14 March 2007 was notable as the first occasion on which Parliament had been given the opportunity to consider whether the UK should remain a nuclear power. The Government secured a majority, but only with Conservative Party support, as 88 Labour MPs rebelled and with former Ministers and Cabinet Ministers among the rebels.

Foreign policy in the general election campaign

Foreign policy was not a significant feature in the General Election campaign as the articles on the parties' campaigns illustrate in this issue. The most concentrated focus on foreign affairs within the campaign came in the second of three televised leaders debates held on 22 April which had an agreed theme of international affairs for its first half.

Three foreign policy questions (four if you include a question on the Pope's visit to the UK) were posed by the audience. The first of the questions focused on Europe. The second asked the three leaders if they would participate in another multinational operation in a failed state to remove Al Qaeda or another terrorist threat. Brown's and Clegg's answers were an unequivocal 'yes'. Cameron was much more circumspect and avoided directly answering the question.

During the debate—and throughout the campaign—each of the three main party leaders made ritualistic tributes to British troops engaged in military operations in Afghanistan but none of the parties indicated their view as to the duration of the commitment of forces. Both Clegg and Cameron criticised the government for its strategy and for the lack of appropriate equipment in Afghanistan. Brown sought to counter these criticisms by seeking to demonstrate that he was fully on top of a situation which had required an evolving set of responses and different types of resources. Clegg sought to cast the debate on resources more widely by pointing to weapons systems such as Eurofighter and the Trident system as a waste of financial resources. The issue of Trident made for the most heated exchanges in the televised debate, with Brown and Cameron heavily criticising Clegg for what they presented as a nuclear disarmament of the UK (when Clegg's argument was that the decision to renew Trident did not need to be taken now). The pro-European Clegg was also attacked—very unconvincingly—by Gordon Brown for being 'anti-American' and for being a 'risk to our security'. Cameron agreed with Brown (a position he admitted he found uncomfortable) that the Liberal Democrats' anti-Trident policies were a risk to Britain. The third question focused on climate change and provided the three party leaders with the opportunity to introduce issues of energy security and to highlight the parties' differences on nuclear power.

A striking characteristic of the debate was that none of the leaders sought to establish a distinctive foreign policy philosophy, or to offer a coherent vision as to how they saw the UK located within changing international relations, and especially how to respond to the rise of the BRICs. Another televised debate on foreign affairs was held as the first of a series of five debates between prospective Cabinet Ministers on the BBC programme The Daily Politics. This debate was much more low-key and much less publicly reported in the media.

The main parties' manifesto commitments to foreign and security policy were marked by their similarities rather than their differences. For Labour this was covered in a chapter entitled 'A Global Future', for the Conservatives 'Protect our national interest' and for the Liberal Democrats 'Your world'. Each party stressed difficulty of separating domestic from international security. Each committed to seeing through the planned Strategic Defence Review. Each also maintained that Britain has a special responsibility to play an active international role and, in differing terms, that the UK is able to punch above its weight. Areas of difference were to be found on European policy and on the appropriate priorities for the defence budget. The Liberal Democrats' manifesto was noticeable for its careful wording on Trident: 'We will strive for global nuclear disarmament, showing leadership by committing not to replace the Trident nuclear weapons system on a like-for-like basis'.

The Labour manifesto was marked by its differences from its predecessors under the leadership of Tony Blair. In the 2010 manifesto there was less stress on an active and assertive interventionism and much more of a focus on other instruments of British foreign policy such as aid, and an interest in conflict prevention through diplomatic means. There are clear echoes of the same position from the Conservative Party with recognition of the contribution that the UK can make to international relations—but within clear limits. One distinctive aspect of the Conservative Party's manifesto commitments was the creation of a National Security Council. This had been flagged up well in advance of the election, and criticised on the grounds that it is about process rather than the ends of British foreign policy.

Conclusion

The General Election campaign was marked by the low-key nature of the debate on foreign, security and defence policy. There was minor skirmishing on the resourcing of Britain's military involvement in Afghanistan rather than the substantive question of whether an ongoing military commitment is in the country's best interests. The only marked disparity between the parties was on the issue of the replacement of the Trident missile system and on which the Liberal Democrats did not place much emphasis in their election campaign. The other area of substantive foreign policy difference between the parties was on the relationship with the European Union (and covered by another article in this issue), but none of the parties sought to devote substantial attention to contrasting their differences on Europe.

With Britain's post-election foreign and defence ambitions being so heavily conditioned by an environment of constrained public expenditure, the lack of clarity in terms of proposals for new directions in foreign policy by the three main parties was perhaps surprising. Each of the parties has recognised that the UK is now operating within a rapidly changing global context which has significant implications for the UK's future security and prosperity. None of the parties sought to convey how this might be addressed in a manner that was cogent and comprehensible to the electorate.

On the basis of the debate within the election campaign the incoming coalition government might be expected to demonstrate a high degree of continuity in foreign policy. However, a key aspect of the early stages of the new administration will be to follow through on the commitment to appraise Britain's foreign and security priorities through the Security and Defence Review, and this looks set to be a major political preoccupation during the early stages of the new Parliament.

1　　C. White, 'Brown's World View: Foreign Policy Under Our New Prime Minister', in M. Rush and P. Giddings (eds), *When Gordon Took the Helm*, Palgrave, 2008.
2　　S. Lee, *Boom and Bust: The Politics and Legacy of Gordon Brown*, One World, 2009 (Chapter 6).
3　　S. Lee, *Boom and Bust: The Politics and Legacy of Gordon Brown*, One World, 2009 (Chapter 6).
4　　The 2006 Queen's Speech has been seen as indicative of the policies Brown will continue as PM. See Adams, 'Clues to Brown's agenda emerge'; Queen's Speech, http://news.bbc.co.uk/2/hi/uk_news/politics/6150274.stm, accessed 27.05.10; interview with Brown by Andrew Marr, Sunday AM programme, 7.01.07; Lionel Barber and James Blitz, 'Security is our top priority, says Brown', interview, *Financial Times*, 25.10.06.
5　　G. Brown, Speech by Brown to UN ambassadors, New York, 20.4 06. http://webarchive.nationalarchives.gov.uk/+/http://www.hmtreasury.gov.uk/speech_chex_200406.htm, accessed 27.05.10.
6　　G. Gordon, Speech to the Labour Party Conference, 25.09.06. http://www.guardian.co.uk/politics/2006/sep/25/labourconference.labour2, accessed 27.05.10.
7　　G. Brown, Lord Mayor's Banquet Speech, 12.11.07. http://webarchive.nationalarchives.gov.uk/20071104170014/http://number10.gov.uk/output/Page13736.asp, accessed 27.05.10.
8　　G. Brown, Kennedy Memorial Speech, 18.04.08. http://webarchive.nationalarchives.gov.uk/20071104170014/number10.gov.uk/page15303, accessed 27.5.10.
9　　Cabinet Office, *The National Security Strategy of the United Kingdom: Security in An Interdependent World* March 2008, Cm 7291.
10　Cabinet Office, *The National Security Strategy of the United Kingdom: Update 2009 Security for the Next Generation* March, 2009. Cm 7590.
11　P. Williams, 'Who's making UK foreign policy?' *International Affairs*, 80, 2004, 909–21.
12　J. Smith, 'A missed opportunity? New Labour's European Policy 1997–2005' *International Affairs*, 81, 2005, 703–21.
13　V. Honeyman, 'Gordon Brown and International Policy' *Policy Studies*, 30, 2009, 85–100.

14 The appointment came as something as a surprise to Beckett herself. See: Philip Webster, 'As he promoted me I replied in one word, with four letters' *Times Online* 28 June 2006. http://www. timesonline.co.uk/tol/news/politics/article680305.ece, accessed 25.5.10.

15 Foreign and Commonwealth Office, *Departmental Report: Better World, Better Britain* May 2008. Cm 7390.

16 D. Miliband, 'The Democratic Imperative' Aung San Suu Kyi Lecture, St Hugh's College, Oxford, 12.02.08. http://www.davidmiliband.info/speeches/speeches_08_02.htm, accessed 27.5.10.

17 The Times online 16.11.07. http://www.timesonline.co.uk/tol/news/politics/article2879884.ece, accessed 27.5.10.

18 'Basra Celebrates British Withdrawal' Times Online, 3.9.07, http://www.timesonline.co.uk/tol/news/ world/iraq/article2378371.ece, accessed 27.05.10.

19 J. Chilcot, Statement by Sir John Chilcot, Chairman of the Iraq Inquiry, at a news conference on Thursday, 30.07.09. http://www.iraqinquiry.org.uk/about/statement.aspx, accessed 27.5.10.

20 J. Ferguson, *One Million Bullets*, London, 2008.

21 On ComRes Polling for the Independent, the Independent on Sunday and the BBC polling results: 'All British Troops should be withdrawn from Afghanistan as soon as possible': 19 July 2009—Agree 64% Disagree 33%; 23 August 2009—Agree 60% Disagree 33%; 'All British Troops should be withdrawn from Afghanistan as quickly as possible': 8 November 2009—Agree 63% Disagree 31%; 'The War in Afghanistan is unwinnable': 23.02.10—Agree 64% Disagree 30%. http://www.comres.co.uk/ search.aspx?q=afghanistan, accessed 27.05.10.

22 A. King, 'Understanding the Helmand Campaign: British Military Operations in Afghanistan' *International Affairs*, 86, 2010, 311–3.

23 House of Commons Foreign Affairs Committee (2007), *Foreign Policy Aspects of the Detention of Naval Personnel by the Islamic Republic of Iran* Sixth Report of Session 2006-07. HC 880.

SEAN CAREY AND ANDREW GEDDES

Less Is More: Immigration and European Integration at the 2010 General Election

On a routine meeting with a voter in Rochdale on 28 April 2010, Gordon Brown had a conversation that would become one of the key incidents of this election campaign. Despite the concentration of media coverage on the Prime Minister's faux pas after his meeting with Gillian Duffy, this incident encapsulates how the issues of immigration and European integration were key concerns for many traditional Labour voters. This contribution unpicks the various factors underlying these concerns through analysis of immigration and European integration as issues during Labour's third term and at the 2010 general election. We also look at connections between these two important issues. The most important of these is that a sizeable part of migration to the UK has been from other European Union (EU) member states in Central and Eastern Europe. We then ask why, when and with what effects Europe and immigration resonated as campaign themes at the 2010 general election and affected party strategies and voting behaviour. Finally, we ask why, given evidence of widespread public scepticism about the EU, hostility to immigration and the mood of 'anti-politics' in the wake of the expenses scandal, the anti-EU and anti-immigration UK Independence Party (UKIP) and British National Party (BNP) failed to make representational breakthroughs? In our conclusions we also explore implications for the Conservative–Liberal Democrat coalition government on immigration and EU policy.

We show that the lesson learned by the Conservative leadership from three successive general election defeats was to talk less about Europe and immigration and a little more about the issues that mattered most to people, particularly the economy and public services. For the Labour Party, despite a busy—if not hyperactive—legislative schedule for immigration policy, there was a powerful perception that the party had failed on immigration and that this contributed to weakening

doi:10.1093/pa/gsq021

support. The Liberal Democrats were notably more progressive and liberal on immigration, including proposals for an earned amnesty for illegal immigrants. There was certainly a considerable distance between the Conservatives and Liberal Democrats on these issues. As election day loomed, Clegg stated that attacks on Liberal Democrats' immigration policy from Cameron and Brown made him 'incredibly angry'.[1] Our analysis of immigration and European integration shows that both immigration and Europe were highly significant in terms of Conservative Party election strategy and repositioning and (particularly on the immigration issue) the erosion of Labour Party support. They both tell us quite important things about the election itself, but also about two of the most pressing and important issues facing the UK.

The politics of control

During general election campaigns, political leaders try to give the impression that they are in control of events. They want to be seen as shapers rather than as hapless victims of circumstance. A quaint illusion this notion of control may be, but much election debate was dominated by the articulation of confidently expressed plans by Gordon Brown, David Cameron and Nick Clegg to mend or resuscitate Britain's economy and society as though the powers needed to effect such change lay squarely in the hands of British politicians. The perception of a leader being shaped by events and losing control—as became a prevailing image of Gordon Brown before and during the campaign—is deeply damaging.

Both European integration and immigration are powerful issues because they represent the potential for loss of control. Writing in his diaries back in the 1960s, the ex-Labour cabinet minister Richard Crossman wrote of immigration's 'powerful political undertow'.[2] This insight was still very relevant for Labour in 2010. Crossman meant a current beneath the surface pulling in the opposite direction. If the undertow is very strong then those on the surface may be swept away. There is ample evidence of deeply engrained Euroscepticism in Britain, particularly in England, while anti-immigration sentiment has been a distinctive feature of public attitudes throughout the first decade of the twenty-first century.[3] Immigration and European integration are both powerful undertows in contemporary British politics that raise profound questions; not least for connections between politicians and 'the people'.

These questions can be put rather straightforwardly. The ceding of sovereignty to collective decision-making structures at EU level may bring advantages, but it also affects the ability of a British government to affect economic and social change.[4] Similarly, relatively large-scale immigration has significant social, economic and political effects, including plugging labour market gaps and providing nurses, doctors and other important public sector workers.

There are also powerful connections between immigration and European integration because much migration to the UK in the last ten years or so has been from other EU member states. These EU migrants have the same rights as British citizens to move within the EU. In fact, the word 'immigrant' does not capture the rights-based dynamic that underpins free movement within the EU. EU migration literally cannot be controlled because such migrants have a right protected by EU law to move to the UK, a reciprocal right also enjoyed by British citizens. This was a point made by Clegg in a tetchy exchange with Cameron at the third leaders' debate when he questioned the Conservative plan to impose a cap or limit on new immigration from outside the EU.

European integration and immigration are also staple issues for UKIP and the BNP. At the 2009 European Parliament elections, UKIP secured 16.5% of the votes, 13 of the UK's 72 seats, and pushed Labour into a dismal third place. At the same elections, the BNP obtained 6.2% of the votes and two seats. Both UKIP and the BNP advocate Britain's exit from the EU and would impose very strict controls on immigration. Both parties were also able to exploit the 'anti-politics' mood in the wake of the expenses scandal at the 2009 European Parliament election. To differing extents—UKIP more than the BNP—both parties have proven able to attract support at low turnout, second-order elections that do not change national governments and where protest voting is a safer option. Would this support be evident at the 2010 general election? UKIP's former leader, the media-savvy Nigel Farage MEP, was standing against the speaker John Bercow in Buckingham and was thought by some to have a reasonable chance of success. The signs were less promising for the BNP. Shortly before the election, a senior party member was arrested for allegedly making death threats against the BNP leader, Nick Griffin. Things got worse when the BNP website went down shortly before the election with a not altogether supportive message from the webmaster condemning Griffin and another prominent party member for being 'pathetic, desperate and incompetent'.

Assets and liabilities

Labour has long been fearful of immigration's 'undertow'. On the EU, Gordon Brown's scepticism while Chancellor between 1997 and 2007 inhibited any ambitions Tony Blair may have held to move Britain closer to the heart of Europe by replacing the pound with the euro. Brown gave the impression of being a reluctant European, as marked not least by his irregular and somewhat grudging attendance at EU Council of finance ministers meetings while Chancellor. As a newly appointed Prime Minister, a powerful image of his lack of engagement with EU issues was his late and solo signature of the Lisbon Treaty in an ante-room long after the other EU leaders had appended their signatures. Brown may well not have wanted to draw people's attention to the Treaty so as to avoid discussion of a referendum, but this could also be seen as a vivid personification of the awkwardness and reluctance that have characterised Britain's EU membership.

On immigration, one of the most distinctive features of Labour rule—certainly of Blair's first term (1997–2001), but with repercussions that were felt in the second and third terms—was the conscious decision to adopt a decidedly liberal approach to labour migration.[5] This set the scene for large increases in numbers of labour migrants as well as the decision to open the doors to nationals of the eight central and east European countries that joined the EU on 1 May 2004. The first decade of the twenty-first century saw the largest scale migration to the UK in its history. Figure 1 shows these levels of net migration (immigration minus emigration).

Britain was one of only three EU member states to adopt this liberal approach and Home Office estimates of 5,000–13,000 annual migrants from the A8 countries proved way off-beam (Figure 2).

Immigration was a highly salient issue among the British public during the 2005–2010 parliament. Opinion polls, such as those conducted by Ipsos MORI each month, frequently found immigration to be 'one of the most important issues facing Britain today'. In each month, immigration was one of the five most important issues, and usually in the top two. Europe, in contrast, was not a highly salient issue with voters during this period, only once receiving more than

Figure 1 Net migration to the UK 2000–2009. *Source*: ONS.

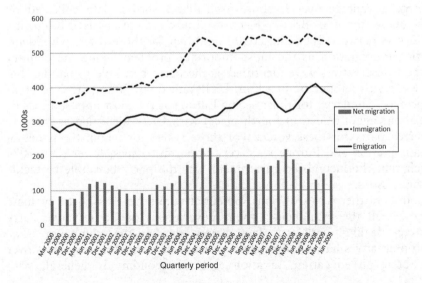

Quarterly period

Figure 2 Net EU migration to the UK, March 2004–March 2009. *Source*: ONS.

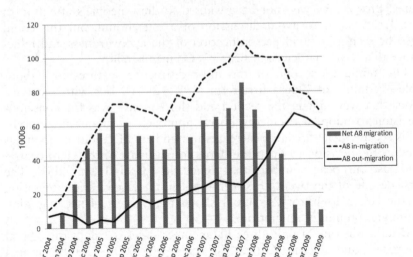

10% of mentions in the Ipsos MORI polls. Figure 3 shows the trend in the salience of immigration and Europe among voters between May 2005 and May 2010. Since September 2008 the economy was far and away the most important issue to a large majority of voters, but immigration remained the most important non-economic issue for voters for the six months prior to the 2010 general election.

For those voters who saw immigration and Europe as important in the run up to the 2010 election, the Conservatives continued to have a large advantage over Labour. As Table 1 shows, data collected by YouGov for the British Election Study's Continuous Monitoring Surveys between 2008 and 2010 found that for those voters who identified immigration as the most important problem facing the country the Conservatives were identified as the party best able to handle that issue, with Labour trailing both UKIP and the BNP in perceived competence. Similarly, for those seeing Europe as the most important issue, Labour again trailed in fourth place, with UKIP identified as the preferred party for these voters. For those voters for whom the issues of immigration and Europe were very important issues, fewer than 10% felt that the incumbent government was the party best able to tackle these issues.

In a further series of polls, potential voters were asked to evaluate how well the incumbent Labour government or Conservative Party were dealing with six key issues during the campaign. The Conservatives had small single-digit leads in favourable responses over Labour on education, taxation and the economy in general, with

Figure 3 Salience of the economy, immigration and Europe, May 2005–May 2010. Questions: What would you say is the most important issue facing Britain today? What do you see as other important issues facing Britain today? (respondents are unprompted, answers are combined). *Source*: Ipsos MORI.

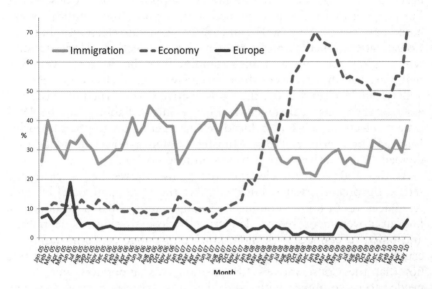

Labour holding similar small leads in perceived competence on health and the financial crisis. In contrast, the Conservatives held a lead over Labour of more than 25% on immigration. This lead was constant for each survey throughout the campaign (Figure 4). However, whether this seriously impacted upon Labour's electoral fortunes is debateable. In mid-March 2010, voters were asked to identify the issues that would be very important in helping decide which party to vote for, with the usual suspects of the economy, health and education far more prevalent

1. Best party to handle the most important problem facing the country: immigration and Europe, June 2008–March 2010

	Immigration (%)	Europe (%)
Conservative	25.2	23.4
Labour	6.3	3.8
Liberal Democrat	1.8	2.4
UKIP	8.5	45.0
BNP	25.0	7.7
Other party	1.3	1.4
None	12.5	10.5
Don't know	19.4	5.7
n	1,983	209

Source: YouGov, British Election Study Continuous Monitoring Surveys.

than immigration, issues where the difference between the preferred policies of the major parties was much closer.

There are some lessons from Britain's recent electoral history that need to be assessed. It could be supposed that Conservative Euroscepticism would have chimed with a prevailing sceptical public mood at the 1997, 2001 and 2005 general elections, but the Conservatives failed to profit at each of these elections. Understanding why is a key component of understanding how the Conservatives eventually learned the lessons of three successive general election defeats.

Between 1997 and 2005, the Conservative Party turned the potential asset of their sceptical stance on Europe into a liability. At the 1997 general election, schisms induced by insurgent Euroscepticism during John Major's term as Prime Minister created a powerful image of a divided Conservative Party that was unfit to govern.[6]

At the 2001 general election, the Conservatives had a clear and settled Eurosceptic stance, but their 'save the £' campaign and Hague's references to Britain becoming a 'foreign land' under a second-term Labour government veered dangerously close to single-issue politics and failed to connect with more important public concerns about the economy and key public services such as health and education. It was not that the Conservative's EU position was unpopular, but that it needed to be combined with issues that were more important to potential Conservative voters.

Figure 4 Best party on immigration (Labour/Conservative comparison), March–May 2010 Questions: How well do you think the present government has handled immigration? How well do you think a Conservative government would handle immigration? % of positive responses, i.e. 'very well' + 'fairly well'. *Source*: YouGov, British Election Study Pre-campaign and Campaign Surveys.

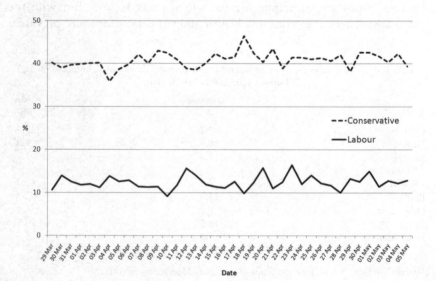

By 2005, Europe had receded in importance as an issue, but immigration had become a far more salient concern in light of increased numbers of migrants, with particular growth in European migration. The Conservatives' 'dog whistle' politics—a technique borrowed from John Howard's Liberal Party in Australia—with the 'are you thinking what we're thinking: it's not racist to impose controls on immigration' message was seen as a coded way of alerting voters to their anti-immigration position. But at the 2005 general election, as in 1997 and 2001, the Labour Party firmly occupied the centre ground and had the most attractive offer to the electorate on the issues that mattered most, namely the economy and public services.

It would seem that the lessons of defeat were that the Conservatives needed to talk a little less about Europe and immigration and a little more about the issues that mattered to people. This was not because the Conservative positions on Europe and immigration were unpopular—the opposite was the case—but that a Conservative campaign focused on these issues would preach to the converted while running the risk of being seen as negative and extreme.[7] This was the argument that prevailed, but there were still voices at the time of the 2010 general election that argued that the Conservatives did need to make more of issues on which they held a considerable advantage.[8] This has been a perennial theme in debates about Conservative election strategy and became prominent too in 2010 when a narrowing of the polls and Cleggmania led some to argue that the Conservatives needed to play to some of their traditional strengths such as immigration and Europe.

The policy focus

The EU was a low-profile issue for the Brown administration. Britain was outside the Eurozone and made it very clear that this was where it intended to stay. Britain is also outside the Schengen area and has insisted on maintaining passport controls for all those entering the UK from another EU member state. In fact, there has been remarkable continuity in Britain's EU policy with themes evident in the 1970s and 1980s continuing to resonate, including unsuccessful calls for reform of the Common Agricultural Policy (CAP); a determination to hang onto the UK budget rebate; a preference for intergovernmental co-operation; and support for a wider Europe, including Turkish accession. New Labour did not break the path of Britain's EU policy. In fact, there is continuity accompanied by a hardening of public attitudes in an anti-EU direction. Brown's interest in the EU seemed only really to be sparked during the financial crisis as it became clear that regional and global action needed to be taken.

Europe had been a key issue in Cameron's election to the Conservative leadership. His announcement that he would take the Conservative group in the European Parliament out of the European Peoples' Party (the mainstream centre-right grouping) was seen as a game changer, but also as a potential hostage to fortune to the Party's Eurosceptic right. Cameron also pledged to hold a referendum on the Lisbon Treaty. This pledge was dropped when the bill was finally ratified by all of the EU member states. This could have been an embarrassing moment for Cameron as he had wrote an open letter to readers of *The Sun* giving a 'cast iron' guarantee to hold a referendum on Lisbon.[9] Helpfully for Cameron, *The Sun* chose not to denounce Cameron for this backtracking, but condemned Brown for signing the Treaty in the first place.

Immigration policy was a far more salient concern for the Brown administration, as it has been for Blair after 2001. Initial openness during Blair's first term to labour migration was accompanied by a distinctly tough stance on asylum. This helps make the point that 'immigration' is very diverse. Relative openness in one area was accompanied by closure in another. The UK was one of only three member states (Ireland and Sweden being the others) that opened its labour market to workers from the eight central and east European countries that joined the EU in 2004. This was accompanied by measures to stimulate recruitment of high-skilled migrant workers and to use what were called 'sector-based schemes' to provide migrant workers in areas with labour shortages such as construction. It is also important to emphasise that migrant workers have long played a key role in delivering public services. Foreign doctors, nurses and care workers were central to the attainment of ambitious plans for NHS improvement. It would thus be mistaken to see Labour's migration policy as entirely driven by liberal, free market principles.

Immigration policy-making tends to be re-active rather than pro-active. This was the case during Brown's time as Prime Minister. Rising public concern about immigration led the government to end sector-based schemes for non-EU migrants because of the apparently ready supply of EU migrants. A Canadian-style points system was introduced, which targeted recruitment of higher skilled workers. By the 2010 general election, there were three main planks of Labour migration policy: a points-based system for higher skilled migrants, a reliance on EU migration to plug labour market gaps in lower skilled employment and a closed door to non-EU, lower skilled migration.

This was accompanied by measures on immigrant integration that emphasised the acquisition of language skills and introduced citizenship tests. From July 2011, it is also planned to introduce 'earned citizenship' for foreign nationals. It had, though, taken nearly 13 years to get to this situation while public opinion seemed to suggest that people had made up their minds that the Labour government had failed on immigration.

Europe and immigration in the campaign

Immigration and Europe were not prominent themes in the manifestos of the major parties or their launches. These documents try to point to the sunny uplands, while immigration and Europe are often seen as negative issues.

The Conservatives did have the ostensibly clearest policy on immigration. They proposed to set an annual limit on the number of non-EU economic migrants admitted into the UK to live and work. They did not say what this cap would be. Too high and it would be meaningless; too low and it could induce complaints from business. The Conservatives stated that immigration policy should be designed to confine access to those who would bring the most value to the British economy. The Conservatives also pledged to apply transitional controls as a matter of course in the future for all new EU Member States. The Labour government did not impose transitional controls on the A8, but did on Bulgaria and Romania, lasting for a maximum period of seven years. The Conservative pledge would apply to Croatia and, if it were to join any time soon, which seems unlikely, to Turkey.

Labour trumpeted their points-based system and said that they wanted to see economic growth translated into rising levels of employment and wages, not rising immigration. This was, perhaps, a more subtle way of re-emphasising the 'British jobs for British workers' line that Brown had used at the 2007 party conference. Labour also reaffirmed its commitment to ensuring that newcomers would 'earn' citizenship.

The Liberal Democrats adopted a markedly more liberal approach to immigration. They talked tough on border controls, but also proposed a regional points-based system to ensure that migrants could work only where they were needed, although it was less clear how this could be implemented. What would stop a migrant given a permit to work in Scotland hopping on a train to London, or *vice versa*? They also proposed to end the detention of child migrants. To manage asylum, the Liberal Democrats proposed a new agency to take the issue out of the hands of the Home Office and also proposed to allow asylum-seekers to work. Most controversially, the Liberal Democrats proposed an amnesty for people who had been in Britain without the correct papers for ten years, but spoke English, had no criminal record and wanted to earn citizenship. This route would not apply to people arriving after 2010. It is impossible to know with precision the size of the population of illegal immigrants in the UK, but some estimates have put the number at between 750,000 and 1 million. It is simply not practical or desirable for all kinds of legal, political, economic and social reasons to round up and deport people on such a huge scale. The problem is that illegal immigrants are 'outside' of the protections of the state and will not be making a full contribution through tax to the society in which they live. Because of their status, they may also be prone to exploitation by unscrupulous employers. The issues are complex, but amnesties deal with the effects rather than the causes of immigration. Amnesties of this kind have been regular features in other countries, such as the USA and in southern Europe. The UK has had smaller scale amnesties in the past (usually to correct anomalies created by new immigration laws), but not on the basis proposed by the Liberal Democrats. As well as the Conservatives, Labour strongly opposed this proposal. Interestingly, the Conservative mayor of London, Boris Johnson, has supported the idea of an earned amnesty, similar to the Liberal Democrats' proposal. Neither the amnesty idea nor regional quotas survived the coalition deal.

All three main parties affirmed the importance of EU membership. The Conservatives pledged that there would be no further transfers of sovereignty to the EU without a referendum, or what they called a 'referendum lock'. A sovereignty bill would also be introduced to make it clear that sovereign authority resided in the UK, a 'sovereignty lock'. Here too there could be difficulties as this would run counter to the principle of the supremacy of European law in areas where there are shared competencies. They also proposed to bring back to the UK powers over legal rights, criminal justice and social and employment legislation. This idea of repatriation of powers is simple to state, but hard to achieve in practice because it would require the agreement of other member states. In fact, the Conservative manifesto sought a 'mandate to negotiate', probably in the knowledge that these would probably be difficult objectives to attain.

Labour's manifesto contrasted their positive view of the EU as a route to achieve policy objectives on issues such as climate change with the 'sullen resistance' that they attributed to the Conservatives. Labour had more to say about bread and butter EU issues such as the CAP, budget reform and enlargement to the Western Balkans. Another difference was that the EU was more 'integrated' into the Labour manifesto as both a domestic and an international issue thus showing the links between domestic and foreign policy that Richard Whitman also explores in his contribution to this volume. For the Conservatives, the EU was squarely located as a foreign policy issue for a 'liberal Conservative government', pursuing 'enlightened national interest'.

The EU has always been a balancing act for the Liberal Democrats. There is a very strong streak of Euro-enthusiasm that runs through the Party. Clegg himself had been a Commission official and an MEP. His own family background is distinctly European and he is happy to display his fluency in other European languages. This compares to Brown's squarely Scottish roots and Cameron's resolutely English background. The problem for the Liberal Democrats is that they have tended to pick up support in areas such as the south west where Euroscepticism runs deep. To square this circle, the EU was not a key Liberal Democrat campaign or manifesto theme. The Labour and Liberal Democrat approaches to the EU were actually quite similar in that they both explicitly sought to bridge the gap between domestic and international politics and saw the EU as a vehicle for solutions to domestic problems and as a route to wider international influence.

UKIP's manifesto and its launch focused squarely on immigration and Europe. They pledged to leave the EU and to end 'uncontrolled mass immigration', to introduce an immediate five-year freeze on immigration for permanent settlement, to regain control of Britain's borders to stop foreign criminals from entering our country, to end what they saw as the abuse of the UK asylum system and to expel Islamic extremists. Migrant workers would be recruited on a bonded basis, meaning that there would be a strict points-based visa system and time-limited work permits.

The BNP manifesto launch in Stoke-on-Trent on St George's day had its bizarre elements. Griffin was led into the room by a man dressed as a knight of St George, but looking more like a disoriented football supporter in fancy dress gearing up for the World Cup. The BNP pledged to leave the EU and to declare Britain a non-immigration country, deport all illegal immigrants, halt what they called the 'asylum swindle', encourage voluntary resettlement and to abolish all 'leftist social engineering projects', which would include multicultural-ism. The 'encouragement' of voluntary resettlement was a slight finessing of extreme right calls for repatriation, but the BNP placed their hostility to immigration, immigrants and foreigners generally at the very centre of their campaign.

Manifestos have their uses in giving us a sense of party positioning, but what matters more is how the issues resonate with the public as campaign themes. Immigration and Europe did feature prominently in the three prime ministerial debates. The opening questions in the first and second debates were on these two issues. The question that was explicitly on Europe asked about continued EU membership, which all three of the major parties favour. Probably the liveliest exchanges on Europe were between David Cameron and Nick Clegg. Memorably, Nick Clegg accused the Conservatives of associating in the European Parliament with 'a bunch of nutters, anti-Semites, people who deny climate change exists, homophobes'. In the third debate, David Cameron clearly saw advantage in demonstrating differences between the Conservatives and the other parties on the Euro, particularly after events of the previous days highlighted the dire economic situation in Greece. He promised that he would never join the Euro in his opening statement, and, with something of a digression following a question about bankers' bonuses, stated that the Liberal Democrats were in favour of joining the Euro. Questions were asked in each of the debates about immigration, and saw the three leaders articulate positions in which each advocated tactics for reducing the rate of immigration. The issues of immigration and Europe were combined when Nick Clegg asked David Cameron three times whether he would confirm that as 80% of people entering the UK came from other EU states then they would not be affected by the Conservatives' proposed cap on numbers. The clearest differences and some of the testiest exchanges between Cameron and Clegg occurred on the immigration issue.

Immigration also hit home as an election issue in another way. The ubiquitous image of the 2010 general election was Gordon Brown's meeting with Gillian Duffy in Rochdale. Much was made of this at the time, although Labour did actually win the Rochdale seat from the Liberal Democrats so its electoral effects might have been over-stated. The incident probably confirmed people's views on Brown rather than led to some dramatic reappraisal.

There may be another way of thinking about Brown's meeting with Mrs Duffy, which helps us to understand how and why immigration and European integration connect and why they proved so damaging to Labour's electoral performance. Mrs Duffy spoke to Gordon Brown about her aspirations for her grandchildren in terms of education and employment. It was in this context that she saw immigration and 'flocking' of east European immigrants. Mrs Duffy was articulating a concern that has also been expressed by liberal-left commentators such as David Goodhart the editor of *Prospect* magazine and Polly Toynbee of the *Guardian*.[10] Jon Cruddas, the MP for Dagenham, also articulated similar concerns about the impacts of immigration on traditional Labour voters.[11] Mrs Duffy was unknowingly echoing concerns expressed by some on the left about the capacity of the labour market and welfare model developed by New Labour, with its conscious liberal and flexible underpinnings, to maintain the bonds of social solidarity necessary to sustain the kinds of redistributive politics that have, in turn, sustained the Labour Party and broader labour movement. As Cruddas and Jonathan Rutherford put it in a post-election *New Statesman* article:

Labour's response was to prepare workers for the global market. It began to promote an entrepreneurial way of life and the aspiration of "earning and owning". The drive towards a more flexible labour market increased the use of short-term contracts, agency work, subcontracting and the hiring of those who were "self-employed". The model encouraged immigration into Britain, but left the British workforce one of the worst protected in Europe.[12]

This view captures some important dynamics of the immigration issue and helps to illustrate why Labour became so vulnerable. It does, though, neglect the public sector rationale also underlying recruitment of many migrant workers.

What we can see, however, is how immigration and European integration connect in powerful ways because they can symbolise loss of control and insecurity. If we try to think in broader terms, then both issues are framed by much bigger debates about the future of the UK social model and the economy that sustains it. It is only if we see the debates about European integration and immigration in terms of this bigger picture that we see how they possess the capacity to hurt a Labour Party that no longer seemed to understand traditional supporters such as Mrs Duffy.

For a certain strand of the British press, immigration and Europe have long been issues of prime importance. The black top tabloid newspapers regularly covered stories about immigration during the campaign.[13] Both the *Mail* and the *Express* stressed that the immigration issue was not being adequately addressed by the major parties. James Slack in the *Mail* commented that 'Politicians of all parties have lamentably failed to tell the truth about how immigration has changed this country beyond recognition during Labour's 13 years in power'.[14] There was a theme running through many of the UK newspapers that immigration was an issue given scant attention by the political parties. This view was reinforced by David Cameron who claimed during the campaign that Labour had attempted to halt any discussion of immigration, stating that 'when anyone does talk about it they get accused of racism or worse'. Cameron's comment was made on the day a number of newspapers led with a story, which originated with the *Spectator* using data procured from ONS,[15] that 98.5% of all new jobs created since 1997 had gone to foreign-born workers. Gordon Brown insisted that was 'not the case' in a radio interview on the Today Programme while Immigration Minister Phil Woolas also vigorously challenged the claim.

The results

After a campaign where the major parties were apparently paying little attention to issues that appeared salient both to a large number of voters and to a significant section of the British press, there was some expectation that two parties that were successful in the European Parliament election a year previously would benefit accordingly. Notwithstanding significant increases in vote share for UKIP and the BNP, the advances made by both parties at the 2009 European Parliament election were not replicated in the General Election. Despite receiving over 50% more votes than in 2005, UKIP's 3.1% vote share was disappointing, especially after their success in the 2009 European Parliament election where they emerged as the second largest party in Britain with a 16.5% vote share. Even former leader Nigel Farage, running against the Speaker in Buckingham, failed to secure second place in a constituency with no Labour or Liberal Democrat candidates standing. There were 21 constituencies where the combined total of the Conservative and UKIP votes was greater than that of the winning Labour or Liberal Democrat candidate. This is not as many as UKIP claimed it had cost the Conservatives in 2005, but enough so that if all of the UKIP voters had voted Conservative in 2010 the Tories would have won an outright majority rather than going into a coalition with the pro-EU Liberal Democrats. However, as David Denver points out in his contribution to this volume, UKIP may actually have cost Labour more votes than the Conservatives at the 2010 general election. There is also little evidence that UKIP or the BNP suffered from a 'debate squeeze' during the campaign with voters' attention focusing on the major parties after the landmark April 15 debate. Daily polls, such as the BES polls by YouGov, demonstrate very little fluctuation away from the eventual vote shares secured by UKIP and BNP throughout the campaign and pre-campaign period.

Despite the BNP's gain in overall vote share and votes, 2010 was a disappointing result for the party. The BNP almost trebled its total number of votes from 2005, and more than doubled its vote share. But this aggregate success is mainly a result of fielding many more candidates and the party failed spectacularly in its key goals of unseating Labour incumbents Margaret Hodge in Barking and Jon Cruddas in Dagenham and Rainham as well as gaining control of Barking and Dagenham council (in fact, it lost all 12 of its seats). The party's average vote share per constituency contested decreased, BNP leader Nick Griffin's highly publicised attempt to unseat Hodge in Barking ended with the BNP actually reducing their vote share from 2005 and they lost 267 deposits (after contesting 339 seats). The BNP's poor performance in East London coincided with a Labour resurgence in these areas. Hodge and Cruddas both comfortably retained their seats, with the former even increasing her overall vote share by 4.7 percentage points.

A mix of internal, external and systemic factors contributed to this BNP wipeout. Internally, there were divisions between the BNP leaders that spilled over into alleged serious criminal offences and the angry denunciations of the leadership by the Party's webmaster. Externally, there was a strong and vigorous counter-mobilisation that led to a large mobilisation of 'hope not hate' volunteers on-the-ground, including high-profile anti-BNP campaigners such as Billy Bragg. The key systemic factor contributing to the poor BNP performance (and UKIP too) was that this was not a second order, low turnout election fought on a proportional electoral system (as had been the case at the 2009 European elections). Both the BNP and UKIP have not yet demonstrated the potential to breakthrough in national, first-order elections and the 2010 result confirmed this.

Conclusions

The 2010 general election saw the Conservatives talk less about immigration and Europe in the hope that by so doing they would secure more votes. The Conservatives sought to develop a broader appeal with messages on both the economy and public services that were designed to resonate with a wider swathe of potential Conservative voters. The overall outcome of this was only partially successful as the Conservatives were not able to secure a majority, but Conservative re-positioning on immigration and Europe is an important element of the story of the 2010 general election.

The story is rather different for Labour, which lost public confidence in its ability to manage migration. Immigration was but one manifestation of a more general public mood that Brown had become the victim of circumstances rather than the shaper of events. The 'Mrs Duffy incident' demonstrated that for many traditional Labour voters 'immigration' was viewed as a threat to jobs and services. Whether this perception was right or wrong, it was real and hurt Labour.

What then for the coalition? On the EU, the Conservative and Liberal Deomcrats would seem uneasy partners, although the crisis in the Eurozone has certainly tempered Euro-enthusiasm on the Liberal Democrat frontbench. Both the immigration and EU portfolios reside with Conservatives. One key looming EU issue is plans for 'economic governance' including tighter regulation of financial services. The coalition government pledges to oppose these plans, but the UK could be out-voted by other EU member states. Another looming issue is renegotiation of the EU budget. The Conservatives claimed that they would like to see repatriation of some powers from the EU to Britain. More likely, however, is concerted pressure from other EU member states to end the British budget rebate secured by Mrs Thatcher in 1984.

On immigration, 2010 may well be 'another 1979' when an outgoing Labour government was replaced by a Conservative government talking tough on immigration. If this historical analogy works then immigration may well fade as a public concern because of the tight regulatory framework. The key constraint, however, is that the migration dynamics have changed. Much migration into the UK is from other EU member states, which - save a fundamental and very unlikely complete revision of the Rome treaty – means that circulation of people within the EU will be out of the government's control. Given that much of this migration is economically driven then the somewhat unpalatable 'solution' would be to ensure that the UK is an economically unattractive destination.

1   Daily Telegraph, Nick Clegg Defends Immigration Policy, 3 May 2010.
2   R. Crosssman, *Diaries of a Cabinet Minister. Volume 1: Minister of Housing 1964–66*, Cape, 1975.
3   L. McLaren and M. Johnson, 'Resources, Group Conflict and Symbols: Explaining Anti-immigration Hostility in Britain', *Political Studies*, 55, 2007, 709–32.
4   A. Geddes, *The Politics of Migration and Immigration in Europe*, Sage, 2003.
5   S. Glover et al., *Migration: A Social and Economic Analysis*, Home Office, 2001.
6   G. Evans, 'Euroscepticism and Conservative Electoral Support: How an Asset Became a Liability', *British Journal of Political Science*, 28, 1998, 573–90.
7   M. Ashcroft, *Smell the Coffee: A Wakeup Call for the Conservative Party*, Politicos, 2005.
8   T. Montgomerie, Leaders Must Speak Up on Immigration, *Guardian*, 31 March 2010.
9   *The Sun*, Cameron's Crusade for UK Rights, November 5 2009.
10 D. Goodhart, 'Population Problem', *Prospect* 24 February 2010; P. Toynbee, Our Borders Are Porous. Why Can't Our Politicians Admit the Problems of Immigration? *Guardian*, 27 February 2010.
11 D. Goodhart and D. Edmonds, Interview: Jon Cruddas, *Prospect*, 14 May 2010.
12 J. Cruddas and J. Rutherford, See the Bigger Picture, *New Statesman*, 31 May 2010.

13 The *Daily Express*, for example, had front page headlines during the campaign including: 'Fury Over 1m Illegal migrants' 26 April 2010, 'Clegg's Crazy Immigration Policy' 22 April 2010, 'Strangers in Our Own Country' 12 April 2010, 'New EU Gestapo Spies on Britain' 26 March 2010, 'Foreign Benefits Scandal' 24 March 2010.
14 J. Slack, Immigration: What None of the Parties Will Tell You, *Daily Mail* 8 April 2010.
15 F. Nelson, British Jobs for British Workers, the *Spectator*, 7 April 2010.

Conclusion: An Absorbing Hanging

On 6 May 2010 the British electorate spoke, but it was not entirely clear what they said. What is apparent is that they pushed British politics on to uncharted terrain and raised fundamental questions about its future. The contributors to this volume have shown us how and why Britain got 'hung'. This concluding section now draws out these key themes and implications.

The 2010 election was marked by novelty in terms of the conduct of the campaign and rarity of outcome, making it a particularly interesting contest, even if the context was one of which party could best prune public expenditure. Stepping back from the content of the campaign we can also ask whether the 2010 general election demonstrates that the current electoral system is broken, that it can no longer deliver single-party majority government and that coalition government is now the norm. This would be a fundamental transformation of British politics. We show that the UK can no longer be understood as a two-party system and that biases within the electoral system make single-party government less likely, particularly for the Conservative Party. The story of the 2010 general election could also be re-interpreted as the story of separate election campaigns and outcomes across southern and northern England and in Scotland, Wales and Northern Ireland. The disunited Kingdom has a disunited electoral system to match. The 2010 general election means that we must rethink key assumptions that have long-informed understandings of British electoral politics.

In terms of the 2010 campaign, this election volume attempted to address several core puzzles; the contribution of Cameronian Conservatism to the election results; the reasons for Labour's loss of support; the transience of 'Cleggmania'; the sharp territorial variations in party support and why some issues became central whereas others failed to register. It also provided a verdict on 13 years of new Labour. The 2010 result showed Cameron to be the heir to Blair in a perhaps unexpected way as he constructed his own version of big tent politics in

© The Author [2010]. Published by Oxford University Press on behalf of the Hansard Society
doi:10.1093/pa/gsq034

bringing the Liberal Democrats into government. The backdrop to the election was, of course, the severe recession which eroded Labour's reputation for economic competence. There was no real difference between the parties during the campaign about the need for cuts, the debate reduced to their timing and the ratio of spending reductions to tax rises. The campaign was accompanied by an air of unreality, due to the unwillingness of any of the parties to talk in any great detail of the dismal post-election vista. The Liberal Democrats leant towards Labour's argument that cuts should be delayed so as not to endanger the economic recovery. These Liberal Democrat doubts were soon cast aside as the coalition government's emergency June budget identified the need for swingeing cuts in public expenditure that, as David Cameron noted, would change the way of life of the British people. How did this grim prognostication tally with the sunny and upbeat Conservative campaign?

At the 2010 general election, Cameronian Conservatism offered a vision of a supposed 'DIY revolution'[1] which marked clear ideological terrain between the Conservatives and the statist approach of the Labour Party. Yet even some party candidates were sceptical over selling the 'Big Society' idea on the doorstep to a puzzled electorate and the anti-state philosophy had serious difficulties in terms of policy detail. Some of the more gimmicky ideas, such as the direct election of local police commissioners, displacing the indirectly elected police authority, surprisingly survived the coalition deal, whilst the outworking of other proposals, most strikingly the formation of local, community-run schools, has yet to be seen. Nonetheless, beyond the overblown invitation to 'join the government of Britain',[2] the 'Big Society' offered a view on how communitarianism and a bolstered civil society could act as a credible substitute for 'Big State' under certain circumstances and contributed to a (limited) debate on how best to organise local democracy and services. The problem for the 'Big Society' idea was its late launch upon the electorate; a big idea which needed sharper definition and a sustained period of inculcation if it was not to either baffle or fail to interest voters.

The key question is how a big society can deal with the swingeing cuts to the big state introduced by the coalition government. The coalition's proposed retreat to a residual welfare state marks a profound re-invention of the relationship between state and society. The scale and extent of cuts announced by the new coalition goes much further than any previous UK government and marks the Thatcher era as one of comparative restraint. A new vision of the relationship between state and society may be consistent with the view of some 'Orange Book' Liberal Democrats, but may well not resonate with non-payroll vote Liberal Democrat MPs, many party members and, in particular, with the bulk of Liberal Democrat voters who self-identify as centrist or on the centre left.

During the campaign, the ideological abstractions of the 'Big Society' quickly became subordinate to the more pressing demands of securing votes in the election campaign, amid the justified fears within the Conservative Party that they would fall short of an overall majority. These concerns reached their nadir with a desperate, ill-judged broadcast attacking the fictional 'hung parliament party', accompanied by apocalyptic warnings from Kenneth Clarke over the consequences for financial stability, and echoed by certain journalists.[3] Yet a hung parliament was the likeliest outcome throughout the 'official' election campaign and was expected by the electorate.[4] This is not to say the opinion polls were perfect guides. They all overestimated the Liberal Democrat vote and (unusually) slightly under-reported Labour's share, but their predictions may be considered broadly accurate, continuing their rehabilitation evident since the 1992 debacle in their most important test since.[5] (We retain some of our earlier mild scepticism over whether polls contribute positively to campaigns, often used by the media as a substitute for policy debate and carrying the risk that they influence voting).[6]

More importantly, the Conservative Party failed to achieve an overall majority due to the modest nature of the party's revival since 2005. In mitigation, the task in attempting to secure an overall majority was Herculean, requiring greater seat gains than those achieved by Churchill or Thatcher. Although the party had enjoyed a strong run of local council election successes and strengthened its organisation and finance since the arrival of Cameron, there was still the 'legacy issue' of the party's unpopularity of the 1990s. There was a lack of warmth towards the party evident in a very modest 'thermometer' rating. The good news, however, was that the electorate had gone from cold to lukewarm in its view of the Conservatives, which constituted progress. Even better was that the electorate was marginally cooler towards other parties, allowing the Conservatives to progress by default. Cameron's net satisfaction ratings, whilst weak, were at least positive, a vast improvement on the pitiful verdicts on Hague, Duncan-Smith and Howard.

Cameron was unimpressed by siren calls from right-wingers (mainly, it should be noted, certain *Daily Telegraph* columnists rather than senior MPs) to fight a campaign upon 'traditional' issues such as law and order, immigration and Euro-scepticism. This was a correct call, highlighted by the fact that Conservative constituency performance is *not* correlated with that of UKIP's. The need for stringent expenditure cuts allowed the party to unite around a clear economic agenda, which also repeatedly criticised Labour's 'jobs tax', the proposed National Insurance rises. The party was broadly united in its Euro-scepticism and the remaining internal divisions, between social conservatives and liberals, did not feature in the campaign. Moreover, Cameron kept room for post-election manoeuvre and doing a deal with the Liberal Democrats. Whilst categorically ruling out ever joining the Euro as Prime Minister, he pointedly refused to rule out discussions on electoral reform, inviting his interviewer to 'put the question in Serbo-Croat if you want, you're going to get the same [non] answer'.[7]

Like devolution itself, the performance of the Conservatives in the devolved nations was asymmetric. Given the importance of Holyrood, it may matter less than in the Thatcher era that the Conservative Party remains isolated and unloved in Scotland, confined to a single seat and with no apparent prospect of a revival in fortunes in a polity where SNP–Labour rivalry will continue to dominate (and vary according to type of election). Without Scotland, the Conservatives would have enjoyed a comfortable overall majority. Yet, notwithstanding continuing Labour overall dominance, the Conservative performance in Wales was impressive, registering the biggest increase in vote share for the party of any region of Britain. Whilst Scottish Conservatives still endure the legacy of the 1980s and, under Cameron, are not seen as defenders of Scottish interests, Welsh Conservatism is not so handicapped. In Northern Ireland, however, the attempt to restore the Conservatives as a UK-wide force and the natural party of the Union, via an alliance with the Ulster Unionist Party (UUP), was ill-judged and embarrassed both parties. Despite the link, the Conservatives brokered talks on prospects for a single Unionist party, indicating a lack of faith in the tired Unionist horse they had backed. Aligning themselves with the Conservatives cost the UUP its only Westminster seat, following the resignation in protest of Lady Sylvia Hermon. Her subsequent crushing victory as an Independent highlighted the folly of the exercise.

What then of the Labour Party and its second-worst share of the vote since 1922, only slightly better than Michael Foot's 1983 performance? It may be intuitive to assume that Labour lost in 2010 because it haemorrhaged the middle class support loaned to the party during the Blair years, but this would be an inaccurate reading of the election. In contrast, Labour's support held up well in all but the lowest section of the middle class and the party suffered a far greater rate of desertion amongst the skilled working class, reminiscent of the Thatcher Conservative triumph of 1979. Labour's support was down by 18% amongst C2 skilled workers, although the Conservatives only gained 6% amongst this class.[8] Amongst *Sun* readers, the switch to the Conservatives was a remarkable 17.5%, bigger than the swing to Labour found amongst that newspaper's readership in the Blair landslide of 1997.[9] Labour's core vote strategy, demonstrable in the latter stages of the election campaign, was thus justifiable in terms of identification of where the party support was slipping, but was insufficient in retaining backing. For the 'elite' of the working class, Labour was no longer seen as the custodian of their material interests. The skilled working class, employed in trades, vulnerable to a drop in customers during a recession and enjoying none of the protections (thus far) enjoyed by the middle class public sector (now the sixth largest in the world in terms of percentage GDP spending), attributed at least part of their plight to the Labour government, despite Gordon Brown's pleas that economic problems were global and that he had made the correct calls. The improvements in public services wrought by Labour in its first two terms were no longer sufficient to offset these resentments.

The feelings of relief amongst some within the Labour party after the election were based upon recognition that seat losses could have been worse amid such a low vote share and a clumsy campaign; that opposition represented safety; that a period of renewal was needed amid political exhaustion and delight that the Liberal Democrats, always regarded with contempt by the more tribal elements within Labour, had sided with the Conservatives. The willingness to head to these tranquil waters contributed to the unwillingness of party leaders to play political 'Top Trumps' and forge a Lab–Lib pact against the emerging Conservative–Liberal Democrat coalition in the days immediately after the election. There were also fears amongst Labour traditionalists of conceding too much on proportional representation.

The acceptance of the inevitability of opposition also diminished the risk of internecine warfare which had passed for post-election defeat 'debate' within the party during the early 1980s, but much more important was that the old ideological ruptures had ended. Contrary to claims, 2010 did not represent the death of New Labour, other than in name, as the party's revisionist tradition remained in the ascendancy and will provide the ideological framework for 'Next Labour'. Yet New Labour managed to lose 5 million votes between 1997 and 2010 and the party was struggling to devise a clear agenda to entice their return.

For the Liberal Democrats, the failure to achieve an electoral breakthrough—the party's 1% increase in vote share was accompanied by a 10% loss of representation in the Commons—was 'rewarded' by the opportunity to help preside over severe cuts in expenditure in a coalition government. The party has now entered office at each level of national election contested, in Wales, Scotland and now Westminster. As such, the credibility of the Liberal Democrats as a party of government continues to grow. Many coalition policies reflected Liberal Democrat priorities. The parties had fairly similar ambitions in terms of deficit reduction; both planned to reduce the underlying deficit by £71 billion over a parliamentary term and on civil liberties, the scrapping of ID cards was readily agreed. There was compromise (i.e. giving way) on key issues—Trident, proportional representation, a 'mansion tax', the Euro, regional immigration quotas and an amnesty for immigrants were all sacrificed, but on many other issues, notably regarding removing the low paid from taxation via an expensive (£17 billion) raising of personal allowances, the scrapping of Conservative plans to reduce inheritance tax; parliamentary reform and ministerial personnel, the Liberal Democrats fared better. Cameron's immediate post-election comment that the coalition offered the 'bulk of the Conservative manifesto and the best of the Liberal Democrat manifesto' had some merit.

The willingness of the Liberal Democrats to forego a referendum on a proportional voting system, in favour of a (risky and coalition-divisive) referendum on the non-proportional AV, surprised those of us who viewed it as a deal breaker, as in 1974. However, AV will clearly benefit the Liberal Democrats if they become the recipients of a large number of second preference votes. Electoral reform could offer consolidation of the party's electoral bloc. It makes the future bypassing of the party amid majority government even less likely, although single-party government is less likely to be the norm in future even if the electorate favours the retention of a First Past the Post system. There are several reasons; the Liberal Democrats' electoral stature, the growth of 'other' parties and system biases, which require a very substantial Conservative lead in terms of vote share due to efficacy issues, notably the large wasted vote majorities in Conservative constituencies and abstentions in safe Labour seats meaning victories with relatively few votes. The electorate has adopted a multi-party outlook for decades, which combined with these factors may be sufficient to prevent a return to majority government in the near future.

Despite further electoral growth for the Liberal Democrats, the party's electoral weaknesses have not disappeared. The lack of a distinctive social base (as ever) allied to vulnerability to the Conservative revival in the South, lacklustre performance against Labour in the North and diminished appeal in Scotland all prevented enthusiasm for Nick Clegg's assured television leadership debate performances securing electoral advance, the problem exacerbated by late swing against the party. The inability of the Liberal Democrats to translate 'Cleggmania' into a serious increase in vote share may have surprised. Nearly one-quarter of television viewers of the first debate claimed that it had changed their mind about who to vote for[10] and Clegg was able to laugh off ludicrous subsequent attacks upon him, including a preposterous *Daily Mail* lead item, as making him 'the only politician who has gone from being Churchill to a Nazi in less than a week'. There was at least one hint, however, suggesting that Clegg's 'support' lacked substance. Asked who was the most 'Prime Ministerial' in the televised debates, Clegg trailed a poor third behind Cameron and Brown each time, polling at only 21% (15 April), 18% (22 April) and 20% (29 April).[11] Moreover, Clegg's biggest reservoir of support after the leadership debate was among young people, who remained the least likely to vote.

We end on the hope that the 2010–2015 (?) fixed-term parliament (there are serious issues of (un)affordability confronting any desire within Labour or amongst Liberal Democrat refuseniks for an early election) leads to the rehabilitation of the House of Commons, whose members, 142 of whom are women and 27 of whom are from ethnic minorities, will at least be modestly more representative of the broader population. There were some encouraging signs in the election that the outcry over expenses was subsiding, given that incumbent MPs performed better across the parties than non-incumbent MPs (admittedly, the worst offenders had retired as MPs) and there was a modest rise in turnout. The outcry against MPs led to welcome reforms of the expenses system, but also contributed to some foolish broader proposals, in terms of culling numbers and giving ill-conceived powers of recall, whilst the petitioning of parliament to trigger debates needs proper regulation. At a time when MPs have never been busier in terms of constituency dealings and legislative scrutiny, the plan to cut their numbers—increasing constituency sizes and making the task of elected representatives in representing us more difficult and remote—smacked of the worst type of populism offered by the Conservatives and Liberal Democrats. Proposals for a reduction in the size of the Commons had been opposed by David Cameron before he became Conservative leader and, given that the electorate has increased by 25% since 1950 yet the number of MPs has risen by a mere 3%, the case for reducing the number of elected representatives was not proven. Whilst the move towards equalising constituency sizes, (removing one form of bias operating largely against the Conservatives) is laudable, kneejerk shrinking of parliament benefits no-one. The 2010 election was hardly a reinvigoration of our democracy given what preceded the contest, but the level of interest suggests that notions of mass disenchantment and disinterest are overblown, whilst the reaction of the leaders of the main parties to a hung parliament was edifying and business-like. The fortunes of the coalition government, operating in difficult economic times, should maintain the modest rise in interest amongst the electorate.

1   *Guardian*, 14 April 2010.
2   Conservative Party, *Invitation to Join the Government of Britain: Conservative Election Manifesto 2010*, Conservative Party.
3   See for example, Camilla Cavendish, 'Voting Lib Dem would be a vote for chaos', *Times*, 17 April 2010.
4   A Populus poll for the *Times*, conducted on 26–27 April, found that 46% of electors believed that a hung parliament was the most likely outcome, compared with 25% who believed the Conservatives would achieve an overall majority and 15% who believe Labour would win such a majority. *Times*, 28 April 2010.
5   See I. Crewe, 'The Opinion Polls: The Election They Got (Almost) Right', *Parliamentary Affairs*, 58, 2005, 684–98.
6   A. Geddes and J. Tonge, *Labour's Second Landslide: The British General Election 2001*, University Press, 2002.
7   *Observer*, 25 April 2010.
8   IPSOS-MORI Final Poll, *Observer*, 9 May 2010.
9   Ibid.
10 *Guardian*/ICMPoll, 17 April 2010.
11 *Sunday Times*, YouGov polls, *Sunday Times*, 18 April 2010, 25 April 2010, 2 May 2010.

INDEX